KT-563-793

THE EUROPEAN DICTATORSHIPS 1918–1945

Stephen J. Lee

London and New York

First published in 1987 by
Methuen & Co. Ltd

Reprinted 1988, 1989, 1990, 1991
by Routledge
11 New Fetter Lane, London EC4P 4EE
29 West 35th Street, New York NY 10001

© 1987 Stephen J. Lee

Printed in Great Britain at
The University Press, Cambridge

All rights reserved. No part of this book may be reprinted or
reproduced or utilized in any form or by any electronic, mechanical
or other means, now known or hereafter invented, including
photocopying and recording, or in any information storage or
retrieval system, without permission in writing from the publishers.

British Library Cataloguing in Publication Data

Lee, Stephen J.
The European dictatorships 1918–1945
1. Dictators — Europe — History —
20th century
2. Europe — Politics and government —
1918–1945
I. Title
321.9   JN12

ISBN 0-416-42270-5
ISBN 0-415-02785-3 Pbk

Library of Congress Cataloging in Publication Data

Lee, Stephen J.
The European dictatorships, 1918–1945
Bibliography: p. 331
Includes index.
Summary: A history of dictatorships
in Europe from 1918–1945.
1. Europe — Politics and government —
1918–1945.
2. Totalitarianism. [1. Europe — Politics
and government — 1918–1945.
2. Totalitarianism. 3. Dictators]
I. Title.
D723.L43   1987   940.5   86-31171

ISBN 0-416-422070-5
ISBN 0-415-02785-3 (pbk.)

025425

21491201

The European Dictatorships 1918–1945

For Margaret and Charlotte

BY THE SAME AUTHOR

Aspects of European History 1494–1789
Aspects of European History 1789–1980

Contents

Contents

Maps

A COMMENT ON THE TERM 'DICTATORSHIP'

'Dictatorship' is not a modern concept. Two thousand years ago, during the period of the Roman Republic, exceptional powers were sometimes given by the Senate to individual 'dictators' like Sulla and Julius Caesar. The intention was that the 'dictatorship' would be temporary and that it would make it possible to take swift and effective action to deal with an emergency.

There appears to be some disagreement as to how the term should be applied today. Should it be used in its original form to describe the temporary exercise of emergency powers? Or can it now be used in a much broader sense?

Let us take two typical views. One is put forward by H. Buchheim in *Totalitarian Rule: Its Nature and Characteristics*.[1] Buchheim argues that dictatorship *should* be seen as a temporary device. It is 'equally present in contemporary democratic republics' and involves the short-term suspension of the democratic process when quick and vigorous action is necessary. An alternative position is adopted by M.R. Curtis in an entry in *Encyclopedia Americana*.[2] He maintains that 'the meaning of the term has changed since Roman times. The essential ingredient of modern dictatorship is power; an emergency is not necessarily present.'

In this book I have opted for the broader approach of Curtis. The reason is not that I consider it to be sounder or more accurate; while preparing my material I came across very different analyses of the term 'dictatorship', most of which were highly convincing and formidably supported. My aim is to reflect common usage and to conform to the approach of general books on the twentieth century and the inter-war period.

Introduction:
The sixteen dictatorships
1918–45

Europe between the two World Wars consisted of a total of 28 states. In 1920 all but two of these could be described as democracies in that they possessed a parliamentary system with elected governments, a range of political parties and at least some guarantees of individual rights. By the end of 1938, no fewer than 16 of these had succumbed to dictatorship; their leaders possessed absolute power which was beyond the constraints of the constitution and which no longer depended upon elections. The dictators sought to perpetuate their authority by disposing of any effective opposition, by severely restricting personal liberties and by applying heavy persuasion and force. Of the remaining 12 democracies, seven were torn apart between 1939 and 1940. Thus, by late 1940, only five democracies remained intact: the United Kingdom, Ireland, Sweden, Finland and Switzerland (see Map 1).

The first dictatorships were those of the far left, and involved the use of the term 'dictatorships of the proletariat' to indicate a temporary but necessary phase in which the basic principles of Communism would be applied (see p. 14).

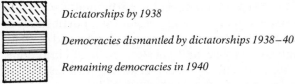

Dictatorships by 1938

Democracies dismantled by dictatorships 1938–40

Remaining democracies in 1940

Map 1 The European dictatorships 1918–38/40

Lenin established the Bolshevik regime in Russia in October
1917 after the overthrow by force of the semi-liberal Provisional Government which, in turn, had disposed of the Tsarist
Empire in March. Lenin's temporary dictatorship was subsequently given a permanent base by Stalin, who came to
power in 1924. Meanwhile, Hungary experienced a Communist revolution in 1919 as Béla Kun tried to repeat the
Bolshevik achievement. His regime, however, lasted only 133

days and eventually fell to counter-revolutionary forces. Although there were to be further attempts at installing a 'dictatorship of the proletariat' in several other European countries during the 1920s and 1930s, none succeeded.

In fact, all the other dictatorships came from the right of the political spectrum. Two of these, the most powerful, have been described as revolutionary. In 1922 Mussolini set the pattern for a number of other leaders by assuming control of Italy, and proceeded to impose the basic principles of Fascism. Eleven years later, in 1933, Hitler was appointed Chancellor in Germany and inaugurated a more ruthless regime – the Nazi Third Reich. Italy and Germany, initially rivals for control over central Europe, developed from the mid-1930s a working diplomatic partnership known as the Rome–Berlin Axis. With this they spread their influence widely in an effort to undermine the remaining democracies on the one hand and, on the other, to checkmate Soviet Russia.

The right also produced a series of more conservative dictatorships; these are often called 'authoritarian', in contrast to the 'totalitarian' regimes of Italy and Germany and, indeed, of Stalin's Russia (see Chapter 6). Central and eastern Europe, completely reorganized after the First World War, succumbed to a series of strong men who promised an escape from the chaos of party conflict or the threat of Communism. Hence, Horthy established control over Hungary in 1920 and Pilsudski over Poland in 1926. Austria moved to the right in 1932 under Dollfuss, whose regime was continued by Schuschnigg from 1934 until Austria's eventual absorption· into Germany (1938). Even the tiny Baltic states adopted an authoritarian system: Lithuania fell to Smetona in 1926, Latvia to Ulmanis in 1934 and Estonia to Päts in the same year.

Dictatorships also emerged in all the states of south-eastern Europe, or the Balkans. Four of these were monarchies: Ahmet Zogu proclaimed himself King Zog of Albania in 1928; King Alexander assumed personal control of Yugoslavia in 1929; King Boris followed suit in Bulgaria in 1934 and, finally, King Carol dispensed with parliamentary government in Rumania in 1938. The fifth Balkan State, Greece, experienced under Metaxas (1936–40) a more systematically organized form of authoritarianism which was influenced to some extent by Nazi methods.

The Iberian peninsula, meanwhile, had produced three 'strong men'. The first was General Miguel Primo de Rivera, Spanish dictator between 1923 and 1930. His regime, it is true, was succeeded by a democratic republic but this, in turn, was brought down by General Franco who led the Nationalists to victory over the Republicans in the Spanish Civil War. This conflict, which lasted from 1936 to 1939, also gave an opportunity to Hitler and Mussolini to pour military support into Franco's war effort and launch a combined offensive against the leftist supporters of the Republic; it did much, therefore, to increase the confidence and aggression of German and Italian diplomacy. Portugal's experience was less turbulent. From 1932 she was under the iron rule of Dr Antonio Salazar, who remained in power until 1968.

Between 1939 and 1941 no fewer than seven dictatorships (Poland, Lithuania, Albania, Yugoslavia, Greece, Latvia and Estonia) came under the direct rule of Germany or Italy. During the same period, seven democracies were dismantled – Czechoslovakia, Norway, Denmark, Holland, Belgium, Luxembourg and France while, from 1941, the Third Reich made substantial inroads into Soviet Russia. Almost the entire continent, therefore, became part of the Nazi order, ruled either by governors appointed by Hitler or by puppet dictators. The latter were often leaders of Fascist movements which had not succeeded in gaining power before 1939 but which now benefited from the military support of Germany. Examples included the Quisling regime in Norway, the Vichy administration in France, the Ustashi movement in Croatia, and Szálasi's 'Arrow Cross' dictatorship in Hungary.

The fate of these regimes was tied to that of Nazi Germany; between 1944 and 1945 they all fell to the invading armies of the Soviet Union or western Allies and to the internal resistance movements. After 1945, parliamentary democracy made a major comeback in western and central Europe, while Stalin's version of Communism prevailed in eastern Europe. Right-wing dictatorship was therefore squeezed out of all but Spain and Portugal, and even here residual authoritarianism ended in 1975.

All the developments outlined in this Introduction will be given more detailed treatment throughout the rest of this book. Chapter 1 will look at the overall situation in Europe between the wars and focus on the general preconditions for dictatorship. Chapters 2, 3 and 4 will examine the main developments in Russia, Italy and Germany, while Chapter 5 will cover the different manifestations of dictatorship elsewhere in Europe. The purpose of Chapter 6 will be to draw together some of the main themes in a comparative survey.

The overall aim will be to examine ideas as well as details. Many of the issues dealt with are highly controversial, and will therefore be looked at from a variety of angles. During the past few decades there has been a vast outpouring of books on the inter-war period, especially on Nazi Germany, and it is intended that the following chapters should reflect at least some of the more important theories.

This approach is based on the conviction, or hope, that most readers will find explanations as interesting and as important to them as factual detail. Where there are several explanations in direct conflict with each other there is plenty of scope for the reader to reflect and come to a personal decision.

Here are a few examples of the sort of controversy dealt with: Why was Lenin not succeeded by Trotsky? Was Stalin's regime merely a continuation of Lenin's, or something totally different? Why did Stalin purge his party even of his loyal supporters? Was Mussolini a statesman or a mere buffoon? Was Hitler's foreign policy based on a master-plan or improvised? Was Hitler a more, or less, effective dictator than Stalin? Was Hitler a 'strong' or a 'weak' leader? Can any of the other dictators legitimately be called 'Fascist'? Which dictatorships were 'totalitarian' and which 'authoritarian'? What was the difference?

1
The setting for dictatorship

Europe experienced, between the wars, an unprecedented upheaval. Boundaries were altered in the most drastic way and numerous new states came into existence. Old fashioned empires and the last remnants of autocracy had been swept away, to be replaced by constitutional democracies and the principle that each major ethnic group should be given the right to form its own nation. Naturally there was a heady optimism about the future and many shared the belief of H.G. Wells that the struggle between 1914 and 1918 had been 'the war to end wars'. Yet the collapse of the old order was also a precondition for movements which were antidemocratic, and there was no guarantee that the new constitutions or boundaries would be indefinitely preserved.

The overall argument of this chapter is that the First World War and the peace settlement acted as a powerful catalyst for change. Initially, this change was expressed in the form of constitutional democracy and national self-determination. These ideals were, however, soon threatened by serious underlying problems which gave a boost to alternative systems in the form of left- or right-wing dictatorship. The process was accelerated by the worst economic crisis in recent history and by a complex international situation which saw the eventual association of dictatorship with militarism and war.

THE IMPACT OF THE FIRST WORLD WAR

The First World War was fought between the Entente powers and the Central powers. The former comprised Britain, France, Russia, Belgium, Serbia, Portugal and Montenegro, joined by Italy (1915), Rumania (1916) and Greece (1917). The Central powers were Germany, Austria-Hungary, the Ottoman Empire and Bulgaria. Both sides expected at the outset a swift victory after a limited, nineteenth-century-style war. What in fact occurred was a massive onslaught, with a mobile front in eastern Europe and stalemate in the trenches of the western front. The total losses amounted to 13 million dead, of whom 2 million were Germans, 1.75 million Russians, 1.5 million Frenchmen, 1 million British and 0.5 million Italians.[1] Economies were drained, resources depleted, armies exhausted. Europe proved incapable of ending the conflict and it took the eventual involvement of the United States to tip the balance in favour of the Entente powers.

The impact of the struggle was considerable. During the 1920s the 'Great War' was regarded as the major catastrophe of the modern era, epitomizing all the evils to be avoided in the future. Twenty years later, however, it seemed to be eclipsed by the Second World War, particularly since the latter involved considerably greater loss of life and destruction. Then, as H.S. Hughes has argued, the further passage of time restored the original perspective. 'The First World War now appears fully as important as the Second – indeed, in certain respects, still more decisive in its effects.'[1] It was, for example, a catalyst for revolution. It has long been accepted that military failure destabilizes a political system, destroys economic viability, mobilizes the masses, and undermines the normal capacity of the regime to deal with disturbances. The European state system was profoundly altered by the collapse of three empires, induced by defeat and privation.

The first of these was Tsarist Russia. By 1916 the German armies had penetrated deep into Russian territory on the Baltic, in Poland and the Ukraine. The Russian military response proved inadequate, and the supply of foodstuffs and raw materials was severely disrupted by communications difficulties. The government proved unable to cope, badly affected as it was by the periodic absences of the Tsar at the front. In February 1917 food riots erupted spontaneously in Petrograd, to which the official response was entirely inadequate; the regime's stability was destroyed by desertions from a destabilized army. The result was the abdication of the Tsar and the emergence of a Provisional Government which aimed eventually at operating a western-style constitutional democracy. But this also made the mistake of seeking to snatch victory from defeat; further military disasters severely reduced its credibility and assisted the Bolsheviks in their revolution of October 1917. Within eight months, Russia had moved from autocracy, via a limited constitutional democracy, to Communism: a remarkable transformation for a state which had historically been renowned for its resistance to political changes. Lenin made peace with the victorious Germans at Brest-Litovsk. The price he had to pay was to abandon Russian control over Finland, Estonia, Latvia, Lithuania and Poland – a very considerable loss of territory.

Of similar magnitude was the collapse of the Austro-Hungarian Empire. This had been Europe's most heterogeneous state, comprising 13 separate ethnic groups, all of whom pulled in different directions. Two of these, the Germans of Austria and the Magyars of Hungary, had benefited most from the *Ausgleich* of 1867 which had created a Dual Monarchy, effectively under their control. The majority of the population, however, had been excluded from this agreement; Austria-Hungary contained a large proportion of Slavs, who could be subdivided into Czechs, Slovaks, Poles, Ukrainians, Serbs, Croats and Slovenes. These were already pressing for full political recognition, even autonomy, by 1914. The First World War wrecked the Austro-Hungarian economy and tore apart the political fabric of the empire as the various Slav leaders decided in 1918 to set up independent states rather than persist with a multi-racial federation. By the time that the Emperor surrendered to the Allies on 3 November 1918, his empire had dissolved into three smaller states, Austria, Hungary and Czechoslovakia, while the remaining areas were given up to Italy, Rumania, Poland and the newly formed Southern Slav nation, eventually to be known as Yugoslavia.

The third empire to be destroyed as a direct result of the First World War was the Kaiser's Germany, or the Second Reich. The German war offensive, so successful against Russia, had been contained on the western front. The western Allies, greatly assisted by American intervention, came close to breaking through the German lines in September 1918. Meanwhile, the German economy was being strangled by a British naval blockade. Under the threat of military defeat, the Second Reich was transformed into a constitutional republic, the Kaiser having no option but to abdicate on 9 November, two days before the German surrender.

By the end of 1918, eleven states covered the area once occupied by the three great empires (see Map 2). All but Russia were trying to adapt to western-style parliamentary systems and this seemed to justify the belief of many that the war had become a struggle for democracy. Victory carried with it an element of idealism. The different peoples of Europe would be guaranteed separate statehood and given democratic constitutions. These, in turn, would ensure lasting peace by removing the irritants which had caused so many of Europe's most recent conflicts: harsh autocracy and unfulfilled nationalism. There is, therefore, a strong case for arguing that the First World War had a liberating effect. Further evidence for this can be seen in the profound social changes which occurred in all the states which took part. Particularly important was the increased influence of the middle class at the expense of the traditional aristocracy, the possibility of agrarian reforms and improved conditions for the peasantry, allowance for a greater political role for the working class and trade unionism and, finally, the emancipation and enfranchisement of women.

There is, however, another side to the picture. The First World War may well have created the conditions for the establishment of democratic regimes. But, at the same time,

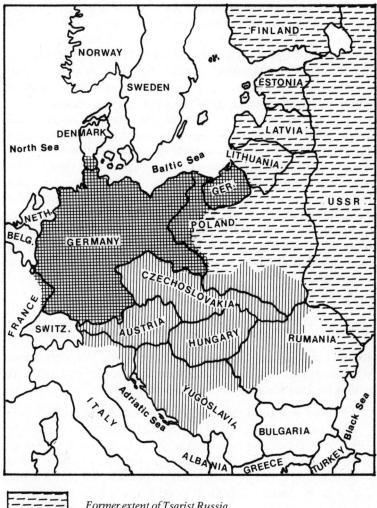

Former extent of Tsarist Russia

Former extent of Austria-Hungary

Former extent of the Second Reich

(*Boundaries shown are those after the First World War*)

Map 2 The collapse of three empires and the emergence of the successor states

it produced a series of obstacles which these new democracies proved unable to surmount. One of these was an underlying resentment of the terms of the peace settlements, which particularly affected Germany, Austria, Hungary and Russia; there was, from the outset, a powerful drive to revise them. Another obstacle was the prolonged economic instability which was aggravated by war debts and reparations payments. Even the destruction of the three empires had unintended side effects. Some of the new dictatorships which emerged between the wars were built upon the mobilized masses and upon the type of ideologies which these autocracies had helped restrain – especially Communism and Fascism. It is arguable, therefore, that the war cleared the way for twentieth-century dictatorships by smashing nineteenth-century autocracies without providing a viable alternative. K.D. Bracher goes so far as to say that 'In spite of their ideological prehistory, there can be no doubt that the new dictatorships of our century were principally a result of the 1914–18 war'.[2]

THE PEACE SETTLEMENT AND ITS SIGNIFICANCE

Ten months before the end of the First World War, President Wilson announced in his 'Fourteen Points' the expectations which he had for any future settlement:

> What we demand in this war ... is that the world be made fit and safe to live in; and particularly that it be made safe for every peace-loving nation which, like our own, wishes to live its own life, determine its own institutions, be assured of justice and fair dealing by the other peoples of the world as against force and selfish aggression.[3]

What was needed, he continued, was a ban on secret diplomacy, guarantees of freedom of navigation on the high seas, the removal of economic barriers, the lowering of armaments levels, the evacuation of all occupied territory, the granting of self-determination to Europe's different peoples and the formation of a 'general association of nations'. This programme provided the set of ideals upon which the peace settlement was to be based.

Idealism, however, mingled with other motives. One was the satisfaction of wartime expansionist ambitions; the Secret Treaty of London (1915) had, for example, promised Italy extensive territorial gains at the expense of the Ottoman Empire and Austria-Hungary – a reward for joining the Entente powers rather than fulfilling an earlier commitment to Germany. Could such promises be squared with the principle of national self-determination? Another factor was public opinion. All the representatives gathering in Paris were under constant pressure from the media at home and from exhortations from politicians like Geddes to 'squeeze the German lemon until the pips squeak'. Finally, some delegates were obsessed with the need for providing security in the future, and regarded their priority as a settlement which would destroy Germany's military strength.

The actual negotiations were carried out in Paris by the Council of Ten. This consisted of two representatives from each of five powers: Britain and the dominions, France, the United States, Italy and Japan. But most of the work was done by President Wilson of the United States, the British Prime Minister – Lloyd George, and the French Premier – Clemenceau. The usual picture of this trio is that Wilson was the idealist, having the advantage of American detachment from European problems. Clemenceau was concerned primarily with French security and revenge against Germany, while Lloyd George adopted a pragmatic approach, endeavouring to steer between Wilson and Clemenceau and to achieve by compromise a moderate and lasting solution. The Paris Settlement, therefore reflected these three broad strategies, which can be seen at work in the individual treaties, named after the ring of towns around the outskirts of Paris or parts of the complex of Versailles.

Germany was dealt with by the Treaty of Versailles, signed on 28 June 1919. It affirmed, by Article 231, the prime responsibility of 'Germany and her Allies' for the outbreak of the First World War and, accordingly, made provision for territorial adjustments, demilitarization and economic compensation to the victorious Allies for the losses they had incurred. Germany was deprived of Alsace-Lorraine, Eupen and Malamédy, Northern Schleswig, Posen, West Prussia, parts of Southern Silesia, and all her overseas colonies. Limits were placed on her naval capacity, her army was restricted to 100,000 volunteers, and the Rhineland was demilitarized. A considerable quantity of rolling-stock and merchant shipping was also removed, while France was given exclusive rights to the coal-mines of the Saar region. Finally, provision was made for the payment of reparations by the German government, the total amount eventually being fixed in 1921 at 136,000 million gold marks. Altogether, Germany lost 13 per cent of her area, 12 per cent of her population, 16 per cent of her coal, 48 per cent of her iron, 15 per cent of her agricultural land and 10 per cent of her manufactures.

Opinion is divided as to whether this was a fair settlement. Historians of the 1920s, like W.H. Dawson, emphasized the harshness of a treaty which cut into German territory in a way which discriminated blatantly in favour of non-German populations. The result was that Germany's frontiers 'are literally bleeding. From them oozes out the life-blood, physical, spiritual and material of large populations.' More recent historiography has tended to redress the balance. Writers like J. Néré, M. Trachtenberg and W.A. McDougall put the case that France suffered far more heavily than Germany from the impact of war and that she therefore had a powerful claim to compensation and security. Indeed, considering that a German victory would have meant German control over much of Europe, the settlement drawn up by the Allies was remarkably moderate.

Time has, therefore, enabled a perspective to emerge. But perhaps the most important point is that contemporary statesmen strongly attacked the Treaty, thereby giving ammunition to the German case that the Treaty should be revised, even evaded. J.M. Keynes, the economist, was particularly critical; he argued that the settlement lacked wisdom, that the coal and iron provisions were 'inexpedient and disastrous' and that the indemnity being considered was far beyond Germany's means to pay. He considered, indeed, that the 'Treaty, by overstepping the limits of the possible, has in practice settled nothing'. This accorded very much with the German view that the Treaty was a *Diktat*, forced upon a defeated power, rather than a genuine negotiated settlement. By 1930 it was evident that a wide cross-section of the German political spectrum was extremely hostile to the Treaty of Versailles and that British politicians were increasingly aware of its shortcomings. The ultimate beneficiaries of both these trends were the parties of the right – the conservative National Party and the more radical Nazis. Hitler, especially, was to exploit the underlying resentment in Germany, while British politicians, affected by a belated attack of conscience, made excuses for his activities against the settlement. As will be shown in Chapter 4, the failure to uphold Versailles in the 1930s contributed greatly to the growing confidence and aggression of Nazi foreign policy.

The rest of the peace settlement concerned central and eastern Europe. Austria-Hungary was dealt with by the Treaties of St Germain (10 July 1919) and Trianon (4 June 1920), which were largely a recognition of a *fait accompli*, the collapse of the Habsburg monarchy. Czechoslovakia was formed out of the provinces of Bohemia, Moravia, Slovakia and Ruthenia; Transylvania and Bukovina were given to an enlarged Rumania; Serbia received the Dalmatian coastline, Bosnia-Herzegovina, Croatia, and Slovenia; while Trentino and South Tyrol were transferred to Italy. Bulgaria, meanwhile, was covered by the Treaty of Neuilly (27 November 1919) by which she lost the Aegean coastline, or Western Thrace, to Greece, parts of Macedonia to Yugoslavia, and Dobrudja to Rumania. Elsewhere in eastern Europe, 1918 saw the emergence of Poland, Finland, Estonia, Latvia and Lithuania as independent states. Although the victorious Allies cancelled the Treaty of Brest-Litovsk between Germany and Russia, no attempt was made to return to Russia the territory which had been given up. Taken as a whole, all these settlements amounted to the greatest territorial transformation in the whole of European history.

The accompanying problems were also considerable. The new nations (or 'successor states') that replaced Austria-Hungary faced a series of crises, examined at length in Chapter 5. They all contained large disaffected ethnic minorities and struggled to achieve economic viability in cut-throat competition against each other. Austria and Hungary sought to revise the whole settlement, Austria by seeking union with

Germany (prohibited by the Treaty of St Germain) and Hungary by trying to extend her frontiers at the expense of her neighbours. The overall result was that eastern Europe was fundamentally unstable and therefore vulnerable to political extremes. Italy, meanwhile, was thoroughly dissatisfied with her meagre gains at St Germain – certainly far fewer than had been guaranteed by the Secret Treaty of London (1915). Indeed, Mussolini found that resentment against the settlement had, by 1922, become a significant factor in boosting support for Fascism. Another resentful, and hence revisionist power was Russia; Stalin had no intention of conceding permanently the territory lost at Brest-Litovsk (1918) or that lost to Poland by the Treaty of Riga (1920). He, too, had no underlying commitment to the post-war settlement and was not averse to helping upset it.

THE CRISIS OF DEMOCRACY

The nineteenth century had seen the growth of parliamentary institutions in almost every European state. In many cases, however, there had been severe constraints on democracy, such as a limited franchise, strong executives, weak legislatures and, in central and eastern Europe, the persistence of royal autocracy. As we have seen, the First World War swept away these constraints, while President Wilson based his views of future stability on entrusting the different peoples of Europe not only with new states but also with the power to run them. A. Cobban argues that 'The key to the understanding of Wilson's conception of self-determination is the fact that for him it was entirely a corollary of democratic theory.'[4] The basic assumption of many was that democracy could work and that it was the best guarantee of lasting peace.

What was meant by the 'democratic' state? H. Kohn has listed some of the main characteristics of the 'democratic way of life'. These include 'open minded critical enquiry' and 'mutual regard and compromise'; an opposition which functions as 'a legitimate partner in the democratic process'; a 'pluralistic view of values and associations'; a refusal to identify totally with 'one party or with one dogma'; recognition of the fundamental values of 'individual liberty'; and 'freedom of the enquiring mind'.[5] These features are common to all open democracies, whether republics or monarchies, and several devices were introduced after the First World War to try to give them effect.

These included the extension of the suffrage and the strengthening of the powers of Parliaments. In much of central and eastern Europe a deliberate decision was made to use proportional representation, in the belief that this was the best means of conveying the popular will. The most influential type was the Belgian system, as adapted in 1918 by the Dutch. This related the number of votes cast to the size of party representation in Parliament while, at the same time, allowing a national pool in which smaller groups could be included alongside the main parties. The general principle here was that the harmony and stability of the new democracies would be best served by a complete range of parties and interests. This device was therefore used in Germany, Poland, Austria, Czechoslovakia, Finland, Lithuania, Latvia and Estonia. Italy, Spain, Portugal and the Balkan states tried other variations on the democratic theme.

Unfortunately, democracy everywhere soon came under serious strain. Economic crises included inflation in the early 1920s in Germany, and a universal depression from 1929 onwards, aggravated by the raising of tariff barriers and the disruption of trade. Some states suffered racial instability as a result of conflicting ethnic groups. Others experienced social disruption caused by the growing hostility towards the regime of the different social classes – the business groups and capitalists, the professional middle class and small traders, peasants, farmers and workers. Economic, racial and social crises had a serious effect on political parties. Liberal parties were drained of supporters, especially in Germany; populist and Catholic parties managed to keep theirs, but consciously moved their policies to the right; conservatives became more and more antidemocratic and authoritarian; and the parties of the left were torn between socialism and Communism. In this state of flux what was needed everywhere was a secure political framework to restore stability and stiffen the resolve to preserve democracy.

This is precisely what was missing. The creators of the

constitutions had been unduly optimistic in assuming that the expression of different viewpoints through party politics would automatically guarantee harmony. The unhappy experience of proportional representation demonstrated quite the reverse. K.J. Newman considers that proportional representation led to the disintegration of Italian democracy and seriously destabilized Germany. In multi-ethnic states like Poland and Yugoslavia it ensured that 'national, religious, ideological and regional groups' were irreconcilable.[6] It could certainly be argued that the majority voting system (or winner takes all) was more likely than proportional representation to maintain harmony. The reason was that it tended to produce a two-party system, in which each party was an alliance of interest groups prepared to compromise in order to present an acceptable image to the electorate; failure to do this would mean severe defeat, as seats in Parliament were not designated in proportion to votes received. Proportional representation, by contrast, removed the necessity for groups to compromise within parties; the emphasis, rather, was on parties presenting as specific an image as possible and making a bid for a place in a subsequent coalition government. In other words, the majority voting system forced co-operation within parties before elections, while proportional representation relied on co-operation between parties after elections.

It is, of course, possible to criticize the majority voting system for being inadequately representative and for distorting the electorate's decision. It is also significant that most European democracies have, since 1945, reintroduced proportional representation. The important point, however, remains that the type of proportional representation adopted between the wars had no means of preventing 'splinter parties' (now largely corrected) and coincided with an unusual number of crises. As a result, democracy became less a matter of how to deal with problems than of how to put together a government.

A considerable amount of time and effort was spent trying to find a majority, necessitating exhaustive negotiation and horse-trading. In the process, the role of the Prime Minister, or Chancellor, changed significantly; instead of acting as the head of a government putting across a package of proposals, he became a mediator between conflicting groups, desperately trying to remain in power. This situation would be difficult enough in normal circumstances. At a time of national crisis it proved intolerable. The result was that, in some cases, the head of the government had many of his powers taken out of his hands by the head of state – the King in a monarchy, the President in a republic.

The trend away from democracy towards authoritarian rule was assisted by another defect which existed in some of the new constitutions. The constitution of the Weimar Republic in Germany was typical in that it provided a 'safeguard' if things went wrong; Article 48 gave the president exceptional emergency powers when he needed them. Thus Germany became authoritarian during the Depression from 1931, providing a more amenable political atmosphere for the rise of Hitler. Over most of Europe it proved possible to graft dictatorship on to earlier democratic foundations. Only one regime, Bolshevik Russia, made a clean sweep of previous institutions. Others, including even Nazi Germany, retained much of the original constitutional framework until the very end. They did, however, amend the constitutions so as to make a mockery of the original principles and intentions. The main amendments were a ban on party politics and the strengthening of the executive at the expense of the legislature.

Finally, democracy was severely weakened by the absence of any really popular statesman during the inter-war years. The talents of men like Briand and Stresemann were unostentatious diplomacy which, although effective, rarely caught the public imagination. Churchill, who eventually did fill this gap, did not come into his own until 1940; indeed R. Rhodes James has called his earlier career 'The Years of Failure'. Almost all the great personalities of the period were critics of democracy – Mussolini, Hitler, Pilsudski, Dollfuss, Primo de Rivera and many others. The masses were tempted by their charisma, sweeping promises and simple solutions. The nations' policies were increasingly taken out of the hands of larger political groups and the key decisions were personalized. This was to be one of the main characteristics of dictatorship and applied everywhere, including Stalin's Russia.

DICTATORSHIP AS AN ALTERNATIVE

It is now time to turn to the main ideas and influences underlying these dictatorships, starting with the Communist left and moving to the more varied radical right.

The Communist movements were based on a carefully formulated set of principles. The original ideas derived from Marx and Engels, who argued that all societies comprised two main parts – the base and the superstructure. The former was the prevailing economic structure, for example capitalism, the latter the political and social institutions of the ruling class. In order to change the institutions, or superstructure, it was essential to transform the base. This, in turn, involved the notion of class conflict, as the exploited classes sought to bring down their oppressors. Indeed, according to the Communist Manifesto (1848) 'The history of all human society, past and present, has been the history of class struggles.' This struggle operated by a 'dialectical' process, by which the capitalist system inevitably developed its own opposite which would eventually destroy it. Hence 'the bourgeoisie produces its own gravediggers'. Revolution, Marx considered, was a necessary function of this change for, in his words, 'force is the midwife of every old society pregnant with a new one'. After the revolution had been accomplished, a period known as the 'dictatorship of the proletariat' would begin, during which the bourgeois superstructure would be dismantled, private property would be abolished, production would be socialized and the proletariat would proclaim its triumph by eliminating all other classes. Gradually the 'dictatorship of the proletariat' would be transformed into the 'classless society' which would see an end to all need for force and coercion. According to Engels 'The interference of the state power in social relations becomes superfluous in one sphere after another, and then dies away of itself.' The result is that state powers would be confined to purely administrative functions. In every other respect the state 'withers away'.

These ideas needed substantial alteration before they could

become the basis for revolutionary action. It was to be the
work of Lenin to develop the practical means for the
proletariat to overthrow the capitalist system. His main
contribution was to develop a revolutionary party to act as
the 'proletariat's advance guard'.[7] Organization he regarded
as essential, for 'Just as a blacksmith cannot seize the red
hot iron, so the proletariat cannot directly seize power.'
Marxism–Leninism, as the new synthesis came to be called,
succeeded in overthrowing the western-style Provisional
Government in Russia in October 1917. Between 1918 and
1919 it looked as though it might, in the wake of the First
World War, make spectacular gains elsewhere. The British
Prime Minister, Lloyd George, said in 1919: 'The whole of
Europe is filled with the spirit of revolution.' Yet, by 1920, the
failure of the non-Russian Communist parties to seize control
had become apparent. Revolutions of the far left had
collapsed in Bavaria, Hungary, Austria and the Po Valley in
Italy. After 1920, Communism, while remaining a 'spectre'
and constant threat, never succeeded in gaining power. A
large part of the reason, examined in Chapter 2, was the
inconsistencies and defects of Stalin's foreign policy, which
eventually weakened Communism everywhere.

The most extreme movement of the right is generally called
Fascism. This was more diffuse than Marxism–Leninism and
certainly much more difficult to define. There were, however,
several obvious characteristics. First, there was a deep hatred
of the British and French traditions of democracy; Hitler
claimed, in *Mein Kampf*, that 'There is no principle which...
is as false as that of parliamentarianism.'[8] Secondly, Fascism
was antagonistic to Marxism, and E. Nolte has argued that
'The origin of the Right lies always in the challenge of the
Left.'[9] Thirdly, Fascism was seen as an alternative economic
strategy to socialism and trade union power on the one hand,
and capitalism and big business on the other. It therefore
offered a 'third way' which would seek to eliminate class
conflict. Fourthly, Fascists believed that traditional social
values, based on Christian morality and ethics, were an
impediment to the achievement of domination and power.
Instead, the emphasis should be placed on conflict. Fascism
applied the theory of the survival of the fittest to the social

and political spheres, justifying both the crushing of the weak and ruthless military expansion. The result was a glorification of war which led to 'hypernationalist' policies. In Germany, this 'Social Darwinism' also underlay Hitler's racism and antisemitism. In terms of organization, Fascist parties were presided over by an absolute leader who, in turn, was surrounded by all the trappings of a personality cult. At the lower levels were cadres and para-military outfits, intended to mobilize the masses and turn them against the establishment: in this sense, Fascism was potentially revolutionary.

Fascist movements drew support from a wide cross-section of the population, although with varying degrees of success from area to area. One receptive social group was the 'lumpenproletariat', the unemployed and displaced, although it should be said that most workers tended to support socialist or Communist parties. Another was the rural population – both the peasantry and the estate owners. A third was the large number of former army officers and demobilized soldiers, veterans who were disillusioned by their treatment immediately after the First World War and, in some instances, shocked by the terms of the peace settlement. In the more industrialized countries, Fascism drew its main support from the middle classes, who were profoundly affected and destabilized by the economic crises of the early 1920s and 1930s. Finally, capital and big business joined the bandwagon to try to find security against the threat of Communism. Overall, Fascism benefited greatly from the instability of the inter-war period and made the most of the 'flabbiness and the failures of the existing regimes'.[10]

As this stage it is necessary to sort out the various regimes of the right and establish which were Fascist. The most obvious instance was Mussolini's Italy, where the term Fascism originated, and which showed all the components already mentioned. Germany may also be included; although Nazism did not consciously imitate Italian Fascism, there was considerable common ground in both organization and ideas. The most important differences were Hitler's emphasis on the racial community and antisemitism – neither of which was an integral part of Italian Fascism until 1938.

The other dictatorships of the right can be divided, before the Second World War, into two types. The first type did have significant Fascist influences but these were mixed, in varying concentrations, with other factors. An example is Spain, where Franco balanced the Fascist Falange with the more traditional interests of the army, Church and monarchists; certainly the Falange never dominated the regime in the way that the Fascist Party prevailed in Italy. Another instance of a regime partially influenced by Fascism can be seen in Austria, where Dolfuss introduced a conservative and clerical-inspired variant which has been dubbed both clerico-Fascist and Austrofascist. A case has also been made for the existence of a 'quasi Fascist' regime under Metaxas in Greece. The second type of dictatorship was fundamentally non-Fascist, although not immune to occasional Fascist influences. These were much more traditional regimes and lacked any mass or mobilized support. They included Poland under Pilsudski, Portugal under Salazar, the Baltic states of Estonia, Latvia and Lithuania, and the Balkan countries of Albania, Rumania, Bulgaria and Yugoslavia.

Fascist movements and Fascist states were not necessarily one and the same thing; before the Second World War the former, more often than not, failed to develop into the latter. In fact, the majority of dictatorships regarded Fascist movements as disruptive and dangerous. Horthy had little sympathy with the Hungarian Arrow Cross, while King Carol of Rumania tried to suppress the Iron Guard. There were also struggles between Päts and the Estonian Freedom Fighters, between Smetona and the Iron Wolf of Lithuania and between Latvia's Ulmanis and the Thunder Cross. Minority Fascist movements also tried to cause upheaval in the democracies: for example, Action Française, the Dutch National Socialist Movement, the British Fascist Movement, Rex in Belgium and Lapua in Finland. There were also, in some countries, subnational or regionally based Fascist parties; these included the Slovak People's Party and, in the Yugoslav province of Croatia, an organization known as Ustashi. Every one of these movements failed to gain power – until an opportunity was provided during the upheaval of the Second World War. From 1941 onwards a series of Fascist regimes came into existence as Nazi puppets – the Iron Guard in

Rumania, Szálasi's Arrow Cross in Hungary, the Slovak People's Party, and Ustashi in Croatia. All proved far more oppressive and vicious than the more traditional dictatorships which they replaced, but none survived the collapse of Nazi Germany in 1945.

THE ECONOMIC CATALYST

J.M. Keynes observed in 1931: 'We are today in the middle of the greatest economic catastrophe – the greatest catastrophe due almost entirely to economic causes – of the modern world.'[11] He was referring to events generally known as the Great Depression. This was the nadir of the inter-war economy but, at the same time was part of a broader economic picture which needs to be examined. It is generally accepted that economic crises had profound political effects; although they were rarely the sole or specific cause of dictatorship, they certainly accelerated the process.

The first major crisis followed the First World War and the peace settlement. Before 1913, Europe had dominated world trade and industrial production. Concentration of four years of total war, however, meant the loss of ground to the United States. Some European countries also experienced major upheavals as a result of revolution or the peace settlement. Russia, for example, went through a period of War Communism, followed by the New Economic Policy. The Bolsheviks also decided to repudiate all of Russia's pre-war debts, which particularly affected France. The emergence of 11 new states in eastern and central Europe destroyed the previous customs union in the area, impeded industrial development and promoted intense rivalry. In western Europe there was a considerable variation in post-war economic conditions. Italy underwent economic collapse which contributed to the rapid decline of effective parliamentary democracy and the rise of Mussolini. Britain and France both experienced post-war booms, but these were followed, after 1922, by a temporary general recession. Germany, meanwhile, was saddled by the Treaty of Versailles with reparations payments. The German government resented these deeply, and defaulted in 1923, at the same time printing paper money and effectively bringing about the collapse of the mark. In fact, the situation in the Weimar Republic epitomized everything which seemed most dangerous to Europe's economies: hyperinflation with threats to jobs and savings and a potential social upheaval.

In many cases, however, this first phase of economic malaise was effectively dealt with. The slump and inflation were both reversed and western Europe experienced a rapid increase in prosperity between 1924 and 1929. Several factors contributed to this. One was a more stable international situation; another was the resolution of the German reparations crisis by the Dawes Plan of 1924. But the most important reason was the beneficent influence of the United States – who contributed between 1925 and 1929 something like $2900 million in the form of investment in Europe. This helped settle the complex problem of post-war debts. American loans enabled Germany to make reparations payments to her former enemies in Europe, who, in turn, could make repayments on war loans to the United States. The more stable and rational system meant that industrial and agricultural output increased, while shipping and transport expanded rapidly. This was also a period of industrial rationalization or 'scientific management', which included the use of assembly-line techniques and the more economic employment of labour. In the international sphere attempts were made to restore a fully functioning and stable exchange. Britain returned to the gold standard in 1925, followed by most other European countries by 1928. Meanwhile, in 1927, a conference met at Geneva to try to remove any remaining impediments to international trade. Overall, it seemed that Europe was experiencing unprecedented – and permanent – prosperity.

Our retrospective knowledge shows just how misplaced this confidence was. The recovery proved extremely fragile and a potential crisis lurked behind every apparent gain.

In the first place, much of eastern Europe was less affected by the upswing in prosperity. The Soviet Union was almost completely isolated, while the less industrialized economies of the 'successor states' and the Balkans suffered severely from lower agricultural prices which benefited the consumer at the expense of the producer. Indeed, Poland, Albania and

Lithuania were all lost to dictatorship during this period, the result of an interaction between economic stagnation and political crisis.

Secondly, western European industrial growth was not accompanied by a proportionate increase in the volume of trade. By 1925 Europe's industrial production was the same as that of 1913, but her share of world trade was down from 63 per cent to 52 per cent. It was clear, therefore, that Europe had not succeeded in replacing fully the markets lost during the First World War. The United States, in fact, hoped to prevent Europe from doing so. Experiencing herself a massive increase in industrial production and fearing competition from Europe, she imposed higher tariffs on imports. European countries, with the exception of Britain, followed suit. The result was a series of major obstacles to international trade which did much to reduce its overall volume.

A third problem was that the agricultural sector in western Europe and the United States went through a period of overproduction, largely because of more efficient farming methods. The result was a fall in agricultural prices of up to 30 per cent between the end of 1925 and autumn 1929. As in eastern Europe, the producer suffered and the erosion of his spending power eventually reduced the market for industrial goods. There were also political implications. In Germany, for example, small farmers had become destabilized and a prey to Nazism long before the onset of the Great Depression.

Fourthly, industrial growth – the great economic achievement of the 1920s – was itself unsteady. It depended too heavily on American loans, mostly short-term, and Germany borrowed at 2 per cent above normal interest rates. Any large-scale withdrawal of this investment would have devastating results. Even industrial rationalization or 'scientific management' had its perils. By making it possible to reduce the size of the workforce, it added, even in prosperous times, to the unemployment figures. Before the onset of the Depression, Britain already had one million out of work and Germany two million.

Finally, even the improvements made in international economic relations proved short-lived. The gold standard, for example, did not provide the anticipated stability, as its operation was distorted by the accumulation of most of the world's gold reserves in the United States. In general, Europe's recovery was so closely linked to the prosperity of the United States that the relationship could transmit infection as well as benefits. To repeat the old metaphor, 'When America sneezes, the rest of the world catches cold'.

The more negative impact of the United States began to be felt from mid-1928. The quantity of American loans to Europe began to slow down, largely because of a boom in the domestic stock market. Investors were convinced that this would last indefinitely and that the prospects for returns on investment were far better at home than they were abroad. European economic growth was, therefore, already affected when, in October 1929, another savage blow was dealt by the Wall Street Crash. The sudden collapse of the US stock market was followed by further restrictions on American lending to Europe, thus depriving the latter of what had been a vital factor in its economic recovery. The real impact, however, was experienced in 1931 when the central European banking system was undermined. The crisis began with the collapse of the Austrian bank, Credit Anstalt, and spread to Hungary, Czechoslovakia, Rumania, Poland and Germany.

The economic impact was devastating. All the underlying deficiencies already referred to now came up to the surface. By the end of 1932, for example, total world industrial production had declined by 30 per cent on 1929 levels and trade in manufactured goods by 42 per cent. During the same period world food output fell by 11 per cent and the extraction of raw materials by 19 per cent. Of the individual countries, Germany was the most seriously affected: her 39 per cent decline in industrial production forced unemployment levels up to over 6 million. Other central European countries were also badly hit, including Austria and Czechoslovakia; the crisis was especially serious in Czechoslovakia's most highly industrialized region, the Sudetenland. Eastern Europe had suffered before the onset of the Depression from a drop in agricultural prices, but the Depression intensified the misery by destroying the trade in agricultural goods. The Soviet Union was, supposedly, insulated from the mainstream of the world economy because of her self-sufficiency and rigid economic planning. But even here the Depression had an impact. The Soviet Union depended for its own industrialization on imports of foreign machinery. These were paid for by exports of Soviet grain, the value of which declined steadily as a result of the fall in agricultural prices. Relatively, therefore, imports became more expensive.

The Great Depression presented a double aspect. In the words of Hughes, 'the crisis of capitalism also appeared as a crisis of liberalism and democracy'. All the remaining parliamentary regimes came under severe strain. Some successfully preserved their political system. The Scandinavian countries, especially Sweden and Denmark, made effective use of consensus politics to contain the emergency. Britain went through a political upheaval, but confined this to the parliamentary context by substituting a National Government for the usual bi-partisan approach. France managed to hang on to democracy through the expedient of broad-based coalitions or Leon Blum's Popular Front of 1936. In most other European countries, however, democracy fell apart. Germany was the classic case. The broad-based coalition government of Müller collapsed in 1929, unable to agree a strategy to deal with the economic crisis. The subsequent shift to the right benefited the Nazis, and made possible the rise of Hitler to power by 1933. In eastern Europe, and in the Balkans and Portugal, there was an almost universal resort to emergency powers to replace already discredited parliamentary governments. The only real exception to this process was Spain, which actually progressed during the Depression from dictatorship to the democracy of the Second Republic. This could, however, be seen as a coincidence and, in any case, the Depression helped destabilize the Republic and lay it open to the eventual counter-attack of the right in 1936.

How did the various governments come to terms with the problems caused by the Depression? Several policies were attempted. France refused to devalue the currency and, like Britain and Germany in 1931, relied on cutting government expenditure and carefully balancing the budget. Italy, Portugal and Austria tried variants of 'corporativism', and Nazi Germany introduced a drive for self-sufficiency, or autarky. The degree of success varied; by 1932 some countries were beginning to pull out of the Depression, and most were emerging by 1934. It seemed, therefore, that capitalism had survived the turmoil. The same could not, however, be said of democracy.

In one area economic recovery was delayed. The complex web of international trade was irreparably torn. The main reason for this was the collapse of any real international co-operation and the adoption of essentially national programmes of survival. There was only one compromise. The 1932 Lausanne Conference agreed to cut reparations by 90 per cent. However, the significance of this was overstated at the time, for Hitler proceeded after 1933 to ignore reparations totally. There were to be no other agreements. The World Economic Conference, convened in London in 1933, achieved nothing. All states were imposing high tariffs and drawing up bilateral or regional agreements which effectively destroyed free trade. Examples included the Oslo Group, comprising the Scandinavian countries, and the Ottawa Agreement of 1932 which covered the British Empire. France made similar arrangements with her colonies, while Germany drew up a series of trade pacts with the Balkan states which had profound political consequences (see Chapter 5).

The failure to provide a common approach to dealing with the world economic crisis also contributed to the rapid deterioration of international relations. The three major powers particularly responsible for this were Japan, Italy and Germany, all of which sought economic solutions in rearmament and aggression. The Italian invasion of Abyssinia, for example, was hastened by the withdrawal of American investments after 1929, which had the dual effect of removing all restraints on Italian foreign policy and encouraging Mussolini to reformulate his entire economic strategy. By far the greatest blow to the international system, however, was dealt by Germany. Hitler's 'Four-Year Plan' was intended to prepare Germany for war by 1940, and the increase in military expenditure contributed greatly to the growing confidence and aggression of Hitler's foreign policy during the late 1930s. Dictatorship had finally forged its association with expansionism and militarism whereas democracy, enervated by the Depression, clung desperately to the hope for peace.

2
Dictatorship in Russia

LENIN'S REGIME 1917–24

Russia between 1917 and 1953 experienced two periods of dictatorship. The first was intended by Lenin to be a temporary 'dictatorship of the proletariat', a phase in the movement towards a communist system. The second was the more permanent and personalized dictatorship imposed by Stalin.

The Revolution of October/November 1917

Soviet Russia was born in October/November 1917, when the Bolshevik Party, under Lenin, seized power in Petrograd and Moscow. In doing so it toppled the Provisional Government, mainly identified with the leadership of Alexander Kerensky. This, in turn, had replaced the regime of Tsar Nicholas II in March 1917.

Nicholas II's government had been severely weakened by a combination of military defeat at the hands of the Germans in the First World War, economic collapse and serious misgovernment. In March 1917 it was confronted by a largely spontaneous movement which began as a series of food riots and ended with the desertion of troops and security forces. When Nicholas II eventually abdicated on 15 March, two institutions claimed political authority. One was the Petrograd Soviet, a workers' council which was elected by soldiers and labourers. The other was the Provisional Government which had been set up by a committee of the Duma, a parliament which had been conceded reluctantly by the Tsar in 1905. The question now arising was: which of the two institutions – Soviet or Provisional Government – would provide the future power base?

There was nothing to indicate at this stage that the Bolsheviks would shortly be adding their bid for the control of Russia. They had played little part in the events of March and had no influence either in the Soviet or in the Provisional Government. The Soviet consisted mainly of Menshevik and Socialist Revolutionary deputies, while the Provisional Government, under Prince Lvov, was dominated by liberals and moderate conservatives – or Constitutional Democrats and Octobrists. Gradually, however, the Bolsheviks made their presence felt. Lenin returned from exile in Switzerland in April 1917 and set about making the Bolshevik Party the major organization of the working class. His intention was to take over the Soviet and use it to destroy the Provisional Government. For a while this seemed an impossible task. The Socialist Revolutionaries and Mensheviks within the Soviet were prepared to form a political partnership with the Provisional Government; this was cemented in the person of the Socialist Revolutionary Kerensky, who succeeded Lvov as head of the Provisional Government on 20 July. Earlier in the same month Lenin had been seriously embarrassed by an abortive Bolshevik uprising; he had actually tried to prevent it on the grounds that it was premature. The Provisional Government ordered the raiding of the Bolshevik headquarters and issued warrants for the arrest of the Bolshevik leaders. Lenin escaped this only by going into hiding in Finland. It seemed, therefore, that the Provisional Government had triumphed and that the Bolsheviks had shot their bolt.

Through much of 1917, however, the Provisional Government faced serious difficulties which eventually worked in favour of the Bolsheviks. It maintained Russia's support to the Allies but, in the process, suffered further losses of territory to the Germans from July onwards. The economy, too, was in desperate trouble and the peasantry were openly seizing the landlords' estates in many of the rural areas. Kerensky, hoping to preside over an orderly land transfer, sent troops to deal with peasant violence, thus antagonizing a large part of the population. The Bolsheviks were able to take advantage of this policy and came out openly in support of the peasants. But the real crisis confronting the Provisional Government was the Kornilov Revolt. General Kornilov, Commander-in-Chief of the Russian army, tried in August/September to overthrow the Provisional Government and to substitute for it a military dictatorship which would, he hoped, drive back the German invader and deal with the internal threat of revolution. Kerensky could rely upon the Petrograd Soviet to mobilize support against Kornilov's troops, but he needed additional help if he were to save the Provisional Government. In desperation he turned to Bolshevik units known as Red Guards and agreed to arm them if they joined the defence of Petrograd. This decision saved the capital but placed the Provisional Government in grave peril. The liberals pulled out of the coalition with Kerensky, who was now left with a small fraction of his original support at a time when the Bolsheviks were growing in confidence.

By September the Bolsheviks had also become the most popular alternative to the Provisional Government. They had won majorities in the Petrograd and Moscow Soviets, and soon came to dominate most of the provincial soviets as well. From this, Lenin deduced that the time had come to seize the initiative and sweep Kerensky from power. The Petrograd Soviet was used as a front for Bolshevik revolutionary activity. Trotsky, its president, was also the overall co-ordinator of the impending coup, directing the activities of the newly formed Revolutionary Military Committee from his headquarters in the Smolny Institute. On the night of 6/7 November, 1917, the Bolshevik Red Guards seized, with surprising ease and minimal bloodshed, the key installations of Petrograd. These included banks, telephone exchanges, railway stations and bridges. By 8 November the Winter Palace and the Admiralty Buildings, the administrative headquarters of the Provisional Government, had also been stormed. Kerensky had left the city to spend the rest of his life in exile.

Why were the Bolsheviks successful?

Lenin regarded the October Revolution as 'as easy as lifting a feather'. He was assisted by two main factors. The first was the social and political situation between March and November, which gradually undermined the Provisional Government. The second was the Bolsheviks' organization and strategy, which enabled them to take maximum advantage of the weakness of their opponents.

The weaknesses of the Provisional Government

The underlying problem of the period between March and October 1917 was the existence of a dual power base, referred to in the previous section. The Provisional Government consisted, at first, of Constitutional Democrats and Octobrists, and stood for the development of a western type of parliamentary system. Established at the same time, the Petrograd Soviet comprised parties of the left, like the Mensheviks, Socialist Revolutionaries and ultimately the Bolsheviks. There were attempts to achieve collaboration between the two institutions. The Soviet, for example, passed an early resolution to co-operate with the Provisional Government laws 'in so far as they correspond to the interests of the proletariat and the broad democratic masses of the people'. Members of the Soviet were also drawn into the Provisional Government; Kerensky, a Socialist Revolutionary, was there from the start and several others joined the coalition governments of May and July.

These developments did not, however, guarantee political harmony. On the contrary, the Provisional Government and the Soviet pulled apart on conflicting policies over the continuation of the war and the distribution of land; to make matters worse, there was also dissension within the Provisional Government itself. The liberals actually pulled out of the government in August over the Kornilov Revolt so that

Kerensky was left virtually isolated, presiding over a mere rump separated by an ever widening gulf from the Soviet. The latter was becoming increasingly radical and assertive, under the growing influence of the Bolsheviks, while Kerensky was becoming more and more vulnerable to the accusation that his own claim to power was still untested by parliamentary election. In the words of one historian, it was a 'pre-legitimate regime'.

The Provisional Government was, therefore, inherently unstable and would have found survival difficult even in favourable circumstances. Its task was, however, rendered impossible by its military commitments. In the summer of 1917 it launched a great offensive against the Germans and Austrians in Galicia. This proved a disastrous failure and, from July onwards, the Provisional Government faced the constant spectre of German advance. The Russian army was in imminent danger of collapse which, in itself, caused problems; mass desertions increased the level of instability while, at the top, officers like Kornilov felt that they had little to lose by taking matters into their own hands. The Provisional Government's commitment to continuing the war was one of the main reasons for its growing rift with the soviets and for the movement of the latter towards the Bolsheviks.

One further issue is worth brief examination. Why did the Socialist Revolutionaries and the Mensheviks in the Petrograd Soviet not take the initiative and set up an alternative to the Provisional Government? The answer is that they stood for different types of socialism which could not easily have been reconciled. The Menshevik commitment was particularly strange. They were tied to a rigid version of Marxism which believed that the proletariat needed to help bring the bourgeoisie to power and then to wait, possibly for a long period, until capitalism had run its course before expecting the arrival of a socialist system. This justified co-operation with the liberals but hardly found favour with the Petrograd Soviet or with the first and second Congresses of Soviets which convened in June and October. (In his study of Menshevik strategy, A. Ascher asks the pertinent question: 'Had any class ever helped to make a revolution and then voluntarily stepped back to allow another to reap most of the benefits?'[1]) The Bolsheviks were presented with a perfect opportunity to appeal to the radicals in the soviets through a series of promises in Lenin's *April Theses*. The result was a steady increase in Bolshevik influence which coincided with the deterioration of the Provisional Government. In the first Congress of Soviets (June 1917) the Bolsheviks had only 150 representatives to the Mensheviks' 248. By October the situation had been reversed; the Bolsheviks now had 300, the Mensheviks 80 at the most.

An incident at the June meeting of the Congress of Soviets shows the contrasting attitudes to power of the Bolsheviks and other parties of the left. Tsereteli, one of the Menshevik leaders, argued that there was no real alternative to the Provisional Government. He concluded: 'At the present moment there is no political party which would say, "Give the power into our hands, go away, we will take your place". There is no such party in Russia.' Lenin was heard to say from his seat, 'There is'.[2]

The strengths of the Bolsheviks

Indeed, Lenin had for many years prepared for just such a situation. He had consistently emphasized the need for a tight party with a core of 'persons engaged in revolution as a profession'. The Bolshevik Party was given a double objective in 1917. The first was to use its organization on behalf of the masses to accomplish what the masses by themselves could not. The second was to take over the soviets, using them as a front to legitimize the Party's revolutionary activities. Lenin, in fact, observed on 22 October: 'If we seize power today, we seize it not against the soviets but for them.'[3]

Effective organization would have been to no avail without a clear overall strategy. The basic principle of the Bolsheviks was to have a fixed long-term objective but a flexible short-term approach to it. The long-term aim was described in Lenin's *April Theses* as 'the transition from the first stage of the revolution, which gave power to the bourgeoisie ... to the second stage, which should give the power into the hands of the proletariat and poorest strata of the peasantry'.[2] The short-term approach, however, would avoid any rigid or doctrinaire commitments. Above all, the right degree of force was essential at the right time; Lenin spoke of a judicious alternation between withdrawal and attack, depending on the strengths and weaknesses of the opponent.

The Bolsheviks were, of course, fortunate in their leadership. Lenin, from the time of his return to Russia in April 1917, was the overall strategist of the revolution; he also dealt with internal divisions within the Party and provided an authoritarian base which promoted a degree of discipline and unity which the other parties lacked. Above all, he was entirely responsible for the timing of the October Revolution. He had realized that the rising of July 1917 was premature and therefore urged restraint on that occasion. But by October he calculated that circumstances had changed sufficiently to warrant immediate action, and he urged: 'We must not wait! We may lose everything!'[3] From this point the initiative passed to Trotsky who, as we have seen, used the Revolutionary Military Committee to effect a smooth and rapid takeover of the key installations in the capital. Western historians are agreed on the vital importance of Trotsky in carrying out the broad aims of Lenin, although modern Soviet historiography predictably regards Trotsky as an impediment who added nothing to Lenin's all-encompassing role.[4]

The survival of Bolshevik Russia: the Civil War 1918–22

Seizing power was accomplished with surprising ease, but retaining it was to prove more difficult, as Lenin himself was all too aware. The most immediate threat was war – in two forms. The first was that the Great War, which had already been the catalyst in destroying Tsarism and the Provisional Government, would bring down the Bolsheviks as well. The second was that counter-revolutionaries, assisted by foreign powers, would destroy the regime in a bloody civil war. Lenin might survive one form of conflict, but he could hardly survive both.

He resolved, therefore, to end the struggle with which he had never agreed and, in 1918, accepted the terms of the Treaty of Brest-Litovsk dictated by the Germans. He justified the enormous loss of territory by pointing to the greater good of saving the regime; hence 'a disgraceful peace is proper, because it is in the interest of the proletarian revolution and the regeneration of Russia'.[5] As a result, he was able to concentrate on dealing with the offensive launched by the 'Whites', or counter-revolutionaries and their Allies.

Early in 1918 the Bolsheviks controlled less than one-sixth of Russia, or an area roughly the size of sixteenth-century Muscovy. The Whites advanced on this from three main directions, before eventually being repulsed by Trotsky's newly formed Red Army. The first attacks, which came from the south, were led by Kornilov, Deniken and Alexeyev. When these were contained in 1918, the southern initiative passed to Deniken and then, in 1920, to Wrangel. The eastern front saw extensive engagements with Kolchak's troops, culminating in the capture of Omsk by the Bolsheviks (1919). In the Baltic sector Yudenitch made a lunge for Petrograd but was driven back from the outer suburbs. Meanwhile, foreign expeditionary forces had landed, in support of the Whites, at Archangel and Murmansk in the north, as well as in the Crimea and the Caucasus. The Japanese penetrated far into eastern Siberia, via the port of Vladivostok. The British, French and United States governments had various motives, including a desire to contain the threat of Communism and, in the case of France, to collect the extensive debts of the Tsarist regime which had since been repudiated by the Bolsheviks. The whole scene was complicated by separatist uprisings, against Bolshevik rule, by the Ukraine and the states of the Caucasus, and by a full-scale war between Soviet Russia and Poland between 1920 and 1921.

By 1921 the Bolsheviks had managed to extend their control from the European heartland to the whole of Russia although, in the process, they had been forced to concede part of the Ukraine to the Poles by the Treaty of Riga. The Whites were everywhere in disarray and the Allied powers had decided to withdraw their expeditionary forces. Why did this transformation occur?

A vital reason was the preoccupation of the foreign powers, elsewhere, which prevented a full-scale invasion of Russia. J.L.H. Keep lays particular stress on this point, attributing Bolshevik survival 'in part to sheer good luck. Neither the Allies nor the Central powers were willing or able to take decisive action against them. To put matters baldly, they were saved by the continuation of the war in the West, which held first priority in the thinking of all the protagonists.'[6] It could also be argued that Allied intervention, where it did occur, was half-hearted and uncoordinated. The western powers eventually lost interest and those statesmen who, like Winston Churchill, wanted to continue an anti-Bolshevik crusade, were very much in a minority. By 1920 Lloyd George's government had heeded the threat of the British trade union movement that it would not tolerate further involvement in Russia, while the French government had decided to switch to a defensive strategy against Bolshevism by bolstering up Poland.

One of the reasons that the Whites were so dependent on foreign support was that they lacked political unity and a clear aim. (P. Kenez, for example, states that the White generals were not intellectuals 'and they did not systematically summarize their goals and beliefs. They never understood the importance of ideology and did not take ideas seriously.'[7]) They had no 'body of doctrine' and no overall leader. Some were active Tsarists, others were more inclined to a republic. There was also an amazing variety of anti-Bolshevik regimes; White-dominated Siberia, for example, had no fewer than 19 separate governments early in 1918. The Bolsheviks, by contrast, had a clear and systematic ideology and used their control over all forms of communication to put across their propaganda. This undoubtedly had some effect on the civilian population. C. Hill stresses the positive support earned by the Bolsheviks from the organized workers and supplemented by the 'patriotism of the peasantry'.[8] The rural populations also tended to support the Bolsheviks as the lesser of two evils; they feared that the Whites would restore the powerful landlords and reimpose the former dues and obligations. Also, the White armies lived off the land during their campaigns and therefore caused immense destruction through their foraging and looting.

In terms of military organization, there was a huge contrast between the growing efficiency of the Bolsheviks and the increasing problems of the Whites. Trotsky accomplished the monumental task of building a new army to replace that which the First World War had smashed, and succeeded in increasing the number of regular troops from 550,000 in September 1918 to 5.5 million. The Whites were never able to co-ordinate their own not inconsiderable supplies and resources in a sledgehammer offensive against Trotsky's recruits. Nor did the Whites and the supporting powers set up an overall war council. The result was that the Bolsheviks could deal with the threats as they occurred, switching their troops as required from one front to another. This was, of course, made possible by geographical factors. The Bolsheviks were defending the heart of the homeland, in which they controlled the main cities and industries and, above all, Russia's main railway network, which radiated outwards from Moscow. By contrast, the Whites had severe transport difficulties and found that the trans-Siberian railway was clogged up as a result of a series of complex political and military disputes.

Finally, the Whites could not even use to their advantage the breakaway movements in the peripheral states. It was not their objective, after all, to win back from the Bolsheviks a state which had decomposed into its national parts. Once it became clear that the Bolsheviks would eventually conquer the whole of Russia, the various nationalities, including the Ukraine and Georgia, were persuaded to accept the principles of national self-determination and federalism which came to be an essential part of the Union of Soviet Socialist Republics.

The Bolshevik state

Shortly after the October Revolution one of the Menshevik leaders, Axelrod, said that the Bolshevik regime's 'days and weeks are numbered'.[1] Events were to prove, however, that the counterpart to military survival against external enemies was the consolidation of internal political power.

The main development was the move away from a mixed democracy, with different types of representative institutions, towards a single or monolithic base. The first casualty was the western-type Constituent Assembly. The elections of November 1917 produced a sweeping majority for the Socialist Revolutionaries, who won 410 seats to the Bolsheviks' 175. In January 1918 Lenin dissolved the As-

sembly and put an end to the hopes of the other socialist
parties that a western democracy would emerge. He saw the
Assembly as 'an expression of the old relation of political
forces'.[9] In his search for an alternative he turned to the
system of soviets, arguing that 'a republic of soviets is a
higher form of democratic principle than the customary
bourgeois republic with its Constituent Assembly'.[1] This was
directly opposed to the policy of the Menshevik leaders, who
saw the soviets as a means of expressing popular opinion only
in exceptional times; after the end of the crisis, they argued,
the soviets would take second place to the more conventional
institutions of democracy. But Lenin was also careful to
control the soviets' powers. Although their number increased
rapidly from 1918, their actual influence declined steadily.
Keep considers that Lenin's intention was quite clear; he
conceived of the soviets as instruments of rule rather than
sovereign bodies.[6]

The hand which controlled these instruments was the
Bolshevik Party, shortly to be renamed the Communist Party.
As far back as 1902 Lenin had decided that the Party should
be the 'vanguard' of the proletariat, based on the leadership
of the few. The result was a structure of authority which led
upwards to the Central Committee. This, in turn, had three
specialized organs in the form of the Politburo, Orgburo and
Secretariat. The Party dominated the soviets at all levels.
Party membership was carefully restricted. This was ensured
by the Control Commission, established in 1920 and placed
under the authority of Stalin. Indeed, according to a Party
resolution of March 1919, 'the strictest centralism and the
most severe discipline are an absolute necessity'.[10] The whole
process was described as democratic, but not in a western or
'bourgeois' sense. Instead, Lenin's term 'democratic centralism' came to epitomize the complete subordination of state
organs to the Party.

How were these changes carried out? Both Lenin and
Trotsky believed in the need for force, although this was to be
conducted 'in the name of the interest of the workers.'[11]
Between December 1917 and February 1922 the secret police,
or Cheka, hunted down opponents of the regime and, by one
calculation, executed over 140,000 people. This compared

with a total of 14,000 dispatched by the Tsarist secret police, the Okhrana. Trotsky, a hardliner on the use of terror, justified the strategy on the grounds that 'we shall not enter into the kingdom of socialism in white gloves on a polished floor'.[12] Not all admirers of the Bolsheviks approved. Victor Serge, a French Communist, referred to the activities of the Cheka as 'one of the most impermissible errors that the Bolsheviks committed'. He added: 'Was it necessary to resort to the procedures of the Inquisition?'[13]

The result was the elimination of all forms of political opposition. The Anarchists were the first to be dealt with by the Cheka, their views of unfettered political liberty being seen as a threat to the Bolshevik theory of the dictatorship of the proletariat.[14] The moderate socialists – Mensheviks and Socialist Revolutionaries – were expelled from the soviets during the course of 1918, while 34 Socialist Revolutionary leaders were put on public trial in 1922. Yet the emergence of the one-party state was not a complete guarantee against dissent and unrest. If anything, the Bolsheviks were confronted by more extensive opposition *after* the elimination of the other parties. The critical year was 1921, when the Cheka reported no fewer than 118 separate uprisings.[14] One example was the Kronstadt Revolt, which carried demands for 'Soviets without Communists', elections by secret ballot and an end to the belief that the only alternative to a 'bourgeois regime' was the 'dictatorship of the Communist Party'. Although the Kronstadt Revolt was suppressed by Trotsky and Tukhachevskii, the threat was taken seriously by Lenin, who referred to it as 'the biggest ... internal crisis'[14] of the period. Since the immediate cause had been the appalling economic situation, Lenin's response was to moderate Bolshevik policy in the way examined in the next section. At the same time, however, Lenin maintained his grasp on political power by ensuring that the opposition parties did not re-emerge. Only when he was fully satisfied did he end the terror by closing down the Cheka in February 1922.

How did the various nationalities fit into this structure? Tsarist Russia had contained many captive peoples who had seized the opportunity provided by the First World War and the Bolshevik Revolution to go their own way. Some, like the

Poles, Finns and Baltic peoples, achieved complete independence as a result of Russian defeat in the First World War. Others, like the Ukrainians and Georgians, stayed out during the Civil War but were brought back into line after the Bolshevik victories over the Whites. Lenin's whole approach to the nationalities was cautious and pragmatic. Originally he had favoured national self-determination in principle but viewed any form of federation with suspicion. Faced with the practical problems of the period 1918–24, he came to the conclusion that the only safe means of allowing for self-determination was *through* federalism. As a result, the Constitutions of 1918 and 1924 established the two largest federations in the world – the Russian Soviet Federated Socialist Republic and the Union of Soviet Socialist Republics. This, however, was only a partial concession, for the total subordination of the organs of each Republic to those of the Party ensured that federalism did not mean decentralization. The USSR, in other words, was controlled by the Communist Party.

The Bolshevik economy

The Bolsheviks came to power intending to introduce sweeping economic changes to wipe out 'all exploitation of man by man' and to eliminate 'the division of society into classes'. The period 1917–24 did not, however, see a phased and systematic approach to this ideal. Instead, Lenin proceeded by a mixture of trial and error.

Between November 1917 and mid-1918 the emphasis was on caution, and nationalization was applied only to banks, foreign trade and armaments works. In particular, Lenin was careful to avoid antagonizing the peasantry and made every effort to win them away from the party which they had traditionally supported – the Socialist Revolutionaries. Hence, by the 1917 Decree on Land he confirmed the peasant takeover of the nobles' estates, without, however, introducing large-scale socialist collective production.[15]

Then, in mid-1918, came a major change of course with his introduction of a policy generally known as 'War Communism'. This was basically an attempt to replace the free market by state control over all means of production and distribution. The Decree on Nationalization, for example, covered all large-scale enterprises, while grain requisitioning greatly reduced the food stocks of the peasantry in order to supply the workers in the cities and the troops fighting the Whites. The result was chaos. The monetary economy disintegrated, to be replaced by barter and black marketeering. Grain requisitioning led directly to a drastic decline in production as the peasantry lost all incentive to labour, while the inevitable shortage of food in the cities provoked strikes and riots which shook the very foundations of the Bolshevik regime. Of these the most serious was the Kronstadt Revolt (1921), dealt with in the previous section.

Why was such a policy introduced at all? There are two possible explanations. One is that it was a genuine emergency measure to mobilize the resources of the state in its struggle for survival against counter-revolutionary forces. Lenin later said: 'War Communism was thrust upon us by war and ruin. It was not, nor could it be, a policy that corresponded to the economic tasks of the proletariat. It was a temporary measure.'[15] Against this, however, is the view that War Communism, far from being a temporary if unpleasant necessity, was a fundamental error. R. Medvedev emphasizes that the New Economic Policy, eventually introduced in 1921, should have been applied from the start instead of War Communism and that it must be concluded that Lenin 'did not at that time arrive at the more correct solution to the economic problems of the post-revolutionary period. It took the hard experience of the civil war and the political crisis of 1921 to accomplish that.'[16]

1921, therefore, saw a second great switch. The basic strategy was now to restore to the economy a degree of capitalism and private enterprise. Introducing his 'New Economic Policy' (NEP), Lenin argued that the road to socialism would be longer than originally thought. 'Our poverty and ruin are so great that we cannot *at one stroke* restore full-scale factory, state, socialist production.'[17] It was also impossible to think only in ideological terms. 'If certain communists were inclined to think it possible in three years to transform the whole economic foundation, to change the very roots of agriculture, they were certainly dreamers.'[18]

Thus the peasantry were now permitted to dispose of their surplus produce on payment of a tax, and 91 per cent of industrial enterprises were returned to private ownership or trusts. The early results of the NEP were disappointing, as economic recovery was held up by famine (1921–2) and a financial crisis (1923). But, by 1924, the year of Lenin's death, considerable progress had been made, and by 1926 the economy had regained the 1913 production level.

In the NEP Lenin left an intermediate strategy which contained a long-term problem. Should the mixed economy be retained indefinitely, as Bukharin argued, or should socialism be accelerated – a course urged by Trotsky? As will be seen, this turned into a major dispute which overlapped the manoeuvring in the struggle for the political leadership.

Lenin: an assessment

Lenin was plagued by ill health during the last two years of his life. He suffered a stroke in May 1922 and, although he made a partial recovery, he never again played a full part in political life. His health deteriorated rapidly from March 1923 with the loss of speech and the onset of paralysis. On his death in January 1924 a post-mortem revealed that one of the two hemispheres of his brain had shrunk to the size of a walnut. The new leadership ignored one of his last wishes by having his body embalmed and placed on open display.

What are we to make of the period 1917–24? How should we interpret the dual process of revolution and consolidation? On the one hand certain positive features are evident. Lenin led a party to electoral victory in the major soviets in Russia by October 1917, replacing the Mensheviks and Socialist Revolutionaries as the real spokesman of the urban workers. He used this new-found popularity to seize power and overturn a temporary regime which had clearly lost its way. He subsequently held the new state together against a series of counter revolutionary attacks which were extensively backed by the major powers; eventually he expanded the frontiers almost to the previous limits of Tsarist Russia, thereby preventing the sort of disintegration which had already overtaken the Ottoman Empire and Austria-Hungary. Finally he brought a dramatic change to the lives of the ordinary Russian people. The last social remnants of the Tsarist regime were swept away as the Bolsheviks confirmed the peasantry in possession of the nobles' estates; while measures were taken to end the exploitation of labour in industry by capitalists careless of such essentials as working conditions and health schemes.

There is, however, another picture. The cost of Russia's transformation was greater than she had ever experienced. Over 20 million lives were lost during a period of unprecedented conflict and destruction which affected the entire country – from the Polish frontier in the west to eastern Siberia, from Archangel in the north to the Caspian Sea in the south. It is possible to absolve Lenin from total responsibility for the ruin caused by the numerous military campaigns, but not from the unnecessary suffering and wastage caused by War Communism. And during the conflict with external enemies Lenin was strengthening the internal apparatus of coercion, establishing a one-party state and dispensing with more moderate forms of socialist democracy. In the process, he demolished one of history's promising 'what-might-have-beens'.

This double-sided view is reflected in the controversies which have arisen over the two components of the period 1917–24: the Leninist Revolution and the Leninist State.

At its most fundamental, the conflict of opinion concerns the very nature of the events which occurred in October 1917. The Bolshevik view was that the revolution was inevitable, part of an historical and dialectical process and representing, in Trotsky's words, the 'transfer of power from one class to another'.[19] A superior form of state was emerging; in this sense the revolution was, according to Lenin, a 'turning point' in history, with the Bolsheviks directing and channelling the 'upsurge of the people'. The other contemporary explanation was advanced by Kerensky, the victim of Lenin's success. He saw the October coup as a freak occurrence and a perversion of Russia's historical trends. He argued that a series of unfortunate events provided the opportunity for the Bolsheviks to 'break up the Provisional Government and stop the establishment of a democratic system in Russia'. Kornilov's attempt at dictatorship 'opened the door to the dictatorship of Lenin'; in fact, far from responding to any popular surge, Lenin succeeded 'only by way of conspiracy, only by way of treacherous armed struggle.'[20]

Lenin's interpretation has since been endorsed by official Soviet historiography. All other parties and types of democracy were mere throwbacks to a lower stage of historical development; hence they could be 'thrown on the rubbish heap of history'. Western historians, not confined to monolithic interpretation, vary in their approach. Some incline towards the 'conspiracy' view of Kerensky. They see the Bolshevik Revolution as a distortion of socialism and Marxism used to construct a dictatorship which was by no means the logical outcome of previous trends. According to R. Gregor, the 'conspiracy' was self-perpetuating, for 'the conspiratorial party of the revolution became a conspiratorial party of legitimacy'.[21] Christopher Hill adopts a western Marxist position; to him 'Lenin symbolizes the Russian Revolution as a movement of the poor and oppressed of the earth who have successfully risen against the great and powerful'.[22]

Another major controversy concerns the nature of Lenin's regime. One extreme has been put forcefully in Solzhenitsyn's *Gulag Archipelago*, published in 1974. One of the central themes of this book is that the October Revolution and the Bolshevik regime led inexorably to Stalinism, that they were one and the same process. In a review of the *Gulag Archipelago*, however, E. Mandel puts the reverse case, emphasizing the fundamental difference between the two regimes, 'the Bolshevik revolution and the Stalinist counter-revolution'.[23]

Some historians incline towards the case for continuity between Lenin and Stalin, although this is a criticism of Lenin rather than a rehabilitation of Stalin. A strong case is established by G. Leggett, who is convinced that terror 'was implicit in Leninism'. Lenin's Cheka led ultimately to Stalin's NKVD (People's Commissariat for International Affairs – the forerunner of the KGB); consequently, 'it was Lenin who laid the police state foundations which made Stalin's monstrous feats technically possible'.[24]

By contrast, E.H. Carr has argued that Lenin was sufficiently different to Stalin to have been likely 'to minimize and mitigate the element of coercion' had he lived to face Stalin's difficulties. Lenin was 'reared in a humane tradition, he enjoyed enormous prestige, great moral authority and powers of persuasion'. By contrast, 'Stalin had no moral authority whatever.... He understood nothing but coercion, and from the first employed this openly and brutally.'[25] Mandel points out that whatever terror did exist under Lenin was a direct response to attempts at counter-revolution, to 'the White terror that came first' and the 'invasion of Soviet territory on seven different fronts'. Unlike Stalin, Lenin and Trotsky did not destroy the basis of justice. They did make mistakes in suppressing other parties and banning factions within the Communist Party itself. But these were a direct response to a desperate emergency and were conceived as temporary measures only.[23] Finally, L. Schapiro maintains that, despite being authoritarian in his methods, Lenin never destroyed the basic machinery of the various Party organs. Stalin, on the other hand, ceased to use the Party as a base of power, depending instead on a personal Secretariat. He therefore exploited and abused Lenin's system – but, of course, the system had no inbuilt safeguards to prevent this from happening. Thus 'Stalinism was not a necessary consequence of Leninism, but it was nevertheless a possible result'.[26]

THE SUCCESSION 1924–9

The struggle for power

During the last months of his effective rule, Lenin seemed increasingly concerned about the problem of his successor. In his 'Testament' of December 1922 Lenin provided comments on the leading contenders. He mentioned, but passed briefly over, Kamenev, Zinoviev, Bukharin and Piatakov. He gave more attention to Trotsky, although he considered that he had become too heavily involved in administrative detail. When he came to consider Stalin he expressed real doubts. 'Comrade Stalin, having become General Secretary, has concentrated unlimited authority in his hands, and I am not sure whether he will always be capable of using that

authority with sufficient caution.' Shortly afterwards, in
January 1923, Lenin added a codicil to the Testament urging
the Party to take action to remove Stalin from his post as
Secretary General. He should, Lenin concluded, be replaced
by someone 'more patient, more loyal, more courteous, and
more considerate of his comrades'. Before Lenin could do
anything to prod the party into action he was incapacitated
by his second and third strokes.

When Lenin died in January 1924 the succession was still
uncertain. At first Stalin's chances seemed remote, particularly in view of Lenin's Testament and its codicil, which were
read out at a meeting of the Party Central Committee. But the
other Party members agreed that Stalin had 'improved' his
reputation during the course of 1923 and therefore voted to
put aside the recommendations of the codicil. Meanwhile,
Kamenev and Zinoviev had come to the conclusion that
Trotsky was the main threat to the Party's stability, partly
because of his forceful personality and partly because of his
close association with the army. Hence they collaborated
with Stalin and a power-sharing Triumvirate emerged, with
Stalin remaining in his post of General Secretary. But the
Triumvirate was to be only a temporary phase in the
succession to Lenin. By 1929 Stalin was in total control,
having disposed of all his possible rivals: Trotsky, Kamenev,
Zinoviev and Bukharin. There appear to have been three
main phases in this development.

The first was the emergence, between 1923 and 1925, of a
major split between the Triumvirate (consisting of Stalin,
Kamenev and Zinoviev) and the isolated figure of Trotsky.
This division was expressed in an ideological debate between
'Permanent revolution' and 'Socialism in one country'.
Trotsky's strategy of 'Permanent revolution' emphasized
rapid industrialization and the abolition of private farming
at home. Abroad, Russia would promote the spread of
revolution to the rest of Europe which would ensure the
survival of Bolshevism. 'Socialism in one country', advocated
by Stalin, stressed the need to maintain the more moderate
economic course of the NEP within Russia and to promote
more positive relations with other countries to increase trade
and attract foreign investment. Stalin was far less deeply

committed to the economic principles of this 'right-wing' strategy than Trotsky was to the 'left', his motive being the political one of isolating Trotsky. In this he succeeded. At the 14th Party Congress in 1925 he received overwhelming support (although not from Kamenev and Zinoviev, both of whom opposed further concessions to the peasantry). Trotsky's political days were clearly numbered.

The second stage was the disposal of Kamenev and Zinoviev, which occurred between 1925 and 1927. Never one to share power for long, Stalin aligned himself with the most obvious 'rightist' elements within the Party, including Bukharin, Rykov and Tomsky. Between 1926 and 1927 Kamenev and Zinoviev made common cause with Trotsky, but it was too late. The Party conference of 1927 gave its approval to 'Socialism in one country' and denounced 'Permanent revolution'. Trotsky was expelled from the Politburo, along with Kamenev and Zinoviev. Trotsky was exiled from Russian in 1929, while both Kamenev and Zinoviev perished in the purges of the 1930s.

The third stage was predictable: the elimination of Bukharin and the rest of the right, which was accomplished by 1929. The end of the 1920s also saw a hardening of Stalin's own economic ideas as he began to associate 'Socialism in one country' with the total transformation of industry at the expense of the peasantry – the programme of Trotsky, in effect, without the insistence on spreading revolution to the rest of Europe. This was strongly opposed by Bukharin, Rykov and Tomsky, who had always supported a moderate policy towards the peasantry. As Stalin gradually introduced measures against the wealthy peasantry, or *kulaks*, Bukharin, Rykov and Tomsky became more outspoken. Stalin accused them of plotting against the Party's agreed strategy and forced them to resign from the Politburo and from their state offices.

By 1929 Stalin dominated the Party more completely than Lenin had ever done and, through the Party, the state. Ahead lay the sweeping economic changes and the purges. Bukharin compared him to Genghis Khan, adding 'Stalin will strangle us. He is an unprincipled intriguer who subordinates everything to his lust for power.'

Why Stalin?

Stalin was probably the least impressive of all the candidates for the succession. He was totally eclipsed by Trotsky in the October Revolution and never succeeded in winning the friendship and confidence of Lenin. He was even regarded as a plodder; Trotsky referred to him as 'The Party's most eminent mediocrity'. This was to prove a serious underestimate. Stalin had skills which were less obvious, but more deadly. He was also able to benefit from a set of objective conditions which favoured mediocrity rather than brilliance.

The most important of these was the failure of Communist revolution in the west. Trotsky and, to a lesser extent, Lenin, had always stressed that Russia would derive strength from contact with Communism in the more advanced economies of western Europe. The first opportunity seemed to come with the German revolution off 1918–19: there was, for a while, the possibility that a Communist regime would replace the socialist government which had, in turn, succeeded the Kaiser. But the outcome was catastrophe for the German Communists – and for the cause of the European revolution espoused by Trotsky. As L. Colletti argues, 'The first rung of the ladder which was to carry Stalin to power was supplied by the [German] Social-Democratic leaders who in January 1919 murdered Rosa Luxemburg and Karl Liebknecht.... The remaining rungs were supplied by the reactionary wave which subsequently swept Europe.'[27] For Stalin was able to put across a more primitive appeal – to Russian self-reliance, even isolationism. This harmonized well with his 'Socialism in one country'. It also provided a solution to one of Stalin's major problems – his intellectual inferiority to most of his Party contemporaries. He alone had no contacts with western ideas or culture; he alone spoke no European language. With the collapse of Communism in Europe, however, Stalin's Slavic background could be seen as a strength rather than as a deficiency. He seemed to have the best qualification to move Russia away from any ideological or economic dependence on the west.

Among Stalin's political advantages was his ability to manoeuvre between factions. He avoided permanent commitments and loyalties to any grouping, as is shown by his treatment of Kamenev and Zinoviev, and then of Bukharin. At the same time he always posed as a moderate, often a centrist, which increased his chance of being misjudged or underestimated by his opponents. Indeed, opponents were unlikely to be aware that they were in any real danger until Stalin had emerged from his 'moderate' cover to launch a deadly offensive. This process was facilitated by certain personal attributes. According to M. McCauley, 'He was a very skilful politician who had a superb grasp of tactics, could predict behaviour extremely well and had an unerring eye for personal weaknesses'.[28] These weaknesses were vital. Trotsky's are dealt with in the next section; Zinoviev, according to Carr, hesitated and had no gifts as an organizer, while Kamenev lacked a 'clear vision' and 'the desire' and 'capacity to lead men'.[29] Bukharin, despite being an economist, failed signally to produce a convincing programme which could have saved the NEP and discredited Stalin. One by one those former associates of Lenin who thought that they could put Stalin in his place found that it was he who put them in theirs – in political exile.

What made this possible was Stalin's supremacy within the Party. His vital appointment was to the post of General Secretary in 1922. Lenin had good reason to be concerned about Stalin's accumulation of power and influence. Stalin controlled the Party administration and was responsible for giving out offices: hence he had the main voice in membership and promotion. Gradually he built up a steady base of support which made it possible for him to manoeuvre so effectively among his political rivals. The process operated as follows. The Communist Party was officially a democratic institution, in which the lowest level – the local parties – elected the Party Congress which, in turn, produced the membership of the Central Committee. The latter, finally, elected the Politburo. The composition of the local parties was determined by the Secretariat, which was under Stalin's control. Over a period of time, therefore, Stalinist supporters moved into the upper levels of the Party. There was an added incentive for these men; if Stalin's opponents could be removed from the highest offices then there would be a series of vacancies. It is hardly surprising, therefore, that Stalin's appointees should have been so willing to support him and that other prominent Bolsheviks were not accorded the respect which their experience perhaps deserved.

Why not Trotsky?

At first sight Trotsky might seem ideally placed to assume the mantle of Lenin. He had been the tactician of Lenin's strategy in October 1917; as President of the Petrograd Soviet he had organized the Revolutionary Military Committee which had actually seized power. During the chaotic months which followed he created the Red Army and, as Commissar for War, was instrumental in overcoming the threats from the Whites and foreign interventionists. He has, indeed, been described as 'the dynamo of the militarised Bolshevik state'.[30] At the same time he made fundamental additions to Bolshevik doctrine, the most important of which was his emphasis on 'Permanent revolution'. He had considerable personal talents. He was unquestionably the greatest orator of the Revolution, and was renowned for his intellect, statesmanship and administrative ability. Yet, for all these attributes, he found himself out of effective power by 1925, out of the Party by 1927 and out of the country by 1929.

Part of the reason has already been provided – Stalin's rapid accumulation of power within the Bolshevik Party which enabled him to outmanoeuvre Trotsky. The rest of the explanation can be sought in a number of serious disadvantages which helped turn some of Trotsky's apparent strengths into liabilities.

The first was his incompatibility with other leading members of the Party. He towered above them intellectually but in a way which brought him suspicion rather than respect. His whole attitude was profoundly influenced by contacts with western Europe. He therefore tended to play down Russian or Slavic achievements in culture and, in particular, in philosophy. After Lenin's death, however, the most influential of the Bolshevik leaders had little experience of the west and were therefore much more sympathetic to Stalin's pro-Slavic line. Hence, in January 1925 a resolution of the Party Central Committee condemned Trotskyism as 'a falsification of communism in the spirit of approximation to "European" patterns of pseudo-Marxism'.[29] As a 'westerner', Trotsky was also regarded as an intruder. He had avoided joining the Bolshevik Party until 1917 and had previously shown more sympathy for the Marxist principles of the Mensheviks. Lenin had found his assistance indispensible and had therefore given him rapid promotion, which was resented by the others.

It was, therefore, crucial for Trotsky to consolidate his own position within the Party. This, however, is precisely what he neglected to do. The revolutionary leader and military organizer was unable to adapt to Party politics; in Mikoyan's words, 'Trotsky is a man of State, not of the Party'.[30] This made him particularly unpopular with men who had tended to sink their own identities into the Party organization. Kamenev, for example, complained that Trotsky 'entered our party as an individualist, who thought, and still thinks, that in the fundamental question of the revolution it is not the party, but he, comrade Trotsky, who is right'.[29] Throughout the period 1917–29 Trotsky persistently underestimated the suspicion in which he was held and took no effective measures to try to dispel it. His capacity for leadership and his ability to persuade were employed *outside* the party; as Carr observes, 'he had no talent for leadership among equals'.[29]

Soviet historians see Trotsky as 'an incorrigible opportunist'. This, however, is an exaggeration as, in many respects, he was just the opposite. He lacked all the essential components of patience, tact and timing and missed a unique opportunity to make a move against Stalin. He failed, in May 1924, to turn the knife in Stalin; he actually voted for the suspension of Lenin's codicil which would have removed Stalin from high office. The picture which emerges is of a politician completely out of his element, with no natural political instinct and no real understanding of how to use a particular situation.

After being expelled from Russia in 1929 Trotsky launched a series of verbal attacks on Stalin's regime. He criticized the growth of Stalin's personality cult; he was outspoken about Stalin's total failure to comprehend the threat of the Nazis in

Germany in the early 1930s; and he wrote extensively on what he saw as Stalin's distortions of Marxism–Leninism. But, lacking a power base, he could be no more than a 'prophet in exile', to use the description of I. Deutscher.

STALIN'S PRE-WAR REGIME 1924–41

The economy under Stalin

Economic change was Stalin's immediate priority once his authority had been confirmed. He intended to transform the Soviet Union into a superpower by equipping it with a huge industrial base. The process began in 1929 and continued, with the interruption of war, until his death in 1953.

His major step was, from 1929, to abandon Lenin's New Economic Policy which had allowed limited private enterprise in the agricultural and industrial sectors. In its place Stalin decided to introduce full state planning to promote heavy industry and enforce the collectivization of agriculture. This, however, would involve mass dislocation and had already been postponed as impracticable by Lenin. Stalin was, therefore, under no ideological compulsion to force the pace of economic change. Indeed, all theoretical solutions seemed to point in the direction of caution and flexibility. What were his reasons for ignoring these?

The first was undoubtedly political. During the 1920s Stalin had no fixed attitude to economic issues, and altered course several times in order to deal with his opponents. He posed as a moderate to eliminate Trotsky and then as a radical to dispose of Bukharin. It could, therefore, be argued that his economic policies developed partly as a result of political needs, and that pragmatism prevailed over ideology.

Nevertheless, Stalin did advance a powerful and logical argument for his programme of industrialization. From 1927 he took over Trotsky's emphasis on the threats which Russia faced from the west and from capitalist encirclement. He then welded this anti-capitalism to a basic commitment to Russia's self-sufficiency, or 'Socialism in one country'. In February 1931 he summarized his position as follows: 'We have lagged fifty to a hundred years behind the leading countries. We must cover this distance in ten years. Either we do that or they crush us.'[31] The method employed was a series of five-year plans, co-ordinated by Gosplan, an institution at the very centre of the Party structure. The priority was the development of heavy industry and armaments.

Industrialization was associated from the outset with the forced collectivization of agriculture. The reason for this was that Stalin perceived the existing organization of agriculture as a major obstacle to his economic strategy. The main problem was the inadequacy of the grain supplies, which were needed partly to feed the industrial workers in the cities and partly to pay for the import of basic machinery from the west – literally the first cogs in the industrialization drive. The reason for this low agricultural productivity was the fragmentation of the land into small individual holdings and the tendency of the peasantry to retain their grain in the absence of any real incentive to sell it; hence less than 17 per cent of the 1926 harvest was marketed.[32] From 1928 Stalin's policies led inexorably to collectivization, although the final decision was not taken until December 1929. In January 1928 he applied pressure on the peasants to release their grain stocks by means of heavier taxation and disguised requisitioning. This, however, caused a collapse in the peasants' food reserves and seed stock, so that less grain was grown in 1928–9. In 1929, Stalin made his coercive measures more systematic and aimed to bring private land into collective farms (*kolkhozy*) or state farms (*sovkhozy*). He justified the programme ideologically by emphasizing the need to eliminate class divisions based on private property. This would be done by the 'liquidation of the *kulaks*', the landowning peasants who had prospered under Lenin's NEP.

Thus by 1931 a 'Great Turn' had occurred in economic policy. Three five-year plans were to be implemented. The first ran from 1928 until 1933, the second from 1933 until 1937, the third from 1938 until its interruption by Hitler's invasion of Russia in 1941. Any examination of their outcome inevitably involves some controversy, and it is possible to see both positive and negative results.

Stalin's positive achievement was concerned almost entirely with heavy industry. Between 1928 and 1941 steel production and coal production increased fourfold and fivefold respectively and, by 1937, the Soviet Union had become the world's second largest manufacturer of heavy vehicles. Stalin had made three vital contributions to industrialization. First, he accelerated the whole process, breaking away from the more cautious mentality of Bukharin and perhaps even of Lenin. Second, he extended the range of industrial centres by equipping the Urals and Siberia with plants and factories. Third, he found the resources to transform Russia's economic base without having to seek western investment. In using agriculture to subsidize industry and in squeezing every drop of money from the ordinary consumer, Stalin devised a ruthless but effective method of accumulating capital. R. Hutchings goes so far as to say that, overall, Stalin's measures were vital in the Soviet Union's capacity to resist the German invasion in 1941. 'One can hardly doubt that if there had been a slower build-up of industry, the attack would have been successful and world history would have evolved quite differently.'[31]

On the other hand, Stalin's industrial measures are open to extensive criticism. There is evidence that he exaggerated Russia's industrial deficiency in 1929. The Tsars had developed a considerable industrial capacity, based on five main centres: Moscow (textiles), Petrograd (heavy industry), the Donetz region (coalfields), Baku (oil) and the Ukraine (iron and steel).[33] In a sense the spadework had already been done and it is not altogether surprising that Stalin should have achieved such rapid results. He was also reluctant to acknowledge that most of his plans for widespread electrification and the development of the Urals were inherited from Lenin. Worst of all was the severe deprivation which accompanied industrial growth. Russia was unique in European economic history in experiencing an industrial revolution without corresponding improvements in the quality of life of the inhabitants. The imbalance between investment in heavy industry and consumer goods was so severe that it had eventually to be redressed by Malenkov after 1953 and again by Brezhnev in the late 1960s. Overall, Stalin's measures can be seen as excessive, in some instances damaging. A. Ulam puts an alternative argument to that of Hutchings: 'I have no doubt that if more humane and more rational policies had been employed, the Soviet economy might have been spared some of its recurrent disasters'.

This certainly applies to Stalin's agricultural changes. At first the policy of collectivization seemed to proceed with great speed but the methods used by Stalin's officials brought serious dislocation. Stalin was forced to call a halt in 1930 and had the nerve to criticize Party activists for being over-enthusiastic and 'dizzy with success'. The campaign was revived in 1931, and by 1932 60 per cent of all land had been collectivized. The figure rose to 90 per cent by 1934 and almost 97 per cent by 1940. Official propaganda pointed to the success of the *kolkhozy* and, indeed, the harvests of 1933, 1934 and 1935 were reasonably satisfactory. But this was only by comparison with the appalling harvest of 1931–2 and the horrific famine of 1932–3. Stalin later admitted to Churchill that collectivization cost, directly and indirectly, the lives of 10 million people. It is hardly surprising that collectivization should, in the early 1930s, have seen massive resistance from the peasantry.

Stalin had made the USSR a major industrial power, but this had been accomplished by crippling agriculture. It was also ironical that the industrialized state which he had built to resist western attacks should have contained millions of inhabitants prepared in 1941 to welcome the Germans as liberators.

Political and constitutional changes

The period 1929 to 1941 saw an apparently contradictory political development. On the one hand Stalin gradually squeezed all signs of democracy out of the Party, confirming his personal power and eliminating any possible rivals. On the other hand, changes in the Soviet constitution appeared to *extend* the range of democracy in the electoral system and some of the state institutions.

During the early 1930s the top levels of the Party, especially the Central Committee, had taken vital decisions concerning economic planning and had greatly accelerated the collectivi-zation of agriculture. At the same time, the Party swelled its numbers and modified its organization to include more

members from trade unions and factories. But the high point
of the Party was reached in 1934. The XVIIth Party Congress
was full of euphoria and self-satisfaction at the scope of the
Party's achievements in industry. The next five years,
however, saw drastic changes as Stalin reduced the top
membership in systematic purges, as described in the next
section; by 1939 none of the original Bolsheviks who had
participated in the 1917 Revolution was left. Stalin also
restructured the Party as a pyramid, with high grades being
conferred as a reward for unquestioning loyalty. He further
consolidated his position during the Second World War,
assuming total civil and military authority within the State
Committee of Defence (1941). After 1945 Stalin ignored the
Party Congress and Central Committee, and eventually
disbanded the Politburo in favour of a larger and less
influential Praesidium. As Khrushchev observed in 1956, in
an apparent understatement, Stalin 'absolutely did not
tolerate collegiality in leadership'.[34]

Constitutional developments presented a strange contrast.
The adoption in 1936 of a more progressive constitution
coincided with Stalin's onslaught on the Party. As part of the
build-up, there was unprecedented preliminary discussion,
with millions of people being consulted. A considerable
change was introduced into the electoral system. Universal
suffrage now applied to all over the age of 18, while voting
was to be secret and direct and no longer weighted (as it had
been in the 1918 and 1924 constitutions) in favour of the
urban workers. The Soviets, or legislative bodies, were also
reformed. The new 'Supreme Soviet' comprised two
chambers, the Soviet of the Union, based on electoral
districts, and the Soviet of the Nationalities, reflecting the
regional and ethnic composition of the country as a whole.
Article 30 of the constitution affirmed that collectively these
were the 'supreme organ of state power'. The Supreme Soviet
elected a series of specialist committees and a 33-man
praesidium for executive functions. The whole structure was
undoubtedly an improvement and remained in existence
until the not very substantial amendments made in
Brezhnev's 1977 constitution.

How can one explain the disparity between developments

in the Party and the constitution? First, the 1936 constitution was made as progressive as possible in appearance in order to attract a favourable response from the west. The mid-1930s, after all, saw a growing concern within the Soviet Union about the spread of Fascism and serious attempts by Stalin to foster popular fronts against it. Secondly, Stalin used the constitution as a means of diverting attention, internal and external, away from his purges. Hence, at a time when the Party was being systematically drained of its top leadership, the real publicity was given to the constitution. This could well explain the remarkably restrained reaction of the west to events in the Soviet Union in the late 1930s. Thirdly, the 1936 constitution was democratic in theory only. Many of the high-sounding principles were not implemented in practice and the supposed power of the Supreme Soviet remained under the direct supervision of Stalin himself. He therefore dominated the proceedings of the Soviet as directly as he controlled the Party.

The purges

The most spectacular and notorious of all Stalin's policies was his deliberate creation of a state of total terror. His direct responsibility for this has never been questioned and plenty of evidence was provided by Khrushchev in 1956.

The earliest purges affected the 'captains of industry' and plant managers, of whom about 75 per cent were eliminated in the early 1930s. From 1934 onwards the purges became more openly political, with the assassination of Kirov, Stalin's main potential rival. There then followed a series of spectacular show trials to deal with the Party's most prominent figures, while below the surface Stalin's NKVD under Yagoda, Ezhov and Beria, hunted down numberless unknowns. The first show trial (1936) disposed of Kamenev and Zinoviev; in the second, in 1937, Piatakov and Sokolnikov were accused of being the 'Anti-Soviet Trotskyist Centre'. The third, in 1938, accounted for Bukharin, Rykov and even Yagoda – all on the charge of belonging to a bloc of 'right-wingers and Trotskyites'. The army was also affected. In 1937 Marshal Tukhachevsky, hero of the Civil War years and now Commissar for Defence, was shot. All 11 deputy Commissars for Defence were executed, together with 75 out of the 80 members of the Supreme Military Council.[35] The navy lost all eight of its admirals. Meanwhile, throughout the Soviet Union, something like 300,000 people were executed and 7 million put through the labour camps. By 1939 Stalin considered that the terror had run its necessary course and decided to call a halt.

Although the enormity of Stalin's purges defy a completely logical explanation, a number of motives have been suggested. One is that Stalin had a disastrously flawed personality. Khrushchev, for example, later emphasized his brutality, vindictiveness, pathological distrust and 'sickly' suspicion. More recently, Tucker has maintained that, in addition to serving a political function, the trials also rationalized 'Stalin's own paranoid tendency'.[36] A second reason for the purges is that Stalin was never one to resort to half measures. He aimed to wipe out the entire generation of Bolsheviks who had assisted Lenin between 1917 and 1924. This alone would guarantee Stalin as the sole heir to Lenin and would secure his position for a lifetime. Most of the threats to his power were latent and would possibly not reveal themselves for several years. They should, nevertheless, be dealt with as soon as possible. Since these latent threats were impossible to identify, a large number of people who would ultimately prove innocent of any form of opposition to Stalin, would also have to go. It was only by having such a clean sweep that Stalin could make sure of eradicating those who *would* be a threat. In contrasting the liquidation programmes of Stalin and Hitler, Ulam points out that, by and large, the latter dealt with individuals and groups clearly identified as enemies of the Nazi regime.[37] Ninety-nine per cent of Stalin's victims, however, were innocent of any opposition to the Soviet system and were actually loyal Soviet citizens.

A third explanation of the purges is that they were ideologically necessary. Stalin argued that he was merely continuing the tactics of Lenin in 1918 and that he was accelerating the move towards a 'classless society'. If this desirable aim of Communism were to be achieved, class conflict would have to be intensified so that it could be ended the more quickly. The state would achieve its objectives 'not through the weakening of its power but through it becoming as strong as possible so as to defeat the remnants of the dying classes and to defend itself against capitalist encirclement'.[38]

This brings us to the most frequently discussed aspect of Stalin's purges: how were they affected by the external situation? Two very different answers have been provided.

The first is that Stalin was obsessed with the fear that the west would smash the Soviet regime before his industrialization programme was complete. It therefore made sense to adopt a pragmatic approach to foreign policy; Germany, the main threat, could be won over by a temporary policy of co-operation. Stalin found it no more difficult to collaborate with Fascism than with any other European system, for he regarded it merely as a variant of western capitalism. The old-style Bolsheviks, by contrast, were profoundly anti-Fascist and saw Hitler as a far more deadly enemy than either France or Britain. According to R. Tucker and R. Conquest, Stalin therefore considered it essential to remove the anti-Hitler element to make possible the accommodation with Germany which eventually materialized in August 1939, in the Nazi–Soviet Non-Aggression Pact.

I. Deutscher puts a different case. Stalin's main worry was that his regime would be destroyed from *within* – by internal revolt. There seemed little chance of this happening in 1936. Unless, of course, some major external catastrophe occurred, which could lead to a revival of the scenario of the First World War; military crisis could well bring about a revolution. Stalin's solution was therefore to destroy any elements within Russia which could possibly take advantage of such a situation. The show trials dealt with these potential threats by magnifying the charge against them. 'They had to die as traitors, as perpetrators of crimes beyond the reach of reason .... Only then could Stalin be sure that their execution would provoke no dangerous revulsion.'[39]

Society and culture

Major changes occurred in both areas. The general trend was away from the brief period of experimentation and relaxed control seen in the 1920s, to a more rigid and authoritarian approach. Stalin placed the emphasis firmly on discipline, imparting a mixture of traditional Russian values and his own interpretation of Marxism.

Perhaps the most basic example of this was his attitude to equality. The Bolshevik Revolution had made an absolute virtue of equality by reducing social distinction and wage differentials. Stalin, however, came to oppose this trend for two reasons. First, he wanted a system of privilege and rewards because this would make it easier for him to retain the support of his subordinates. Hence he reintroduced all the distinctions in army rank, together with epaulettes, and developed a hierarchy in industry and the Party. Secondly, he believed that equality, taken to excess, undermined the prospects for economic growth. He attacked the practice of 'wage equalization', arguing that it had nothing to do with Socialism. Indeed, it was essential to 'abolish wage equalization' and draw up scales which would 'take into account the difference between skilled and unskilled labour'.[40] Hence the old Marxist principle of 'from each according to his ability, to each according to his needs' was modified. Under Stalin the maxim was 'from each according to his ability, to each according to his work'.

The family also received Stalin's attention. Official policy between 1917 and 1926 had been to encourage the break-up of traditional institutions associated with the old order, of which the family was typical. In her treatise *The New Morality and the Working Class* (1918) Alexandra Kollontay had stated: 'The old type of family has seen its day.'[41] Divorce was made extremely easy and free love was sanctioned. A decree in Vladimir made every virgin over the age of 18 state property, but this went beyond official Party policy.[41] Stalin restored the family to its full status within society partly because this was one of many Russian traditions he favoured and partly because the family provided a useful means of political socialization. A series of laws therefore reversed early Bolshevik policy. In 1935 divorce was made difficult and expensive and in 1936 abortion was made illegal.[41] There was also a return to a strict form of morality, with a complete ban on any mention, in fiction, of pre-marital or extra-marital love affairs.

Education underwent a similar tightening after initial experimentation. During the 1920s educational theory had favoured relaxed discipline and group activity in schools. In fact, this was not unlike the trend in the United States and Great Britain, popularized by educationalists like Dalton and Dewey. Stalin, however, ended this libertarian approach and reintroduced formal learning, examinations and grades, and the full authority of the teacher. He also reversed the tendency of the 1920s to base access to higher education on social criteria. Thus, instead of favouring applicants from the proletariat, Stalin insisted that the demands of technology would be best served by selecting candidates with the highest academic qualifications.

The official line intruded also into culture. The arts, especially literature, were subjected from the early 1930s to the doctrine of Socialist Realism. During the 1920s censorship had, on the whole, been negative: writers were told what to avoid. Socialist Realism laid down direct guidelines so that writers would mobilize the masses and aim consciously to be 'engineers of the human soul'. All literary works must also provide 'a truthful, historically concrete depiction of reality in its revolutionary development'.[42] The writer Sholokhov provided, in 1958, a more straightforward description of Socialist Realism as 'that which is written for the Soviet government in simple, comprehensible, artistic language'.[43] Stalin was also susceptible to Russian tradition, showing a liking for Russian stories and folk tunes. His own view of Socialist Realism, therefore, was that it was 'National in form, Socialist in content'.[44]

SOVIET FOREIGN POLICY 1918–41

The foreign policy of Lenin and Stalin was highly complex, and involved numerous zigzags. At its best, it was skilful, confident and effective; at its worst, it was blundering, uncertain and ruinous. Throughout the period there was an internal conflict between ideological motives on the one hand and, on the other, a pragmatism which bordered on cynicism.

The period 1918–24

The underlying issue was how the new Bolshevik leaders displayed an intense ideological hostility to the western powers, believing in the inevitability of their eventual collapse and also in the necessity of this as a precondition for the survival of Communism. Trotsky argued that this collapse must be accelerated by Russia: 'Either the Russian Revolution will create a revolutionary movement in Europe, or the European powers will destroy the Russian Revolution'.[45] At the same time, Lenin had to take into account the immediate situation in which he found himself and make policy adjustments as he considered necessary. He therefore evolved a dual approach. He encouraged foreign revolutionary activity, as ideology seemed to demand, while also pursuing a pragmatic diplomacy which seemed to owe as much to Machiavelli as to Marx.

The immediate priority in the first year of the new regime was the withdrawal of Russia from the First World War. Lenin had always opposed Russia's involvement in what he regarded as a conflict between monopoly capitalists and, on coming to power, he issued a Decree which called upon 'all warring peoples and their governments to begin immediately negotiations for a just and democratic peace', a peace 'without annexation and indemnities'. Unfortunately, Russia's negotiations with Germany at Brest-Litovsk at the end of 1917 hit a major snag. The Germans insisted that Russia surrender, as the price for peace, Finland, Lithuania, Poland and the Ukraine. The Russian delegation withdrew from talks in February 1918 but was forced to return when the Germans renewed their military offensive. In March 1918 the Soviet government ended up by conceding, in the Treaty of Brest-Litovsk, to all the German demands. It was this experience which impressed upon the Bolsheviks the need for the utmost flexibility in dealing with the capitalist powers.

Relations with the other European powers and the United States also started on a disastrous footing. Western reactions to the new Bolshevik regime and to Russia's separate peace with Germany were thoroughly hostile. Russian capitulation at Brest-Litovsk enabled the Germans to launch a new offensive on the western front and the Allies were determined that Russia should be brought back into the conflict even if this should require military intervention. As explained on pp. 31–3, the Bolsheviks managed to overcome the threat of the White counter-revolutionaries and their foreign support.

But they were less successful in dealing with a Polish invasion in 1920 which conquered much of the Ukraine. The Red Army did launch a counter-attack and came within striking distance of Warsaw, but a second Polish offensive was made possible by extensive reforms carried out by Marshal Pilsudski and French help provided through General Weygand. By the Treaty of Riga (1921) Russia suffered its second territorial amputation in three years. This was a further incentive for Lenin to resort to cunning and diplomacy.

What, in the meantime, had happened to the revolutionary flame which would save Russia by consuming its enemies? 1919 had brought high hopes but eventual disappointment. The left-wing socialist regimes of Bavaria and Hungary were overthrown, while the Communist uprising in Berlin was put down, in January 1919, with considerable bloodshed. Clearly world revolution was further off than had originally been hoped. Yet Lenin was determined to use revolutionary activity and propaganda as a device in his foreign policy. In March 1919 he established Comintern (Communist International) to co-ordinate Communist movements and to bring them under the overall direction of Moscow. In 1920 Comintern based its whole structure on that of the Soviet Communist Party and declared itself to be 'a single Communist Party having branches in different countries'.[46] Its purpose was to promote radical activity and to weaken anti-Soviet policies pursued by western governments. At the same time Lenin established relations with countries of the East (a term which has now been replaced by 'Third World') to encourage them to throw off Western influence. It did not matter that most of these countries were themselves anti-Communist. The important thing was that they were also anti-imperialist; wars of liberation in the colonies could be just as damaging for the western powers as internal revolution.

The lessons of Brest-Litovsk, the Civil War and the Treaty of Riga were, however, that Russia would have to rely for the moment more on diplomacy than on revolution. The priority by 1921 was to end the isolation of the Soviet State and to coexist, for the time being, with the west. This would enable Soviet Russia to concentrate on industrial growth and thereby increase its armaments and create a balanced economy. It might even be necessary to attract western investment. According to Kamenev in 1921: 'We can, of course, restore our economy by the heroic effort of the working masses. But we cannot develop it fast enough to prevent the capitalist countries from overtaking us, unless we call in foreign capital.'[47] Lenin also intended to work on the differences between the various capitalist states to Russia's benefit. In a speech to Moscow party activists in December 1920, he argued: 'So long as we have not won the whole world, so long as we remain economically and militarily weaker than what is left of the capitalist world, we must stick to the rule: be able to exploit the contradictions and oppositions between the imperialists.'[48] He saw three particularly important areas of discord – in the Pacific between the United States and Japan, the differences between the USA and Europe and, above all, the gap between the wartime Allies and defeated Germany.

Between 1921 and 1924 the Soviet Government endeavoured, with some success, to fulfil these two objectives of acquiring western economic aid and driving a wedge between capitalist states. In March 1921, for example, a trade agreement was drawn up with Britain. But the real target for Soviet activity was Germany, isolated and resentful after the harsh terms of the Versailles Settlement. As Lenin had stated in his 1920 speech: 'Germany is one of the strongest advanced capitalist countries, it cannot put up with the Versailles Treaty. . . . Here is a situation we must utilize.'[48] He did. The Soviet Foreign Minister, Chicherin, conducted secret negotiations with Rathenau, his German counterpart. These reached their climax in Genoa in 1922. Ostensibly, Russia and Germany were themselves objects of discussion among the other powers, but the tables were turned when the Russo-German treaty of Rapallo was announced. Germany became the first state to extend full diplomatic recognition to Bolshevik Russia; both countries agreed to expand trade, and Germany would provide credits and investment for Russian industry. Rapallo is usually seen as a diplomatic victory and a vindication of Lenin's approach. It succeeded in splitting the western powers and destroyed any immediate chance of a united western response to Communism. The question which arose on the death of Lenin in January 1924 was: would his successor follow a similar pragmatic course?

The period 1924–39

Stalin's foreign policy was so complex that it is the subject of considerable controversy even today. This section will, therefore, provide a brief outline of the main developments and then present two contrasting interpretations of their meaning.

At first the Soviet government succeeded in extending its respectability. It gained diplomatic recognition, in 1924, from Britain, France, Italy and Japan. In 1926 a second agreement was drawn up between Russia and Germany; the Berlin Treaty was, in effect, a neutrality pact which also renewed the various agreements made at Rapallo. There were, however, complications in Soviet relations with the west. In 1927, for example, the British government broke off diplomatic relations after ordering the Soviet embassy in London to be raided. By the end of the 1920s Stalin was deliberately playing down friendship with the west. He argued that the Soviet Union no longer needed any form of western economic assistance and that, in any case, capitalism would be destroyed by an economic crisis. He decided to keep open the contact with Germany by renewing, in 1931, the Treaty of Berlin. But he made no attempt to assist the Weimar Republic to prevent the rise of Nazism between 1931 and 1933 and actually restrained the German Communist Party (KPD) under Thälmann from collaborating with the German Social Democrats (SPD). Indeed, Stalin saw the latter as merely another manifestation of that same crisis of capitalism which had increased Hitler's support; hence 'social democracy' was the 'moderate wing of Fascism'.[49] Stalin's insistence that the SPD were unworthy of power because they were 'Social Fascists' certainly played a part in destroying any meaningful opposition to the Nazis, who came to power in January 1933.

Between 1933 and 1934 Stalin attempted to maintain close relations between Russia and Germany. In 1935, however, he appeared to change course and to draw up agreements to contain Germany. Two examples are the Soviet – French and

Soviet–Czechoslovak Treaties of Mutual Assistance. Meanwhile, Stalin had also secured Russia's entry into the League of Nations and from 1935 he sponsored the growth of popular fronts throughout Europe in which Communists, socialists and liberals were encouraged to resist Fascism. By 1938, however, Stalin was clearly envisaging further alterations in Soviet foreign policy, while 1939 saw separate negotiations between Russia and, on the one hand, Britain and France and, on the other, Nazi Germany. In August 1939 Stalin eventually settled for Germany and the foreign ministers of the two powers, Molotov and von Ribbentrop, formally signed the Nazi–Soviet Non-Aggression Pact.

This somewhat tortuous route to Soviet security has often puzzled western observers. The problem of interpretation is increased by the lack of detailed documentary evidence. The Politburo is hardly to be expected to release the relevant information after an appropriate time lapse, as western Chancelleries tend to do. Hence there is more scope than usual for historians to generalize about underlying aims. In the case of Stalin's diplomacy there are two important but very different interpretations.

One is that Stalin's policy was entirely consistent. Any zigzags detected in the sequence of events were not basic changes in principle but temporary alterations of course. In an influential article in the *Slavic Review* (1977),[48] Tucker argued that Stalin's emphasis was on safeguarding Russia from the west by industrializing, and preparing in the long term for war. This conflict should be postponed for as long as possible but, when it came, could be used to destroy capitalism and promote Communist revolution. In 1925 Stalin outlined the general scenario he envisaged – a war between capitalist states in which Russia would become involved at her own convenience:

> Our banner remains, as before, the banner of peace. But if war breaks out, we shall not be able to sit with folded hands – we shall have to make a move, but the move will come last. And we shall act so as to throw the decisive weight onto the scales, the weight that could be preponderant.[48]

His main hope, it is often argued, was that Germany and the

west would tear each other apart and that Russia would be well placed to pick up the pieces. One of the main reasons for Stalin's willingness to see the Nazis in power in Germany was that they would be much more likely than a democratic regime to attack the west. Another reason was that the alternative – a collaboration between the SPD and KPD would be highly embarrassing to Stalin. The SPD were pro-western and were therefore likely to *reduce* the chance of a split between capitalist powers. Hitler's rise, it would seem, suited Stalin perfectly. Of course, Hitler's policies from 1934 onwards were more forceful than Stalin had anticipated and it was therefore necessary to take steps to contain Germany and to remind Hitler that Germany had no option but to consider an eventual deal with Russia. But the collaboration between the Soviet Union and the western powers was never more than a temporary expedient, designed to last until Stalin was able to return to his preferred policy. The opportunity came in August 1939 and the Nazi–Soviet Pact represented, in Tucker's words 'the fruition of Stalin's whole complex conception of the means of Soviet survival in a hostile world and emergence into a commanding international position'.[48] A new war was now inevitable, a war which Stalin could help start. Then, from a position of neutrality, he could watch the combatants exhaust themselves. He could then involve Russia, claim territory and sponsor revolutionary movements to create a ring of socialist states.[48]

There is an alternative and more traditional explanation. This also places heavy emphasis on Stalin's desire to turn the western states against each other, enabling Russia to benefit from their mutual destruction. It also accepts Stalin's implication in the use of Hitler and his profound dislike of the SPD. It is argued, however, that Stalin never really took Hitler seriously as a future threat. He thought that the Nazi Party would never come to power. Or, if it did, it would soon succumb to a revolution from the Communist left. Then, within two years Stalin realized his error: Nazism proved far more resilient than he had expected and Hitler looked as if he might actually try to implement the aggressive and expansionist policies referred to in *Mein Kampf*. The only answer was a total change of strategy, to end the connection

established with Germany in the 1920s and to seek accommodation with the west and Czechoslovakia. Stalin also
ordered Communists everywhere to collaborate with
socialists, in direct contrast to his previous policy towards
the German Communists and Socialists. During the Spanish
Civil War he was even concerned that any far-left government
might lose Russia the co-operation of France. It seemed,
therefore, that he was prepared to make some profound
ideological changes to keep open relations with the west.

Then why the eventual switch back to Germany? The
argument continues as follows. The events of 1938, especially
the Anschluss and the crisis over Czechoslovakia, showed up
the west in the worst possible light. Stalin was forced to the
conclusion that the western powers were unreliable allies.
The Anglo-French response to German territorial expansion
was the policy of appeasement, and Stalin was shocked by the
ease with which Hitler absorbed Austria and the Sudetenland
into the Reich.

It appeared, therefore, that Germany would be allowed to
rearm and expand without hindrance from the west. In 1939
Stalin had two options open to him. He could maintain the
Soviet friendship with France and extend it to Britain – but
with more definite and specific military commitments. Or he
could seek agreement with Germany and draw up a territorial settlement which would eliminate any possible cause of
conflict. During the first half of 1939 Stalin seemed willing to
incline towards either alternative but was eventually infuri-
ated by the unwillingness of Chamberlain, the British Prime
Minister, to meet his terms. In August, 1939, therefore, he
informed the Politburo of his decision to do a deal with
Hitler. In this perspective, the Nazi–Soviet Non-Aggression
Pact can be seen as one of two last-minute alternatives, rather
than as the logical outcome of all Stalin's previous policies.

The period 1939–41

The terms of the Pact may be summarized as follows.
Germany and Russia undertook 'to desist from any act of
violence, any aggressive action, and any attack on each other,
either individually or jointly with other Powers'. Should
either become involved in any conflict, the other would

remain strictly neutral. Neither would 'participate in any grouping of Powers whatsoever that is directly or indirectly aimed at the other party'.[50] Accompanying the Non-Aggression Pact was a 'Secret Additional Protocol' which provided for the demarcation of spheres of influence in eastern Europe and the possibility of the division of Poland between Russia and Germany. This, in effect, was a death sentence to the new Polish state.

How necessary was this Pact for Russia? As usual, two cases have been put. One is that the measure was fully justified. Soviet historians today make little mention of Stalin but do argue that 'subsequent events revealed that this step was the only correct one under the circumstances. By taking it, the USSR was able to continue peaceful construction for nearly two years and to strengthen its defences.'[51] The alternative view, however, is that the Pact was not necessary. W. Laqueur argues that it should not be assumed that without the Pact Germany would have attacked Russia in 1939.[52] Hitler was too preoccupied with Poland, Britain and France to draw off divisions for yet another campaign. More telling is the observation that even if Hitler *had* moved immediately, the Soviet Union would actually have been better off. By 1941 German military production had grown, proportionately, more rapidly than Russia's, enabling Hitler to launch, in operation Barbarossa, the sort of offensive which would have been impossible in 1939.

Stalin invaded Poland on 17 September 1939, two weeks after the start of the German *Blitzkrieg* from the west. The Red Army encountered comparatively little resistance, for the Polish airforce had been obliterated by the *Luftwaffe* and the Polish cavalry had destroyed itself in heroic but futile attacks against German tank divisions. A further agreement followed between the two powers, partitioning Poland for the fourth time in that unhappy country's history. The Soviet Union regained the Belorussian and Ukrainian areas lost to Poland in the war of 1920–1. It might appear that Stalin had a sound historic case for reclaiming what had, after all, been integral parts of Russia until the Treaties of Brest-Litovsk and Riga. On the other hand, G. Kennan points out that the Soviet Union's case was destroyed by the great brutality with which it treated the conquered peoples.[53] Poles and others became caught up in a wave of purges and deportations which meant that the number of deaths in the Soviet sphere of eastern Europe rivalled that in the Nazi sector.

Meanwhile, Stalin was using the lull offered by the Nazi–Soviet Pact to deal with the problem of Finland. He did not intend to try to reverse the Treaty of Brest-Litovsk and force Finland back into Russia but he did mean to extend the boundary back from the outer suburbs of Leningrad and to gain facilities for a Soviet naval base near the mouth of the Gulf on Finland. The Finnish government had, since 1938, rejected all proposals for exchanges of territory or Soviet leases. There were those in Helsinki who thought that the Russian requests were not unreasonable, but Stalin's ruthless policy towards Poland stiffened Finnish determination not to compromise. On 30 November 1939 twenty Soviet divisions were launched against Finland's fifteen, opening what soon came to be known as the Winter War. The task proved far more difficult than Stalin had envisaged and the Red Army experienced a number of humiliating reverses before the Soviet Union extracted the desired territory from Finland in February 1940. The Winter War had important results. First, it completed the destruction of Russia's reputation abroad; Russia was expelled from the League of Nations for aggression against a fellow member. Secondly, the war showed up Russian military deficiencies. Stalin learned this lesson by introducing sweeping reforms in the army and recalling many officers who had previously been dismissed. In fact, Marshal Zhukov, the Soviet hero of the Second World War, went so far as to call 1940 'the year of the great transformation'.[54]

During the rest of 1940 and the first half of 1941 relations between the Soviet Union and Germany deteriorated rapidly. The Germans regarded Stalin's Winter War as entirely unnecessary and they openly expressed their sympathy for the Finns, with whom, indeed, they eventually allied. Stalin, for his part, was openly dissatisfied with the amount of territory in eastern Europe which had come under Soviet influence and was putting pressure on Hitler to make further concessions, especially in the Balkans. Meanwhile, there were also diplomatic complications. In September 1940 Germany, Japan and Italy concluded a Three Power Pact, which Stalin was invited to join. When Molotov, the Soviet Foreign Minister, visited Berlin in November 1940, he refused to adhere to this Pact until the remaining Soviet demands in eastern Europe had been met. According to I. Grey, this meeting probably confirmed Hitler's decision to invade Russia in 1941.

From this stage onwards, Stalin's behaviour was highly puzzling. He seemed to follow a contradictory policy of pressurizing Germany and yet failing to prepare Russia to receive a German attack. For this he has been heavily criticized from two contrasting sources. Khrushchev said in 1956: 'The threatening danger which hung over our Father-land in the first period of the war was largely due to the faulty methods of directing the nation and the Party by Stalin himself'.[55] Earlier, Churchill had described Stalin and his commissars at this stage as 'the most completely outwitted bunglers of the Second World War'. Incredibly, Stalin failed to deploy the Red Army properly and, as will be shown in the next section, ignored all intelligence warnings of Hitler's intended invasion.

And yet there is a certain logic to Stalin's policy. It could be argued that his appraisal of the situation was wrong, not because it was irrational but because it was based *too* heavily on logical reasoning. Stalin doubted that Hitler had any real motive to attack Russia. Germany, after all, was still involved in a struggle with Britain and opening up a second front would be sheer folly. As for provoking Germany, Stalin intended to avoid this at all costs. He was careful to stress that 'the friendship of the peoples of Germany and the Soviet Union, cemented by blood, has every reason to be lasting and firm'.[56] Besides, as long as the Soviet Union provided Germany with essential raw materials, this co-existence could be maintained indefinitely. It is true that Stalin had pushed Soviet interests in eastern Europe particularly hard, but this had been necessary to show Hitler that Germany was not dealing with a strategy of appeasement (Chamberlain had already demonstrated in 1938 that Hitler responded to concessions by further demands). Stalin's approach would gain Hitler's respect through its firmness and, should the two countries appear to be drifting towards war, the signs would be instantly recognizable and Stalin could make well-timed concessions to satisfy Hitler. What Stalin felt he had to avoid was being put under pressure by alarmist rumours of an impending German attack, spread by agents of Churchill who had excellent reasons to see Russia embroiled in a conflict with Germany. Stalin was therefore convinced that Hitler could not possibly have a single sound reason for wanting to break the Nazi–Soviet Pact. What he failed to realize was that Hitler was pursuing a totally different set of objectives based upon an entirely different logic.

THE GREAT PATRIOTIC WAR 1941–5

Reverses 1941–2

Operation Barbarossa was launched by Hitler on the Soviet Union on 22 June 1941. Other states soon followed in declaring war on Russia, especially Rumania, Italy, Slovakia, Finland and Hungary. The invasion force totalled 3 million men, the greatest in the whole of human history to that date. The objective was no less than the complete destruction of the USSR.

At first, German troops were remarkably successful. Their advance divided into three prongs – against Leningrad in the north, Moscow in the centre and Kiev in the south. By the end of 1941 the whole of the Baltic coastline had been conquered, Leningrad was almost surrounded and the Germans were within 25km of Moscow. Although the attempt to take the capital failed, most of the Ukraine was occupied, including Kiev, Kharkov, Odessa and the Crimea. When the offensive was resumed in the spring and summer of 1942 the main advances came in the south with the crossing of the Don and the capture of the oilfields and agricultural areas of the Caucasus. By August 1942 the Germans had reached the Volga and Stalingrad. During the early phases of this advance the Soviet armies folded up like cardboard. German tanks, for example, advanced an unprecedented 250km within the first three days and, within the first few months, killed one million

Russians and took one million prisoners. Hitler had told his generals at the outset: 'We have only to kick in the door and the whole rotten structure will come crashing down.'[57] Events seemed to justify his confidence. How can this amazing Soviet collapse be explained?

Undoubtedly the main factor was Stalin's complete failure to take the most elementary defensive precautions. We have already examined his concern to maintain good relations with Germany between 1939 and 1941. This clouded his judgement so that he ignored all intelligence reports of impending attack. There are numerous examples of these, which can be divided into two main types. One consisted of warnings from foreign governments; Churchill's personal message of April 1941 gave details of German troop movements in eastern Europe and warned of Hitler's intentions.[54] Stalin, it could be argued, was not being unreasonable in supposing that Churchill was trying to provoke a confrontation between Russia and Germany and his decision to discount this type of warning is therefore understandable. A second form of intelligence report, however, came from Soviet agents and there are instances of information being ignored. On 20 March, for example, General Golikov, the head of military intelligence, forwarded to Stalin information he had received about the build-up of German troops in the border areas, but added that he did not believe it to be genuine; this confirmed Stalin's own views. Similarly, in May, Admiral Kuznetzov quoted the Soviet naval attaché in Berlin that war was imminent, but again the warning was thought to have been 'planted'.[54] Vital information was also received from the famous pro-Soviet German agent in Japan, Richard Sorge, as well as from the Soviet Embassy in Berlin. Both gave the precise date of the intended attack – 22 June 1941.

Stalin's decision to ignore all these reports meant that the Red Army was taken totally unawares; most of the troops were still in their barracks when the news of the invasion broke. This was particularly devastating because of the mechanized nature of the German advance. Hitler repeated the *Blitzkrieg* strategy he had employed so successfully against Poland and the element of surprise meant that most of the Soviet airforce was destroyed on the ground. Hence the Soviet army had no air cover and no leadership of the quality needed to stiffen the defence at such short notice. Part of the reason for this was Stalin's purges, which deprived Russia of many experienced commanders.[58] To make matters worse, parts of the Red Army deserted, the best known example being the second-in-command on the Volkhov Front, Vlasov.

Stalin's initial reaction to this evidence of his blunders was total shock; he is believed to have had a nervous breakdown and he confined himself to his Kremlin flat. This would have been the ideal time to depose Stalin and institute a more collective form of leadership based on a revival of Party power. Yet Stalin had done his job too effectively in the purges for this to happen. There was literally no one to take his place and, despite his evident shortcomings, he was now needed more than ever. To do him justice, he did show a swift personal recovery and on 30 June he set up the State Defence Committee (GKO) to co-ordinate the war effort. He also moved quickly to a decision to transfer major industries from the war zone eastwards. Above all, he was driven by an all-consuming hatred of Hitler which had replaced his previous ill-judged trust.

Revival 1943–5

The furthest extent of the German advance was reached towards the end of 1942. From this stage onwards the occupying forces were slowly but steadily driven back by the unremitting counter-offensive of the Red Army, made possible by a remarkable national revival.

The first major Soviet achievement was the successful defence of Moscow by Marshal Zhukov. This was made possible by the withdrawal of Soviet troops from the Far East to strengthen the capital. (It seems that this time Stalin decided to believe the news of the Soviet agent in Tokyo, Richard Sorge, that Japan was about to launch an attack on the United States, not on Russia.) The Battle for Moscow tested the German army to its utmost and, although the German advance continued in 1942, it was directed against the south, not against the capital. Stalin decided to focus the Soviet counter attack on the city of Stalingrad, which was eventually captured by Zhukov early in 1943. This was undoubtedly the turning-point of the war and was followed in July 1943 by a Soviet victory in the tank battle at Kursk. From this time onwards the Soviet advance proved irresistible. Kiev was liberated by November 1943 and Leningrad early in 1944. During the first half of 1944 the Germans were finally forced out of Russian territory while, in the second half, the Red Army advanced into the Nazi-occupied states of eastern Europe. Most of Poland was captured, although virtually no assistance was provided by Stalin to the Warsaw revolt against the Germans, which was eventually put down with great brutality. Rumania was forced to surrender in August and Bulgaria in September, while in October the Yugoslav resistance forces under Tito were assisted by the Russians to liberate Belgrade from German occupation. A final effort from the north-east resulted, in January 1945, in the fall of Warsaw and the conquest of the rest of Poland.[59] From February 1945 Zhukov concentrated on the advance on Berlin. The capital was besieged and heavily bombarded, eventually falling in April after savage street-to-street fighting.

One of the reasons for this remarkable Soviet success was the errors committed by the Nazi regime. The Führer made a series of appalling military blunders which are analysed in Chapter 4. He also alienated huge sections of the Soviet population, missing a unique opportunity to mobilize them against Stalin's dictatorship. His deliberate policy of extermination and enslavement gave Stalin the chance to project himself as the saviour of Mother Russia.

After the initial disasters of 1941, Stalin showed more obvious powers of national leadership. He made numerous direct appeals to the people and placed particularly heavy emphasis on patriotism. In November 1941, he urged: 'Let the brave example of your great ancestors, Alexander Nevsky, ... Alexander Suvorov, Michael Kutuzov, inspire you!'[60] Also, on his orders, newspaper bannerheads were changed. 'Proletarians of All the Countries Unite' became 'Down with the Fascist Invader'. He managed to link Russian nationalism directly to Marxism, even arguing that Hitler was not a genuine nationalist, but an imperialist.

Stalin's leadership was also apparent in the actual organization of Russia's war effort. The two major institutions established specifically to deal with the emergency were the *Stavka* (a general headquarters) and the State Defence Committee (GKO). The latter, which was given full powers to conduct all aspects of the war, consisted of Stalin, Molotov, Voroshilov, Malenkov and Beria. It had total control over all Party bodies and branches which were obliged to carry out all instructions without delay or question. Stalin himself became People's Commissar for Defence in July 1941, Marshal of the Soviet Union in March 1943 and Generalissimo in June 1945. Among his more important military contributions were the reorganization of the army, the institution of a new system of incentives and decorations, and the promotion of young and able officers to supreme command; examples included Zhukov, Tolbukhin, Konev, Malinovsky, Vatutin and Rokossovsky. Stalin avoided the mistake made by Hitler. He did not dictate detailed military strategy to his marshals, allowing Zhukov to develop the detailed application of Stalin's broad concepts.

The result was a flexible approach to dealing with the occupation forces. The overall plan was to wear down the more highly tuned Nazi war machine and to rely on exhaustion plus, of course, the size and climate of Russia to do the rest. Zhukov told Stalin in April 1943:

> I consider it inadvisable for our forces to go over to the offensive in the very first days of the campaign. . . . It would be better to make the enemy first exhaust himself against our defences, and knock out his tanks and then, bringing up fresh reserves, to go over to a general offensive which would finally finish off his main force.[61]

The campaigns of 1944 were carefully planned and co-ordinated – and highly successful. Deutscher comments on the flexibility used in shifting forces from north to south and then to the centre 'with astonishing regularity, power and circumspection, like a boxer who systematically covers his opponent with telling blows without expecting that a single blow would knock him down'.[62] This strategy was also ideally suited to partisan warfare, in which hundreds of guerrilla detachments launched surprise raids and blew up key installations.

The Soviet forces were provided with an amazing array of advanced weapons and equipment which enabled them to overwhelm the German *Wehrmacht*. Among the most important of these were the *Katyusha* rocket-launchers, the SUS (self-propelled artillery), heavy mortars, and the T-34 tank which was admitted by one of the German commanders, General Guderian, to be superior to anything in the panzer divisions. German vehicles were not equipped for winter conditions and did not even have antifreeze (something that the Soviet vehicles did not need as they ran on diesel). The initial German superiority in the air was soon reversed as the Soviet airforce was provided with 14 new types of aircraft, including the II–2, nicknamed the 'Golden Plane' by Soviet pilots and the 'Black Death' by the Germans.[63]

Underlying this war effort was a massive industrial base with an expanding capacity. This was due partly to Stalin's first three five-year plans which had concentrated on heavy industry and had set up industrial centres in the Urals and Siberia. But equally important was the wholesale transfer of factories and production plants from the war zone to the safety of Siberia and Central Asia. The whole process was organized by the GKO and involved the transportation of 1500 factories in 1.5 million wagon-loads. As a result, the areas beyond the Urals developed huge industrial complexes which were well beyond the range of German bombing raids and which fed the Red Army with an ever increasing supply of war material. Despite the occupation and destruction of a large part of European Russia, the productive capacity of the Soviet Union eventually far exceeded that of Nazi Germany. In 1942, for example, the Soviet Union produced 25,000 aircraft to Germany's 14,700, and 24,700 tanks compared with 9300. The workforce was placed under even more intensive discipline by a Soviet decree on 'The Working Hours of Factory and Office Employees in Wartime' which resulted in a reduced labour force providing a 25 per cent increase in production. Overall, it does appear that of the two totalitarian regimes, Communism was more effectively geared than Nazism to a prolonged struggle for survival, a theme which will be explored in Chapter 6.

Relations with the west 1941–5

When Germany attacked Russia in June 1941 Stalin's whole attitude to Hitler underwent a profound change. He hastened to seek the co-operation of those western countries which he had previously suspected. Hence, in 1941, the Anglo-Soviet Mutual Assistance Pact was drawn up, followed in 1942 by the 20-year Anglo-Soviet Treaty of Alliance. Stalin also concluded a lend–lease agreement with the United States worth $11 billion. When the United States entered the war against Germany, the Grand Alliance was formed (although no document was actually signed) aimed at bringing down the Nazi regime. However, collaboration was never complete. Throughout the war there existed an undercurrent of distrust which grew stronger as the need for unity receded. This distrust went back as far as the foundation of the Bolshevik state and was largely ideological: Trotsky, for instance, had once referred to Lenin and Wilson as 'the apocalyptic antipodes of our time'.[45] But there were also specific irritants throughout the period 1941–5 which were particularly apparent at the major wartime conferences – at Teheran (November to December 1943), Yalta (February 1945) and Potsdam (July to August 1945).

The first of these irritants was military. Stalin wanted an active alliance and no repetition of the '*sitskrieg*' which had been the west's response to Hitler's *Blitzkrieg* against Poland in August 1939. He considered it vitally important for the western Allies to open up a second front in France to draw off between 40 and 60 German divisions from the Russian sector. He made his first request for this to Churchill in July 1941. In August 1942 Churchill visited Moscow to disclose his plans for 'Operation Torch' – to be opened up, however, in North Africa. Stalin's reaction was bitter disillusionment. 'All is clear', he told his associates. 'They want us to bleed white in order to dictate to us their terms later on.'[64] The Anglo-American landings in North Africa did help matters but Stalin did not regard them as a justifiable substitute for an attack on France. This finally came in June 1944, although by this stage Stalin was accusing the Anglo-American forces of advancing into Germany as quickly as possible in order to minimize Soviet conquests in central and eastern Europe.

The second main breach concerned the frontiers and regimes of eastern Europe. The most significant of these was Poland. Britain and the United States were prepared, at Yalta and Potsdam, to concede the Curzon line as Poland's frontier, thus allowing the USSR to retain all the Polish territory conquered in 1939. But at the same time they were profoundly unhappy about the possibility of permanent Soviet control over Polish institutions; hence their insistence on the Yalta Declaration on Liberated Europe, by which the powers undertook to assist the liberated states to create democratic institutions of their own choice. This, of course, produced an inevitable difference of interpretation between the western powers, who hoped for the installation of liberal democracies, and the Soviet Union, which had always intended to promote revolutionary Communist regimes. Above all, Stalin was determined to develop a buffer zone between Russia and the west, or a 'glacis' of friendly socialist states. Clearly this would be a major post-war issue.

The outcome of the war, and of the disagreements with the western Allies, was clearly in Russia's favour. Stalin had, by the middle of 1945, every reason to feel satisfied with the Soviet position in Europe. Nazi Germany had been smashed and partially dismembered by the principle of zoning agreed at Yalta and Potsdam. All the gains made by Russia as a result of the Nazi-Soviet Pact of 1939 were retained, namely eastern Poland, the Baltic states and part of Rumania. Indeed, Soviet expansion went beyond the 1939 limits, also encompassing parts of East Prussia and Czechoslovakia. In the Far East, Russia had gained, in return for minimal participation in the war against Japan, Sakhalin and the Kurile Islands, which had been ceded by Tsarist Russia in 1905 and 1875 respectively. The sphere of Soviet control extended far beyond these enlarged frontiers. Moscow now dominated a huge socialist arc comprising Poland, Czechoslovakia, Hungary, Romania and Bulgaria, together with the Soviet zone of Germany. At last the USSR seemed to have both security and the means to spread Communism into the heart of Europe. Many of Stalin's expectations had therefore been realized. The capitalist states *had* come into conflict with each other and the end result *had* been the strengthening of the Soviet Union and the opportunity to spread Soviet influence.

The cost

It was not until 1956 that the full extent of Soviet losses in the Second World War were revealed. It is now known that they are the heaviest suffered by any country in history as the result of an invasion by another power.

The most devastating impact was on the population, both military and civilian: 5.7 million Russian soldiers surrendered to the Germans, of whom 3.3 million subsequently died in captivity. The German High Command bore direct responsibility for the appalling conditions faced by Russian prisoners-of-war; an order stated that 'The Bolshevik soldier has lost all claims to treatment as an honourable opponent in accordance with the Geneva Convention'. The occupying forces also treated Russian civilians with extreme brutality. The Slavs were seen as a sub-human race and the *Reichsleiter* of the east, Rosenberg, aimed at no less than the 'national disintegration of the USSR'. Overall, the Soviet Union lost 23 million dead, compared with 375,000 Britons, 405,000 Americans and 600,000 Frenchmen. The total looks even worse when placed in the context of previous losses. Ellenstein's figures[65] have been tabulated as follows:

1931–21	(First World War, Civil War and epidemics)	13.5 million
1930–9	(Famine and purges)	7.0 million
1941–4	(Second World War)	23.0 million
Total 1913–45		43.5 million

To this total can be added the 'shortfall in births', an estimated 45 million. By 1945, therefore, the population was about 90 million less than it should have been.[65] Even today this deficiency continues to cause concern to the authorities who consider the USSR to be severely underpopulated.

Destruction of property was also on a massive scale. Details were released as early as 1947. According to Molotov, the Germans destroyed 1710 towns and 70,000 villages, 31,850 industrial enterprises and 98,000 collective farms. The sufferings of two Soviet cities are particularly well known. Leningrad experienced a siege which lasted for 900 days and the eventual casualty figure for this one city was greater than that of all the western Allies combined. The suffering was the direct result of starvation, dystrophy and scurvy, as well as German bombing and bombardment. Stalingrad, meanwhile, was totally devastated. Russian and German troops fought over each street, and then in the ruins and rubble. An official Soviet description reads as follows:

> In the trenches carved out in the steep banks of the Volga, in gullies and the shells of ruined houses, in the cellars of bombed buildings the Soviet soldiers fought to the last to defend the city. The German forces launched 700 attacks and every step forward cost them tremendous losses.... Between 500 and 1200 splinters of bombs, shells and grenades per square metre were found on the slopes of Mamai Hill, one of the main centres of the fighting, after the Battle of Stalingrad had at last come to an end.[66]

R. Hutchings[67] has placed Soviet sufferings in perspective by comparing the losses inflicted in the two World Wars. Population losses in the Second World War were 50 per cent larger, but the population of 1941 was much greater than that of 1913. Russia during the Second World War experienced greater economic destruction than in the First, but substantially less disruption, largely because the industrial base of 1941 was much greater than that of 1913. There was a significant contrast in the pattern of destruction; in the First World War industry suffered more severely than agriculture, while the reverse was true in the Second. Indeed, after 1945, agriculture remained a serious problem long after factories and houses had been rebuilt.

MATURE DICTATORSHIP 1945–53

Stalinism 1945–53

Stalin was unique among the dictators covered by this book in that he emerged as a victor in 1945. For the next 8 years, until his death in 1953, his ascendancy was total. During this period he launched a campaign of reconstruction and finally achieved his original objective of making the Soviet Union a superpower. He also extended Russian control, for the first time, over most of eastern Europe and established a series of satellite states. Meanwhile, he took measures to consolidate his authority which meant that the Stalinist dictatorship was actually more severe than it had been during the war.

Stalin's main priority after 1945 was the reconstruction of Soviet industries and agriculture. He decided at the outset, however, that this recovery would be based entirely on Soviet efforts. This meant a return to his policy of isolation from the west, which had been so evident in the 1930s, and the end of wartime dependence on US aid. He returned to his economic strategies of the 1930s, including central planning and collectivization. In the fourth and fifth five-year plans (1946–1950 and 1950–1955) the emphasis was placed, once again, on heavy industry, especially for defence. Much of the investment was directed towards the steel, construction and armaments industries. At first the results were disappointing, but by 1950 it was announced that all the targets of the fourth five-year plan had been exceeded and that the overall industrial base was now substantially larger than it had been in 1940. Considerable investment was also channelled into the nuclear industry, again for military reasons. By 1949 the Soviet Union possessed the atomic bomb and, by 1951, the hydrogen bomb.

There were, however, several deficiencies in the post-war economy. The emphasis on heavy industry meant the continuing neglect of the Soviet consumer. The conditions of the workforce were also very harsh. The 48-hour week was regarded as a minimum; workers were unable to choose their jobs or to move to other areas; industrial discipline remained especially severe; and wages were based on piece work. But the Achilles' heel of the Soviet economy was undoubtedly agriculture. The 1946 harvest, for example, produced only 40 per cent of the crop of 1913. The problem was aggravated by low investment, as agriculture received only 7.3 per cent of the total available in the fourth five-year plan. There was also widespread discontent with the *kolkhozy*, or collective farms, with the artificially low prices for agricultural produce and the lack of incentives. Stalin's response to these problems was further centralization and more bureaucratic controls. He tried to consolidate the *kolkhozy* by reducing their number from 252,000 to 76,000.[68] There was, however, little evidence of widespread recovery and the 1952 harvest was only marginally better than that of 1913. One is left with the conclusion that Stalin must take personal blame for much of what is wrong with Soviet agriculture and that part of the problem was total ignorance. He had, after all, last visited a collective farm in 1929.

Despite these continuing problems, the Soviet Union was now the major power of the European continent. Stalin was determined to spread Soviet influence wherever possible, but especially to those areas liberated by the Red Army from Nazi rule. Stalin's hegemony was gradually enforced and institutionalized by four main methods. The first was the establishment in 1947 of the Communist Information Bureau (Cominform). This was intended to ensure Moscow's complete control over international Communism and especially to guarantee conformity to Stalinism in eastern Europe. The second was the takeover of the governments of the eastern European states. Originally these had been broad fronts, consisting of Communist and non-Communist parties. Stalin, however, tightened the control of the former and ensured total Communist domination from 1948. The catalyst was the fear of President Tito of Yugoslavia, the one genuinely independent Communist leader in eastern Europe. Stalin accused Tito of wanting to spread 'National Communism' and therefore instituted purges to prevent other states being infected by the Titoist heresy. The third means of achieving Soviet control was the formation in 1949 of the Council for Mutual Economic Assistance (Comecon). This was designed to co-ordinate the economies of eastern Europe and to direct Czech, Polish and Hungarian trade towards the Soviet Union, thereby creating an almost self-sufficient commercial bloc. The fourth method was military dominance; the number of Soviet troops in eastern Europe stood at 5.5 million during the early 1950s. It remained, however, to Stalin's successor to create a multilateral military alliance in the form of the Warsaw Pact (1955).

Stalin's control over eastern Europe was to be an important dimension in the development of the Cold War. The last seven years of his rule saw the further deterioration of relations between the Soviet Union and the west, after the wartime differences explained in the previous section. The ideological confrontation was now more intense than at any time since the creation of the Bolshevik state. In a major speech on 9 February 1946 Stalin announced that he would abide by the basic principles of Marxism–Leninism, and proceeded to attack the capitalist powers as instigators of the Second World War. In the following month Churchill openly criticized Stalin's policy in eastern Europe. His speech, delivered in Fulton, Missouri, contained the famous sentence: 'From Stettin in the Baltic to Trieste in the Adriatic an iron curtain has descended across the continent'. The Cold War was subsequently hardened by two open declarations of policy. One was the Truman Doctrine (1947) which promised military or economic aid to Greece and Turkey and support for 'peoples who are resisting attempted subjugation by armed minorities or by outside pressures'.[69] The promise of economic aid was subsequently implemented by the Marshal Plan. Stalin's response was the so-called Zhdanov Line. In a speech in 1947 Zhdanov warned of the new threat of the capitalist west. 'The cardinal purpose of the imperialist camp is to strengthen imperialism, to hatch a new imperialist war, to combat socialism and democracy, and to support reactionary and anti-democratic pro-Fascist regimes and movements everywhere'.[70] The only answer, he concluded, was to tighten Soviet control – in the ways already outlined.

Tension between the Soviet Union and the west was also apparent in areas beyond eastern Europe. One of the earliest confrontations was the Iranian crisis (1945–6), in which the continued Soviet occupation of the northern part of Iran was challenged by the United States and Britain. The threat of armed conflict was eventually averted when, in 1946, Soviet troops were withdrawn in return for oil concessions. Back in Europe, the Cold War entered a particularly dangerous phase in 1948 with the Berlin crisis. Stalin attempted to squeeze out the western presence from Berlin by closing off the supply routes which connected West Berlin to the western zones of occupied Germany. This policy, however, backfired. The

British and Americans airlifted sufficient quantities of food and fuel to supply West Berlin, and Stalin was unable to prevent this for fear of American nuclear retaliation. The Berlin blockade had another undesirable side-effect for Stalin. It convinced the west of the need for a more systematic defence pact against Soviet aggression in Europe: hence the formation of the North Atlantic Treaty Organization (NATO). Soviet involvement in the Far East met with mixed success, especially over the Korean War (1950–3). When Soviet-backed North Korea invaded the South, the latter was assisted by United Nations forces, comprising mainly Americans. Stalin was forced to watch while the newly established Communist regime in China came to the rescue of North Korea. From now on the Soviet Union had a major rival in the Communist world.

Confrontation with the capitalist countries was accompanied by a tightening-up within the Soviet Union itself. President Roosevelt had once believed that contacts with the west in wartime would soften the Soviet dictatorship; he had been greatly encouraged by Stalin's relaxation of censorship and by his more positive attitude to intellectuals and religious minorities. But this policy proved to be the exception rather than the norm. After 1945 Stalin returned to all the restrictions which had underpinned the totalitarian regime during the 1930s. There seem to have been two basic motives for this. One was to put the Russian people under sufficient discipline and constraint to ensure rapid recovery after the appalling experience of the war with Germany. The other was to cut off all contacts with capitalism and thereby prevent the contamination of Soviet society and of the new eastern European satellites. Dictatorship was consolidated by a number of political changes. Stalin ended the crucial role played during the war by the army; fearing that war heroes like Zhukov might eventually rival his own popularity, he downgraded them. He also wound up the State Defence Committee (GKO) and took measures to guarantee that he remained in full control of the Party. He rarely summoned the Central Committee and the Politburo; in fact, they probably did not convene at all between 1947 and 1952 when, in any case, the Politburo was replaced by a larger Praesidium with few effective powers. The Party Congress did not meet at all before 1952. The overall trend was for Stalin to accumulate even more personal power than he had possessed before 1941.

While fully restoring the components of political dictatorship, Stalin was also seeking to dominate all aspects of Russia's social and cultural life. In 1946 several decrees signalled a tightening of discipline by defining in detail working practices and reimposing Socialist Realism in the arts. The latter was the work of Zhdanov who, in a speech in 1946, stressed the importance of cutting all connections with the corrupting bourgeois influences of the west. As usual, writers were the main target, but composers and scientists also had to bow to Party wisdom. In deference to Marxist teaching, all genetic studies were banned, and the existence of genes and chromosomes officially denied. All biologists were obliged to accept the theories of Lysenko, who maintained that cells could develop within their lifetime certain characteristics which could then be passed on. Party ideology demanded that environment should at all times triumph over heredity.

The most sinister development after 1945 was the revival of the type of repression experienced in the late 1930s. The NKVD became more active under Beria, and there were several instances of purges and persecutions. In the so-called 'Leningrad Affair', Party leaders like Voznesensky, who had resisted the German siege, were shot. Antisemitism reached a new peak with the execution of prominent Jewish intellectuals. Then, in 1953, several doctors, mostly Jewish, were accused of having hatched a monstrous plot to kill, by medical means, all the prominent Soviet leaders; they had, it was claimed, already murdered Zhdanov in 1948. It was now clear that a new purge was about to break.

There are three possible reasons for this. First, a new élite had developed within the Party, which Stalin felt needed to be cut down. Second, the Cold War and the bitter hostility towards the capitalist world made it seem imperative that any internal 'bourgeois' influences be eliminated. Third, there is evidence that Stalin was becoming increasingly paranoid and unbalanced; after 1948 his mental and physical health deteriorated rapidly.

The new purge was, in fact, prevented only by the death of Stalin in March 1953. He was staying at his country *dacha* in Kuntsevo, where he suffered a stroke. When he did not make an appearance on 1 March, none of his staff dared find out the reason. As Stalin's absence lengthened, the officer on duty contacted Stalin's senior associates – Beria, Malenkov, Khrushchev and Bulganin. They came quickly to the residence to find Stalin lying on his bedroom floor at the point of death. Stalin's body was embalmed and placed next to Lenin's in the mausoleum. There it remained until 1961 when, on the orders of Khrushchev, it was cremated and buried in the Kremlin wall.

Reflections on Stalin's dictatorship

Chapter 2 has considered the merits and defects of Stalin's individual policies before 1941, during the Great Patriotic War, and after 1945. This final section will provide some overall views of Stalin's rule, concentrating on two questions.

What was the basis of Stalin's power?

We have seen that Stalin rose to power through his control over the Party and maintained it by means of social discipline and purges. Throughout his rule, however, there were three factors which gave Stalinism its distinctive character: ideology, historical tradition and personality cult.

Stalin was not originally renowned as a philosopher, but he aimed to establish himself as an authority on Marxism and to adapt Marxism to the needs of an industrializing society. He wrote four major works: *Marxism and the National Question* (1913), *Foundations of Leninism* (1924), *Marxism and Linguistics* (1950) and *Economic Problems of Socialism in the USSR* (1952). He always prefaced any major policy statements with ideological references, even in his speeches to the people during the Second World War. He even succeeded in turning Marxist principles upside-down in order to justify his enormous personal powers. As a result, Stalin has been disowned by most Marxists, who denounce his use of their ideology to construct a totalitarian state.

Stalin did not, however, base his power entirely on ideology. Most of the early Bolsheviks, especially Lenin,

Trotsky, Bukharin, Kamenev and Zinoviev, had been westernized Russians who had turned against their Slavic inheritance – political, social and cultural. Stalin, by contrast, was profoundly Slavic and quite deliberately revived an interest in an earlier phase of Russian history. He was particularly fascinated by Ivan the Terrible (1533–84), with whom he seemed in many ways to identify. Ivan had been confronted by opposition from the landed nobility, or *boyars*, under their spokesman Prince Andrei Kurbsky; this paralleled Stalin's problems with dissidents within the Party, led by Trotsky. Ivan tackled the problem by initiating a series of purges carried out by the *oprichniki* (horsemen who carried, as the emblem of their special authority, brooms and dogs' heads attached to their saddles). This may well have been one influence behind Stalin's purges and the activities of the NKVD. Stalin insisted on the offical rehabilitation of this most unpopular of tsars and ordered Eisenstein to produce an epic film. He also restored pride in other periods of the Russian past and, during the Second World War, patriotism was deliberately linked to ideology. In the words of Tucker, Stalin 'merged Marx with Ivan the Terrible'.[71] He also developed an almost tsarist attitude to power, but with his version of Marxism taking the place of Divine Right.

This brings us to the personal basis of Stalin's power. During the period 1929–53 Stalin constructed the most elaborate personality cult in history. An extract from an official history read:

> Stalin is the brilliant leader and teacher of the Party, the great strategist of the Socialist Revolution, military commander and guide of the Soviet state. With the name of Stalin in their hearts, the collective farmers toiled devotedly in the fields to supply the Red Army and the cities with food, and industry with raw materials. Stalin's name is cherished by the boys and girls of the Socialist land.

On Stalin's 70th birthday so many letters of congratulations and greetings were sent to *Pravda* that it took three years to publish them. The Soviet Union was filled with Stalin statues and busts, and numerous cities and towns were named after him.

In part this cult of personality was developed to cover Stalin's personal deficiencies and lack of charisma. Mediocrity and facelessness had assisted his rise to power, as his contemporaries had not seen Stalin as a danger until it was too late. But mediocrity bred insecurity, and insecurity was certainly a factor in Stalin's campaign to eliminate the entire 1917 crop of Bolsheviks and to project himself as the only true successor to Lenin – the 'best Leninist'.[72] Ulam provides another explanation for the cult. Stalin was 'a butcher, who had sent tens and hundreds of thousands of men, women and children to be tortured and shot on the strength of a diseased imagination'. The cult acted as a safeguard or a 'barrier keeping him from stepping over into actual insanity'.[37] He needed, it could be argued, to be reassured by overwhelming acclamation that he was pursuing the right policies after all. In effect, therefore, Stalin practised the ultimate in self-delusion, and indoctrinated *himself*.

Was Stalin necessary?

This is a second question which is frequently asked about the period 1924–53. Stalin has always had both critics and defenders. Most western historians have tended to follow an argument which runs something like this. Stalin constructed the most brutal dictatorship and used appalling methods, but his achievement was considerable. His industrialization drive, in particular, made possible eventual victory against Fascism and the subsequent development of the Soviet Union into one of the two superpowers. McCauley states:

> One may dismiss Stalin as a tyrant, as an evil man whom the USSR could have done without. On the other hand, it is possible to argue that he rendered the Soviet people a service which may eventually be seen as his greatest achievement. It is quite probable that had the USSR not gone through the forced industrialisation of the 1930s she would have succumbed to the German onslaught of 1941.[73]

Carr believes that Stalin was necessary, in that he was 'an agent of history', produced by the circumstances following the Bolshevik Revolution. If Stalin had not set in motion the process of industrialization, someone else would have done.

In this respect, Stalin was 'the great executor of revolutionary policy'. He was, however, a man of opposites. He combined immense achievements with utter brutality: he was, in Carr's words 'an emancipator and a tyrant'.

This interpretation, with its emphasis on the overlap of positive and negative, has recently been challenged from two angles. Ulam has chosen to lay much more stress on Stalin's deficiencies, believing that Russia would have been much better off without him. He refutes the argument that Stalin's industrialization programme dragged Russia into the twentieth century; on the contrary, much faster progress would have been made by an alternative regime – possibly even by Tsarist Russia. It is also inappropriate to argue that Stalin paved the way for victory in the Second World War; if anything, he impeded it by his earlier liquidation of vast numbers of people who would have been useful to the war effort.

The opposite view has been put by I. Grey, who deliberately set out to redress what he considered a longstanding bias against Stalin. 'There has been a paucity of studies of his positive achievements.' Many historians, he argues, have been influenced by Trotsky's vilification of Stalin. In reality, Stalin may have had defects, but he also possessed a 'great and highly disciplined intelligence' together with 'single-mindedness' and 'implacable will'. He was totally dedicated to 'the two causes of Russia and Marxism – Leninism', in the service of which 'no sacrifice was too great'. His ruthless measures were therefore applied for a higher objective. Throughout the purges Stalin 'showed an extraordinary self-control and did not lose sight of his purpose'. In the last analysis, Stalin could claim that 'Soviet Russia had become stronger as a result of his grandiose campaigns of industrialization, collectivization and social transformation'.[74]

The Soviet leadership since 1953 has also reacted in different ways. On the one hand, Stalin's influence was profound. The Soviet Union continued to possess a tightly controlled and monolithic party, an autocratic leadership, a constitution almost identical to Stalin's and, under Brezhnev, a continuing commitment to Socialist Realism. On the other hand, Stalin's excesses were openly condemned by Krushchev, who used the

1956 Party Congress to initiate the 'destalinization' campaign. Gorbachev, who came to power in 1985, went considerably further. He introduced 'glasnost' to remove the residue of Stalinist repression and 'perestroika' to combat the weaknesses of the centralized economy. He also presided over the rehabilitation of those Bolsheviks who had opposed Stalin and who had been eliminated in the purges. More than any of his predecessors, therefore, Gorbachev genuinely acknowledged the excesses of Stalinism and sought to alleviate their influence.

3
Dictatorship in Italy

Italy was the first of the major European states to seek salvation in the policies of the radical right, and Mussolini was the first of a succession of 'Fascist' dictators. Yet there has always been a puzzling element about Mussolini's rule. Although his influence was profound, he is often derided as a buffoon. In 1919, for example, the Socialist, Giacinto Serrati, described him as 'a rabbit; a phenomenal rabbit; he roars. Observers who do not know him mistake him for a lion.'[1] More recently A.J.P. Taylor called him a 'vain, blundering boaster without either ideas or aims'.[2]

This chapter will examine how Mussolini captured, held and lost the Italian nation; the reader should be able to decide whether or not these views are justified.

THE RISE OF MUSSOLINI TO 1922: AN OUTLINE

From the beginning of his stormy career in journalism and politics until he became Prime Minister in 1922, Mussolini underwent a series of major shifts in the direction of his beliefs and tactics.

His original radicalism was of the left, not of the right. He leaned towards revolutionary socialism, thought in terms of class struggle and uncompromisingly condemned nationalism and imperialism, particularly Italy's conquest of Tripoli in 1912. He was a member of the PSI (Italian Socialist Party) and in 1912 was appointed editor of the newspaper *Avanti* by the Party's militants. Through *Avanti* he aimed to promote popular revolutionary fervour, while at the same time he attempted to enter Italian politics legally; he failed, however, to win a parliamentary seat in the 1913 elections. Throughout 1914 he devoted his energies to putting the case against Italian involvement in the Great War.

Then occurred the first of Mussolini's changes. By 1915 he was pressing openly for Italy to join the fighting; clearly his ideological views were built on shifting sands. He was promptly deprived of his editorship of *Avanti* and was expelled from the PSI. He succeeded, however, in acquiring his own paper, *Il Popolo d'Italia*, in which he wedded war with revolutionary fervour using slogans like 'Who has steel has bread' and 'Revolution is an idea which has found bayonets'. His own personal contribution to the Italian war effort was a spell of loyal but undistinguished military service, ended in 1917 by wounds received after a grenade exploded in his trench.

In March 1919 Mussolini presided over a meeting in Milan which gave birth to the *Fascio di Combattimento*. The *Fasci* soon spread to some 70 other cities and towns, where they established themselves as local political movements with local programmes. At the national level, the *Fascio di Combattimento* identified as its enemies a surprisingly large number of groups: organized labour (especially the trade unions and the PSI), capitalism and big business, the monarchy and even the Church. Not surprisingly, the Fascists failed to win a single parliamentary seat in the 1919 elections, and the Socialists mocked Mussolini by burying an effigy of Fascism in Milan.

These developments induced Mussolini to undergo, in 1921, a second change. This time he was prepared to abandon his revolutionary inclination and prepare Fascism for a parliamentary struggle. Hence he set up a political party (the PFI or

Partito Nazionale Fascista) and appealed to as wide a cross-section of society as he could by narrowing down the enemies to socialism and the threat of 'red' revolution. For reasons which are examined in the next section, this strategy was more successful, and in 1921 the Fascist Party won 35 parliamentary seats.

But broadening the appeal and abandoning open revolution did not mean less violence. On the contrary, black-shirted Fascist squads launched numerous attacks on the left. They were given their opportunity by a wave of strikes organized in the cities by the trade unions and the PSI, as well as by action taken in rural areas by peasant leagues against land owners. Throughout 1920 and 1921 militant workers and peasants were intimidated into submission, through beatings and being forced to consume castor oil and live toads. All over Italy Fascist activities were directed by local leaders (or *ras*). One of the most successful of these was Balbo, who captured Ferrara and much of Romagna from the Socialists in May, 1922. The Socialists responded in August with an appeal for a general strike as a protest against Fascist violence, but this played further into Mussolini's hands. It took the Fascists only one day to smash the threat and thus to emerge as the main safeguard against industrial disruption.

Meanwhile, the post-war Italian governments had become increasingly unstable and unpopular. A succession of Prime Ministers sought to contain what they saw as a threat from the left and, in the process, came to depend on the parliamentary support of the Fascist Party. Even so, Mussolini had nowhere near sufficient electoral backing to establish an alternative government; the best he could reasonably have expected was an invitation to play a minor role in Prime Minister Facta's cabinet. Yet 1922 saw a spectacular political development: the replacement of Facta by Mussolini.

This occurred as the result of a threat of force from Mussolini and a reaction of near panic from the government. On his way to the Fascist Party Congress in Naples in October 1922, Mussolini stopped off in Rome to demand at least five cabinet ministries. In Naples he made preparations for a Fascist 'March on Rome' to seize power if his conditions were not met. Facta urged King Victor Emanuel III to declare martial law so that the threat could be countered by force. The King refused and, mindful of the Fascist contingents gathering outside Rome, invited Mussolini to join a coalition government. Sensing the possibility of total capitulation, Mussolini declined. On 29 October Mussolini, then in Milan, received a request from the King to form his own government. This was followed shortly afterwards by the much heralded 'March on Rome' as Mussolini, now Prime Minister, paraded his henchmen through the streets and announced the beginning of a new era.

THE RISE OF MUSSOLINI TO 1922: AN EXPLANATION

Three reasons can be given for Mussolini's success by the end of 1922. First, Italy had undergone a prolonged crisis before 1914 which was so aggravated by the First World War that conventional political and economic solutions no longer worked. Second, this situation favoured the emergence of a new movement able to attract the support of a cross-section of a society thoroughly disillusioned with the existing establishment. Third, Mussolini's leadership and strategy gave to this movement a versatility and vitality which contrasted all too obviously with a tired and dull government.

Underlying instability 1861–1922

Italy had been united as a liberal-parliamentary regime but, in the era between Cavour and Mussolini, lacked political stability. There was a rapid succession of ministries: 22 between 1860 and 1900 (an average of 1.8 years each), 9 between 1900 and 1914 (1.6 years each), and 7 between 1914 and 1922 (1.1 years each). At first, parties were not clearly defined and government depended on a consensus reached between the different political groups, a process known as *trasformismo*. Unfortunately, this could be maintained only by the distribution of favours and offices, a corrupt system which kept political power in the hands of the very few. In the decade before 1914 Giolitti (Prime Minister 1903–5, 1906–9 and 1911–14) tried to reform the whole process by seeking the co-operation of the Catholic Church and the Socialists, and by introducing universal manhood suffrage in 1912.

Critics of Giolitti argued that his efforts were already in trouble by 1914 and that Italian politics had not been able to adjust to mass participation. Governments continued to be regarded with scepticism and distrust by the majority of the electorate. Then came the First World War which, in the words of A. De Grand, 'marked a rupture in the course of Italian political development'.[3] In effect, it pushed Italy from instability into crisis. The traditional governing groups were split in their attitude to the war. Giolitti remained consistently opposed, while the wartime Prime Ministers, Salandra, Boselli and Orlando could neither co-operate with him nor do without him.[3] The result was a 'paralysis' of parliamentary government, which was worsened by Italy's military defeat at the hands of the Austrians at Caporetto in 1917. The regime was reprieved only by the Italian victory in 1918 at Vittorio Veneto against an Austria which was falling to pieces internally.

The war also produced the threat of economic collapse and social disruption. The total cost of the war was 148,000 million lire, over twice the total expenditure of all Italian governments between 1861 and 1913.[4] The economic base was weakened by huge budget deficits and by unbalanced trade and industrial production. It has been estimated that, by 1919, exports covered only 36 per cent of Italy's imports.[5] Furthermore, the growth of industrial production between 1915 and 1918 had been geared so directly to the war effort that it could not be maintained by the requirements of the post-war home market. Unemployment soared, with demobilization mainly responsible for the total of 2 million by the end of 1919.[5] Inflation had also become a fact of life, with the cost of living in 1919 about four times that of 1913. With this gloomy economic background, it appeared that Italy had emerged from the war with all the makings of violent social confrontation. On the one hand, the urban and rural working classes were desperate to prevent any further decline in their standard of living. On the other, the industrialists and landowners feared that demands for increased wages and employment protection would raise costs and threaten productivity and profits. The situation was further complicated by the impoverishment of a large part of the lower middle class which became radical and assertive, distrusting labour and capital alike.

The question arising in 1919 was this: could the post-war governments pull these conflicting forces together for the collective national good? Giolitti, Prime Minister between June 1920 and July 1921, made some attempt but found that all hope of consensus politics had been dashed by the war. The Socialist Party (PSI) and the majority of the unions were militant in their demands, the lower middle classes were no longer dependable as moderate voters, and the whole political scene was further complicated by the emergence of the Italian Popular Party (PPI), a large Catholic grouping. The only real hope for stability was a coalition which included Italy's two largest parties, the Socialists and the PPI. However, the gap between them was unbridgeable. Giolitti and his successors, Bonomi (1921–2) and Facta (1922) therefore operated in a political vacuum. Increasingly, they came to depend on the Fascists – but in a way which was underhand, unparliamentary and ultimately suicidal. Unable to resolve the growing crisis between labour and capital, and ever conscious of the threat of revolution, the governments tacitly allowed the Fascists to take direct and often brutal action against unions and peasant leagues. This was the resort of a government which seemed to have lost the will to govern.

Support for Fascism

The emblem eventually adopted for the Fascist Party was the *fasces*, a bundle of rods with a protruding axe-head, carried by magistrates in ancient Rome. These rods came to symbolize the various groups supporting Fascism, individually weak but deriving a collective strength from being bound together. Certainly Fascism appealed to a wide cross-section of society at a time when the prevailing atmosphere was one of political instability and economic insecurity. To many people Fascism offered an alternative to a narrowly based and discredited government on the one hand and, on the other, the upheaval of a socialist revolution.

The original support for Fascism came from war veterans – young, aggressive and, according to A.J. Gregor, 'irretrievably lost to organized socialism and ill-disposed toward the commonplaces of the traditional parties'.[6] Most of them were fiercely patriotic; they denounced the 'mutilated peace' of the Paris Settlement and their ardour was fired by the occupation of Fiume in 1919–20 by the poet and adventurer, D'Annunzio. The Italian army was generally sympathetic towards the Fascists, although two attitudes tended to prevail. The lower levels participated enthusiastically in Fascist rallies and diverted a considerable amount of military equipment and arms, while the officer corps tried to keep discipline within the army without actually attacking Fascism. On the civilian scene, the *carabinieri* which, as the constabulary, was the main force of law and order, openly sympathized with Fascism and stood aside when attacks were directed at trade unionists.

The backbone of Fascism, however, was the lower middle class, especially small shopkeepers, artisans and clerical workers.[7] This normally moderate sector of society had been destabilized by the process of industrialization and by the economic difficulties caused by the war. They were the casualties of changes occurring all over central Europe, and the sociologist Seymour Lipset has called them the 'displaced masses'. They were caught between the rival forces of labour and capital and spurned the solutions of the socialist left, for these would involve a further depression of their status and their being levelled down into the working class. Hence they saw the Fascist movement as 'the long sought instrument of bourgeois resurgence' (De Grand),[5] since it promised an end to industrial disruption and revolutionary socialism on the one hand while, on the other, it seemed ready to curb the power of big business.

The agrarian sector also became involved in the Fascist movement. At first most of the support came from the landlords and estate owners who were greatly assisted by the Fascist attacks on peasant strikers in 1920. During the first half of 1921 Fascist squads destroyed 119 labour chambers, 107 co-operatives and 83 peasant league offices.[5] Yet there is evidence that even some of the peasantry could be won over. Recent studies have shown that a proportion of the peasantry came to prefer the later Fascist policy of small land grants given to individual cultivators rather than the socialist alternative of land collectivization.[8]

Industry produced the most dramatic class rupture in post-war Italy and it is scarcely surprising that the great industrialists should have backed Fascism. Because Mussolini's followers battered the unions into submission, the industrialists were willing to provide large donations; two examples were Alberto Pirelli, the tyre magnate, and Giovanni Agnelli of Fiat. Then, during the course of 1921, a number of workers joined the Fascist movement. The main reason for this was the growing crisis of socialism. The PSI split in 1921 and a separate Communist Party was established under the influence of Gramsci. The organization of the socialist movement became even more decentralized and provincial, which meant that the attacks of the Fascists rarely met co-ordinated resistance. Those workers who defected from what they saw as a sinking ship were also attracted by the emergence of alternatives to the unions – the Fascist syndicates.

Finally, there were sectors who assisted Fascism indirectly: although they could not bring themselves to support Fascism openly they were at least prepared to tolerate it in a way which would have been out of the question with, for example, socialism. One of these groups was the political establishment, whose attitude has already been examined. Another was the aristocratic class, who were appeased by Mussolini's willingness to end his attacks on the monarchy. In fact, the Queen Mother, Margherita, and the King's cousin, the Duke of Aosta, were admirers of Fascism. A third sector was the Catholic Church, taking its cue from Pope Pius XI who, from the time of his election in 1922, remained on good terms with Mussolini. The Church undoubtedly considered a Communist revolution to be the main threat. Mussolini, by contrast, had abandoned atheism and had come to accept Catholicism as one of the sources of 'the imperial and Latin tradition of Rome'.[9]

The role of Mussolini

A distinction is often drawn between Italian Fascism and Mussolini. The former possessed considerable independent momentum, as was shown by the widespread local support gained in 1920 and 1921. But Fascism was also diffuse and incoherent, likely to dissipate unless given a national structure and identity. This is what Mussolini provided.

His first contribution to Fascism was its organization. It is true that he had an enormous struggle to achieve any sort of centralization in 1921 and that local activism would continue, undisciplined, for several years to come. He did, however, give Fascism its vital foothold in Parliament, and the PFI gained respectability and political credibility which transcended purely local interests. He was also able to establish links between local activist groups, so that Fascism could claim to be a national *movement* as well as a national *party*.

Secondly, Mussolini showed the importance of opportunism and action rather than a fixed ideology. Admittedly, he sometimes hesitated: Balbo, for example, is supposed to have prodded him into action over the March on Rome by telling him: 'We are going, either with you or without you. Make up your mind.'[10] He was also strongly inclined to intuitive behaviour and he lacked a policy or a programme.[11] He did, however, succeed in projecting himself as a flexible pragmatist and he managed to cover up any erratic or inconsistent views. He once explained: 'Only maniacs never change. New facts can call for new positions.'[12] He claimed that his was a 'doctrine of action', and he saw his strength as having neither an overall 'system' nor, after 1919, an ideological straitjacket. This pragmatism enabled him to make full use of the chaotic conditions in post-war Italy. He could use the largely spontaneous Fascist campaigns of pressure and violence in order to satisfy the popular craving for positive action; at the same time, he could pretend that Fascism was moderate in Parliament, so winning the grudging approval of the government.

This brings us to Mussolini's personal leadership. His career has been presented as one of bluster and bluff – in huge proportions.[13] But then the early 1920s were a period in which outrageous bluff had a better than usual chance of success. Mussolini applied all his journalistic skills and tricks to attract popular attention and support. He also learned, from D'Annunzio during the Fiume escapade, how to create a sense of power among his followers, even incorporating into the Fascist movement the war-cry of the *arditi* (shock-troops): 'Ayah, ayah, alala!' His personal attributes, according to C. Hibbert, included 'a physical stance not yet devitalised by illness', a 'style of oratory, staccato, tautophonic and responsive, not yet ridiculed by caricature' and 'a personal charm not yet atrophied by adulation'.[14] With this presence, he was able to act his way into power.

For this is what really happened. He played upon the postwar crisis, making it appear that Fascism really *did* have the strength to smash socialism and remould society, and that it really *could* disrupt the functioning of parliamentary politics. No chances were taken by the politicians, and Mussolini was given more respect than his real strength perhaps deserved; this would explain the capitulation of Facta and Victor Emmanuel when they were put under threat in October 1922. The counterpart to Mussolini the destroyer was the constructive statesman who, alone, could reconcile, rally and unite; under his leadership Fascism would 'draw its sword to cut the many Gordian Knots which enmesh and strangle Italian life'.[15] This personification of power had inherent dangers as, eventually, the bluff turned inwards and, as D. Mack Smith argues, Mussolini fell victim to his own delusions.

MUSSOLINI'S DICTATORSHIP 1922–43

Between 1922 and 1943 Mussolini established, at least in theory, all the institutions and devices associated with the totalitarian state. The foundation was the Fascist ideology, upon which was set a one-party system and all the paraphernalia of the personality cult. Popular support was guaranteed by indoctrination and, where necessary, coercion, while the economy was brought under a corporative system and geared to the needs of war.

This is a fairly conventional picture of Fascist Italy. It is not untrue but it *is* incomplete. Below the surface there are indications that the totalitarian state was actually quite precarious. Fascist ideology was a makeshift alliance of different interests, the political institutions retained a surprisingly large number of non-Fascist influences, and the processes of indoctrination, coercion and corporativism were never completed.

The rest of this section will illustrate this contradiction between the strengths and weaknesses of Mussolini's dictatorship.

The ideology of Fascism

In 1932 Mussolini defined the basic ideas of the movement, clearly and emphatically, in his *Political and Social Doctrine of Fascism*. Fascism, he said, was anti-Communist, anti-Socialist and strongly opposed to an 'economic conception of history'. He denied that 'class war can be the preponderant force in the transformation of society'. Fascism was also antidemocratic, denouncing the 'whole complex system of democratic ideology'. It was certainly authoritarian: 'The foundation of Fascism is the conception of the State. Fascism conceives of the State as an absolute.' Finally, it promoted territorial expansion as 'an essential manifestation of vitality'.[16]

On the negative side, this definition was a hotchpotch of the ideas of conflicting sub-movements and sub-ideologies, of which De Grand has identified no fewer than five.[17] The first was 'National Syndicalism' which, in its emphasis on creating syndicates of workers and managers, was initially 'republican, anticlerical and vaguely socialistic'. The second was 'Rural Fascism', which was 'anti-urban, anti-modern and anti-industrial'. The third was 'Technocratic Fascism'; because it accepted industrialization, and all the implications of modernization, it differed markedly from Rural Fascism. The fourth was 'Conservative Fascism'; with its 'industrial, agrarian, monarchist and Catholic' connections, it was basically traditional, pragmatic and non-ideological. The fifth was 'Nationalist Fascism', perhaps 'the most coherent version' with an emphasis on an aggressive foreign policy and an authoritarian political system.[17]

In addition to this five-way division between the strategies of these groups, there were other gaps. National Syndicalism and Technocratic Fascism were both radical. They regarded themselves as the logical outcome of western Europe's revolutionary heritage, although they restored the emphasis on order and social harmony rather than individualism and liberal democracy.[17] By contrast, Conservative and Nationalist Fascism rejected Europe's revolutionary tradition altogether; their purpose was not to rationalize the French Revolution but to do away with it. This wide range of attitudes may originally have helped Fascism to gain popular support but, once the Fascist regime had been established, it proved a source of weakness. The Fascist state lacked the sort of monolithic base which Stalin's version of Marxism–Leninism gave to the Soviet Union.

Political power and institutions

When he was appointed Prime Minister in October 1922 Mussolini presided over a cabinet in which there were four Fascists and 10 non-Fascists. Since his Party had only 7 per cent of the seats in the lower chamber of Parliament, Mussolini had, at first, to be cautious and conciliatory. He lulled the other deputies into a sense of security by promising that he would defend, not destroy, the constitution. The former governing parties seemed to have given up completely. Nitti, an ex-Prime Minister, was convinced that 'The Fascist experiment must be carried out without interference: there should be no opposition from our side.'[18] The King, meanwhile, was prepared to grant Mussolini emergency powers for one year.

The first step in the constitutional process establishing a Fascist dictatorship was to achieve a permanent parliamentary majority, so that there was no possibility of an alternative government being installed some time in the future. Mussolini managed to persuade the Chamber that his intention was constructive, not revolutionary. In a mood of revulsion against Italy's habit of producing brief and unstable ministries, the Chamber passed the Acerbo electoral law in 1923. This stated that the party, or bloc, with a 25 per cent poll would automatically have a two-thirds majority in the Parliament and would therefore form the government. The Italian electorate confirmed Mussolini's power in the election of April 1924 by giving the Fascists 4.5 million votes (64 per cent of the total) and control over 404 seats. The combined vote for the opposition was about 2.5 million. From this time onwards Mussolini could claim a genuine electoral mandate and therefore pursue more radical policies with fewer inhibitions.

The next stage was the elimination of all parliamentary opposition parties. The occasion which made this possible started as a serious embarrassment to the regime. In June 1924 an outspoken Socialist deputy, Matteotti, was seized outside his house, bundled into a Lancia and stabbed to death. His body was discovered two months later in a shallow grave on the outskirts of Rome. It soon became evident that the crime had been committed by over-zealous Fascists, and Mussolini feared that their activities could permanently taint his Party in Parliament. His recovery, however, was rapid and his subsequent actions illustrate his opportunism. Most of the non-Fascist deputies withdrew from the Assembly, as a protest, in what came to be known as the 'Aventine Secession'. Their intention was to show the King that parliamentary democracy was dead. In fact, the gesture showed that the opposition had given up. Mussolini hammered home his advantage by refusing to allow the Aventine Secessionists to return and by imposing a ban on all other parties.

The one-party state was formalized in May 1928 by the introduction of a new electoral law; this ensured that all parliamentary candidates would be selected by the Fascist Grand Council from lists submitted by confederations of employers and employees. The final list had to be voted for as a whole by the electorate. In effect, parliamentary elections had been replaced by a plebiscitary dictatorship. The process was completed when, in 1939, the Chamber of Deputies was abolished and replaced by the Chamber of Fasces and Corporations.

The Fascist Party itself also underwent modification. Originally it had been localized in its composition, and there was a faction which demanded a permanently decentralized organization and a limited membership. Eventually, however, the centralist viewpoint prevailed. The radicals of the Party, led by Farinacci, wanted a carefully organized machine to ensure that the policies of Fascism could be uniformly implemented. The first step was the establishment in 1922 of the Fascist Grand Council, under the control of Mussolini himself. Then, during the Matteotti crisis, the original Party bosses at local level were purged and a new structure came into being, based on the principles of centralized direction and widespread Party membership. In theory, at least, the Party was being adapted to reach the masses.

Meanwhile, Mussolini was also aiming to consolidate his personal powers. A fundamental law, passed in 1925, altered the constitution to make him responsible to the King rather than the legislature. Then, in January 1926, he was empowered to govern by decree, a process which was to be used over 100,000 times by 1943.[19] During the late 1920s he also accumulated offices on an unprecedented scale. In 1929, for example, he was personally responsible for eight key ministries: foreign affairs, the interior, war, navy, aviation, colonies, corporations and public works. This authority was accompanied by the deliberate inflation of Mussolini's own image in the creation of the cult of the Duce.

So far we have been left with a picture of the institutions of parliamentary democracy being eroded and replaced by those of a Fascist dictatorship. A closer look, however, reveals some surprising inconsistencies between theory and practice which made for serious inefficiency within the regime.

For one thing, Mussolini left a considerable part of the previous political structure intact, especially the system of local prefects. In a circular issued on 5 January 1927, he ordered that the provincial prefects must be obeyed completely by all citizens, including Fascists.[20] The result was that the prefects exercised more control over the Party than the Party possessed over the administration. Indeed, the Fascist Party contributed little to the formulation of policy, and Mussolini played off the members of the Grand Council against each other. He also insisted on widespread membership of the Party, thus deliberately devaluing the privilege. Finally, he made the administrative machine more complex, increased the number of departmental personnel and, in A. Lyttelton's words, 'deliberately fostered untidiness and illogicality in the structure of government'.[8] Why did he do all this?

The main reason was that Mussolini intended to rule by

balancing the different elements which made up the state and the Party. His basic fear was that one or more of these elements might eventually challenge his authority, and the greatest immediate threat seemed to come from the Fascist Party itself. Hence he took the drastic but logical step of depoliticizing the regime. The result was a strange paradox: the strength of Fascism depended on the weakness of Fascist organizations. Or, to put it another way, a movement which was famed for its activism was encouraged by its leader to show inactivity. Mussolini was deliberately creating a vacuum in the political and administrative structure where one would normally expect to find a ruling class or élite. The explanation of this was that Mussolini was actually opposed to the emergence of any group which was likely to compete with him for power and public support. The gap was filled by the cult of the Duce,[20] or Mussolinianism, and Fascism was restrained so that this could predominate. The cult of the Duce was not an essential part of the Fascist programme, but rather an elaborate superstructure imposed on top of it. As far as Mussolini was concerned, however, it was the whole point of his rule; after all, he had once said, 'If Fascism does not follow me, no one can make me follow Fascism.'[9]

Is it therefore surprising that the Fascist political dictatorship was only half implemented? The whole trend worked against efficiency, as Mussolini introduced new institutions but then refused to let them function properly in order to protect his own popular image.

The use of indoctrination and coercion

While altering the base of political power, Mussolini also sought to establish a new national identity for the Italian people. In the *Enciclopedia Italiana* (1931) he wrote: 'The Fascist conception of the state is all-embracing, and outside of the state no human or spiritual values can exist, let alone be desirable.'[21] All allegiance was to be focused on the Duce himself, which meant that the personality cult, already referred to, became a major priority in the indoctrination process. Mussolini's short stature and partial baldness were disguised by a ramrod straight stance and shaven head, both of which were intended to give him a 'Roman' appearance.

His demagoguery remained impressive, based on the unsubtle belief that 'The crowd loves strong men'. He was also portrayed as an expert rider, fencer, racing driver and violinist. The public were constantly assailed by slogans like 'Mussolini is always right!' and 'Believe! Obey! Fight!' Eventually, Mussolini hoped, there would be created the 'New Fascist Man' who would live in the 'century of Fascism'.

The first systematic measures were tried in education, the intention being to use the schools as the main channel of indoctrination. In 1923 the Education Minister, Gentile, introduced a new structure specifically intended to create a new élite; technical education was separated from the classical courses which became the passport to university education, and a rigid examination system was applied. This, however, came under universal criticism from parents and was so difficult to operate that Fedele, Gentile's successor, had to modify it from 1925 onwards. The most important attempt to 'Fascistize' education was initiated by Bottai in 1936. Textbooks became a state monopoly; the number of approved history texts, for instance, was reduced from 317 to one, while a junior Italian reader informed solemn eight-year-olds that 'the eyes of the Duce are on every one of you'. From 1938 racism was openly practised and taught in the classroom, while 1939 saw the introduction of the Fascist School Charter. By and large, however, education was not one of the more successful examples of indoctrination. There were too many loopholes and evasions and, in the universities, underground resistance to and contempt for Fascist values.

Hence the regime came to place more emphasis on the organization of youth groups outside the school sector. At the age of four, boys became 'Sons of the She-Wolf'; at eight they joined the *Balilla*, before moving to the *Avanguardisti* at 14 and finally the Fascist Levy at 18. The creed of the *Balilla* blatantly superimposed a doctored version of Italian history on a twisted religious format:

I believe in Rome the Eternal, the mother of my country, and in Italy, her eldest daughter, who was born in her virginal bosom by the grace of God; who suffered through the barbarian invasions, was crucified and buried, who descended to the grave, and was raised from the dead in the nineteenth century, who ascended into heaven in her glory in 1918 and 1922 and who is seated on the right hand of her mother Rome; who for this reason shall come to judge the living and the dead. I believe in the genius of Mussolini, in our Holy Father Fascism, in the communion of the martyrs, in the conversion of Italians and in the resurrection of the Empire.[19]

A large proportion of Italy's youth responded enthusiastically to Fascism. It should, however, be pointed out that membership of these para-military organizations was by no means universal, as some 40 per cent of the age group between eight and 18 managed to avoid joining them.

That Mussolini considered the control of the press to be a major priority was hardly surprising, in view of his own experience as a newspaper editor. Early measures included the suppression of many papers by the Exceptional Decrees of 1926 and, in 1928, the compulsory registration of all journalists with the Fascist Journalist Association. By the mid-1930s a measure of uniformity had been achieved and the Press Office managed to exert effective control over what was and was not published; in difficult cases the government called upon the local prefects to enforce its decisions. By and large, Mussolini's 'regime of journalism' was more successful than most other elements of the totalitarian state. There was, however, a price; constant distortion of the facts about Italy's record in her three wars led eventually to the entire government being misinformed. Mussolini, in particular, lost all contact with reality, even though – or because – he spent several hours each day reading the newspapers.

The government's policy towards culture shows a particularly large gap between expectation and achievement. Mussolini's initial intention was to create a series of Fascist cultural forms. Hence Gentile's Conference on Fascist Culture, convened at Bologna in 1925, produced the Manifesto of Fascist Intellectuals. This was promptly ridiculed by dissidents, mostly in exile, who lampooned Fascist cultural pretensions as an 'incoherent and bizarre mixture of conflicting ideas'.[22] Attempts were also made to institutionalize the control of culture through the Ministry of Popular Culture, which tried to regulate music, literature, art and the cinema. Eventually, however, the government had to reduce its influence over cultural forms in return for a degree of political orthodoxy. This was in marked contrast to the more successful measures used by Goebbels to 'Nazify' German art and literature and the 'Socialist Realism' of Stalin.

One of the more popular forms of culture was the cinema which, according to Mussolini, was the 'strongest weapon'.[23] This provides a more detailed example of the incomplete nature of Fascist control. On the one hand there was an increase in institutions and regulations. A film institute was set up in 1925, followed, in 1934, by the Office for Cinematography. The government insisted on quotas (100 films were to be made in 1937) and tried to dictate the themes of major epics. On the other hand, such controls were far from total. Most films were produced by private enterprise and were not geared to the state's propaganda requirements. Indeed, Fascism's lack of cultural awareness alienated the younger generation of film directors, like De Santis and Visconti, who aimed at realism rather than distortion. Thus, ultimately, 'Mussolini's strongest weapon...was turned against Fascism itself.'[23]

The overall impression, therefore, must be that the Fascist state failed to exert the type of control over ideas which is normally associated with totalitarianism. The more traditional liberal culture proved impossible to eradicate so that the authorities had to resort to a series of unsatisfactory compromises.

Indoctrination is invariably linked to coercion. The use of force had been implicit in the Fascist movement from the beginning and a system of repression was gradually constructed. This included, in 1926, the OVRA (*Opera voluntaria per la repressione antifascista*) and a Special Tribunal for the Defence of the State. The dissidents who experienced the full pressure of these organs were mainly ex-politicians who refused to take the oath of loyalty to the regime. From the late 1930s the apparatus was also used to enforce a policy of antisemitism (see p. 106). At no time, however, was coercion

as systematic as in Hitler's Germany or Stalin's Russia.
Torture was used more sparingly and the death sentence was
rarely imposed for political offences. As Fascism established
itself and eliminated opposition parties it became, if anything, less violent, the very reverse of Nazism and Stalinism.
As A. Cassels observes, 'The Fascist regime used terror, but
was not in any real sense based on terror.'

The policy of antisemitism

In July 1938 a *Manifesto on Race* was drawn up by Mussolini
and 10 'professors' as a 'scientific exposition' of Fascist racial
doctrine. It proclaimed that 'the population of Italy is of
Aryan origins and its civilization is Aryan', that 'there now
exists a pure Italian race' and that 'Jews do not belong to the
Italian race'.[24] It was followed by decrees banning inter-
marriage between Jews and non-Jews and removing Jews
from prominent positions in finance, education and politics.
Property restrictions were also imposed and any Jews who
had entered Italy since 1919 were to be repatriated.

This was a major switch in Fascist policy. Italy had always
been less affected than other parts of Europe by antisemitism,
largely because Jews had never amounted to more than one
in a thousand of the total population. Also, Mussolini had
originally denounced Nazi racism as 'unscientific' and
'absurd'[25] and several prominent Fascists were of Jewish
origin. Therefore 1938 saw the reversal of a tolerance which
had been generally accepted.

Two explanations are normally advanced. One is that
Mussolini's Ethiopian War (1935–7) made race a public
issue, while several Jewish organizations drew attention to
themselves by condemning Italian aggression.[25] The other
explanation is that Mussolini felt under increasing pressure
to compete with Hitler for seniority within the partnership
between Italy and Germany. This involved creating an Italian
counterpart to the German 'master race', and Mussolini's
special ingredient was 'racial purity'. Hence, 'While the racial
composition of the other European nations has altered
considerably even in recent periods, the grand lines of racial
composition have remained essentially the same in Italy
during the last thousand years'.[26] The only blot on this record

were the Jews, who were 'constituted of non-European racial elements' and had never been 'assimilated in Italy'.

It is possible, therefore, that Mussolini's antisemitism was the unfortunate by-product of an inferiority complex and not the focal point of the type of obsessive hatred shown by Hitler. As a policy it was neither popular nor accepted – it was only resented. In asking 'Why, unfortunately, did Italy have to go and imitate Germany?'[25] Pope Pius XI was voicing both the Catholic conscience and the secular misgivings of those who saw the creeping influence of Nazism in Italy. In the event, the racial decrees were never applied effectively, another illustration of the incomplete nature of the totalitarian state. During the Second World War there were no large-scale shipments of Italian Jews to Nazi camps until the Germans occupied northern Italy in 1943; elsewhere antisemitic legislation gradually lapsed, especially after the fall of Mussolini. This has been hailed as 'the triumph of old humanitarian values over new Fascist principles'.[25]

Relations between Church and state

There was no natural affinity between the Church and Fascism. After all, Mussolini had once been a strident atheist and very few of the Fascist leaders were practising Catholics. Both sides, however, had much to gain from ending the deep rift between Church and state which went far back to the era of Italian unification. Mussolini claimed the credit for this reconciliation ('This serenity of relations is a tribute to the Fascist regime');[27] in fact the healing was started by Orlando, Prime Minister between 1917 and 1919. It could, however, be argued that the process was greatly accelerated by a Fascist government in need of the approval of Italy's Catholic population.

The highlight was the three Lateran agreements of 1929. The Lateran Treaty settled the question of the Pope's temporal power by restoring the Vatican City to his sovereignty. The Concordat defined more carefully the role of the Church in the Fascist state. Catholicism was to be 'the sole religion of the state', religious instruction would return to schools, and Church marriages would be given full validity. In a third agreement the papacy was compensated for financial losses, incurred in the nineteenth century, by the payment of 750 million lire in cash and 1000 million in state bonds.

This is usually seen as one of Mussolini's more durable achievements. He had, after all, succeeded in gaining the support of a power which had been hostile to successive governments for a period of 50 years. Pius XI claimed that the Lateran Accords 'brought God to Italy and Italy to God'.[28] In foreign policy, there was to be a considerable overlap of interest between the government and the papacy.[29] Cardinal Shuster, for example, compared the invasion of Ethiopia with the Crusades, while Pius XI openly justified Mussolini's participation in the Spanish Civil War on the grounds that he was helping contain the main enemy of Christianity: 'The first, the greatest and now the general peril, is certainly Communism in all its forms and degrees.'[30] This attitude met with the overwhelming approval of the upper levels in the Church hierarchy.

On the other hand, Mussolini never succeeded in subordinating the Church to the full control of the state; it could even be said that the Church came eventually to threaten the Fascist state. In 1931 Catholic Action, an organization for laymen, clashed with the government over the type of education intended for Italy's youth. An agreement was reached whereby Catholic Action would confine its recreational and educational activities to a purely religious content and would not try to undermine Fascist ideology. By 1939, however, Catholic Action had developed a number of institutions for youth which drew membership away from the Fascist para-military organizations and which directly competed with official social and cultural groups. It seemed that while approving Mussolini's fight against alien beliefs abroad, within Italy the Church competed aggressively with Fascism for the soul of the people.

There were also political implications. Two other organizations sprang up in the 1930s – the FUCI, for university students and staff, and the *Movimento Laureati* which aimed, quite deliberately, at fostering a 'new order'. Together with Catholic Action, these proved to be a potential opposition. Indeed, according to a police report in Milan in 1935, *Movi-*

mento Laureati could form, 'in a few hours, the strongest and most important political party in Italy'.[28] As the Fascist regime entered a period of crisis after 1939, Catholic leaders began to take a direct initiative. Aldo Moro, for example, revitalized the FUCI, and what was almost an alternative government formed around De Gasperi in 1943. Bitterly disillusioned by military defeat, Italians eventually shook off Fascism and returned in part to the traditional left, in part to Catholic politics – this time in the form of the Christian Democratic Party.

Economic policies

The overall trend in economic policy was from initial free enterprise to state intervention and control. During the 1920s this process was gradual, but accelerated from 1930 onwards as a result of the Great Depression and Italy's involvement in four wars.

The main development was the emergence of the 'corporate state'. The idea of corporativism was not new; it was based partly on medieval guilds and corporations and partly on the revolutionary syndicalism of Georges Sorel, an early influence on Mussolini. The basic intention was to replace the old sectional interests (such as trade unions and employers' organizations) which so often produced conflicts between labour and capital. Instead, the Rocco Law of 1926 recognized seven branches of economic activity: industry, agriculture, internal transport, merchant marine, banking, commerce and intellectual work. These were formed into syndicates, under the control of the Ministry of Corporations, also established in 1926. The system was further refined by the creation in 1930 of the National Council of Corporations and the organization of economic activity into 22 more specialized corporations by 1934. By 1938 this process was brought into the political system with the creation of the Chamber of Fasces and Corporations in place of the old Chamber of Deputies.

In theory, corporativism was the Fascist alternative to socialism on the left and undiluted capitalism on the right. The so-called 'third way' would increase state control over the economy without destroying private enterprise and it could be adapted to the new Fascist institutions. In practice, however, the whole system proved inefficient and cumbersome. It failed to provide any sort of consensus between employers and workers (see p. 112) and was almost entirely excluded from any real decision-making on the economy. As Cassels remarks, 'the corporative state was a true child of Mussolini: the great poseur brought forth an organism which was a travesty of what it purported to be'.[31]

The other major developments within the economy concerned finance, industry, agriculture and population. Between 1922 and 1925 Finance Minister De Stefani followed a traditional course of balanced budgets, avoided price fixing and subsidies, and withdrew government involvement in industry. From the mid-1920s, however, the views of Mussolini became more influential. These were based as much on the dictates of national prestige as on sound economic thought. He was obsessed, in particular, with the value of the Italian currency, declaring: 'I shall defend the Italian lira to my last breath'. In 1929 the lira was reflated to the level of 90 to the £ sterling, a decision which seriously undermined Italy's competitiveness as an exporter and which probably brought on recession even before the impact of the Great Depression. During the 1930s the government imposed increasingly tight financial controls which, from 1936, became an integral part of the policy of autarky (self-sufficiency) necessitated by war.

Fascism always favoured heavy industry at the expense of light (or consumer) industry, because of the former's close association with armaments. At first the emphasis was on encouraging private enterprise and leaving untouched private concerns like Fiat, Montecatini Chemicals and Pirelli Rubber. With the onset of the Great Depression, however, the government became more heavily involved by introducing schemes for job-sharing and for rescuing those industries in difficulty. In 1933 it set up the IRI (*Istituto per la recostruzione industriale*) to channel state investment into those industries which were considered most vital. The policy of autarky brought more rigid controls and centralization. By 1939, according to De Grand, the IRI controlled 77 per cent of pig iron production, 45 per cent of steel production, 80 per cent of naval construction and 90 per cent of shipping.[32]

In some respects, industry recovered reasonably well from the impact of the Great Depression. Between 1936 and 1940 it overtook agriculture for the first time in Italian history as the largest single contributor to the GNP (34 per cent as opposed to 29 per cent).[33] Imports had dropped considerably by 1939 when compared with the levels of 1928: raw materials by 12 per cent, semi-finished articles by 40 per cent and finished articles by 48 per cent. Meanwhile, industrial production as a whole had risen by 9 per cent. These figures were, however, offset by the persistence of serious weaknesses in the Italian industrial sector. Mussolini's policies failed to remove the huge disparity between north and south, while Italy remained affected by low productivity, high costs and a decline in domestic consumption. Overall, Italy's recovery from the effects of the Depression was slower than that of any other European power, and her industrial deficiencies were to become glaringly obvious under the strains of the Second World War.

The most important development in agriculture was the drive for self-sufficiency in grain which was intended to improve Italy's balance of trade with the rest of Europe and with North America. Characteristically, Mussolini introduced the 1925 campaign as the 'Battle for Grain' and, amid massive publicity, was photographed reaping, or driving tractors. The 'Battle' succeeded in increasing grain production by 50 per cent between 1922 and 1930 and by 100 per cent between 1922 and 1939. This was, however, largely at the expense of other crops like fruit and olives which would have been more suited to the additional land given over to grain.

Mussolini also sought to create extra arable land, through reclamation schemes, and extra people, through a higher birth rate. The former was accomplished by schemes like the draining of the Pontine Marshes. The latter was attempted by the 'Battle for Births', the aim of which was to double Italy's population within a generation. The reasoning behind such a dramatic demographic change was that a static population reflects a decay of national 'vitality' and that a larger population would be essential for the empire which Mussolini was in the process of creating. The incentives for larger families included the payment of benefits for children, the imposition of extra taxation on single people and giving priority in employment to fathers. The whole scheme, however, failed in its objective: between 1921 and 1925 there had been 29.9 births per 1000 people, whereas between 1936 and 1940 this had declined to 23.1 per 1000, due partly to the mobilization of men to fight in Mussolini's foreign wars.

The social consequences of Mussolini's regime

We have seen that the Fascist dictatorship was, in almost every respect, less totalitarian than it purported to be and that its economic policies met with very mixed success. The final, and most fundamental, issue to be examined is its impact on the Italian people. Before 1922 Mussolini claimed that Fascism represented the interests of all classes. By 1939, however, it was evident that any real benefits had accrued only to a small minority – the great industrialists, the estate owners and those members of the middle class serving in the Fascist bureaucracy. For the majority of Italians, by contrast, the quality of life deteriorated.

The industrialists were able to depend on a permanent alliance with the government. The 1925 Vidoni Pact and the Charter of Labour (1927) greatly increased their powers while destroying the capacity of the trade unions to resist. The corporate state, too, was loaded in favour of employers, who continued to be represented by their traditional spokesmen, while the workforce had to depend on government lackeys. Thus all forms of industry, from mass production to small-scale sweatshops, were free from official regulations. Of course, parts of industry were adversely affected by the Depression, but they were given top priority by the government after 1933, either through investment from the IRI or through official approval of the spread of cartels. The latter effectively reduced competition between the industrial giants, making life easier at the top but also preventing any real modernization.

The landed gentry also maintained their status despite the Depression. They were helped by government policies which were intended to maintain a large rural labour pool. In 1930, for example, the movement of rural workers to cities was allowed only by permission of local prefects, while in 1935 special workbooks (*libretto di lavoro*) were introduced. Also, despite Mussolini's original belief that Italy was a country of small landholders, the large estates were maintained undiminished. By 1930 the large landowners, who accounted for 0.5 per cent of the population, owned nearly 42 per cent of the land; the small landholders, 87 per cent of the rural population, owned a mere 13 per cent.

The lower middle class experienced mixed fortunes. Those in private enterprise were adversely affected by the economic circumstances of the 1930s, but those who entered state service did reasonably well for themselves. The complexity of the administration and the growth of the corporate state produced large numbers of civil service jobs. On the whole, wages were reasonably high and the fringe benefits considerable.

The rest of Italian society suffered severely, mainly for the same reasons that the upper classes benefited. The urban workers were tied down by the regulations introduced by the industrialists with government approval, and were also intimidated by the fact of high unemployment (about 2 million by 1932). The peasantry were so badly affected that many defied government edicts and moved to the cities (particularly Rome, Milan and Turin) to swell the slum population. They were driven to this by a reduction in agricultural wages of up to 40 per cent during the 1930s. The working masses as a whole experienced a comparable decline in living standards; it has been estimated that the index of real wages fell between 1925 and 1938 by 11 per cent. Food became more expensive because, although retail prices moved downwards, they did not correspond to the reduction in wages. Moreover, Mussolini's obsession with the 'Battle for Grain' meant the neglect of other foodstuffs and the wasteful use of marginal land. Hence, a whole range of essentials like meat, fruit, vegetables, butter, sugar, wine and coffee became too expensive for many urban and rural workers. Mussolini recognized this development; he also justified it and, in the process, turned his back on his original guarantee of material well-being for all. 'We must', he said in 1936, 'rid our minds of the idea that what we have called the days of prosperity may return.'[34]

The status of women was also depressed by Fascism, this time more deliberately and systematically. Again, a change of official policy was involved. At first Mussolini had anticipated that women would take part in 'every sector of human activity'. Then his 'Battle for Births' placed women firmly in the roles of childbearing, family management and the 'homemaking sciences'. During the 1930s a spate of edicts restricted the participation of women in most branches of employment. By 1938 women were permitted to take up no more than 10 per cent of the total jobs available. Mussolini used this trend to control the levels of unemployment among men, but his justification was offensive and contemptuous: naturally a woman 'must not be a slave, but...in our state women must not count'.[35]

It has been argued that the Fascist state did provide positive benefits. According to Gregor,[35] 'Fascist social welfare legislation compared favourably with the more advanced European nations and in some respects was more progressive.' To take some examples, old-age pensions and unemployment benefits were both increased; medical care improved to the point that there was an appreciable decline in infant mortality and tuberculosis; and the state spent 400 million lire on school building between 1922 and 1942, compared with a mere 60 million spent between 1862 and 1922.[35] On the other hand, state benefits, valuable though they were, could not in themselves make up for the heavy loss in earning power. In any case, many Italians dropped through any safety nets spread by the state. About 400,000 people lived in hovels made of mud and sticks, while others lived 10 to a room.[34]

Was it entirely the fault of the Fascist regime that so many Italians faced impoverishment? After all, the Italian economy had always been vulnerable and during the 1930s other industrial nations also suffered severely as a result of the Depression. While allowing for this, it is still possible to attribute many of Italy's problems directly to Fascist policy. The policies of the 1920s, especially the revaluation of the lira, pushed Italy into recession *before* the Depression, and possible recovery in the 1930s was slowed down by preparation for war. It could be argued that even the population policy contributed directly to the falling standard of living. When the United States cut its annual quota of Italian immigrants to 4000 in 1924, Mussolini did everything possible to promote migration from the United States to Italy. This reduced the remittances sent to Italy by workers in the United States by something like 90 per cent: from 5 billion lire per annum to 500 million.[34]

The mass of the population was still tacitly loyal to the regime in 1939, despite the hardships faced. From 1941, however, discontent grew rapidly. This was the result of Italy's catastrophic involvement in the Second World War – the result of an adventurist foreign policy, to which we now turn.

MUSSOLINI'S FOREIGN POLICY 1922–39

The period 1922–9

In his first speech as Prime Minister to the Chamber of Deputies (1922), Mussolini proclaimed that 'Foreign policy is the area which especially preoccupies us.' His intention, he said on another occasion, was simple: 'I want to make Italy great, respected and feared.'[19] He undertook to end Italy's traditional backstage role in European diplomacy; instead of picking up the scraps left by other powers in their rivalries with each other, Italy would seize the diplomatic initiative. As a result, she would be able to secure a revision of the post First World War settlement – that 'mutilated victory' – and extensive territory in the Mediterranean and Africa.

During the 1920s, however, Mussolini's foreign policy appeared somewhat erratic, alternating between aggression and conciliation. This, it would seem, was because he was constantly seeking to put pressure on the diplomatic fabric to see where it would yield. He aimed to be pragmatic and opportunist but sometimes became irrational, unable to resist the chance of swift glory cheaply bought. Where no such chance existed he had to moderate his activities.

The first instance of aggression was the Corfu incident. On

21 August 1923 General Tellini and four other Italians were assassinated by terrorists while working for a boundary commission which was marking the border between Greece and Albania. Mussolini seized the opportunity to browbeat Greece, demanding compensation of 50 million lire and an official apology. When these did not materialize, he ordered the occupation of the Greek island of Corfu, clearly his original intention. Greece, however, appealed to the League of Nations which, in turn, referred the whole matter to arbitration by the Conference of Ambassadors. The outcome was a compromise which Mussolini accepted, with extreme reluctance, under strong British diplomatic pressure. Italian marines were pulled out of Corfu on 27 September and the Greek government paid 50 million lire, but without the apology. Within two weeks of the settlement of the Corfu crisis, Mussolini tried again, this time more successfully. He installed an Italian commandant in Fiume, a city whose status was in dispute as it was claimed by both Italy and Yugoslavia. In this instance, Yugoslavia had no alternative but to agree to the Italian occupation as her main ally, France, was militarily involved in the Ruhr. Mussolini's 'victory' was formalized in 1924 by the Pact of Rome.

By 1925, however, Mussolini was showing a more reasonable face – this time to the European powers. Stresemann, Briand and Austen Chamberlain, Foreign Ministers of Germany, France and Britain, were committed to international co-operation and the construction of a system of 'collective security'. Mussolini was at first reluctant to involve Italy in any specific scheme, as it would limit his chances of a future diplomatic coup. Increasingly, however, he came under pressure from two directions. Externally, he was persuaded by French and British diplomats and was courted by Chamberlain, who particularly wanted Mussolini's participation. Internally, the more traditional and non-Fascist career diplomats of the Italian Foreign Ministry brought all their persuasiveness to bear.[36] The result was Mussolini's signature on the Locarno Pact. Partly as a result of this concession, British opinion of Mussolini became more favourable. Over Corfu he had shown a petulant outburst which seemed to go against the pragmatic trend of Italian diplomacy; Locarno seemed to indicate that he had at last moved to a more moderate and sensible course – in the tradition of Cavour.[37]

Or had he? Elsewhere in Europe Mussolini was doing what he could to destabilize the international scene. It could be argued that he was trying to make up for his lack of influence in western Europe by pressing particularly hard for advantages in the Balkans. He was resolutely hostile to French efforts to influence eastern Europe through a series of alliances. More fundamentally, Mussolini had conceived a deep dislike for France. This was partly ideological, as France harboured most of Italy's anti-Fascist exiles. It was also partly strategic, as France seemed to block the way to Italy's expansion in the Mediterranean and Africa. Hence he tried to destroy the French 'system' in eastern Europe and, in the process, to penetrate the Balkans. His main target was the French-sponsored 'Little Entente' of Yugoslavia, Rumania and Czechoslovakia. At first it appeared that he might break this by peaceful means. In 1924 he drew up a commercial agreement with Czechoslovakia and a treaty of friendship with Yugoslavia. But then he overreached himself in a sudden lunge for territory and glory. He became involved in the Albanian Civil War, supporting the rebel Noli against Yugoslavia's protégé, Zogu. Although Italy came to establish a virtual protectorate over Albania, Mussolini lost the chance to detach Yugoslavia from the French 'system'. Indeed, the Little Entente tightened and Mussolini felt obliged to attempt to sponsor a counter-bloc consisting of Albania, Hungary and Bulgaria.

How successful had Mussolini been by 1929? On the one hand, he was being seen by British leaders in an increasingly positive light. Churchill called him 'Roman genius in person' and Austen Chamberlain said: 'I trust his word when given and think we might easily go far before finding an Italian with whom it would be as easy for the British Government to work.'[38] On the other hand, Italy had not benefited materially from Mussolini's diplomacy. She was still outflanked by French influence in the Balkans and there were times when the Locarno Pact seemed a major disadvantage; in helping guarantee the Rhine, Mussolini had freed French and German attention, which could now wander to central Europe – and Austria.

The period 1930–5

Between 1930 and 1935 Mussolini aimed to make a more definite mark on European diplomacy by a more consistent and less random policy. In this way he would emerge, as he had always intended, as Europe's senior statesman and arbiter. It has been argued that, at this stage, 'Mussolini was capable of a shrewd and realistic assessment'[39] of the European scene. His new device was to promote rival blocs, with Italy acting as a mediator and maintaining a calculated equidistance between the powers involved. On one side would be France and Britain. On the other would be Germany, increasingly revisionist and determined to undermine the Versailles Settlement. Mussolini would commit Italy to neither; instead he would create tensions or, alternatively, promote détente in such a way that Italy would always be the beneficiary. He may even have thought that Britain and France would become so dependent on Italian co-operation in containing Germany that they would have to grant major concessions in the Mediterranean and Africa. Should they ever take Italy for granted, Mussolini could always exert diplomatic pressure on them by producing the 'German card' – or backing German revisionist claims.

Before long, however, Mussolini found this card unplayable, for Germany came to pose an even greater threat to Italian interests than had France. The source of the trouble was Austria. It was well known that the German right had long favoured the absorption of this rump of the former Austro-Hungarian Empire, a danger which increased with Hitler's appointment as Chancellor in January 1933. Mussolini was desperately anxious to avoid this *Anschluss*, since he regarded Austria as an Italian client state and as a military buffer zone. A crisis occurred in 1934, when the Austrian Nazi Party was involved in the assassination of the Austrian Chancellor, Dollfuss. Fearing that Hitler would use the chaos within Austria as an excuse to annex it, Mussolini sent Italian troops to the frontier. Meanwhile, he was forced to swallow his previous prejudices and seek closer ties with France – who also dreaded the prospect of an enlarged Germany. He therefore dropped his designs on the Balkans, and in January 1935 formed an Accord with France. This was followed, in April, by the Stresa Front in which Mussolini joined Britain and France in condemning German rearmament.

Could this be the answer? Although forced by events in Austria to give up his preferred strategy of equidistance, Mussolini seemed, nevertheless, to have recovered a degree of diplomatic security. Could he now seize the initiative which had so long eluded him?

The period 1935–9

Mussolini certainly seemed to think so. Italy now entered a period of hectic activity, behaving in every way like an expansionist power (see Map 3). In the process, however, Mussolini committed Italy irrevocably and disastrously to an alliance with Germany.

The first step was the Italian conquest of Ethiopia (1935–6). The motives were partly internal; as is shown in the next section, the cult of the Duce required a boost which only a successful war could provide. But there was also a powerful ideological impetus: a Fascist yearning for expansion and conquest which accentuated the traditional Italian commitment to colonies. The diplomatic scene seemed to favour a swift and decisive stroke. Britain had acknowledged an Italian role in the Horn of Africa ever since 1906 and the French appeared willing in 1935 to grant a *carte blanche*. As far as the German threat was concerned, an Italian victory in Africa would deter Hitler from any further action over Austria and could be accomplished sufficiently rapidly to restore an Italian military presence in the Danube area.

The Ethiopian War was sparked by the Wal Wal incident. In December 1934 a party of Italians was fired upon at an oasis on the Ethiopian side of the border with Italian Somaliland. An immediate apology was demanded from Ethiopia, since Italy claimed the right to use Wal Wal. The matter was, however, referred to the League of Nations, while Italy prepared, over the next 10 months, for a full-scale invasion of Ethiopia. All seemed well for Mussolini, particularly since Britain and France were unwilling to condemn his attitude. When the League eventually refused to apportion blame for the Wal Wal incident, Mussolini decided to go

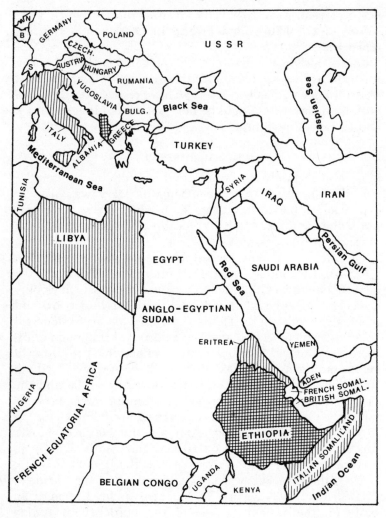

 Possessions before 1930

Acquisitions during the 1930s

Map 3 The Italian overseas empire by 1939

ahead with the invasion; this commenced, from Eritrea, in October 1935, under the leadership of Graziani and De Bono. Italian troops won a major victory at Adowa, erasing the humiliating memory of defeat there in 1896. In November, however, a sinister development occurred with Badoglio's use of poison gas against Ethiopian troops and civilians. This time the League responded more decisively by applying, from October, economic sanctions against Italy. Unfortunately, these were largely ineffectual since they excluded vital materials like oil, coal, iron and steel. It also appeared that Britain and France were willing to connive at Mussolini's conquests. The Hoare-Laval Pact of December 1935 would have given Italy northern and southern Ethiopia, leaving an independent state in the centre. This scheme was leaked to the press and eventually howled down by public opinion. Nevertheless, nothing was done to prevent the Italian advance on Addis Ababa, which fell in May 1936.

The Ethiopian War had momentous results. For example, it narrowed the range of Mussolini's future diplomatic options. Britain and France were alienated by the method of conquest and were never to trust Mussolini again. Germany was considerably strengthened, as Hitler used Mussolini's involvement in Africa, together with the diversion this caused to Britain and France, to remilitarize the Rhineland in 1936. Mussolini had seriously miscalculated; Hitler had reacted far more rapidly than he had expected and, to make matters worse, Austria was more vulnerable than ever before. From 1936 Germany exerted a profound influence on Italy, based on growing diplomatic confidence and military strength. Within Italy this influence took the form of a racial programme, while externally Mussolini was hoping to synchronize his own ideology with Hitler's Nazism to produce a 'century of Fascism'.

From 1936 a policy of consolidation would have made most sense, giving Italy the chance to replace losses caused by the Ethiopian War. Yet even before this conflict had ended Mussolini had made another commitment – this time to assisting Franco's National Front against the Spanish Republic.

Involvement in the Spanish Civil War was motivated partly

by an obsessive hatred of left-wing popular-front governments. The future, he wanted to proclaim, lay with Fascism,
nationalism and right-wing militarism. It might well be
possible to establish Italian influence over a series of Fascist
or semi-Fascist states in the Mediterranean; influence over
Spain, for example, could well lead to control over Salazar's
Portugal. In strategic terms, this would weaken Britain's
naval position in the western Mediterranean and make
Gibraltar extremely vulnerable. It would mean that the
Soviet Union would lose Spain as a potential ally and that
France would be outflanked by three hostile states – Spain,
Italy and Germany. There was also a military motive for
involvement, as Italy could test the efficiency of her armed
forces in a different theatre of war.

Italian contributions to the Nationalist cause were considerable. By 1937 50,000 Italian troops were active in Spain
and the total death-toll had reached 6000. Mussolini also
provided 763 aircraft and 1672 tons of bombs, 950 tanks and
7663 motor vehicles, 1930 cannon and 240,747 small arms,
and the use of 91 warships – all at a total cost of 14 billion
lire.[40] Admittedly, other governments became involved;
Hitler also supplied Franco, and Stalin assisted the Republic.
There is no doubt, however, that Italy's sacrifices were by far
the largest.

To what effect? Italy's involvement can be seen as a serious
blunder. Certainly Mussolini was unable to make up the loss
of equipment before the outbreak of the Second World War.
This was to prove very serious. Both Britain and France,
convinced that Italy was now irrevocably hostile, began from
1937 to rearm at a pace which Italy, with her smaller
industrial base, could not match. While all the other major
powers were stronger in 1939 than they had been in 1936,
Italy was undeniably weaker. The full extent of her vulnerability was not yet known, but clues were provided by the
humiliation of the Italians by Spanish Republican forces at
Guadalajara. Nor was there any real gratitude from Franco,
who would agree only to guarantee Spanish neutrality in any
conflict between Italy and another power. More than ever,
Mussolini had to depend on Germany. He tried to ignore the
uncomfortable truth that war, and the policy of autarky

which accompanied it, had disrupted Italian trade and allowed Germany to penetrate Italy's markets in the Balkans. He therefore had to swallow his personal dislike of Hitler and give Italy up to what F.W.D. Deakin has termed 'the Brutal Friendship'.

This connection between Italy and Germany was formalized by the 'Rome–Berlin Axis', a term first used by Mussolini in a speech delivered in Milan on 1 November 1936. This followed a visit by the Italian Foreign Minister, Ciano, to Berlin and Berchtesgaden to secure an agreement on joint intervention in Spain. Both Germany and Italy were well satisfied. Germany had succeeded in pulling Italy into her corner. As von Hassell, German ambassador in Rome, had observed, the Spanish Civil War was reinforcing the lesson of the Ethiopian War and Italy was realizing 'the advisability of confronting the western powers shoulder-to-shoulder with Germany.[41] The Axis was further tightened by the signing of the Anti-Comintern Pact with Germany and Japan in November 1937 and the Pact of Steel (May 1939) which committed Germany and Italy to mutual support in any offensive or defensive war. Italy, for her part, was momentarily enjoying the sensation of power. In 1937 Ciano exulted: 'The situation of 1935 has been transformed. Italy has broken out of her isolation: she is in the centre of the most formidable political and military combination which has ever existed.'[42]

Unfortunately for Mussolini, Germany's seniority in the Rome–Berlin Axis soon became obvious. Hitler forced the pace, and some of his actions showed open contempt for Mussolini. In March 1938, for example, he gave Rome only a few hours' notice before sending German troops into Austria. This has been seen as 'the beginning of the end of Fascist Italy' as 'the shadow of the predatory and overwhelming force of pan-Germanism'[38] fell over her. It is true that Mussolini managed to regain some of his stature as a mediator at the Munich Conference in September 1938. But this was because it suited Hitler to cast Mussolini temporarily in this role, before returning to his customary offhand manner. On two occasions in 1939 Mussolini was given virtually no advance notice of German intentions: the occupation of Bohemia in March and the conclusion of the

Nazi-Soviet Pact in August. Yet, amazingly, Mussolini's government failed to monitor the wording of the 'Pact of Steel' which bound Italy militarily to Germany; instead, Ciano virtually gave to his German counterpart, von Ribbentrop, a blank cheque. Mussolini was also deceived over Hitler's timetable. He had assumed in May 1939 that Germany was not intending to fight a war before 1943 at the earliest. When Germany invaded Poland in September 1939, Mussolini was severely embarrassed by Italy's total inadequacy to meet the commitments of the Pact of Steel. Ciano had to submit to Berlin a list of strategic materials urgently needed by Italy. When Germany offered only a small quantity, Mussolini had no option but to seek from Hitler a temporary release from his military obligations. Part of the problem was that Italy's resources had been over-extended by Mussolini's attack on Albania in April; he could not afford now to rush into a conflict with France and Britain which Hitler had so inconveniently provoked. Even so, for a man with such a huge ego this peace was a humiliation, to be reversed at the earliest opportunity.

The connection between foreign policy and domestic issues

It has become increasingly common in historical writing to point out the close links between foreign and domestic policies. Much has been made of the attempts made by rulers like Napoleon III and Wilhelm II to mobilize popular support and maintain domestic harmony through the deliberate use of aggressive diplomacy, territorial expansion and war.

Most observers see the same tendency in Mussolini's policy, although they differ over the extent of his calculation. Perhaps the grandest conception has been put forward by the Italian historian Renzo De Felice, who sees Fascism as a 'revolutionary phenomenon' which aimed at 'the mobilization of the masses and the creation of a new kind of man'.[43] This had not been accomplished during the 1920s by domestic policies and clearly a new impetus was needed. This would be external expansion; hence 'the Ethiopian question was not only one of waging war, but also principally of creating the new Fascism after the conquest of the empire'.[43] In terms of generating a new spirit and mobilizing support behind the Duce, the Ethiopian War was Mussolini's 'political masterpiece' and his 'greatest success'.

Another Italian writer, G. Carocci, emphasizes the search for an instant remedy rather than the achievement of a grand design. By 1935, he argues, the situation at home was potentially dangerous:

> People all over the country felt indifferent to the regime, detached from it. In order to overcome these feelings, in order to galvanise the masses and try to break the vicious circle of economic crisis, more drastic and more attractive measures were needed.[44]

Mack Smith agrees that the purpose of Mussolini's foreign policy was to bolster Mussolini's prestige, which by the mid-1930s had been affected by economic strain. The device used was propaganda on a massive scale; indeed, 'any history of Mussolini's foreign policy has to be...a history of propaganda'.[45] The whole process created an addiction; the addiction led to self-delusion. Increasingly Mussolini was misled by his own pronouncements, pursued erratic policies and ignored basic facts. Such an argument was also adopted by contemporaries of Mussolini. Salvemini, an exile from Fascist Italy, identified Mussolini as a buffoon, a 'sawdust Caesar', living hand-to-mouth in a desperate effort to make his foreign exploits rally support for his domestic measures and to stabilize the base of his regime.

Some historians remain unconvinced about this type of argument. M. Knox,[46] for one, sees in Mussolini's expansionism a genuine vision – equivalent to Hitler's quest for *Lebensraum*. Foreign policy did not proceed from 'internal social or political pressures'. Indeed, what happened in the 1930s was the opposite of 'social imperialism'. To extend this line of reasoning, it might be said that Fascism was an ebullient ideology which had to turn outwards in order to seek sublimation in struggle, militarism and conquest. This approach would reduce the emphasis on domestic problems in the mid-1930s. It could be argued that Mussolini's personality cult had already won the battle for popular acceptance and support; it now had to be justified by action.

After all, Italians had been led to believe, it was better to 'live one day as a lion than a thousand years as a lamb'.

WAR AND COLLAPSE 1940–5

Italy in the Second World War

Italy's neutrality, announced by Mussolini on 3 September 1939, came to an end with his declaration of war on Britain and France on 10 June 1940.

During the intervening months the situation in Europe had been transformed. Hitler's *Blitzkrieg* had crushed Poland within four weeks and his offensive in the west had brought the collapse of Norway, Holland and Belgium. Mussolini, therefore, felt that he had little to fear. Italy would not be committing herself to a prolonged struggle, as France was on the point of defeat and it was only a matter of time before Britain fell. Hence there was a chance for Mussolini to erase the humiliating memory of 'non-belligerence' by joining Hitler as an equal partner in a great Axis offensive. He envisaged a short conflict, lasting perhaps only a few weeks, and followed by a conference at which Italy would receive the spoils due to a victorious power.

These expectations were not fulfilled. Italian troops made slow progress in the Alpine War against a severely weakened France, managing to win only a few square miles of territory. The main disappointment was that Hitler was unwilling to hand France's north African colonies to Italy, preferring to leave them and the French Mediterranean fleet under the puppet Vichy regime to ensure the latter's permanent collaboration. Nor could Mussolini expect easy compensation in the form of British territory in Africa: the Royal Navy was still active in the Mediterranean and the long-awaited German invasion of Britain had not materialized. Once again there was the danger that Italy would play a totally subordinate role to Germany – unless, of course, Mussolini could regain the initiative.

He attempted to do so in the 'parallel war'. The intention was to develop an Italian sphere of influence in the Balkans and north Africa, leaving Germany to dominate northern

Europe. Hence, in September 1940, he launched an Italian invasion of British Egypt from Libya and, in October, attacked Greece. But his hopes of a new Roman Empire covering most of the eastern Mediterranean were swiftly shattered. The Greeks repulsed the Italian attack and Hitler had to mount an extensive rescue operation in the Balkans in 1941; when, eventually, Greece and Yugoslavia did fall, it was to the Germans not the Italians. The British, meanwhile, counterattacked from Egypt, achieving major successes under Wavell early in 1941. Again, the Germans had to take over and Mussolini was partly relieved, partly humiliated, by the successful campaigns of Rommel. No rescue was, however, possible in the Horn of Africa where, during the course of 1941, Italy lost to British Empire troops her prized colonies of Somaliland, Eritrea and Ethiopia.

Floundering badly in the sort of prolonged war which he had not anticipated, Mussolini became increasingly desperate and irrational. He proved entirely willing to go along with Hitler in widening the scope of the war. In 1941, for example, he pressed on Hitler a total of 61,000 Italian troops to assist the German invasion of the Soviet Union. In the same year he declared war on the United States in the naive belief that America was a degenerate power which could never adapt a consumer-based economy to military needs. He placed more and more emphasis on ideology, envisaging an ultimate Fascist triumph over the forces and theories of Bolshevism and liberal democracy. Yet, despite his attempts to retain at least some influence over the Axis alliance, the reality was that Italy's dependence on Germany was now total.

The trouble was that Germany was now beginning to lose ground. From late 1942 German forces in north Africa and on the eastern front were heavily assailed by Montgomery, Eisenhower and Zhukov. Hitler's priority was the Russian campaign, which involved drawing off German troops and supplies from north Africa. This sealed Italy's fate. The western Allies won back north Africa early in 1943 and, at the Casablanca Conference, agreed that the first attacks on Axis-controlled Europe should be directed against Italy as its 'soft underbelly'. Consequently, British and American troops landed in Sicily in July 1943. Even before they crossed over to mainland Italy, Mussolini had been removed from power. On 8 September the new Italian government officially surrendered to the Allies. The Germans, however, occupied northern Italy, delaying final victory for the next 18 months.

Reasons for Italian defeat

One of the main factors in the Italian defeat was the series of disastrous decisions taken by Mussolini, often against the advice of his ministers. The first of these was to commence hostilities in June 1940 with the full knowledge that the Italian Commission on War Production had warned that Italy could not sustain a single year of warfare until 1949. The second was to initiate a parallel war when it seemed unlikely that Germany would co-operate with Italian designs on French colonies; Mussolini's invasion of Greece in October 1940 went directly against his belief in 1922 that Italian policy 'has not and never can have as objectives continental European territory except Albania'.[47] The third error was to commit Italy so lightly and with so little thought of the consequences, against the world's two industrial and military giants, the United States and the Soviet Union. The former played a vital part in rolling back the Axis occupation of north Africa, while the latter drained off the Axis troops needed to prevent this. Of the three mistakes, the first was the most catastrophic, as it made Italy entirely dependent on German military success. Hitler destroyed Mussolini's chances of swift victory by broadening his own objectives to fit into his own visionary scheme, and the invasion of Russia doomed Fascist Italy long before it brought about the collapse of the Third Reich.

Italy's armed forces were inadequate to the demands placed upon them by Mussolini. Earlier losses incurred in the Ethiopian War (1935–7) and the Spanish Civil War (1936–9) had not been made up and there was, by 1940, a hollow ring to Mussolini's boast that Italy could mobilize 8 million men within hours. In fact, the Italian army in 1940 comprised a total of 3 million men, who were inadequately supplied with 1.3 million rifles (of 1891 design);[48] the most reliable weapons proved to be those captured from the Austrians at the end of the First World War. The army had only 42,000 vehicles, including obsolete tanks and armoured cars which could be pierced by rifle fire. Ignorant of these deficiencies, Mussolini gambled everything on a lightning war – or *guerra lampo* – the equivalent to Hitler's *Blitzkrieg*. In practice this strategy was inoperable, partly because Italy had no equivalent to Germany's panzer divisions and partly because Italian generals were intensely suspicious of such methods; they regarded the tank as having little practical application to the demands of warfare either in Europe or in north Africa. The army was also poorly organized and the mobilization of August 1939 was so inept that it is doubtful whether Italy could have entered the war at that stage even if Mussolini had decided to do so. There was virtually no co-operation with either the German government or the German High Command, in complete contrast to the joint planning undertaken by the western Allies in their conquest of north Africa and France.

Of the other two services, the navy was the better equipped and had actually been admired by Hitler in the mid-1930s. Yet here, too, there were serious deficiencies. Italian warships were designed essentially for speed, which meant that their heavy fuel consumption limited their effective range to 6500 miles. No aircraft carriers were built, as Mussolini believed that Italy was herself a 'natural aircraft carrier'. Although eight battleships were under construction in 1939, the incredible fact remains that not one of them hit an enemy ship with its shells.[48] Italy did possess the world's largest fleet of submarines but they were notoriously slow to submerge and losses amounted to 10 per cent within the first weeks of war. Italy's airforce was also defective. Mussolini had once boasted that he could make the skies black with Italian aircraft, but in reality Italian production was far below that of the other Axis powers, Germany and Japan. The quality was also suspect, and the RAF had comparatively little difficulty in knocking out the Fiat CR 42, the Fiat G 50 and the Macchi MC 200. Matters were made even worse by the refusal of the airforce leadership to co-ordinate its plans with the other services. Unlike the *Luftwaffe* and the RAF, the Italian airforce always demanded, and received, special autonomy.

Underlying Italy's military weakness was a severely limited economic and industrial base. Mussolini's policy of self-sufficiency had failed to solve the problem of the shortage of strategic materials and, as we have seen, Germany was slow to respond to Ciano's appeals for help in August 1939. Italy went against the overall trend for industrial nations by experiencing between 1940 and 1943 a decrease in production of 35 per cent in industry and 25 per cent in agriculture. The figure which most effectively conveys Italy's limitations as an industrial power is that for steel production: 2.4 million tons in 1939, compared with Britain's 13.4 million and Germany's 22.5 million.[46] The problem was, of course, partly historic, as Italy had industrialized at a later stage than her competitors. But the responsibility rests also with the policies of Fascism, as Italy was less prepared for war in 1940 even than she had been in 1915.

The fall of Mussolini

Military disaster provoked a wave of disillusionment with Mussolini's regime. Taken in by his own propaganda, the Duce was totally unaware of the dangers; as Mack Smith observes, he had 'got used to living in cloud-cuckoo land'.[49] There was increasingly widespread opposition to German ideological and military influence. There was resentment at the rapid fall in living conditions: Italians had to put up with some of the worst hardships suffered by civilians anywhere in Europe. There was pressure for peace from those traditional groups which had once collaborated with Fascism – the industrialists and military leaders like Badoglio and Caviglia. The Fascist Party proved incapable of rallying the population to face adversity and was itself demoralized by the internal convulsions brought about by Mussolini himself.

Indeed, Mussolini set in motion the chain reaction of events which led to his collapse. In February 1943 he sacked Grandi, Bottai and others from high office within the Fascist Party. This provoked a set of conspiracies in which De Grand has identified two main elements. The first involved the traditionalist 'pre-Fascist' politicians and military leaders, the second the 'moderate Fascists' who hoped to dump Mussolini and replace him with Caviglia. With the Allied landings in Sicily the conspirators decided on drastic measures. At a session of the Fascist Grand Council in July 1943 Mussolini was attacked by Grandi, Bottai and Ciano for his conduct of the war. They called for the full restoration of the legal organs of the state and the dismissal of Mussolini himself. This motion was eventually carried by 19 votes to 7 and Grandi explained the decision to the bewildered Duce: 'You believe you have the devotion of the people.... You lost it the day you tied Italy to Germany.'[50] The following day Mussolini was dismissed by King Victor Emanuel and imprisoned at the Gran Sasso. Marshal Badoglio was appointed as the new Prime Minister.

Why was Mussolini so powerless to prevent this startling turn of events? The answer lies in the delicate balance between the different powers and institutions within Italy, which Mussolini had been so careful to maintain. Under the strain of war this balance was destroyed and Mussolini was left without any political protection. During the 1930s he had missed the opportunity of giving the Fascist Party greater unity and had deliberately encouraged the growth of cliques in order to pursue a policy of 'divide and rule'. This recoiled on him in 1943; he could rely on only a single group led by Farinacci, while the majority of the Fascist leaders turned against him, charging him with having deliberately distorted the Fascist movement. As Grandi observed, 'It is dictatorship, not Fascism, which has lost the war.'[51]

Mussolini's vulnerability was intensified by the existence of an alternative form of leadership in Italy. Unlike Hitler, Mussolini had never assumed all the powers of head of state. The monarchy, which had been left intact, became a rallying point for the Italian army in 1943, while the coup against Mussolini was backed by Victor Emanuel himself. In addition, Mussolini never placed his personal stamp on the Italian army. The oath of allegiance, for example, was still to the state and not to the Duce in person. Nor had he managed to create an entirely loyal military élite like Hitler's *Waffen SS*. He had also been less careful than Hitler in anticipating trouble from his generals, and had not taken the trouble to shuffle their positions to prevent plotting or the build-up of opposition. Even his intelligence service was defective, for he was taken completely by surprise by the July coup. Despite his known contempt for Mussolini, Hitler was astounded by the suddenness of the Duce's fall and asked: 'What is this sort of Fascism which melts like snow before the sun?'

The Italian Social Republic 1943–5: a return to the beginning?

Mussolini was rescued from the mountain stronghold of Gran Sasso on 12 September 1943 by a German glider-borne expedition. He was taken to Germany, where plans were made for the formation of a new Fascist state in that part of Italy which had not yet been occupied by the Allies. The headquarters of the regime were at Lake Garda, while the leadership was provided by three main types of Fascist. There were pro-Nazis like Pavolini, Ricci, Farinacci and Preziosi; opportunists like Graziani, who had no military future under the Royal government in Rome; and those who, like Pini, remained devoted to Mussolini himself.

It has been said that the new Italian Social Republic (alternatively known as the Salo Republic) represents a return to the beginning of the Fascist movement. The plot of 25 July showed Mussolini how treacherous the monarchy and the old establishment could be. Shorn of his alliance with those traditional institutions, the argument continues, Mussolini was free to revive his early ideological preferences. Once again, he became anti-monarchist and displayed the kind of radicalism which had been absent from Fascism for many years. He also returned to a type of socialism which once again attacked capitalism. Instead of allying with industrialists, he now intended to 'annihilate the parasitic plutocracies and...make labour the object of our economy and the indestructible foundation of the state'.[52] A new programme was devised at Verona in November 1943, followed by the 'socialization' law of February 1944. Key industries were to be nationalized, workers were to participate in factory and business management, land reform was to be initiated and there were to be wage and price controls.

From the start, however, the Italian Social Republic proved a pale imitation, even a mockery of the early Fascist movement. For one thing, it had lost all control over its own destiny, as Mussolini was now heavily dependent on Germany.

For another, it no longer had the old attractions for the various parts of the population. Workers and peasants, who had once deserted the left for Fascism, now abandoned Fascism to return to the Socialist and Communist left. They took part in strikes and demonstrations and joined the Italian resistance movement. Industrialists saw no advantages in Mussolini's new radicalism and did everything in their power to prevent the implementation of the 1944 Decree Law. By 1945, therefore, only a few dozen enterprises had actually been nationalized. Finally, the mainstay of Fascism, the lower middle class, became resentful at the decline in living standards caused by prolonging the war against the Allies. They, too, switched their allegiance and once more craved parliamentary politics. It seemed, therefore, that Italy had been jolted back into its pre-Fascist course and that the Social Republic had become totally inappropriate.

The end

The collapse of the Italian Social Republic, although delayed by 18 months, was inevitable. It was rent with dissension as extremists like Farinacci and Pavolini hunted down the 'traitors of July 25th', to the alarm of the moderates. The Republic seemed to focus on revenge rather than unity; at Verona, for example, Ciano and several others were found guilty of treason and executed. Mussolini himself became bitterly disillusioned and cursed the Italian people for their soft character and dislike of vigorous action. He came to the conclusion that Italy was not, after all, the historical heir to ancient Rome, but a nation of serfs. As for his government, it was almost entirely in foreign hands. Northern Italy had been divided into two sectors – one under direct German administration, the other under German influence. In the latter, which included the Republic, the German army introduced a set of institutions which ran parallel to those of Mussolini and also controlled the entire network of communications between Mussolini's ministries.

Mussolini's survival now depended entirely on German military fortunes. In April 1945, however, German resistance collapsed as the Allies broke through the Commacchio Line and the Argento Gap. Mussolini fled from Milan with his mistress, Clara Petacci. They were picked up by partisans on the Lake Como road and, on 28 April, were shot against the gates of a villa. The final indignity was the public exhibition of the mutilated corpses, along with those of Farinacci and other leading Fascists, at a petrol station in Milan. By a cruel irony, Mussolini had once said (referring to the martial spirit of Fascism) that 'Everybody dies the death that corresponds to his character.'[53]

4
Dictatorship in Germany

Adolf Hitler was appointed Chancellor on 30 January 1933. His rise to power and the decline of the Weimar Republic are sufficiently complex to justify a preliminary section relating the main developments before proceeding to look at explanations.

THE WEIMAR REPUBLIC AND THE RISE OF HITLER 1918–33

The formation and development of the Weimar Republic 1918–29

The Weimar Republic was born of military defeat and revolution at the end of the First World War. Under the threat of military collapse the Kaiser's Second Reich was transformed into the Weimar Republic during what has come to be known as the 'German Revolution'.

This occurred in two phases. The first was a revolution from above as, early in October 1918, the military establishment handed over power to a civilian cabinet. The High Command, under Ludendorff and Hindenburg, sensed the inevitability of defeat and tried to ease the way towards an armistice with the Allies by advising Kaiser Wilhelm II to appoint Prince Max of Baden as Chancellor. A powerful underlying motive was the army's desire to avoid any direct blame for Germany's surrender, when it came. The Allied response, however, was unfavourable; President Wilson argued that the German power structure was still intact and that he could deal only with a genuine democracy. Prince Max now prevailed upon the Kaiser to dismiss Ludendorff from his command and it seemed that, despite the Allies' reservations, the Second Reich had the most genuinely representative government since its formation in 1871.

The second phase was a revolution from below which brought down the Second Reich altogether. In late October and early November the sailors of the German fleet mutinied in Kiel and Wilhelmshaven, while military discipline was also subverted in Hamburg and Cologne. Similarly dramatic events occurred in the south, as Kurt Eisner declared Bavaria an independent republic. Prince Max, fearing the complete disintegration of Germany, resigned on 9 November, to be replaced as Chancellor by the leader of the Social Democrats, Friedrich Ebert. On the same day the Kaiser and the lesser German rulers abdicated, and a republic was proclaimed by another Social Democrat, Philipp Scheidemann, from the balcony of the Reichstag building in Berlin. Scheidemann's concluding words were: 'The old and rotten – the monarchy – has broken down. Long live the new! Long live the German Republic.'[1] Two days later, on 11 November, Germany signed an armistice with the Allies.

But the German Revolution was not yet complete. The country now experienced a brief period of civil war as rival groups of the left competed for power. The main contenders were the Social Democrats (SPD) and two more radical groups, the Independent Socialists (USPD) and the Spartacists. At first a Provisional Government was established, comprising both the SPD and the USPD. The former, however, were much afraid that Germany might follow the example of Russia the year before, and that the Provisional Government would be destroyed by a coup from the radical left – perhaps from the Spartacists. To prevent this, Chancellor Ebert made a controversial deal with the army commander, General Groener, to put down any Bolshevik-style revolution which might occur. The test was not long in coming. In December the Independent Socialists withdrew from the government, while the Spartacists (who now called themselves Communists) demanded the 'sovietization' of Germany and the continuation of the revolution. The SPD put down subsequent Spartacist demonstrations in January 1919, and in the violence and bloodshed the two Communist leaders, Karl Liebknecht and Rosa Luxemburg, were killed. A second Spartacist uprising was suppressed, with much greater bloodshed, in March, while, in April, troops were sent to overthrow the Republic of Soviets which had just been proclaimed in Bavaria. Moderate socialism now appeared safe from the far left, but the latter neither forgot nor forgave the experience of 1919.

During this crisis a move was made towards establishing permanent institutions. Elections were held in January 1919 and a Constituent Assembly convened in Weimar, away from the street violence of Berlin. Three of the moderate parties formed a coalition government – the Centre Party (Z), the Democratic Party (DDP) and the Social Democrats (SPD). In opposition to the coalition were the parties of the right – the Nationalists (DNVP) and the People's Party (DVP), as well as the Independent Socialists (USPD) of the far left. The Communists (KPD) did not contest this election. Ebert now became the first President of the Republic, with Scheidemann his Chancellor until June 1919.

Meanwhile, a constitution was being drafted by a special committee under the jurist Hugo Preuss. Eventually promulgated in August 1919, this embodied many advanced principles of democracy and borrowed freely from the experience of England, France and the United States. The main terms were as follows. The head of state was to be the President, elected every 7 years by universal suffrage. He was given, by Article 48 of the constitution, emergency powers: 'In the event that the public order and security are seriously disturbed or endangered, the Reich President may take the measures necessary for their restoration.'[2] The head of the government was to be the Chancellor, appointed by the

President and needing the support of the majority of the legislature, or Reichstag. The Reichstag, elected by universal suffrage by means of proportional representation, would be able to deal with legislation, defence, foreign policy, trade, finance and security. The last section of the constitution carefully itemized the various 'rights and duties of the Germans'.[2]

By the end of 1919, therefore, the Repubic had overcome pressures from the far left and had acquired a legal framework. The question now arising was: could it survive? The next 14 years saw, in succession, a period of instability and severe problems (1919–23), a remarkable recovery and a period of consolidation (1923–9) and, finally, the crisis which eventually destroyed the Republic (1929–33).

The most serious obstacle to the new government in 1919 was the signing of the Treaty of Versailles with the victorious Allies. The German delegation was horrified by the harshness of the terms but the Allies were determined not to make major modifications. In June, Scheidemann resigned as Chancellor in protest but his successor, Bauer, eventually agreed to accept the treaty. Versailles was to prove a millstone around the neck of the Republic, and had much to do with the second problem of this early period – inflation. The devaluation of the mark started during the war but was aggravated by demobilization and by the stiff reparations imposed, under a provision in the Treaty of Versailles, in 1921. Speculation, massive overprinting of paper money, and the French occupation of the Ruhr in 1923, all completed the collapse of the mark in November 1923 to 16,000 million to the £. Savings were wiped out overnight and, for a few weeks, barter unofficially replaced the use of coinage. During the same years, political challenges compounded the difficulties of the Republic. One example was the Kapp *putsch* (1920), an unsuccessful but frightening attempt by the far right to seize power in Berlin; another *putsch* was tried by Hitler in Munich (1923) in circumstances described in the next section.

Nevertheless, the period 1923–9 saw a remarkable recovery and greater stability. This is generally known as the 'Stresemann era' because of the profound influence exerted by this leader of the DVP, first as Chancellor in 1923 and then as Foreign Minister until 1929. Vital economic developments included the stabilization of the currency in the form of the Rentenmark and an agreement on reparations with the Allies in 1924 known as the Dawes Plan. Massive investment followed, mostly from the United States, which enabled German industry to recover almost to 1913 levels, despite the loss of resources and land in 1919. At the same time, Stresemann stabilized Germany's relations with the rest of Europe. He followed the 1922 Treaty with Russia with another in 1926, participated in a collective defence pact with four other countries at Locarno in 1925, and took Germany into the League of Nations in 1926. Underlying these achievements was a period of relative political stability as coalition governments functioned more or less effectively, lubricated by the political diplomacy of Stresemann himself.

These halcyon years did not last. Stresemann died in 1929, a year in which Germany was suddenly confronted by economic catastrophe. Meanwhile, lurking in the background, and preparing to take advantage of any such change of fortune, were Hitler and the Nazis.

The early years of the Nazi movement 1918–29

Many Germans were bitterly opposed to the Revolution of 1918, blaming Jews, socialists, liberals and Catholics for the fall of the Second Reich and military defeat. Particularly resentful were the *'völkisch'* groups which sprang up all over the country and issued racialist and anti-liberal propaganda.

One of these was the German Workers' Party (DAP), formed by Anton Drexler in Munich in January 1919. It was joined, in September 1919, by an Austrian with unfulfilled artistic pretensions who had fought in a Bavarian regiment in the German army throughout the First World War. Hitler blamed the Republic for Germany's surrender and openly expressed his 'hatred for the originators of this dastardly crime'.[3] He rose rapidly to the position of the Party's theorist and chief propaganda officer, and his talent as a public speaker was apparent even at this early stage. In February 1920 he headed a committee which devised the Party's 25-point programme, consisting of a variety of nationalist, socialist, corporativist and racialist principles. Meanwhile, the name was extended to 'National Socialist German Workers' Party' (NSDAP), commonly abbreviated to 'Nazi'. Branches were organized beyond Munich and support came from disbanded soldiers and from some elements of the army, or *Reichswehr*. The mouthpiece of the NSDAP was the *People's Observer* (*Völkischer Beobachter*), acquired in 1920.

The next stage was Hitler's rise to the leadership of the Party. By mid-1921 he was in dispute with the Committee under Drexler over the question of organization and strategy. Eventually he outmanoeuvred Drexler and was elected Party Chairman in July. He immediately decided to demonstrate that the NSDAP was radically different from all traditional 'bourgeois' parties and to centralize everything, especially propaganda, on Munich. The movement was given teeth by the formation, in July 1921, of the *Sturmabteilung* (SA), a violent para-military organization intended, in the words of the newly named *Völkischer Beobachter* 'to develop in the hearts of our young supporters a tremendous desire for action'.[4] The SA proceeded to intimidate opponents, disrupt other meetings and engage in bloody clashes in the streets. Hitler developed a sense of irresistible power and overwhelming confidence, prepared to prove the *Beobachter's* maxim that 'history does not make men, but men history'.

Mussolini, it seemed, had demonstrated this in his 'March on Rome' in 1922. Could Hitler do the same in 1923? The Republic was experiencing a many-sided crisis at least as serious as that confronted by the Italian monarchy. Hitler hoped to march on Berlin with the support of the right-wing commissioner of Bavaria, Gustav von Kahr, and the Bavarian armed forces; the majority of the *Reichswehr* would then be won over. In November 1923, 600 SA men, under Hitler's command, took over a meeting being addressed by Kahr in the *Bürgerbräu Keller*, one of Munich's largest beer halls. Kahr, even at gunpoint, refused to support the 'Putsch' and an SA street demonstration the following morning was dispersed by the Bavarian police. Hitler's attempt at power therefore ended in ignominious failure and he was put on trial for treason. He was, however, treated leniently by sympathetic judges, and was sentenced to five-years imprisonment in Landsberg Castle. He actually served just over one year, in comfortable conditions which enabled him to write the first volume of *Mein Kampf* (My Struggle). On his emergence from captivity in December 1924 he found the NSDAP in total disarray; in his absence it had disintegrated into warring factions. Hitler was not displeased with this, as it guaranteed his own indispensibility and meant that he was well placed to resume control.

When he refounded the NSDAP in February 1925, Hitler emphasized the need for a change in strategy. The failure of the Munich *putsch* had shown that violence alone was unlikely to succeed; the best course, therefore, would be to participate in regular politics. This did not mean a fundamental conversion to the principles of constitutional democracy; on the contrary, parliamentary politics would be the means, not the end. On the surface, therefore, the NSDAP assumed the role of a parliamentary party, aiming at gaining electoral support at the expense of its rivals. At a deeper level, however, the NSDAP remained a mass movement. Hitler still hoped to emulate Mussolini, given the right circumstances, and concentrated in the late 1920s on taking over the key cities. The Party therefore had a Jekyll and Hyde appearance which Hitler made no attempt to conceal.

Despite this new approach, the period 1925–9 proved exceptionally difficult for the Nazi Party and the movement. In the first place, Hitler was confronted by opposition from north German leaders, especially Gregor Strasser who considered that the Party's ideology should place heavier stress on socialism and the nationalization of key industries. Hitler eventually gained unquestioned ascendancy over the northern units of the Party at the Bamberg Conference[5] (February 1926) in which he out-argued Strasser and, by the force of his rhetoric, won over one of his arch-critics, Josef Goebbels. (The latter had, only a short time before, demanded the expulsion of the 'petty bourgeois Adolf Hitler'!) The overall result of this victory was that Hitler tightened his control and established the monolithic structure he had always sought. In the subsequent reorganization, cadres of dedicated activists were set up in the basic Party units – the *gaus*, under the control of the officials, or *gauleiters*, who were appointed by Hitler himself.

The second and more intractable problem of this period was the stability of the Republic and the poor electoral performance of the NSDAP. In the Reichstag election of December 1924, for example, the NSDAP acquired only 14 seats, making it the least significant of the national parties in terms of electoral support; its performance in 1928 was even poorer, resulting in only 12 seats. Yet the Party was nothing if not resilient. It showed a remarkable capacity to survive these hard times and switched its campaign from the cities to the rural areas, which agricultural depression had made more volatile. The *Völkischer Beobachter* observed in May 1928: 'The election results from the rural areas in particular have proved that with a smaller expenditure of energy, money and time, better results can be achieved there than in the big cities.'[6] The Party therefore developed an electoral base which expanded rapidly as Germany came under the grip of economic recession.

The years of crisis 1929–33

The origins of the Great Depression are dealt with in Chapter 1. Of all the industrial states, Germany was undoubtedly the most vulnerable to a sudden downturn in economic conditions. Her industry was heavily dependent on foreign investment – to the tune of 5 billion marks per annum by 1928. Her banking system was geared to the use of short-term loans for long-term enterprises and, as a result, was potentially very vulnerable. As the Depression deepened, foreign loans were withdrawn and the banking system eventually collapsed in 1931. Meanwhile, industrial output had to be cut back through lack of investment and the contraction of overseas markets. The boom years of the late 1920s came to an abrupt end with a dramatic rise in the number of bankruptcies. The inevitable result was a rapid increase in unemployment, from 2 million in 1929 to 3.5 million in 1930, 4.4 million in 1931 and over 6 million in 1932.

The Depression dealt a devastating blow to democracy in Germany. Chancellor Müller's coalition fell apart on 27 March 1930 over the question of cutting dole payments. Since the power of the Chancellor depended on the support of the Reichstag and the economic crisis had made collaboration between political parties more difficult, the initiative now passed to the President. The Republic's second President, elected in 1925, was Field Marshal Hindenburg. Very much a product of the old establishment of the Second Reich, he had an authoritarian approach to politics. During the stable years he had had no option but to play an inactive role in the manoeuvring for power between the various parties. From 1930, however, he was able to fill the vacuum left by the sudden death of consensus politics. Under the influence of one of his main advisers, General Schleicher, Hindenburg appointed the Centre Party leader, Brüning, as Chancellor. When Brüning tried to introduce a deflationary budget it was rejected by the Reichstag. Hindenburg sought to enforce it by Presidential decree, under Article 48 of the constitution. The Reichstag objected to this course, with the result that Hindenburg agreed to Brüning's request for an election in September 1930. The results proved disappointing to Brüning and he was forced to carry on without the support of the Reichstag. He resorted increasingly to the use of Presidential decrees so that, by the time of his fall in May 1932, parliamentary democracy had virtually disappeared.

Meanwhile, the NSDAP was rapidly expanding the base of its support. It was geared to take full advantage of the Republic's crisis, as Hitler arranged mass rallies, travelling speakers and a flood of material from the propaganda department. Below the surface the violence and intimidation intensified, although Hitler sometimes considered that the activities of the SA were too extreme. The Reichstag election of 1930 was a triumph for the NSDAP which secured 6.5 million votes and increased its representation from 12 to 107 seats, thus becoming the second largest party in the Reichstag. Hitler capitalized on this success by cultivating connections with the traditional right, including the Nationalists (DNVP), the army, industralists like Thyssen, and agriculturalists; this alliance was formalized in the Harzburg Front of October 1931, directed against the Republic's policies and record. In January 1932 Hitler made a direct appeal to German industrialists in his Düsseldorf speech, denouncing parliamentary democracy and highlighting the 'Bolshevik threat'. He was carefully establishing his credentials as an anti-revolutionary and providing the sort of reassurance which cancelled out the reservations caused by the obscene violence of the SA.

Hitler's self-confidence was now at its peak and he challenged Hindenburg for the Presidency. The 1932 election ran to two ballots. On the first, Hindenburg obtained 18.7 million votes (49.6 per cent of the total), Hitler 11.3 million (30.1 per cent) and Thälmann, the Communist leader, 5 million (13 per cent). On the second ballot Hindenburg secured an overall majority with 19.4 million (53 per cent) to Hitler's 13.4 million (26.8 per cent) and Thälmann's 3.8 million (10.2 per cent). This result was a disappointment to Hitler, who had expended a massive effort – to no avail. The only other possibility was now to try for the second most important office – the Chancellorship.

In this he was to prove more successful, and ultimately he came to power by the back-door methods of diplomacy and intrigue rather than over the threshold of electoral support. The process was highly complex, involving President Hindenburg, General Schleicher and an aristocrat, Franz von Papen.

The first stage was the collapse of Brüning's government in May 1932, largely because it had lost the support of those who mattered, namely the President and his retinue. Schleicher had been alienated by Brüning's decision to ban Hitler's SA, and Hindenburg by a proposal to take over bankrupt Junker estates for use by landless peasants. Hindenburg therefore pushed Brüning into resignation and Papen was installed as the new Chancellor, the first in the history of the Republic not to have the basis of Party support. Hitler agreed not to oppose the new government in exchange for the removal of the ban on the SA and new Reichstag elections. The latter, held in July 1932, showed another sensational swing to the NSDAP which now became easily the largest party, with 230 seats and 37.3 per cent of the popular vote. When Hitler was invited by Papen to join his cabinet he demanded, instead, the Chancellorship. This was, however, refused by President Hindenburg. Papen then tried to weaken the position of the NSDAP by calling yet another Reichstag election in November 1932. This time the NSDAP lost electoral support, declining to 196 seats in the Reichstag and 33.1 per cent of the vote. Clearly Hitler's popularity had peaked and it would have come as no great surprise if the Nazi phenomenon had faded to its semi-obscurity of the late 1920s.

Then events swung back in Hitler's favour. Papen proved incapable of holding power for very long and the Chancellorship went to Schleicher, who had managed to convince Hindenburg that he could broaden the base of his support by detaching members of the NSDAP from their support for Hitler. In this he failed dismally; the only Nazi who seemed interested in his offer was Strasser, who was promptly thrown out of the Party. Meanwhile, Papen felt sufficiently slighted by Schleicher to intrigue against him with Hitler. In January 1933 Papen persuaded Hindenburg to appoint Hitler as Chancellor in a coalition government which would contain only three Nazis and which would be carefully monitored by Papen as Hitler's deputy. Schleicher had tried to keep his own government afloat by asking for further emergency powers. These Hindenburg was not prepared to grant, since he now had an alternative. On 30 January 1933 he confirmed Hitler's appointment, believing that sufficient precautions had been taken to tame the radicalism of the NSDAP. In fact, Hitler proceeded to destroy the Weimar Republic within weeks of his coming to power. Only one more election was to be held before Germany was subsumed into the Third Reich.

EXPLANATIONS OF THE RISE OF HITLER

The rise of Hitler involved two distinct processes which, although connected, did not lead inevitably from one to the other. The first was the collapse of democracy within the Weimar Republic and the development after 1930 of an authoritarian regime which was hostile to the whole basis of the Republic. The second was the emergence of an entirely new form of right-wing movement which, under Hitler, eventually replaced this authoritarian system with a totalitarian regime. The latter could not have occurred without the former: Hitler's rise was accomplished through the collapse of the Republic. But this collapse was not necessarily tied to an historical trend leading inevitably to Nazism; it could have been followed by an alternative system.

Any explanation as to why Hitler became Chancellor must, therefore, focus on the weaknesses leading to the collapse of the Republic on the one hand and, on the other, the strength and appeal of Nazism. The whole picture is complex, and it is necessary to avoid any one-sided or over-simplified view.

The vulnerability of the Weimar Republic

The bedrock of any democracy is its constitution. As we have seen, the constitution of the Weimar Republic had certain advanced democratic features, including the enfranchisement of all men and women at 20, and a form of proportional representation which guaranteed one seat in the Reichstag for every 60,000 votes cast. It also made it necessary for the Chancellor and his cabinet to have the support of a majority in the Reichstag, thus ensuring that the executive would at all times be responsible to the legislature. Yet several problems soon emerged to negate these positive features, making the constitution extremely difficult to operate.

One was the tendency of proportional representation to encourage the proliferation of parties. When this was associated with the need for majority government, it became evident that everything would depend on the assembling of coalitions. At first this seemed theoretically simple. The three parties most responsible for the formation of the Republic – the SPD, the Centre and the DDP – earned in the 1919 elections 76 per cent of the vote, which translated into 78 per cent of the seats. But in the election of 1920 their support dropped to only 48 per cent of the vote which meant that government became dependent on other parties as well. The eventual solution was the support of Stresemann who brought in part of the DVP. Unfortunately, this was offset between 1923 and 1928 by the withdrawal of the SPD into opposition. It even became necessary to bring into two cabinets several right-wing politicians from the DNVP. This, of course, meant that the base of the government was broadening all the time, which made more difficult any concerted decision-making. Serious enough in the favourable economic climate between 1924 and 1928, this became an intolerable handicap when Germany was struck by the Great Depression. The result was the collapse of the normal process of democracy as, under

Brüning and his successors, the government no longer sought the regular mandate of the Reichstag.

This led, between 1930 and 1933, to the authoritarian phase of the Weimar Republic. Ironically, this was made possible by the constitution itself which, in Article 48, allowed the President to assume emergency powers should he consider these necessary. The first President, Ebert, had used Article 48 constructively to maintain the stability of the new democracy. But his successor, Hindenburg, was a very different proposition. His election in 1925 has been seen as a major disaster for the Republic: he was an authoritarian and military figure, with a considerable suspicion of the whole parliamentary process. E. Eyck comments that 'No matter how Hindenburg might comport himself in the immediate future his election as president of Germany was a triumph of nationalism and militarism and a heavy defeat for the Republic and parliamentary government.'[7] As we have seen, Hindenburg brushed aside the problem of finding a parliamentary majority by exercising Presidential decree powers allowed by Article 48. According to H. Boldt[8] the use of decree laws increased from 5 in 1930 to 44 in 1931 and 60 in 1932, while sittings of the Reichstag declined from 94 in 1930 to 41 in 1931 and a mere 13 in 1932. This trend effectively ended the role of party politics. The situation deteriorated further after the fall of Brüning in 1932 as Papen and Schleicher were both determined to avoid any return to parliamentary sovereignty. This was the environment which produced the squalid manoeuvres described on p. 145 and which helped place Hitler in power.

Some historians and recent German politicians have identified an undercurrent of antidemocratic feeling which severely damaged the fabric of the Republic. According to L. Snyder, the new regime was seen as a 'stopgap' and 'from the days of its origin the Weimar Republic was unwanted and unloved'. Theodor Heuss, the first President of West Germany, maintained that 'Germany never conquered democracy for herself.'[9] It could certainly be argued that democracy was handed down from above in 1918 (see p. 133), without any serious attempt to change the existing civil service or the judicial and military élites. Below the surface of a democratic constitution, therefore, was a profoundly conservative base, with no commitment – emotional or intellectual – to a republic. Certain sections of the community could have become permanently reconciled to the new system – for example the proletariat and the middle classes. These, however, were severely affected by the impact of the 1923 and 1929 economic crises. Much of the population was highly vulnerable to right-wing ideas and organizations. A strong tradition of anti-western and antidemocratic thought was maintained by writers and activists like Moeller, van den Bruck and Junger, who induced widespread nostalgia for the Second Reich and anticipation of a Third. The response of much of the population was to criticize the Weimar politicians for their facelessness and to turn to more authoritarian figures like Hindenburg and, ultimately, Hitler. Throughout the period 1918–33, therefore, the onus was always upon democracy to show that it was a better system than the authoritarian models of the past. Many people remained highly sceptical.

Unfortunately, the image of democracy was not strengthened by the performance of the political parties. According to E. Fraenkel, these failed to fulfil 'the functions which devolve upon them in a constitutional pluralistic Parliamentary democracy'.[10] The traditional right – the DNVP – maintained a consistent hostility to the Republic and eventually welcomed its demise. Indeed, in collaborating openly with Hitler's NSDAP, they actually accelerated the process. The more moderate Centre Party did manage to keep a respectable level of support from the Catholic population, but it lurched to the right under the leadership of Brüning and also assisted the re-election of Hindenburg as President in 1932. It was certainly no aggressive defender of parliamentary democracy, Brüning being only too willing to make use of the Presidential power of decree. The liberal part of the political spectrum showed the greatest deficiency. Germany had developed the unique phenomenon of two varieties: right-wing liberalism in the form of the DVP and the more left-wing DDP. Both had promising beginnings and a substantial share of the vote in the early years of the Republic. But both experienced a dramatic collapse with the defection of middle-class support, which will be analysed later in this section. The type of constitution which Germany possessed depended very heavily on a strong liberal performance; liberals were, after all, likely to be the cement holding together any coalition. What Snyder calls the 'feebleness of the German brand of liberalism' was, therefore, catastrophic.[11]

It might be thought that the best chance of upholding the Republic came from the left wing. After all, the parties of the left had fairly consistent support, ranging from 45.5 per cent of the vote in 1919 to 36.9 per cent in November 1932. Unfortunately, the left was also fragmented into two segments (three for the brief period 1919–23). The bitter rivalry between the SPD and the KPD was the legacy of the German Revolution of 1918–19 (see pp. 136–7). The KPD never forgot the bloodshed of January 1919 and regarded the SPD, who had put down their attempted coup, as class enemies. There was also a profound ideological gap. Thalmann, the KPD leader, was influenced by Stalin's belief that social democracy was not essentially different to Fascism and that they were both manifestations of capitalism (see p. 61). He argued, indeed, that the greatest threat to German Communism lay in the SPD, 'in the social democracy which gains the trust of the masses through fraud and treachery'.[12] He believed that the Depression would act as a great catalyst for changes in the voting pattern and that the KPD would pull in the working-class vote in much the same way as the NSDAP was benefiting from the support of the middle classes. (The KPD did make certain inroads; for example, in July 1932 it reduced the SPD's share of the vote to 21.6 per cent and boosted its own to 14.3 per cent. But it never became a mass party to rival the NSDAP.) Thälmann also hoped that, if Hitler were to achieve power, he would soon be overthrown by a proletarian revolution organized by the KPD; in this sense, a Fascist regime would be a 'temporary intermediate development'. As far as Thälmann was concerned, therefore, there was no reason to co-operate with the other parties in preventing the accession of Hitler.

The leadership of the SPD was, of course, aware of this line of reasoning and therefore hated the KPD as much as it did the NSDAP. It refused to seek any common ground and even allowed the right to increase power by default. Papen, for example, managed to extend his authority in Prussia in 1932, even though there was still considerable support in this state for the parties of the left. The SPD decided against calling a general strike in protest because the leadership felt that the subsequent chaos might benefit the KPD. A similar inactivity occurred on a national scale because the attention of the SPD was fixed for most of the time on the Communists rather than on the right.

Chapter 1 referred to the importance of a catalyst in the breakdown of parliamentary systems. This was particularly important in the case of Germany, where economic crisis destabilized the whole social structure, with serious side effects for the political system. Two stages were involved in the process – inflation and depression. General Morgan of the Disarmament Commission said of the former:

> Inflation has destroyed the equipoise of society. It has ruined the middle classes and impoverished the workers .... Inflation has undermined the political basis of the Republic and concentrated all real power in the hands of a few – namely the great industrialists.

In fact, a period of recovery followed this perhaps premature diagnosis. But the real significance of inflation was that any future economic crisis would be bound to have a doubly serious impact. Hence from 1929 the Depression radicalized sections of the population which inflation had already rendered unstable, turning them either to the extreme right or to the far left. It also destroyed any possibility of political consensus and, as we have seen, returned Germany to the practice of authoritarian government.

There is a final irony. Hitler came to power as the impact of the Depression was beginning to lessen and as the support for the Nazis was starting to ebb. The reason for this seems to be that the conservative and authoritarian politicians were determined that the parliamentary democracy destroyed by the Depression should never be reintroduced. It seemed preferable to hand over power to Hitler, especially now that an impending improvement in the economy seemed likely to reduce his appeal and therefore his power. Even Hindenburg, who initially disliked Hitler, was won round to the argument that Hitler could be controlled, even manipulated, within the context of a carefully constructed coalition. The authoritarian regime, in other words, would continue to function as it had done since 1931. The politicians who gave Hitler power in this way made the worst political blunder in the whole of German history.

The strength and appeal of the Nazis

The rise of Hitler was also due to a number of positive factors. To be examined in this section are the role of propaganda and organization, Hitler's strategy and identification of key issues, and the importance of his own personality and influence. Also of vital importance is the support given to the NSDAP by different sections of the population.

The success of the Nazi movement is inevitably associated with the highly skilled use of propaganda and the development of an efficient organization. In these respects it was far ahead of all the other German parties, including the KPD. The importance which Hitler attached to propaganda and organization can be seen clearly in several extracts from *Mein Kampf*. 'The function of propaganda', he argued, 'is to attract supporters, the function of organization is to win members.' He continued:

> Propaganda works on the general public from the standpoint of an idea and makes them ripe for the victory of this idea, while the organization achieves victory by the persistent, organic, and militant union of those supporters who seem willing and able to carry on the fight for victory.

Or, to put it another way,

> The first task of propaganda is to win people for subsequent organization; the first task of organization is to win men for the continuation of propaganda. The second task of propaganda is the disruption of the existing state of affairs and the permeation of this state of affairs with the new doctrine, while the second task of organization must be the struggle for power, thus to achieve the final success of the doctrine.'[13]

The manifestations of propaganda were numerous. Albert

Speer later asserted that 'Hitler was one of the first to be able to avail himself of the means of modern technology.' Admittedly he was unable to make effective use of the radio until after coming to power and establishing a monopoly over this medium. But he did use numerous other trappings, including loudspeakers, provocative posters and bands. Above all, he depended on the power of the spoken word, which he always considered more important than written material. He had a profound insight into the collective emotions of crowds and believed that his message to them had to be kept simple, striking and memorable. 'The receptivity of the great masses is very limited, their intelligence is small, but their power of forgetting is enormous.' Hence propaganda 'must be limited to a very few points',[14] which must be constantly repeated to establish them as incontrovertible facts. It was also vital to make the individual feel important only in the context of the crowd and to establish stereotyped enemies and targets by means, if necessary, of 'the big lie'. Organization, of course, was essential for the maintenance of mass commitment: hence the vast number of marches and rallies, the uniforms and para-military drill, and the street fights with Communists and Social Democrats. The whole process was intended to prepare the movement to seize power when the opportunity arose.

The identification of this opportunity depended on Hitler's strategy and timing. As shown on pp. 140–1, his first bid for power was defective. He believed that he could imitate Mussolini's successful March on Rome. But the failure of the Munich *putsch* in 1923 was followed by a more skilful adaptation to a dual role of legality in party politics which drew attention away from the radicalism of his mass movements (see pp. 141–2). This course lulled the suspicions of the Republican government, which considered the KPD as a more serious threat and, as a result, underestimated the revolutionary potential of the Nazis. It also enabled Hitler to appear as a more moderate politician to those sectors of society who had previously been put off by the gutter politics of the early years of the movement. Along with this overall change in strategy, Hitler aimed constantly to reformulate the Party programme so as to appeal to different parts of the population as they became alienated from the Republic. In 1927 he told his economic adviser, Keppler, that the economic goals of the original programme were now 'unusable'. He considered that some of the details of the 1920 document were too doctrinaire and he was more prepared than some of the more orthodox Nazi leaders to be flexible and pragmatic in the presentation of a Party image. He went so far as to establish a section within the organization to identify the reasons for different types of public discontent and to develop specific remedies which would appeal to different social groups. As P.D. Stachura has put it, the 'NSDAP revealed itself to be perhaps the most tactically flexible and opportunistic political movement in the Republic'.[15]

In developing a broad appeal for the Nazi movement, Hitler relied on the projection of general issues for the consumption of the population as a whole, and specific issues for the different classes. An example of the former was his attack on the Republic's foreign policy. Taking advantage of the unpopularity of the Versailles Settlement, Hitler was able to implant upon the national consciousness terms like 'November Criminals' and the 'stab in the back'. He also slammed the policy of détente pursued by Stresemann: 'our people must be delivered from the hopeless confusion of international convictions and educated consciously and systematically to fanatical Nationalism'. Another mainline policy, guaranteed to be taken seriously across most of the political spectrum, was anti-Communism; in fact, this is seen by R.F. Hamilton[16] as one of the most important of all Hitler's appeals. Finally, he made effective use of the deep undercurrent of antisemitism in Germany, making the Jews a scapegoat for all of Germany's evils, whether in the form of callous capitalism or revolutionary Communism. Above all, he made a permanent and intentionally damaging connection between the regime and the detested minority, developing the concept of the 'Jew Republic'.

What was the importance of the personal role of Hitler in the rise of the Nazi movement? Emphasis is usually placed on his charismatic leadership and an almost demoniac will-power. H. Trevor-Roper, for example, maintains that 'His own firm belief in his messianic mission was perhaps the most important element in the extraordinary power of his personality'.[17] He also possessed, according to A. Bullock, a 'sense of opportunity and timing'. This was the right combination of characteristics to take advantage of the troubles of the Weimar Republic since Hitler was at his best when destroying a system by exploiting its crises. He later experienced much greater difficulty when he had to defend his own system which, in turn, came under threat in the second phase of the Second World War (see pp. 214–17). At this stage, Hitler's personality was to become a major liability to the Nazi movement and to Germany's military survival (see pp. 217–20).

The final issue which needs to be examined is the basis of support for National Socialism. Many observers agree that most of this support came from the middle classes; this argument is advanced, for example, by Bullock, K.D. Bracher, W. Knauerhase, W. Kornhauser and S. Martin Lipset. The middle class, often referred to as the *Mittelstand*, comprised two main sections, old and new. The old *Mittelstand*, who consisted of artisans, small retailers and peasant farmers, formed the core of Nazi support, and some were throwing in their lot with Hitler even before 1929. The new *Mittelstand*, or non-manual employees, civil servants and primary school teachers, added their support between 1930 and 1932. In both cases the *Mittelstand* deserted those parties which they had previously supported, especially the DDP and the DVP, to help boost the Nazi vote from 810,000 in 1928 to 13.5 million in 1932.

The main reason for this was that the *Mittelstand* feared a catastrophic decline in their status unless drastic action were taken to uphold it. During the Second Reich (1871–1918) the *Mittelstand* had been a much honoured part of the population; they were also predominantly Protestant and clearly differentiated from the more humble proletariat. The problem came with the change of regime in 1918, for, according to J. Noakes, 'the establishment of the Weimar Republic represented, to some extent, the triumph of the values of the Catholics and the working classes over the previously dominant culture with its monarchist, Protestant, bourgeois, nationalist and militarist attributes.'[18] To make matters worse, intolerable pressure was exerted by a combination of hyper-inflation and serious depression. The result was a 'crisis of the *Mittelstand*' in which a previously stable part of the population was radicalized. They now feared being squeezed between the two extremes of big business and the socialist or Communist preferences of the proletariat. The middle class parties seemed to offer no solution, whereas the Nazis had geared their appeal to catch just such a disillusioned section of the population. Hitler made a series of promises guaranteed to attract distressed groups within the *Mittelstand*, whether urban or rural, old or new. He undertook, for example, to control the impact of the great department stores on small businesses, to end farm foreclosures, and to reduce interest payments on agricultural debts.[18]

The role of the other classes appears less clear cut. The majority view seems to be that the working classes were far less important than the *Mittelstand* in the Nazi movement. Stachura, for example, argues that 'The Party was unable to establish a significant working-class constituency because it did not develop a coherent interpretation of "German Socialism".' One reason for this was that 'Hitler had amply demonstrated his lack of genuine interest in the proletariat.' Indeed, his 'innate contempt and distrust of the proletariat remained paramount and constituted one of the few constants in his emotional and political make-up'.[15] Other reasons could be cited for the resistance of many workers to the appeal of Nazism. The SPD and KPD were much stronger than the liberal parties and more adept at organizing class-based support. In any case, the majority of workers remained loyal to the parties of the left because of their membership of trade unions. In fact, if radicalization did occur as a result of the Depression, it tended to deflect votes from the SPD to the KPD rather than to the Nazis. Yet a great deal more research needs to be done on this subject. D. Mühlberger, for example, challenges the 'middle-class thesis of Nazism'[19] as does Hamilton.[16] The former argues that the proportion of working-class members of the Nazi movement has been much understated: it could have been as high as 35 per cent of the Party's total. Membership of specific Nazi organizations could have been much higher: the SA recruited 63 per cent of its members from the working class between 1929 and 1933. There could well be a case, therefore, for arguing that the NSDAP did not completely abandon its earlier proletarian base but managed to retain vital links.

The attitudes to Nazism of the upper levels of society are also difficult to pin down precisely. The upper middle class, generally regarded as politically the most stable social group, remained moderate in its outlook. On the other hand, a significant number of landowners, businessmen and industrialists defected to Nazism. The main attraction in their case was undoubtedly Hitler's undertaking, from 1931 onwards, to maintain the essence of capitalism and do everything in his power to eradicate the threat of Communism. Even so, most of the electoral support of the wealthy sectors of society tended to arrive *after* Hitler had been appointed Chancellor, making itself felt in the election of March 1933 rather than in those of 1930 and 1932.

To some extent, the appeal of Nazism transcended class barriers altogether. The three more general categories usually considered most important are religious denomination, gender and age. There is no doubt that the Protestants were more likely than Catholics to vote Nazi. They had no existing party base, whereas the Centre Party held the Catholic vote even at the height of the economic and political crisis. Many were also profoundly suspicious of the Weimar Republic which, as we have seen, they identified mainly with Catholic and working-class values. On the whole, they had far more affection for the memory of the Kaiser's rule and were not, therefore, averse to another change of regime. As far as gender is concerned, the Nazis managed to make up for an early imbalance in their support. Before 1930 the majority of women were more right-wing in their voting behaviour than men; yet the majority of Nazi votes came from men rather than women. By 1933 there was a more even split as many women became convinced that Hitler was the best prospect for bolstering the institution of the family in troubled times; this probably counteracted the earlier and well-founded suspicion that Nazism was profoundly anti-feminist. Finally, the Nazi movement had a powerful generational impact. It appealed directly to youth, partly through its dynamism and attack on traditional ideas and institutions, partly through the over-simplified solutions to the problem of unemployment. Young men, more than any other section of the community, were prepared to submerge their identity and to respond to Hitler's appeal to the crowd instinct.

It is difficult to escape the conclusion that during the later period of the Weimar Republic the NSDAP was the most heterogeneous party in Germany. It included people from the complete range of social backgrounds, even though the precise proportion of these may be open to debate and controversy. Hitler alone managed to create a radical movement with which he could transform into fanaticism the desperation of a profoundly disturbed people.

THE THIRD REICH 1933—45

Dictatorship established 1933

When he was appointed Chancellor on 30 January 1933, Hitler's power was by no means absolute. He had only three Nazis in his cabinet and he was constrained by Papen who, in his position as Vice-Chancellor, had to be involved in any contacts between the Chancellor and President. Another problem was that Hitler had no emergency powers beyond those which Hindenburg was prepared, under Article 48 of the constitution, to grant him. It seemed, therefore, that Papen was fully justified in believing that Hitler could be tamed. Within two months, Papen argued, 'we will have pushed Hitler so far into a corner that he'll squeak'.[20]

Yet, within six months, all constraints had been eliminated. Hitler was able to kick away the ladder by which he had ascended to power and establish a dictatorship based in effect on a permanent state of emergency. Part of the process was accomplished, technically at least, within the ambit of the constitution; the results, however, were so devastating that they amounted to a 'legal revolution'.

Hitler's first priority was to strengthen the position of the NSDAP in the Reichstag so that he could use the latter to force through measures to change the constitution. He intended, in other words, to use the democratic process to destroy democracy. He therefore demanded immediate elections, and the Reichstag was dissolved on 1 February, two days after his appointment as Chancellor. In the election campaign which followed, Hitler had two major advantages over the other parties. First, he had more direct access to the media, especially the radio; this he used more effectively than any previous politician, thereby enhancing the electoral appeal of the NSDAP. Secondly, he was able to use emergency powers to weaken the position of some of his opponents. For example, the decree of 4 February made it possible to control the meetings of other parties. It also enabled Goering to draft a special police order in Prussia to the effect that the 'activities of subversive organizations are...to be combated with the most drastic measures'. Indeed, 'failure to act is more serious than errors committed in acting'.[21] Even more extreme measures were allowed by the decree of 28 February which suspended many personal liberties 'until further notice'. The pretext for this was a much publicized attempt to burn down the Reichstag building on 27 February. It used to be thought that this was a deliberate ploy by the Nazis to cast the blame on the Communists and SPD. It is now generally believed that the fire was the work of a single individual, van der Lubbe, and not part of an organized plot. Whatever the truth, however, the event was exploited by Hitler to the utmost. He was empowered to suspend various articles of the constitution and to take over the power of the state governments if necessary.

The election results were announced on 5 March. They showed considerable gains for the NSDAP when compared with the results of the elections of November 1932. The Nazi vote increased from 11.7 million to 17.2 million and its percentage of the total from 33.1 to 43.9. Hitler's partners, the DNVP, gained 200,000 votes and an extra seat. The Centre Party made marginal increases and the SPD remained about the same. Real losses were experienced by the DVP and other middle-class parties, and also by the Communists.

Three reasons can be given for Hitler's gains. The first is that his tactic in calling an immediate election completely unsettled his opponents. Most of the non-Nazis in his first cabinet had meekly submitted to this demand for a dissolution and, according to Broszat, 'were guilty of the first fateful blow against the concept of containing Hitler'. Secondly, there appears to have been a degree of resignation in the

Reichstag itself as the deputies failed to use effectively the Committee for the Protection of Parliamentary Rights; this might have challenged Hitler's demand for an election as being too hasty. And thirdly, the Nazi monopoly of the state media and extensive use of emergency decrees cut away much of the opposition's capacity to present an effective case against Hitler.

But the process of establishing a dictatorship was not yet complete, for the NSDAP still lacked an overall majority in the Reichstag. What happened next was a new offensive as the constitution was stormed from below, at the level of local government, and from above, within the Reichstag itself.

Recent historical studies have drawn attention to the importance of Nazi pressure in the individual states or *Lander*, in many cases amounting to a 'terrorist, revolutionary movement'.[22] In March 1933 SA and SS squads went into action, taking over town halls, police headquarters and newspapers. The resulting chaos was usually so serious that the central government had to intervene via the Minister of the Interior, Wilhelm Frick. Nazis were appointed to the local office of Police Commissioner and, on 7 April, a new law allowed for the installation of special Reich governors in all states. In effect, therefore, Nazi rule was imposed at the local level throughout Germany even before dictatorship had been completed at the centre. Nevertheless, Hitler was conscious of the need to restrain some of the wilder Nazi activists in case they should actually impede the revolution from above – which was now well under way.

The Reichstag reconvened on 21 March 1933. Hitler now intended to secure the passage of an Enabling Act which would radically reduce the Reichstag's powers. Such a major constitutional change, however, needed a two-thirds majority vote, which the NSDAP and their allies, the DNVP, did not between them possess. Hitler's solution was ingenious. First, he used the Emergency Decree of 28 February to expel from the Reichstag all Communist deputies. He then negotiated with the Centre Party an agreement whereby the latter would vote for the Enabling Act in return for special guarantees for the Churches. Hitler was very reassuring on this point. He saw in Christianity 'the most important factors for the maintenance of our society' and would therefore 'permit and guarantee to the Christian denominations the enjoyment of their due influence in schools and education'.[23] On 23 March 1933 the Enabling Act secured its required majority, with only the SPD voting against it. Its terms virtually destroyed parliamentary powers by allowing the Chancellor to issue laws without consulting the Reichstag.

The 'legal revolution' now gathered momentum as the new power was used to eliminate other political parties. Between March and July all parties apart from the NSDAP were forced to wind themselves up. The whole process culminated in the Law of 14 July 1933 – 'Against the Establishment of Parties' – which declared it a criminal offence to organize any political grouping outside the NSDAP. Another election was held in November 1933, in which a single party list was put to the electorate for its approval. The result was that the NSDAP took all the seats in the Reichstag. Germany was officially a one-party state.

Why did the opposition give up? The most obvious reason is that it had no choice. The parties of the left were smashed by the government's emergency powers. The Communists, for example, were prevented from taking their seats in the Reichstag, and the SPD were banned outright in June. The Centre Party gave up any pretence at political opposition in return for a guarantee of religious freedom; it actually liquidated itself voluntarily. Even the DNVP was unable to keep itself afloat as its leaders found it increasingly obvious that they no longer had any hold on the political monster they had helped create. President Hindenburg, no admirer of the party system, made no attempt to interfere with Hitler's assault on the opposition, for fear of provoking a more violent and radical constitutional upheaval. By the middle of 1933 the only remaining obstacle between Hitler and total power was the German army. The question now to be decided was whether the military leadership would make a stand against Hitler. Or would they too fall into line?

Dictatorship consolidated: relations with the army

Hitler was not yet completely secure. His position could be upset either by the radical wing of his Party or by the army.

The most likely threat was that undisciplined action by the former could provoke a counter-blow from the latter.

The destructive capacity of the Nazi radicals had been evident in March 1933 when the rank and file had brought about at local level changes which were far more sweeping than Hitler had intended. The SA were especially violent and the Party leadership regretted its earlier failure to tame them. By the middle of 1933 there were also demands for a new Nazi revolution. Ernst Röhm, for example, wanted to extend the scope of the SA so that the German army would be absorbed into it. Röhm expressed the disillusionment of the radical Nazis with Hitler's apparent caution. 'A tremendous victory has been won', he argued. 'But not absolute victory.' He added: 'The SA and SS will not tolerate the German revolution going to sleep.'[24]

Hitler was unimpressed by such views. He was particularly anxious to keep the support of those very interests under attack by Röhm. He was also opposed to radicalism for its own sake. 'Revolution is not a permanent condition. . . . The stream of revolution once released must be guided into the secure bed of evolution.'[25] Further provocative activities were therefore to stop. Accordingly, Frick's circular of 6 October 1933 instructed the activists that 'These infringements and excesses must now cease once and for all.'[26] What made Hitler particularly wary of antagonizing the army was that he hoped shortly to become President. Hindenburg was approaching death and the army, if threatened by the Nazis, might prevail upon Hindenburg to nominate a successor. Alternatively, the army might attempt a coup against Hitler, with or without Hindenburg's approval. Hitler *would* be able to counter this coup with the help of the SA, but this would make him a virtual prisoner of the radicals. He could, however, adopt another course. He could crush the SA with the support of the army and, over a period, establish the same influence over the military commanders as he had over the politicians. There would be more chance of total penetration and control if Nazification was slow and cautious.

The army had good reason to co-operate with Hitler. It hated the programme of the SA and was particularly averse to Röhm's aim to see 'the grey rock' of the *Reichswehr* submerged in the 'brown flood' of the SA. The dislike was mutual. The SA despised the aristocratic connections of the army officers, while the army regarded the SA leadership as uncouth upstarts. The *Reichswehr* commanders saw Hitler as the moderate who would seek to preserve at least some of the traditional values. They were therefore prepared to do a deal with Hitler; they would stand back while Hitler took whatever measures he considered necessary against his own delinquents. They would even intervene to save Hitler from the SA if necessary. As events turned out their help was not required. By the beginning of July, 1934, the SA leadership had been cut down by Hitler's élite corps, the SS. The 'Night of the Long Knives' claimed the lives of Röhm, Strasser and many other Nazis who were considered disruptive.

The results of this bloodbath were twofold. First, a grateful army was now prepared to concede to Hitler the office of head of state. When Hindenburg died five weeks later, Hitler succeeded him as Reich President, adding the title of *Führer* for good measure. The army took an oath of personal allegiance: 'I swear before God to give my unconditional obedience to Adolf Hitler, *Führer* of the Reich and of the German People, Supreme Commander.'[27] The second result of the Night of the Long Knives was the rapid emergence of the SS as the most important political influence in Germany. It gradually infiltrated the key organs of the state, including even the civil service and the army, in the manner examined on pp. 168–9. The SA, by contrast, was a mere shadow of its former self.

Having neutralized the army as a potential threat to his position, Hitler was now determined to Nazify it. This process seems to have occurred in two main phases. The first, between 1934 and 1938, saw the army's gradual loss of control, culminating in 1938 in sweeping changes of personnel. The second phase saw the total subordination of the army to Hitler's foreign policy and war objectives.

Between 1934 and 1938 the army still considered that it was an equal partner with the Nazi regime. Gradually, however, it lost the initiative. By 1934 it had already agreed to accept the swastika insignia on uniforms as well as the oath of personal allegiance to the Führer. It was now obliged to put up with Nazi instruction and indoctrination. Worse, Hitler was determined to pursue an active foreign policy which in some ways differed substantially from the preferences of the general staff. The latter objected to the risk involved in the remilitarization of the Rhineland in 1936 and, when in 1937 Hitler revealed his intentions for the territorial expansion of Germany, the likes of Blomberg and Fritsch were horrified at the thought of provoking Britain and France into retaliation. Hitler's response was forceful; he announced on 4 February 1938: 'From henceforth, I exercise personally the immediate command over the whole armed forces.'[27] He proceeded to reorganize the entire command, establishing under his own leadership the OKW (*Oberkommando der Wehrmacht*). He also dismissed or retired 16 generals and relocated 44 others. Blomberg and Fritsch were dismissed for personal reasons, the latter incriminated by an SS file alleging homosexual offences.

These changes, it has been argued, finally cast off the last constraints of the Hindenburg era. From 1938 onwards Hitler was in total control of military strategy as well as foreign policy. At first he was still prepared to use the professional expertise of the Wehrmacht. The invasion of Poland, for example, was planned and executed by the generals. Hitler, however, became increasingly confident of his own abilities. He was largely responsible for the attack on France in 1940, which succeeded brilliantly, and the invasion of Russia in 1941, which did not. Once he started to experience defeat he showed bitter resentment of the high command, regarding his generals as effete, unadventurous and cowardly. He therefore encouraged the penetration of the Wehrmacht by his own fanatical followers in the form of the *Waffen SS*. This completed the Nazification of the German military machine.

Why did the army not take more positive action to prevent Hitler's domination? The main reason was that the military commanders made the same mistake as the right-wing politicians. Their dislike of the Weimar Republic was so strong that they were prepared to go along with the Nazis, confident that they could ultimately control Hitler. Indeed, the Night of the Long Knives seemed to show that Hitler was moving to a more moderate position. After 1934, however, the army was inundated with a wave of younger, pro-Nazi officers being turned out by the military academies. The sweeping structural changes of 1938 further emasculated the military élite; it now proved too late to try to regain the initiative. It is true that there were some instances of dissent and plotting – for example, Beck's involvement in the plans to remove Hitler in 1938 and 1944. But these did not achieve sufficient support within the army to be really effective. The majority of officers were unwilling to take action, even when Hitler's military deficiencies became really apparent. This was partly because of what Rosinski has called the psychological fetters of the oath of personal allegiance[28] which made any action against Hitler seem treasonable. Another explanation is that throughout the entire period the army displayed only a blinkered vision of self-interest. According to Grunberger, 'It is no exaggeration to say that Pontius Pilate achieved multiple reincarnation in gold braid and field-grey.'[29]

Party, government and leadership

By the end of 1934 Hitler had, to all intents and purposes, destroyed the Weimar Republic. The constitution of 1919 was never formally abrogated but all opposition parties had been eliminated, individual rights withdrawn, the Reichstag's control over the government ended, and all the major offices of state concentrated in the hands of one man. Democracy had been superseded by dictatorship and institutionalized terror. The traditional view is that this was efficient and tightly organized, with Hitler in total control. This view has, however, undergone recent modification. It is now argued that the German dictatorship was far less orderly than used to be supposed; indeed there were elements of chaos. Basically, there existed in the Third Reich two competing trends. One was the revolutionary activism of the Nazi movement, the other the persistence of traditional institutions and structures. The result was duplication, overlapping and conflict, evidence of which can be seen at the levels both of central and local governments.

Despite the so-called 'Nazi Revolution', central government experienced a surprising degree of continuity. All the former ministries were retained, and their powers were actually increased by the Enabling Act. The civil service continued to function; in the words of Noakes and Pridham, it was a 'bureaucracy of high competence and long traditions'.[30] There was certainly no attempt to destroy existing institutions and to replace them with new NSDAP organs. In fact, Hitler was never over-enthusiastic about the idea of undiluted Party rule. He preferred to develop parallel institutions, which generally competed with each other.

There were several examples of this process. One was the appointment of Special Deputies which were outside the government ministries but fulfilled similar functions. Hence Todt, as General Inspector for German Roads, overlapped and came into conflict with the Minister of Transport, while the Youth Leader of the Reich had powers which impinged on those of the Minister of Education. Another example was Hitler's use of personnel completely outside the scope of the normal ministries – for instance the newly created office of Deputy Führer. Above all, there emerged within the Third Reich an autonomous empire, the SS. Under the control of the Reich SS leader and responsible ultimately to Hitler alone, this assumed functions which went far beyond security, spreading into the economy, industry and education.[31]

Untidiness and overlapping were also apparent in local government, where two main types of authority jostled for power. The first type were the traditional authorities, under the Minister-President of each state. This office was retained even when the Reich was reconstructed in January 1934 and the federal system ended. The Minister-President was regarded as a useful post in the Nazi regime and subordinated to the central government's Ministry of the Interior. Meanwhile, a second type of official had emerged – one which was based more directly on the Party. Hitler decided to appoint ten Reich Governors from among the most prominent of the Party *gauleiters*; their purpose was to enforce the Führer's edicts and orders. What happened was open competition and conflict between the Ministers-President and the Governors, each complaining regularly to central government about the activities of the other.

What was the reason for this curious state of affairs? There are two broad possibilities. One is that the Führer did whatever was necessary to maintain his personal authority by deliberate manipulation, by a process of divide and rule. Hitler's real strength, in other words, depended upon his being the only one who could sort out the 'jurisdictional thicket of party agencies and state machinery'.[32] A second possible reason is that the overlapping and inefficiency was the result of a completely haphazard exercise of power; far from being systematic and manipulative, Hitler came close to being administratively incompetent. Which of these interpretations is the more likely? To a large extent the answer depends on how one sees the leadership of the Führer himself. Was he strong and decisive or weak and uncertain?

This is one of the most interesting of recent historical debates.[33] For the majority of historians, German and Anglo-Saxon, there is no question about Hitler's overriding authority. N. Rich is particularly emphatic: Hitler 'undoubtedly possessed one of the most forceful leadership personalities in recorded history...and was indeed the Führer'. Again, according to Rich, 'the point cannot be stressed too strongly: Hitler was master in the Third Reich.' Some, like Bullock, would emphasize the opportunist nature of Hitler's power; others, like Trevor-Roper, his commitment to an ideology and the gradual unfolding of an overall purpose. But most would agree on his authority. There is therefore a logical step to the much respected argument of K.D. Bracher that Hitler kept himself aloft by deliberately weakening any possible rivals. Thus, 'the antagonisms of power were only resolved in the key position of the omnipotent Führer.... the dictator held a key position precisely because of the confusion of conflicting power groups.'[32] Haffner even goes so far as to refer to the deliberate destruction of the normal functioning of the state and the apparent paradox of 'controlled chaos'.

Quite the reverse is argued by Broszat, who has played an important part in cutting Hitler down to size. Despite the oath of personal loyalty to him, the Führer's control over government actually declined as he became increasingly dissociated from its daily routine. Cabinet meetings virtually ended, to be replaced by separate and sporadic negotiations with individual ministries. Hence, according to Broszat, 'The authoritative Führer's will was expressed only irregularly, unsystematically and incoherently.'[33] Hitler was inclined increasingly to withdraw from active decision-making in government, a process which became even more pronounced during the war years. H. Mommsen goes still further. He argues that Hitler allowed Germany to deteriorate into 'an unparalleled institutional anarchy' increasingly divorced 'from practical reality'. The main influence was Hitler's own defects: his reluctance to make decisions, his uncertainty and his concern about his prestige. He was, therefore, in some respects a 'weak dictator'.[33] D. Irving goes the whole way and claims that Hitler was 'probably the weakest leader Germany has known this century'.[34]

The debate is surely not exhausted and is a fascinating example of how even the most basic assumptions – like the absolute power exercised by Hitler – are open to reinterpretation.

The apparatus of coercion and terror

Changes in the political system were accompanied and reinforced by the transformation of the institutions of justice and of law and order. The basic principles of the law were radically altered while, at the same time, there developed an enormously powerful apparatus of coercion and terror. In effect, the Third Reich was under a perpetual state of emergency.

The legal system was profoundly altered, in both theory and practice. Hitler disliked the 'liberal' and 'formalistic' elements of legal theory. Instead, he insisted that the basis of law should be 'healthy popular feeling' and 'welfare of the national community'.[35] In other words, more attention was to be given to social influences. Naturally these were to be directed by the Party and expressed as 'the will of the Führer'. In practice, the 'legal revolution' brought government control over the whole judiciary. Judges were appointed on the basis of loyalty and part of their training 'must include a serious study of National Socialism and its ideological foundations'.[36] For a while the process of Nazification was incomplete. The Minister of Justice, Gürtner, was not himself a Nazi. On his death in 1941, however, he was succeeded by Thierack, and the whole judicial system slid under the control of the SS.

The SS, or *Schutz Staffel*, had been formed in 1925 as an élite corps within the unruly SA. Himmler was appointed its leader in 1929. Its membership grew rapidly thereafter, from 290 in 1929 to 52,000 by 1933.[37] It was responsible for the elimination of the SA leadership in the Night of the Long Knives, for which it was rewarded by being made the paramount security force in Germany. It had close links with the Gestapo (*Geheime Staatzpolizei*) set up by Goering in Prussia in 1933. In 1934 the Gestapo came under Himmler's overall direction, although Heydrich was its administrative head until his assassination in Prague in 1941. Heydrich was also in charge of the security service of the SS, known as the SD. The SS came to comprise three broadly distinct components. One was Hitler's own bodyguard, the *Leibstandarte*. The second was the *Waffen SS*, the vanguard divisions within the army. The third was the *Totenkopfverbände* or Death's Head Units who manned the concentration camps.[38] The SS were therefore directly involved in the mass extermination programme and in working to death 'anti social elements' such as 'Jews, gypsies, Russians and Ukrainians, Poles with sentences of more than three years, Czechs and Germans with sentences of more than eight years'.[39]

There is general agreement among historians that the SS wielded enormous influence in the Third Reich. It could even be argued that the SS/Gestapo/SD complex was far more a manifestation of the 'Nazi Revolution', than the administrative changes, which were relatively limited. Neumann and Hüttenberger maintain that the Third Reich was in fact a 'power cartel' based on three parts: a 'Nazi bloc', big business and the army. The Nazi bloc gradually weakened the others. Within the Nazi bloc were two main divisions – the party organization, and the SS and related bodies; it was the latter which experienced the real growth.[40] D. Schoenbaum points to the almost limitless involvement of the SS: 'in one form or another the SS made foreign policy, military policy and agricultural policy. It administered occupied territories as a kind of self-contained Ministry of the Interior and maintained itself economically with autonomous enterprises.'[41] It also frequently trespassed on the work of the ministries; Noakes and Pridham argue that the state authorities now formed a façade, 'the substance of which was progressively being eaten away by the cancerous growth of the new organization under individuals appointed by Hitler'.[35]

The control of the mind

In a speech at a Nazi Party Congress in Nuremberg on 7 September 1934 Josef Goebbels emphasized the importance of 'total' propaganda; 'Among the arts with which one rules a people, it ranks in first place .... There exists no sector of public life which can escape its influence.'[42] The Nazi leadership certainly made a major attempt to foster ideological commitment to the regime. It began by bringing the cultural roles of the different ministries into the new Ministry for People's Enlightenment and Propaganda, set up under Goebbels in March 1933. This controlled the Reich Chamber of Culture which, in turn, subdivided into sub-chambers for the fine arts, music, literature, the press, theatre, radio and films.[43] An elaborate educational system also evolved, overlapping the various youth organizations and combining indoctrination with mass mobilization. The results were often startling, but success was far from total. There were major deficiencies in all areas of culture and education, and where persuasion failed the regime frequently had to resort to coercion. Twelve years of philistinism also led inevitably to the impoverishment of German culture.

Of the arts, literature was the most immediately vulnerable to state interference, since it offered great potential either for official indoctrination or for resistance. The Nazi mass movement was profoundly anti-intellectual and went in for book-burning with a zeal which greatly reduced Germany's literary output. Over 2500 important writers, like Thomas Mann, were proscribed, while the regime promoted propagandist literature like Hans Grimm's *People Without Space*. Music was also a target. Following the golden age of Weimar, the Nazis 'disastrously interrupted the flow of musical life',[44] banning any works by Jewish composers like Mendelssohn and Mahler, and promoting *völkisch* music and the grand operas of Wagner. Art was thoroughly purged of all 'degenerate', modernist and Jewish influences. The personal tastes of the Führer demanded a new 'Aryan' art showing rustic and martial themes and focusing on physical power. Of all the art forms, however, it was architecture which held the deepest interest for Hitler; it would, after all, be the visible measure of the expected millennium of Nazi rule. Hitler made the revealing comment in 1937 that 'the greater the demands the state makes upon its people, the more imposing it must appear to them'. He therefore became obsessively involved in designs for the rebuilding of Berlin and Nuremberg – plans eventually scrapped because of their unsurpassed ugliness.

A prime target for any dictatorship is the mass media. This had two main components in the 1930s – the press and radio. The Nazis made extensive efforts to gain control over both. Taking over the press was the more gradual. In 1933 Nazi papers accounted for only 2.5 per cent of the total, reaching 82 per cent by 1944.[45] Great care was taken to ensure a 'correct' presentation of material. Individual news agencies were amalgamated to provide only one source of information. Journalists were made responsible to the state rather than to their editors, and regular conferences were held by the Press Department of the Propaganda Ministry. These efforts were not entirely successful and, on the whole, the government proved more adept in the use of radio In 1933 it established complete control over the Reich Broadcasting Corporation and used Germany's 16 million receiving sets to maximum effect; Hitler broadcast 50 radio speeches in 1933 alone. Yet, even though radio had a major impact on morale, especially in wartime, there was a tendency to pour out, with constant repetition, the light music of Lehar and Strauss.

One of the most obvious channels for Nazification was education. The main intention was to indoctrinate, to implant fixed ideas and doctrines rather than to open minds. Hence, Hitler once said, 'When an opponent declares "I will not come over to your side," I calmly say, "Your child belongs to us already".' The subjects primarily affected were history, which emphasized Nordic, Nazi and military themes; science, based strongly on Nazi race theories; and literature, which was virulently antisemitic. Teachers were recruited and kept for their ideological conformity, their main obligation being 'to defend without reservation the National-Socialist state'.[43] To guarantee this degree of loyalty, membership of the *Nationalsozialistische Lehrerbund*, or Nazi Teachers' Association, was compulsory. The impact of these measures was considerable, creating among the young an emotional commitment to the regime which was often absent in the adult population. Yet here there were also major deficiencies. One was the lack of administrative co-ordination, as various authorities interfered with each other. The educational roles of three officials were never precisely defined: Baldur von Shirach as Youth Leader, Frick as Minister of the Interior and Rust as Minister of Education. There was also a serious decline in educational standards. A typical complaint – expressed by the army – was that 'Many of the candidates applying for commissions display a simply inconceivable lack of elementary knowledge'.[46] Vocational and technical schools frequently claimed that basic ignorance seriously impeded normal coverage of the curriculum.

The universities were also the target of a regime which both despised and feared the academic world. Again the emphasis was on ideological conformity. The Minister of Culture told the universities in 1933: 'From now on, it will not be your job to determine whether something is true, but whether it is in the spirit of the National Socialist revolution.'[42] To enforce this new approach to higher learning, the government deprived university senates of their authority and assumed control of the appointment of rectors. It also displayed a staggering ignorance, typified by the remark of Robert Ley on the subject of university research: 'A roadsweeper sweeps a thousand microbes into the gutter with one brushstroke; a scientist preens himself on discovering a single microbe in the whole of his life.'[47] The inevitable result was a decline in the standard of scientific research, especially with the abolition of the 'Jewish Physics' of Albert Einstein. Ultimately Germany paid a heavy penalty for this strait-jacket on academic freedom, losing against the western allies the race to develop the atomic bomb.

Finally, the Nazis aimed to mobilize Germany's youth to provide a new base of mass support. All young people were to be trained for a future role. In the case of boys this was military service, while for girls the emphasis was on preparation for marriage and motherhood. To ensure the martial and marital message did get through, boys and girls were co-opted into the Hitler Youth. This was subdivided into several components. Boys joined the *Jungvolk* at the age of 10, proceeding at 14 into the *Hitlerjugend*. Similarly, girls became *Jungmädel* (Young Maidens) at 10 and went into the *Bund Deutscher Mädel* at 14. Baldur von Shirach, the *Reichsjugend-führer*, made the whole organization fervently nationalist and unashamedly racist; in this respect it was a remarkably effective vehicle for Nazi influence. There were, however, several defects. It failed, for instance, to bring about one of the major Nazi objectives: complete social fusion and the blurring of class distinctions. Despite the powerful influences on it, the Hitler Youth remained a microcosm of a still traditional social structure.

Racism and antisemitism

Fundamental to all Hitler's policies was his absolute belief in the superiority of the 'Aryan' race and the need to prepare the German people for their role as masters of Europe. He categorized mankind into three separate groups, 'founders' of culture, 'bearers' of culture and 'destroyers' of culture. The Aryans, of course, formed the highest group. According to Nazi race theorists, the essential characteristics of the typical Aryan included a tall and slim build, a narrow face and nose, a prominent chin, a fresh complexion, and gold or blond hair. (It is ironical that the only one of the Nazi leaders to fit this description – Heydrich – was obsessed with what he considered to be the 'taint' of a Jewish ancestor.) Hitler aimed gradually to purify the German race so that the majority of people would eventually conform to this ideal appearance. This would be achieved by eliminating racial mixing (miscegenation) and by special breeding programmes undertaken by the SS. Race therefore became a vital part of all indoctrination, the purpose being in von Shirach's words to create 'the perfect and complete human animal – the superman!'

The main obstacle to this was what Hitler called 'subman', who threatened to 'pollute' the Aryan race. Among 'submen' were the 'eternal enemy' of the German people, the Jews. Antisemitism was undoubtedly Hitler's major obsession and permeated his entire thought; indeed, it is difficult to find a page in *Mein Kampf* which does not have some reference to Jews. There was nothing new in the existence of this type of prejudice. European history is stained with instances of persecution; these include the use of the Spanish Inquisition by Ferdinand and Isabella against the Jews in the 1490s, the anti-Jewish pogroms in Tsarist Russia, and the injustice committed against the Jewish officer, Captain Dreyfus, in France. What *was* unprecedented was the lengths to which antisemitism was taken in the Third Reich.

Nazi policy unfolded in three main stages, each more radical than the last. The first, between 1933 and 1938, saw extensive legislation imposing a series of disabilities on the Jews. In April 1933 Jews were excluded from the civil service, prevented from working in hospitals and removed from the judiciary. The Nuremberg Laws of 1935 deprived Jews of German citizenship and banned marriage or sexual relations between Germans and Jews. Between them, these measures were the most comprehensive in modern history. Yet, at this stage, there were still some constraints on Nazi action. President Hindenburg, for example, managed to keep civil service jobs for those Jews who had fought or lost relatives in the First World War. Also, Frick issued a memorandum from the Ministry of the Interior instructing authorities not to *exceed* the instructions on the Jews. In some instances the authorities were actually embarrassed by the excesses of militants like Julius Streicher with his virulent tabloid *Der Stürmer*. On the occasion of the 1936 Olympics Hitler ordered the removal from Berlin of all anti-Jewish notices. He was clearly playing safe so as not to alienate the establishment while secretly preparing more comprehensive measures for the future.

After 1938 antisemitism became more violent and all remaining constraints on persecution were swept aside. In July 1938 they were banned from participating in commerce, their last preserve. The authorities also attempted to identify and control the movement of Jews by decrees on compulsory 'Jewish' names, identity cards and passports. The law no longer offered any protection, as was all too evident on the night of 9–10 November 1938. '*Kristallnacht*' saw the smashing of Jewish shops and other property all over Germany by the SA and the SS in retaliation for the assassination by a Polish Jew of an official in the German Embassy in Paris. The mob violence caused some irritation at top levels in the administration which preferred a more systematic and less messy approach like the confiscation of Jewish assets. At Hitler's instigation several possibilities were now examined for removing the Jewish population from Germany altogether, including a scheme for its resettlement in the island of Madagascar.

But Hitler soon came to the conclusion that emigration was not feasible. Between 1941 and 1945 Hitler's anti-Jewish obsessions were sublimated in the most extreme measures seen in the whole of human history. The programme of extermination appears to have begun in July 1941 with instructions to Heydrich to implement the 'Final Solution'. The first step was the Decree of Identification which forced every Jew to wear a yellow Star of David. This was followed by the mass deportation of Jews to the concentration camps at Chelmo, Auschwitz-Birkenau, Belzec, Sobibor, Treblinka and Maidenek. Exterminations began in earnest from mid-1942 and, by the time that the Russians liberated the camps in Poland, and the Allies those in the west, some 3 to 4 million Jews had been sent to the gas chambers. Organized by Eichmann, the whole process was conducted with industrial efficiency, leading German firms competing for contracts to manufacture the gas chambers. Yet the Nazis were constantly aware of the need to maintain secrecy for fear of a public backlash. Himmler referred to the process as 'a page of glory in our history which has never been written and must never be written'.

The 'Final Solution' has been the subject of controversy among historians – especially after the trial and execution of Eichmann in Israel in 1960. The traditional view is that Hitler intended extermination from the outset. J. Toland, for example, maintains that Hitler advocated such measures in 1919. The same point is made by G. Fleming, who adds that Hitler started to develop a plan to realize his policy as early as the 1920s. K. Hildebrand has no doubt as to the underlying commitment of Hitler to extermination: 'Fundamental to National Socialist genocide was Hitler's race dogma.'[48] An alternative viewpoint, however, is that extermination was not an inherent policy of the Nazi regime but, rather, one carried out when other policies had failed and, furthermore, under the pressure of war. M. Broszat states that the possibility of massive deportations eastwards was ended when the German invasion of Russia became bogged down at the end of 1941. Hence, according to Broszat, 'the extermination of the Jews came about, it would seem, not only because of the professed intention to destroy them but also as a way out of the impasse into which the regime had manoeuvred itself.'[49] Furthermore, annihilation was 'not a steady, planned operation but was of a more improvised and fitful character, carried out by intensified *ad hoc* measures from time to time'.[49] This argument does not lessen the enormity of the crime committed between 1942 and 1945 but it does tend to reduce the emphasis on long-term plans for extermination. Only one historian seriously seeks to rehabilitate Hitler. D. Irving argues that the killing of Jews was initiated on Himmler's authority and that Hitler did not learn of it until 1943. Irving bases his claim on the lack of any specific evidence that Hitler had given an order for the extermination. Other historians, however, reject Irving's conclusion on the grounds that for Hitler not to have known would have been inconsistent with every other feature of the Nazi regime.

The Nazi economy

The main priorities in Hitler's economic policy were to maintain the support of as much of the population as possible while, at the same time, to revive Germany as a military and industrial power. This involved balancing the needs of the consumer and of the army. The result was generally a piecemeal approach, involving a considerable amount of confusion. According to Bracher, 'At no time did National Socialism develop a consistent economic or social theory.'[50]

There appear to have been four main phases in the emergence of an economic policy, although these did not follow on logically from each other. The first, lasting from

1933 until 1936, has been called a period of 'partial Fascism'. The state moved into a programme of job creation to reduce the levels of unemployment while, at the same time, seeking to control wages and eliminate trade union powers. In these respects there is some similarity to Mussolini's corporativism. But in other respects the government's economic policy was highly pragmatic, especially while it was under the direction of Schacht (President of the Reichsbank from March 1933 and Economics Minister from June 1934). He gave priority to developing a favourable trade balance by means of a series of bilateral trade agreements with the Balkans and South American states. These underdeveloped areas provided Germany with essential raw materials in return for German investment and credits for German industrial products. The complexities of foreign exchange were dealt with by the New Plan (September 1934) which regulated imports and the allocation of foreign exchange to key sectors of the German economy. Overall, Schacht was convinced that it was essential to raise the level of exports if Hitler's objective of increased military expenditure were to be realized.

By 1936 Hitler had begun to show impatience with Schacht's somewhat cautious approach and opted openly in his 'Memorandum' for 'military and political rearmament',[51] to be promoted by 'economic rearmament and mobilization'. The second economic phase therefore opened with the introduction of the 'Four Year Plan'. Under the direction of Goering, this completely undermined Schacht's position so that the latter felt compelled to resign his post in November 1937. The basic purpose of the Four Year Plan was to achieve self-sufficiency or autarky, in both industry and agriculture, through increased productivity and the development of substitutes for oil and other key items.[52] The Plan was not, however, entirely effective. Although some progress was made in the manufacture of substitutes, targets were not met for the production of rubber and synthetic fuels; synthetic petrol, for example, covered only 18 per cent of Germany's needs[51] and it was still necessary to import one-third of all the raw materials needed by industry. In many respects, the Four Year Plan was an improvised measure and there has been some controversy as to whether it was even intended as a preparation for war. W. Sauer[53] considers that there was a direct correlation between the Four Year Plan and the Second World War because Hitler, in effect, created a 'plunder economy' and 'committed himself also to starting a war in the near future'. B.H. Klein[53] and others, by contrast, maintain that Hitler tried as long as possible to buy both guns and butter and that he was not prepared to risk damaging the economy and thus alienate the ordinary consumer from the regime. Statistical evidence seems to point in both directions. Sauer's case would appear to be strengthened by the figures for military expenditure between 1933 and 1939:

1933	1.9 billion marks
1936	5.8 billion marks
1938	18.4 billion marks
1939	32.3 billion marks

On the other hand, there was an overall growth in the Nazi economy, so that the 1938 expenditure amounted to not more than 15 per cent of the gross national product.[53]

Whatever Hitler's real intentions, in 1939 the Nazi economy entered its third phase – armed conflict. Some historians feel that the outbreak of war was due less to deliberate planning than to an economic crisis from which there was no other escape. Rearmament was putting intolerable pressure on exports and foreign currency earnings and creating a shortage of labour in other sectors of the economy. Goering considered that Germany could move in one of only two directions. She could either return to the mainstream of world trade – at the cost of her commitment to rearmament. Or she could fight a successful war and plunder other economies. It was, however, vitally important that this war should be swift, as the German economy would not respond favourably to prolonged mobilization. The answer appeared to be the concept of *Blitzkrieg* – lightning war – which was as much an economic policy as a military strategy. A successful *Blitzkrieg* would, through a series of rapid victories, enable Germany to develop the means of more prolonged and complete mobilization in the future.

The fourth phase (1942–5) was the result of Hitler's drastic miscalculation. *Blitzkrieg* had worked brilliantly against Poland in 1939 and France in 1940, but it had not defeated Britain and, from the end of 1941, became bogged down in Russia. 1942 found Hitler with a major dilemma. He was obliged to contemplate reducing German armaments for the Russian campaign in order to construct a larger airforce and navy to deal with Britain. But, despite the destruction which she suffered at German hands in 1941, Russia had succeeded in fully mobilizing her economy. Germany had now no option but to respond. War production came under the control of Albert Speer and the Central Planning Board. The result was a more rapid increase in armaments, despite the heavy allied bombing of German cities between 1943 and 1944. Yet, even at this point, Germany was massively outproduced by the two peripheral industrial giants – the Soviet Union and the United States. As will be shown on pp. 217–18, this was a major factor in the eventual destruction of the Third Reich.

The social impact of economic policies

How were the German people affected by Nazi economic policies? There were a few overall advantages. By 1938 Germany had completely recovered from the impact of the Depression, and national income was 20 per cent higher than the previous peak of 1928. There had also been, since 1932, a rise in wages, a reduction in unemployment, an increase in food consumption by one-sixth, and a growth in the turnover of clothing by a quarter and household goods by a half.[54] Two further observations, however, somewhat lessen the impact of these figures. One is that the German consumer did not keep pace with those in Britain and the United States; Germany, for example, possessed only 500,000 cars, compared with 1 million in Britain and 23 million in the United States. Secondly, wages declined as a proportion of national income as a whole which meant the real benefits of economic growth accrued to the better-off.

In fact, different sections of the population were affected in different ways. The largest single group – the industrial workers – certainly benefited from the decrease in unemployment from 6 million in 1932 to 0.4 million in 1938. It has, however, been shown that the trend was already downwards before Hitler came to power in January 1933. Wages increased slowly, but were held down to the level of price rises and were fixed to a longer working week; in 1939 the number of hours worked per week averaged 47.8, an increase of 15.2 per cent on the 1932 level.[55] The collective influence of working-class organizations was steadily eroded, the trade union movement coming under a general ban from May 1933. The gap was filled by a pro-Nazi German Labour Front (DAF) under Robert Ley. Two other organizations were established: *Schönheit der Arbeit* (Beauty of Labour) and *Kraft durch Freude* (Strength through Joy), which had the overall effect of regulating leisure as well as working hours and increasing the possibilities for exploitation by employers.

Germany's rural population comprised three sections, all pro-Nazi at the outset of the regime. The peasants, or small landowners, were upheld by Nazi ideology as the backbone of the German race but there was a tendency to paint an idealized and highly unrealistic picture. The result was a series of damaging attempts by the government to freeze the peasantry into an unchanging class. The Reich Entailed Farm Law of 1933 severely limited the subdivision and sale of peasant plots, which inevitably prevented consolidation, mechanization and more effective use of fertilizers. The second group, agricultural workers, made very few substantial gains. Many continued to experience grinding poverty and migrated in desperation to the towns at a rate of 2.5 per cent per annum (compared with 1.5 per cent per annum before 1933). The third category, the wealthy landlords, were the only real beneficiaries of Nazi rule. The rapid increase in land values enabled them to retain their economic prominence, which partially offset the loss of some of their political influence.

The business sector comprised two main groups. The small businessman, usually from the middle class, was attracted at an early stage by Nazi promises to protect the 'small man' from the burden of monopolies. This group did benefit initially, mainly from the much tighter control over the labour force. On the whole, however, the NSDAP preferred to cultivate the support of big business which increased its ownership of industry from 40 per cent of the total in 1933 to

70 per cent by 1937; this was accomplished mostly through the absorption of the smaller enterprises. It is true that the state exercised greater influence and control during the period of the Four Year Plan. The new Hermann Goering works, for example, became a major state-owned steel producer. But some of the great names in private enterprise rapidly increased their profits. I.G. Farben, Germany's largest company, raised its profits by 150 per cent between 1938 and 1942. Great industrialists also collaborated closely with the government over the war effort – and worse: several, for example, supplied Auschwitz with equipment for the gas chambers. This co-operation between the government and big business has led some historians to see the Nazi regime as a bastion of capitalism. It would, however, be more appropriate to argue that Hitler decided at the outset to avoid confrontation with capitalism, even if, in the process, it meant swallowing a number of earlier economic principles.

Women, as a distinct social group, had a clearly defined place in the Nazi world. In a rally at Nuremberg in 1934 Hitler said that 'man's world is the State', while 'the world of woman is a smaller world. For her world is her husband, her family, her children and her house.'[56] According to Goebbels: 'The mission of woman is to be beautiful and to bring children into the world...the female prettifies herself for her mate and hatches the eggs for him.'[57] The initial policy was to ease women out of the top levels of the civil service, law, medicine and politics. Women were induced to stay at home by new 'marriage credits' and child bonuses.[58] The gradual decline of unemployment, however, created a new demand for labour. The result was the steady recruitment of women into both agriculture and industry, the total reaching 5.2 million by 1938. But the highly qualified never regained their former status. They were the real victims of Nazi policy.

Relations with the Churches

Germany has, since the Reformation, been divided between the Protestant north and the mainly Catholic south. Both denominations had been highly suspicious of what they saw as the blatant secularism of the Weimar Republic and were prepared to do a deal with the Nazi regime. Hitler's initial attitude was reassuring. He said in the Reichstag on 23 March 1933 that Christianity was 'the unshakeable foundation of the moral and ethical life of our people'.[57] There was, however, some doubt as to whether this was the real policy of the Nazis or merely a precaution to maintain a measure of support while the regime consolidated. The passage of time soon pointed to the latter.

The Protestant churches were prepared to welcome the arrival of the Nazi regime, regarding the Weimar Republic as unGerman and unGodly. Hitler took only six months to exploit this. In July 1933 the 28 provincial Protestant churches (*Landeskirchen*) were centralized into a single Reich Church, which soon came under Reich bishop Müller. Then, in 1935, the Reich Church was placed under the control of Hans Kerrl, minister of Church Affairs. There was also increasing evidence of the infiltration of Nazi values, with the establishment of the DC (German Christians). This sect managed to combine Christian beliefs with racism, anti-semitism and Führer-worship, laying itself open to the accusation that it was the 'SA of Jesus Christ'. In opposition to the DC there emerged the Confessional Church, under the leadership of Pastor Niemoller. It retained its political detachment from the Nazi regime and, perhaps because of this, was banned in 1937, Niemoller himself being interned in a concentration camp.

The Catholic Church was also willing to collaborate with Hitler in 1933. The Centre Party, still a political arm of Catholicism, had supported Hitler's Enabling Act (March 1933) in return for certain religious guarantees from the government. This compromise was followed, in the same year, by the Concordat, drawn up by Cardinal Pacelli for the Church and by von Papen for the political authorities. This promised continuing freedom of worship, the protection of denominational schools and the right to publish and distribute pastoral letters. In exchange, the Church agreed to withdraw totally from active politics; the Centre Party, for instance, dissolved itself voluntarily. The Nazis, however, soon subverted the agreement. Various organizations, like the Cross and Eagle League and the Working Group of Catholic Germans, sought to disseminate Nazi values, while the government deliberately discredited the clergy by holding public 'immorality' trials involving nuns and monks. By 1937 the situation had deteriorated so badly that Pope Pius XI abandoned his earlier neutrality and issued an encyclical called *'Mit brennender Sorge'* ('With Deep Anxiety') which was strongly critical of government measures. This was followed by growing disillusionment within the Catholic Church and real doubts about ultimate Nazi intentions towards religion.

By the late 1930s these intentions had come out into the open. As the Churches reacted with hostility to government attempts to Nazify them, many Party officials inclined increasingly to non-Christian forms of religion. One example was the German Faith Movement, which introduced pagan ceremonies (widely used by SS officials) and virulently attacked the most sacred tenets of Christianity. According to *Sigrune*, the journal of the German Faith Movement, 'Jesus was a cowardly Jewish lout who had certain adventures during his years of indiscretion'.[59] Two prominent Nazis were particularly anti-Christian. Julius Streicher, notorious anti-Semite and pornographer, claimed that the Crucifixion was an instance of Jewish ritual murder.[59] Martin Bormann declared in 1941 that 'The concepts of National Socialism and Christianity are irreconcilable.... Our National Socialist ideology is far loftier than the concepts of Christianity, which in their essential points have been taken over from Jewry.'[57] Given these extreme viewpoints, it is hardly surprising that the Nazi regime was considering banning the Churches altogether as soon as the war had been won.

Did Nazi persecution inflict any lasting damage? I. Kershaw provides several examples of the resilience of Christianity in Germany. During the 1930s there was no significant decline in Church membership, while an actual increase occurred during the war years. Meanwhile, the clergy managed to maintain a considerable influence over the laity.[60] In the long term, the impact of the Churches on politics was actually strengthened, as was shown in the Catholic base of post-war Germany's CDU (Christian Democratic Union). Everything, therefore, 'points to the conclusion that Nazi policy failed categorically to break down religious allegiances'.[60]

The opposition

During the twelve-year history of the Third Reich there was no means of expressing a political or ideological choice. Support for the regime was built up in three ways. First, the Nazis had a diverse and genuine appeal to different sections of the population, as has been shown elsewhere in this chapter. The middle classes, big business, the landowners, peasantry, the army and youth were attracted by a combination of growing prosperity, reduced unemployment, strong leadership and successful foreign policy. Second, support was induced through the twin processes of propaganda and indoctrination, which aimed at creating total acquiescence. The third method was applied where the other two failed: the SS and Gestapo dealt with any signs of dissent through a system of organized terror.

The longer the regime was established the more difficult it became to resist it. The opposition was never a united force and comprised different groups with conflicting interests and objectives. To make matters worse, *any* opposition carried with it the taint of treason rather than, as in wartime France and Yugoslavia, the aura of patriotism. This was one of the disadvantages of living under a home-bred rather than a foreign-based dictatorship.

There were, nevertheless, two major groups prepared to take the chance. One was the opposition based on the left, according to R.O. Paxton 'the earliest and, at least numerically, the largest.'[61] The Communists had been taken completely by surprise by Hitler's rise to power in 1933, but managed gradually to build up a propaganda campaign and organized secret cells in an attempt to penetrate the factories. The Social Democrats also disseminated material and had an efficient *émigré* organization under Ernst Schumacher, initially in Prague and, from 1937, in Paris. There were, however, several major obstacles to successful resistance by the left.

The most serious was the negative influence which Stalin continued to impose on the KPD (German Communist Party); he effectively abandoned it to the Gestapo and SS when in 1939 he moved closer to Germany and agreed eventually to sign the Nazi–Soviet Non-Aggression Pact. In addition, the long-standing mutual distrust between Communists and Socialists continued undiminished, even while both were being persecuted by the Nazis. The Communists still regarded the SPD as 'Social Fascists', while the SPD associated the KPD with the unacceptable totalitarianism of the Soviet Union. The KPD and SPD had not been willing to combine to save the Weimar Republic; nor could they now do so to threaten the Third Reich.

At the other end of the political spectrum, Germany's conservatives – civilian and military – also took a stand against Nazi philosophy and policies. They showed a predominantly Prussian and traditionalist distrust of the revolutionary right and were also influenced by prominent Christian dissidents. The first actual attempt to change the regime occurred in 1938, when General Beck tried to persuade the General Staff to remove Hitler and, at the same time, requests were made to the British government to take a firm line over Hitler's claims to the Sudetenland province of Czechoslovakia. This conspiracy never got off the ground: the Commander-in-Chief, Brauchitsch, refused to become involved, while the British Foreign Office preferred to solve the Czech crisis by doing a deal with Hitler. Completely isolated, Beck resigned his post, fortunate perhaps that his scheme was not divulged to the Führer.

After the outbreak of war opposition acquired a greater urgency while, at the same time, becoming more difficult. The traditional right now felt that Hitler was set on a course for military defeat. Ulrich von Hassell, former German ambassador to Italy, warned that 'among informed people there is a growing awareness of our impending disaster'.[62] Other prominent opponents included Goerdeler, von Koltke and von Wartenburg. The most famous example of a resistance organization was the Kreisau Circle, which convened at Moltke's estate in Silesia. The most serious blow to the regime was struck on 20 July 1944, when Stauffenberg placed a bomb in Hitler's military headquarters at Rastenberg in East Prussia. Hitler escaped shaken, but alive, and exacted a terrible revenge on all suspected participants in the plot against him. Generals Beck and Rommel committed suicide, while many other known opponents of the regime were put through a mockery of a trial, presided over by Judge Roland Freisler, and hanged with nooses of piano wire from meat-hooks. The trial and execution were filmed for the personal viewing of Hitler and his immediate circle. According to K. Hildebrand, 'The Prussian nobility, which had led the conspiracy, paid a high price in blood.'[63]

In retrospect, there seem to be two views about the importance of the conservative opposition to Hitler. One is that it was a major failure. 'In the end Hitler was removed only by the kind of military defeat and disintegration of the German state at the hands of invading armies that the conservative opposition had tried desperately to avoid.'[61] On the other hand, it could be argued, the martyrdom of this opposition was vitally important for the salvation of post-war German self-respect, providing at least one genuine note in the process of deNazification.

GERMAN FOREIGN POLICY 1919–39

Background: the period 1919–33

By far the most important influence behind German foreign policy before the rise of Hitler was the Treaty of Versailles. Since this was fundamental to the mainstream of European diplomacy, its terms and significance have already been examined (see pp. 6–10).

The Treaty of Versailles caused great bitterness in Germany. There it was condemned by the entire range of political opinion, from far left to extreme right. It was seen by Hugo Preuss, a prominent politician and legal expert, as a severe blow to the new Republic; he referred to the 'criminal madness of the Versailles *Diktat*'[64] and claimed that the new constitution 'was born with this curse upon it'. It was hardly surprising, therefore, that the major objective of the Republic's foreign policy was to lift the burden of Versailles and seek a revised settlement. The question, of course, was how could this be accomplished?

One of the earliest strategies was that devised by Joseph Wirth, Chancellor for two brief periods in 1921 and 1922. This was the policy of 'fulfilment', a strange approach which, according to J.W. Hiden, was 'a necessary expedient based on the premise that to show determined good faith in trying to carry out the peace terms properly would not only demonstrate how impossible a task this was, but would therefore also induce the Allied powers to be more lenient in interpreting the treaty'.[65] In other words, let the Treaty discredit and destroy itself through its very harshness. The British government was not unsympathetic, but the French were determined that the Treaty should be applied to the letter. Hence, when Germany defaulted on a reparations payment of a specified number of telegraph poles, French troops entered and occupied the Ruhr in 1923. The policy of 'fulfilment' was immediately replaced by one of passive resistance called for by the chancellor, Wilhelm Cuno. Relations between Germany and the western powers had therefore reached a dangerous low.

Elsewhere, Wirth had been more successful. He succeeded in opening up diplomatic relations with Europe's other isolated power, Bolshevik Russia. Page 60 describes how representatives of Germany and Russia used the international conference at Genoa (1922) as a front for their own Treaty of Rapallo. This established diplomatic relations between the two states and laid the foundations for commercial contacts and economic co-operation. Rapallo was a diplomatic triumph for the Weimar Republic in eastern Europe, but clearly something had to be done to improve relations with the west.

This was to be the work of Gustav Stresemann. Chancellor in 1923 and Foreign Minister between 1923 and 1929, he pursued a skilful combination of aims. He intended, on the one hand, to rebuild cordial relations with other states and to remove the underlying international tensions which Europe had experienced in the early 1920s. He even saw Germany as 'the bridge which would bring East and West together in the development of Europe'. For his promotion of *détente* and his condemnation of war, Stresemann has sometimes been called a 'good European'. On the other hand, he was also a patriot who was as convinced as anyone that the Treaty of Versailles must eventually be revised. Much of his diplomacy was therefore double-edged. He once observed: 'We must get the stranglehold off our neck. On that account, German policy, as Metternich said of Austria, no doubt after 1809, will have to be one of finesse.'[66] More specifically, he had three objectives. One was 'the solution of the Reparations question in a sense tolerable for Germany'. A second was the 'protection of Germans abroad, those 10 to 12 millions of our kindred who now live under a foreign yoke in foreign lands'.[66] Thirdly, he hoped eventually for 'the readjustment of our eastern frontiers'. The other face of the 'good European' was, therefore, the 'good German'.

There are three particularly important examples of Stresemann's policy of reconciliation between Germany and the rest of Europe. These were Germany's accession to the Locarno Pact (1925), her membership of the League of Nations (1926) and her involvement in the Kellogg–Briand Pact of 1928. These all seemed to indicate that Germany was now a reformed and rehabilitated power. Yet, at the same time, Stresemann was pursuing covert policies which benefited Germany at the expense of the rest of Europe and which were clearly revisionist in intention. H.W. Gatzke refers to Stresemann's 'appeasement abroad' and 'rearmament at home'. A good example of the latter was the 1926 Treaty of Berlin between Germany and Russia. This extended the earlier relationship established by the Treaty of Rapallo. Both powers now agreed to remain neutral if either were involved in a war with a third country. Even more significant, however, was Germany's use of her special relationship with Russia as a means of evading the rearmament restrictions imposed by the Treaty of Versailles. The German army (*Reichswehr*), under von Seeckt, derived a great deal from secret training and manoeuvres on Russian soil. Stresemann's attitude to Germany's secret rearmament ranged, in the words of Gatzke, 'from passive acceptance to active assistance'.[67] This was because co-operation and *détente* needed, in Stresemann's view, to be accompanied by an increase in self-confidence and strength. Hence, in Stresemann's words, 'The main asset [of a strong foreign policy] is material power – army and navy'.[67]

What was the extent of Stresemann's success? Between his

death in 1929 and the accession of Hitler in 1933, Germany experienced several positive developments. The Allied powers removed in 1930 all the occupying troops still in the Rhineland and, in 1932, the Lausanne Conference judged it expedient to alter radically the method by which Germany should pay reparations. It might, therefore, be thought that revisionism had made substantial inroads into the Versailles Settlement. Yet, during this same period, the Weimar Republic's foreign policy experienced a profound crisis. The Great Depression upset the Republic's political stability and caused a swing to the parties of the right (see pp. 142–5) and 154–5). These had always opposed Stresemann's policies of *détente* and collaboration with the west. Hitler, especially, increased the intensity of his attacks on the Republic, reviving the myth that the German army had been 'stabbed in the back' in 1918 and that the Republic had always been dominated by the 'November Criminals', the 'traitors' of the First World War. The way was therefore open for the more intensive pursuit of revisionism by a regime which took full advantage of the head-start provided by the Stresemann era but which rejected Stresemann's moderation.

The period 1933–9

Hitler assumed responsibility for German foreign policy in January 1933. Although he had a considerable number of preconceived ideas, he decided that his initial strategy should be cautious and moderate. The main reason for this was Germany's still vulnerable position in Europe. She was still regarded by the western powers as a defeated state, under the constraints of the Treaty of Versailles. Furthermore, the German government still had to contend with the manifest distrust shown by France and with the extensive system of alliances constructed by France in eastern Europe. Germany had not yet developed a counter-alliance, unless the pact with Russia, renewed in 1931, is included. Fascist Italy, perhaps the most likely prospect for an alliance with Germany, was at this stage hostile to Germany's designs on Austria, since Mussolini had not yet abandoned the possibility of expanding Italy's frontiers into the Alps. Between 1933 and 1935, therefore, Hitler had little option but to make conciliatory diplomatic gestures and to lull the suspicions of the rest of Europe. At the same time, he clearly intended to revive Germany's military power; the problem was, he said to his generals, that this 'building of the armed forces' was also 'the most dangerous time'.[68] He must, therefore, avoid any possibility of retaliation.

An example of Hitler's early diplomacy was his attitude to the Geneva disarmament conference (1932–3) and its immediate follow-up. The politicians of the Weimar Republic, especially Stresemann, had shown interest in the case for a general reduction of armaments throughout Europe, since this would help offset the one-sidedness of the Versailles provisions. Hitler, however, was less interested in this type of approach for, as G.A. Craig points out, he intended to *exploit* Germany's grievance over arms, not deprive her of it.[69] He certainly wanted to avoid any future limitations on German rearmament but without being blatantly provocative. His opportunity came when the British Prime Minister, Macdonald, proposed a reduction of French troops from 500,000 to 200,000 and an increase in German troops to parity with the French. This was far below Hitler's expectations; he knew, however, that the French would reject the proposal and was therefore able to project a moderate image in supporting Macdonald. When the French did decline the offer, Hitler withdrew from the Disarmament Conference and then from the League of Nations. Realizing that this might provoke some sort of retaliation, he decided to cover his tracks with bilateral agreements which could later be broken. In 1934, therefore, he drew up a Non-Aggression Pact with Poland. This was partly to break the French system of alliances in eastern Europe and partly to allay the suspicions of western Europe that he had long-term designs on Polish territory. In reality, of course, he had no intention of keeping to the Pact. He declared, privately, 'All our agreements with Poland have a purely temporary significance.'[69] For the time being, however, he decided to conceal his hand.

Hitler's pretended moderation encountered a setback in 1934 when the Austrian Nazis assassinated Chancellor Dollfuss in an abortive attempt to seize power and achieve a political union with Germany. Hitler was seriously embarrassed by this development which set back the possibility of closer relations between Germany and Italy. He was therefore obliged to play down the activities of the Austrian Nazis, since he was not yet strong enough to use such opportunities to further a more aggressive course. Much would depend on the success of his rearmament policy. What stage had this reached by 1935?

There had never been any question of Hitler abiding by the disarmament provisions of the Treaty of Versailles. When he came to power in 1933 he inherited 10 divisions; by the middle of 1934 he had increased the total to 240,000 men, more than twice the number allowed by Versailles. By 1935 there was no longer any point in pretending. On 11 March he formally announced the existence of a German airforce. On 16 March he issued a decree introducing conscription and warning that the military provisions of Versailles would no longer be observed. The reaction of the other powers posed a major diplomatic problem which Hitler needed to resolve. The League of Nations formally censured Germany's unilateral decision to rearm and, in April 1935, Britain, France and Italy formed the Stresa Front. In the following month, France responded of her own accord by drawing up a mutual assistance pact with the Soviet Union. It seemed that Germany had reached the critical phase of almost total isolation.

The period 1935–7, however, provided Hitler with a series of opportunities. He was able to end German isolation, put pressure on Britain and France and bring together a formidable diplomatic combination in central Europe. He was greatly assisted in accomplishing all this by favourable external trends and events.

The first of these was the reluctance of the British government to become involved in continental obligations, which meant that it was always receptive to a deal on armaments levels. In June 1935 Hitler secured an Anglo-German Naval Pact by which he undertook not to build a German fleet beyond 35 per cent of the total British strength. This was another example of Hitler's preference for bilateral agreements and it ruined any chance that the Stresa Front might be able to put concerted pressure on Germany: France and Italy were both furious with Britain's co-operation with Hitler. But the real windfall for Hitler was the involvement of Italy, from 1935 onwards, in Ethiopia (see pp. 119–21). This had several beneficial results for Germany. Imperial expansion diverted Italian attention away from Austria, Hitler's target to the south. It also had considerable diplomatic repercussions as Britain and France antagonized Italy by applying economic sanctions. Above all, Britain now saw Italy as a potentially hostile power and became more apprehensive than ever about commitments in Europe; she needed to be free to deal, if necessary, with Italian threats in the Mediterranean or Africa. Hitler therefore gambled that Britain would not be prepared to back any military action by France to prevent any further breaches of the Treaty of Versailles. He decided to remilitarize the Rhineland ahead of his original target. This he accomplished in March 1936 with only 22,000 troops, against the advice of his generals who feared instant retaliation. His judgement proved correct. The British government, anxious not to become involved, took no action and persuaded the French government to do likewise.

From this stage onwards Hitler was able to construct a new network of partners and satellites. Italy, involved in the Ethiopian adventure and the Spanish Civil War (see pp. 121–2) was no longer a rival in central Europe and gravitated towards Germany in the 'Rome-Berlin Axis' of 1936. At the same time, Hitler extended the scope of his diplomacy to outflank France. He assisted Franco to replace the Spanish Republic with a far right regime deeply hostile to the French Republic. Russia, France's partner since 1935, was the target of the Anti-Comintern Pact, draw up in November 1936 between Germany and Japan and eventually including Italy. Meanwhile, Germany was also implementing the Four Year Plan and a policy of autarky which involved the economic penetration of Rumania, Yugoslavia, Bulgaria and Greece (see pp. 174–5). By the end of 1937, Hitler's position was sufficiently secure for him to consider adopting a more openly aggressive policy.

Therefore, in November 1937, Hitler summoned to a special conference the War Minister (Blomberg), the Commander-in-Chief of the navy (Raedar), Commander-in-Chief of the army (Fritsch), Commander-in-Chief of the airforce (Goering), and Foreign Minister (Neurath). The sixth person present was Colonel Hossbach whose unofficial record of the meeting is generally known as the Hossbach Memorandum. According to this document, Hitler revealed the underlying purpose of his foreign policy and his hopes for the future, including schemes for the enlargement of Germany. Hitler added that there was some urgency because his plans would be resisted by Britain and France, and Germany's military superiority could not be expected to last beyond the period 1943–5. The Hossbach Memorandum, therefore, clearly indicates a change in the tempo of Hitler's diplomacy. It has been argued that Hitler was now willing to run high risks to attain his objectives and that he was prepared, if necessary, to launch a series of swift military campaigns. His new approach came as something of a shock to some of his subordinates, who inevitably tried to point out the dangers involved. Hitler's response to this was to reorganize the structure of the army and to replace Blomberg, Fritsch and Neurath. He was clearly determined to remove any obstruction to the next phase of his foreign policy.

Two targets were particularly prominent in 1938: Austria and Czechoslovakia. In March he accomplished the long-intended *Anschluss* and, in defiance of the Treaty of Versailles, incorporated Austria directly into the Reich. The result was a radical change in the balance of power in central and south-eastern Europe. Germany now had a joint border with Italy, completely outflanked Czechoslovakia and had gained direct access to Hungary and the Balkans. Hitler had also scored a major personal triumph: once again he had ignored warnings that his action would provoke foreign intervention and once again he had been proved right. Indeed, the ease with which the *Anschluss* had been accomplished led inexorably to the next undertaking. This was the removal of the German-populated Sudetenland from Czechoslovakia and its incorporation into the Reich (see p. 293). Again, this has been seen as a 'virtuoso performance'.[69] Hitler used a variety of expedients; these included the use of Henlein's Sudeten Nazis as an internal pressure group, and the serious differences between the provinces of Bohemia and Slovakia (see pp. 293–4). According to Noakes and Pridham, 'Hitler now proceeded to use the ethnic diversity of the country as a lever with which to break it up into its ethnic components.'[70] Above all, he exploited the unwillingness of Britain and France to take direct action in support of Czechoslovakia. The result was the Munich Agreement (29 September 1938) which allowed Hitler to annex the Sudetenland to the Reich. In return Chamberlain, the British Prime Minister, secured a promise that Britain and Germany would 'never go to war with one another again'. The whole episode showed the bankruptcy of collective security, of Franco-Soviet co-operation and of the British policy of appeasement. The Munich Agreement, conversely, built up Hitler's image within Germany and convinced him absolutely of his ability to accomplish the objectives outlined in the Hossbach Memorandum.

There is a school of thought that Hitler actually saw Munich as something of a failure – that he had allowed himself to be talked into making a diplomatic agreement instead of going ahead with the military option which he had threatened throughout the crisis. He certainly made up for this during the course of 1939. Once again working on an internal crisis, he engineered the break-up of Czechoslovakia (see p. 293) and, in March, incorporated Bohemia and Moravia into the Reich. Having accomplished his objectives in central Europe, Hitler turned his attention eastwards, gaining Meme from Lithuania. He was now determined to complete the union of all Germans within the Reich, recover the last vestiges of territory lost at Versailles, and begin the process of *Lebensraum*.

This meant that his next victim was Poland. Hitler swiftly stepped up the pressure by demanding Danzig and the Polish corridor, only to meet determined resistance from the Polish Foreign Minister, Beck. By this stage, Poland was bolstered up by an Anglo-French guarantee. This had been delivered in March and was a clear indication that the western powers had finally come to recognize the futility of appeasement. Hitler was, however, utterly confident that he could continue to outwit Britain and France. He was convinced that the British government was bluffing and that France would not go to war alone against Germany. In any case, he made his own position more secure by drawing up in May 1939 the Pact of Steel with Italy (see pp. 123–4) and in August the Non-Aggression Pact with the Soviet Union (see pp. 64–5). The latter was a major diplomatic turnabout which made a nonsense of any undertaking by the west to protect Poland. Hitler still expected to avoid a conflict with Britain by seeming to negotiate further with the Polish government and, through a series of manufactured border incidents, providing evidence of Polish 'aggression'. But his invasion of Poland on 1 September 1939 provoked declarations of war from both Britain and France, much to Hitler's surprise. He was also let down at the last minute by his most important ally: Mussolini felt obliged to inform Hitler that Italy was insufficiently equipped at this stage to undertake direct military action (see p. 124). Despite these unexpected obstacles, Hitler was supremely confident of success and proceeded to demonstrate the awesome power of the new German army operating a *Blitzkrieg* strategy.

The aims of Hitler's foreign policy

While the statesmen of the Weimar Republic were trying in the 1920s to achieve a revision of the Versailles Settlement and, at the same time, effect a reconciliation with the other powers, Hitler was already devising more elaborate schemes, to which he added substantially in the 1930s and early 1940s. There are three major sources for discerning Hitler's ideas. The first, of course, is *Mein Kampf*, written in Landsberg Prison, and subsequently published; it achieved a mass circulation and was read by millions of Germans. The second is Hitler's *Zweites Buch*, which dealt explicitly with foreign policy but remained unpublished in his lifetime. The third source is a series of spoken remarks made by Hitler and edited by Dr Henry Picker as Hitler's *Tischgespräche* (Table-Talk). Because of the undisciplined and often rambling nature of these works it is difficult to put together a carefully structured outline of his policy. The basic aims, however, seem clear enough.

He maintained that all previous governments had been

restricted in their foreign policy by the notion of the 'fixed frontier'. Even the conservatives and neo-Bismarckians were wrong to aim at recreating the territorial arrangements of 1914, for 'the German borders of the year 1914 were borders which presented something incomplete'. As an alternative to the 'border policy' of the 'national bourgeois' world, the Nazis would follow a 'territorial one', the whole purpose of which would be 'to secure the space necessary to the life of our people'. The limited policies of Bismarck had, perhaps, been necessary to establish and build up the 'power structure' for the future. But Bismarck's successors had denied Germany her natural process of expansion and had pursued an 'insane' policy of alliance with Austria-Hungary and maritime conflict with Britain. Now the mistakes of history should be rectified, *Lebensraum* could be achieved, and the 'inferior races' could be deprived of the territory to which their low productivity and potential gave them no natural right. 'According to an eternal law of Nature, the right to the land belongs to the one who conquers the land because the old boundaries did not yield sufficient space for the growth of the population'. Returning to the theme of struggle which had permeated *Mein Kampf*, Hitler affirmed: 'Every healthy, vigorous people sees nothing sinful in territorial acquisition, but something quite in keeping with its nature.' The intended direction of this expansion was made abundantly clear in *Mein Kampf*: 'We put a stop to the eternal movement of the Germanic people to Europe's South and West and we turn our eyes to the land in the East.' More specifically, 'In speaking of new territory in Europe, we can, above all, have in mind only Russia and its subjugated border states.'[71]

Did these ideas gradually evolve into an overall programme, a blueprint which Hitler intended to follow? This question has produced one of the major historical controversies within the theme of Nazi foreign policy.

On the one hand, some historians emphasize the fundamental logic of Hitler's designs and acknowledge that he did develop a definite programme and set of intentions. These so-called 'programmists' and 'intentionalists' owe much to the pioneering work of Trevor Roper, who maintained that *Mein Kampf* was 'a complete blueprint of his intended achievements'.[72] More recently, it has been argued, by A. Hillgruber, that Hitler pursued his aims systematically 'without, however, forfeiting any of his tactical flexibility'.[73] Similar views are expressed by E. Jäckel, who claims that Hitler's 'programme of foreign policy' can be divided into three phases:

> During the first phase, Germany had to achieve internal consolidation and rearmament and to conclude agreements with Britain and Italy. During the second phase Germany had to defeat France in a preliminary engagement. Then the great war of conquest against Russia could take place during the third and final phase.[74]

Jäckel also maintains that there is 'ample documentary evidence to prove that he always kept this outline in mind'.[74] There is an alternative 'programme', pointed to by other historians but overlapping that deduced by Jäckel. Hitler's first priority was to destroy the Versailles Settlement and rearm Germany. This would be followed by the creation of an enlarged Reich which would incorporate all of Europe's German population. This, in turn, would be the prelude to the achievement of *Lebensraum* from conquered territory in Poland and Russia.

The 'intentionalist' school is in broad agreement on Hitler's formulation of a programme or series of objectives. There is, however, a sub-debate between what might be termed the 'continentalists' and the 'globalists'.[75] The former maintain that Hitler's objective was the conquest of *Lebensraum* in the east. According to Jäckel, 'Hitler's main aim in foreign policy was a war of conquest against the Soviet Union.'[76] But a considerable number of German historians now claim that Hitler had an aim which transcended the defeat of Russia and the achievement of *Lebensraum*, namely world conquest. These include Hillgruber, who believes that Hitler's policy geographically 'was designed to span the globe; ideologically, too, the doctrines of universal anti-semitism and social Darwinism, fundamental to his programme, were intended to embrace the whole of mankind'.[77] Thies is in broad agreement with this; 'at no time between 1920 and 1945 did [Hitler], as his statements prove, lose sight of the aim of world domination'.[75] Other 'globalists' include Hildebrand

and Hauner; according to the latter, Hitler's power would be spread 'in a series of blitz campaigns, extending stage by stage over the entire globe'.[75] As events turned out, of course, Hitler was never able to achieve 'more than the opening moves of the continental phase of his programme'.[77]

There is a school of thought which denies that Hitler pursued a particular programme in his foreign policy. Rather, he was profoundly influenced by the needs of the moment. This case has been put most forcefully by A.J.P. Taylor, who argues that Hitler's projects, as outlined in the Hossbach Memorandum, were 'in large part day-dreaming, unrelated to what followed in real life'. In his opinion, 'Hitler was gambling on some twist of fortune which would present him with success in foreign affairs, just as a miracle had made him Chancellor in 1933.'[78] There has been qualified support for this line of thought, although for different reasons. Mommsen, for example, argues that Hitler did little to shape his foreign policy and that his whole approach was spontaneous – a series of responses to specific developments: 'in reality the regime's foreign policy ambitions were many and varied, without any clear aims and only linked by their ultimate goal: hindsight alone gives them some air of consistency'.[79] M. Broszat, too, points to the lack of any fundamental design and maintains that *Lebensraum* was basically an expression of the need to sustain a dynamic momentum.[75]

An overall synthesis was suggested by one of the earliest and best known historians on the Hitler era, A. Bullock. He submits that both claims – whether for preliminary planning or disorganized spontaneity – have to be combined. Hitler, after all, 'had only one programme: power, first his own power in Germany, and then the expansion of German power in Europe'.[80] Elsewhere, Bullock maintains that 'he was at once both fanatical and cynical'.[81]

Another major debate on Hitler's foreign policy is whether there is an underlying continuity with early periods. The original argument was that there was a fundamental break, both with the foreign policy of the Weimar Republic and with that of the Kaiser's Second Reich. But this earlier consensus was shattered during the late 1960s by F. Fischer who, in *Germany's Aims in the First World War*,[82] claimed that

Germany deliberately engineered the conflict in order to pursue expansionist aims which were really a prelude to those of Hitler. These aims had included: economic dominance over Belgium, Holland and France; hegemony over Courland, Livonia, Estonia, Lithuania and Poland, as well as over Bulgaria, Rumania and Turkey; unification with Austria and the creation of a Greater Germany; control over the Eastern Mediterranean; and rule over a dismantled Russia. Clearly, in the light of such a programme, Hitler's objectives would appear far from new; they could more appropriately be called a continuation than a radical departure.

Of course, these 'war plans' were never actually implemented. The Second Reich lost the First World War and was itself replaced by the more moderate Weimar Republic. Here, surely, would be a case for denying continuity? Yet certain trends can be detected linking the Weimar Republic and the Third Reich. In the first place, there was considerable continuity of military and diplomatic personnel which lasted until Hitler's radical changes in 1938. The Weimar Republic had contained, within the foreign ministry, men like Neurath and Bülow, who also served Hitler for the first 5 years of the Third Reich. Much the same applied to Germany's ambassadors abroad, drawn as they were largely from the former aristocracy. This continuity of personnel at first lessened the likelihood of any sudden and dramatic switch of policy. In any case, it could be argued, Hitler was able to continue with the objectives of the Republic as long as he concentrated on whittling away the Versailles Settlement. Indeed, by 1938 he had accomplished the targets of the Republic's revisionists; Germany had regained full sovereignty over all internal territories, including the Saar and Rhineland; the restrictions on armaments had been ignored since 1935; and the Germans of Austria and the Sudetenland had been incorporated into the Reich.

In retrospect, however, it is obvious that the continuity between the diplomacy of the Weimar Republic and the Third Reich can be misleading. The crucial point which showed that Nazi foreign policy was as revolutionary as its domestic counterpart was that Hitler saw revisionism merely as a step towards projects which were well beyond the ambitions of the Republic's statesmen. Although the Republic's politicans had a strong element of opportunism, even ruthlessness, they did not share Hitler's Social Darwinism and racialist vision. They also respected the traditions of European diplomacy and, under Stresemann, contributed much to international co-operation. One of Hitler's aims was to smash the multilateral agreements, like the Locarno Pact, which had been carefully built up during the 1920s. As for the continuity of personnel, it suited Hitler to retain the appointments made by the Republic, so that he could give his regime a facade of moderation and respectability during the period of maximum vulnerability. As soon as he had accomplished safe levels of rearmament he instituted radical changes, both in his policy and his appointments. The turning-point was clearly the Hossbach Memorandum of 1937 and its follow-up. The developments of 1939, too, went far beyond any Republican revisionism. According to Noakes and Pridham, 'It is in the policy pursued in Poland after 1939 and in Russia after 1941 that the distinction between Nazism and conservative German nationalism emerges clearly for the first time.'[83]

Hitler and the outbreak of the Second World War

The Nuremberg Judgement maintained that the Second World War was the outcome of Nazi policy and of Hitler's determination 'not to depart from the course he had set for himself'.[84] This raises the fundamental question: was the conflict really Hitler's war?

The majority opinion is that it was. The previous section provided an outline of the various arguments about Hitler's plans for European and world mastery, which are clearly relevant to the debate on the origins of the Second World War. There has also been much emphasis on what Hitler himself had to say about struggle and war. *Mein Kampf*, the *Zweites Buch* and the *Tischgespräche* all focus on militarism and unlimited expansion, together with the notion that struggle and war were fundamental human activities and needs. 'War is the most natural, the most ordinary thing. War is a constant; war is everywhere. There is no beginning, there is no conclusion of peace. War is life. All struggle is war. War

·is the primal condition.' The logical conclusion, therefore, is that Hitler *wanted* war, not only to achieve the objectives of his foreign policy, but also to purify and strengthen the Aryan race. Hitler's responsibility for the outbreak of war is emphasized by a variety of British, German and American historians. R.J. Sontag, for example, argues that Hitler's policy in 1939 was, 'like the annexation of Austria and the Sudeten districts of Czechoslovakia, merely preliminary to the task of winning "living space" '.[85] Trevor-Roper believes that 'The Second World War was Hitler's personal war in many senses. He intended it, he prepared for it, he chose the moment for launching it.'[86] J. Fest, one of the most recent German biographers of Hitler, affirmed the orthodoxy that 'who caused the war is a question that cannot be seriously raised'.[87] Much the same conclusion has been arrived at by Hillgruber, Hildebrand and G.L. Weinberg.

There is, however, an alternative view, pioneered by A.J.P. Taylor. Again, this relates to his argument that Hitler lacked any specific programme or long-term objectives, as outlined in the previous section. Instead of pursuing policies which led inevitably to war, Taylor argues, Hitler was, by and large, continuing those of the Second Reich and the Weimar Republic. He goes further. 'Hitler was no more wicked and unscrupulous than many other contemporary statesmen', although 'in wicked acts he outdid them all'. Hitler's diplomacy was based on short-term expedients and he doubted that a major conflict would be the outcome. According to part of the Hossbach Memorandum: 'He was convinced of Britain's non-participation, and therefore he did not believe in the probability of belligerent action by France against Germany.' According to Taylor, the Hossbach Memorandum contained no plans for war.

> and would never have been supposed to do so, unless it had been displayed at Nuremberg. The memorandum tells us, what we know already, that Hitler (like every other German statesman) intended Germany to become the dominant Power in Europe. It also tells us that he speculated how this might happen. His speculations were mistaken. They bear hardly any relation to the actual outbreak of war in 1939.[78]

He also maintains that Germany was not really ready for war in 1939 – the levels of armaments confirm that Germany had not developed an advantage over Britain and France.

There has been considerable criticism of the Taylor thesis, both from historians convinced that Hitler *did* have long-term objectives which included war (for example, Trevor Roper) and those who, although less convinced about this, feel that Taylor's approach is too narrow. One method of criticism is to remove the debate from the predominantly diplomatic ground which Taylor preferred to occupy and focus, instead, on the economy. T. Mason, for example, argues that Taylor's view 'leads to an overwhelming concentration on the sequence of diplomatic events', that his judgements 'rest very largely upon the diplomatic documents' and that

> these documents were primarily the work of conservative German diplomats, who, in dealing with their specific problems, were able to cover up or ignore the distinctive language and concepts of National Socialism. This helps to nurture the illusion that the foreign policy of the Third Reich was much the same as that of the Weimar Republic.[88]

Instead, Mason argues, Hitler deliberately chose war in 1939 as a way out of the difficulties faced by the German economy.

There is, finally, an approach which would apportion at least part of the responsibility for the outbreak of war to the other powers. In this case, however, responsibility is associated less with 'guilt' than with 'misinterpretation', 'inconsistency' and 'default'. It has been argued that Hitler's progress towards war was unintentionally accelerated by western leaders, paradoxically, because of their very hatred of war. Daladier and Chamberlain, who found war morally repugnant, assumed that the rationale of all diplomacy was the pursuit of peace. Chamberlain, in particular, made the crucial mistake of assuming that even Hitler had fixed objectives and that if these were conceded to him, the causes of international tension would be removed. Hitler, of course, was greatly encouraged by the pressure exerted on the smaller states by the British and French governments and mistook forbearance in the interests of peace for weakness and diplomatic capitulation. This explains the increasingly aggressive stance which he adopted during the Sudeten crisis of 1938. By 1939 Chamberlain had at last got the true measure of Hitler and decided to extend guarantees to Poland. This sudden switch appeared to be a desperate turn within a bankrupt policy and clearly failed to convince Hitler of Chamberlain's seriousness. B. Liddell Hart compared the pre-war crises with allowing someone to stoke up a boiler until the pressure rose to danger level – and then closing the safety valve. It could certainly be said that the western powers let Hitler accomplish so many of his objectives before 1939 that they actually precipitated conflict by eventually trying to stand firm. On the other hand, according to R. Henig, one cannot argue

> that firmer action before 1939 would have prevented war. It might have precipitated it earlier. Evidence seems to suggest fairly clearly that Hitler was determined to fight in October 1938 to gain Sudeten Czech territory. It might have been better, from a military point of view, for Britain and France to have fought then rather than later. This would not have prevented war but it might well have localized it.[89]

GERMANY AT WAR 1939–45

Introduction

German involvement in the Second World War is often divided into two distinct phases.

The first was the period of *Blitzkrieg* or 'lightning war'. This saw a series of rapid military victories over Poland, western Europe and the Balkans, as well as initial success against Russia (see pp. 203–7), bringing most of Europe under German control (see pp. 207–14). The main reasons for the *Blitzkrieg* strategy are dealt with on p. 177; Hitler's basic intention was to make the most efficient use possible of Germany's limited economy and, through a series of swift conquests, build up a new and more powerful basis for future operations, possibly on a world scale.

The second period was one of total war (1942–5). By this time *Blitzkrieg* had clearly failed to defeat Britain and the Soviet Union and proved helpless against the United States. During this second phase, Germany was slowly but inexorably ground down by the overwhelmingly greater industrial capacity of the Allies (see pp. 214–17), who were much more effectively geared to fight a prolonged war. In retrospect, it is surprising not that Germany lost the war but that she survived so long.

Blitzkrieg and the expansion of the Third Reich 1939–41

German armies invaded Poland on 1 September 1939, secured by the Non-Aggression Pact from possible retaliation by the Soviet Union. Although Britain and France had both declared war on Germany in support of Poland, they were unable to take direct military action; for them the period 1939–40 was one of inactivity, generally known as the 'phoney war'. The German attack on Poland was the last to be planned entirely by the German generals. It was highly professional and was the first completely mechanized invasion in history, comprising armoured vehicles, tanks and preliminary air attacks on selected targets. The Polish cavalry was routed and Warsaw was taken after a converging drive from East Prussia, Pomerania, Silesia and Slovakia. When Stalin intervened on 17 September to claim the territory set aside for Russia by the Non-Aggression Pact (see pp. 64–5), Poland's fate was sealed. She was partitioned for the fourth time in her history and ceased to exist as an independent state.

The strategy of *Blitzkrieg* was applied next to the west, with even more spectacular success. The first targets were Denmark and Norway, chosen to consolidate Germany's position before the major assault on France, long considered by Hitler to be Germany's 'natural enemy'. Norway was especially important as it was a major outlet for Swedish iron ore supplies and had enormous potential for North Atlantic naval bases. Besides, it dominated Germany's submarine route past the Shetlands and could well be used by Britain unless quickly taken. The task, accomplished in April 1940, demonstrated a new version of *Blitzkrieg*, namely combined land and sea operations. It seemed that the German war machine was irresistible and there was clear evidence of a sense of defeatism in the Low Countries and France – Hitler's next victims.

The Netherlands, Belgium and Luxembourg all fell to a renewed German onslaught in May 1940. This, however, was only the preliminary to Hitler's major objective – the conquest of France. Again, this was accomplished by a variation of *Blitzkrieg*. This time Von Kleist's panzer divisions punched a hole through the Ardennes, supposedly impassable and therefore lightly defended. Guderian's forces then over-whelmed the French Ninth Army. In the subsequent race to the Channel ports, the Germans captured most of Flanders, and the British army was evacuated at Dunkirk. The German offensive then flowed southwards, culminating by the end of June in the capture of Paris and the capitulation of France.

Why was France defeated so easily? It used to be thought that the French armies were overwhelmed by superior numbers. More recent estimates have shown that this was not the case. Against the 103 German divisions on the western front, France mustered 99 which were also supported by British contingents. The Allies had a definite superiority in tanks (3000 against 2700), in warships (107 against 13) and in artillery pieces (11,200 against 7710). The only real deficiency of the Allies was in air power, where the *Luftwaffe* had the advantage. The real reason for Germany's success has to be sought, therefore, in vastly superior strategic thinking. Hitler's campaign was based on the '*Sichelschnitt*' (sickle cut) through the northern plains of France via the Ardennes, as explained above. According to Noakes and Pridham, 'It was perhaps the most brilliant military plan of modern times.'[90] The French, by contrast, were stuck in the mould of their First World War strategy. They assumed that any conflict with Germany would again be defensive and slow moving, a belief which was symbolized by the vast and ultimately useless Maginot Line, constructed at enormous expense between the wars.

By June 1940 Hitler had achieved in the west all his objectives but one – a satisfactory settlement with Britain. Hitler did not intend, at this stage, to undertake a fight to the

finish with Britain: his first priority was the quest for
Lebensraum in eastern Europe. In any case it might be
possible to produce honorable peace terms. His interpretation of recent history was that Britain had always distanced
herself from Europe unless she could rely upon particular
power to act as her 'continental sword'.[90] The collapse of
France had now removed this sword. It would make sense,
therefore, for Britain to resume her traditional position of
neutrality and isolation. Hitler did everything possible to
encourage this. He made a series of statements that he had no
hostile intentions against Britain and that he certainly never
intended to seek to destroy the British Empire.[91] When his
peace approaches were contemptuously rejected by Churchill, the new British Prime Minister, Hitler considered that
he had no option but to give the directive for the invasion of
Britain. This would be the most ambitious *Blitzkrieg* to date,
starting with an all-out preliminary air offensive, followed by
a massive landing operation which would be codenamed
'Operation Sealion'.

The events of 1940–1 were to prove the first setback in
Hitler's war. This was due in part to a lack of total
commitment to the task which he had undertaken. He
overestimated the possibility of reconciliation with Britain
on the one hand while, on the other, underestimating the
British capacity for resistance. The result was that Hitler
seriously misused Germany's resources and undermined the
whole purpose of *Blitzkrieg*. In the first place, he mismanaged
the invasion plan. According to Craig,[92] Goering's direction of
the preliminary campaign to knock out resistance from the
RAF was amateurish: he frittered away Germany's strength
in the air by hitting too wide a variety of targets and not
concentrating on British airfields. Hitler's decision to go for
British cities also contributed to the survival of the RAF in
the early and crucial stage, making possible its eventual victory in the Battle of Britain. The RAF also had the advantage
of more effective aircraft in the Spitfire and Hurricane, more
experienced pilots, and a better warning system. Once the
RAF had confirmed its superiority in the air by 1941, Hitler
was forced to postpone Operation Sealion.

But, despite the failure of Hitler's plans, Britain posed no *direct* threat to Germany in 1941. She did not possess sufficient resources to engage in a major continental war and, in 1941, suffered a number of reverses which built Hitler's confidence to a new peak. The opportunity was, in a sense, unsought. Mussolini had made a series of disastrous mistakes in North Africa, Greece and Yugoslavia (see pp. 126–7), resulting in temporary incursions by British troops. In order to consolidate Germany's southern flank and to rescue Mussolini from defeat, Hitler despatched Rommel to North Africa and German panzer divisions to the Balkans in 1941. Within weeks the British were forced back into Egypt and had to evacuate Greece and the Greek islands in the Mediterranean.

These reverses did not, however, make the defeat of Britain any more imminent. Hitler had already decided to approach the problem from a different angle and to unleash another *Blitzkrieg*, this time against Russia. In retrospect, this decision seems to be the ultimate in folly. Yet, at the time, it must have had a certain compelling logic. Ideologically, of course, Hitler had a longstanding urge to smash what he regarded as the centre of international Bolshevism and world Jewry – in his eyes synonymous evils. At the same time, Germany would at last achieve *Lebensraum* in eastern Europe, a design frequently mentioned in *Mein Kampf* and *Zweites Buch*. The defeat of Russia would also enable him to dominate the Eurasian land mass and accumulate sufficient strength to accomplish the next stage in his quest for world supremacy.

One question is frequently asked about this decision. Why did Hitler open up a second front, thereby bringing into action a new enemy, before disposing of Britain? This could be seen as a monumental blunder, one which eventually cost Hitler the war. After all, he had once argued in 1939 that 'we can oppose Russia only when we are free in the West'.[93] On the other hand, it has been argued that he took the decision to invade Russia precisely because he had not managed to defeat England. According to G.L. Weinberg, this was 'Hitler's answer to the challenge of England – as it had been Napoleon's'.[91] By means of another swift and decisive campaign Hitler was certain that he could deprive Britain of any lingering hope that she might in future be able to use a 'continental sword'. There would also be wider advantages. As early as 31 July 1940 Hitler told his army chiefs: 'If Britain's hope in Russia is destroyed, her hope in America will disappear also, because the elimination of Russia will enormously increase Japan's power in the Far East.'[94] On 18 December 1940, he therefore issued Directive no. 21 for Operation Barbarossa and ordered that 'The German armed forces must be prepared to crush Soviet Russia in a quick campaign even before the end of the war against England.'[94]

The actual invasion was delayed until June 1941 to enable Hitler to rescue Mussolini in the Balkans and North Africa. When it came it was to be a *Blitzkrieg* on an unprecedented scale, consisting of 4 million men, 3300 tanks and 5000 aircraft. At first the Germans encountered little resistance and advanced more rapidly than had any previous invasion force in history. Russian resistance folded up (see pp. 68–9) and, by September 1941, the Germans held a line extending from Leningrad to the Black Sea. Hitler now intended to capture the rest of European Russia at least as far as the Urals.

By the end of 1941 Hitler had reached the peak of his power in Europe. *Blitzkrieg* had been applied in a succession of waves, each more extensive than the last. Poland had been crushed in the initial assault of 1939, followed in 1940 by western Europe. His attempt to apply it to Britain had failed, but the second *Blitzkrieg* in the east produced even more stunning results than the first. There was, however, one major shortcoming, which was ultimately to prove fatal to the Third Reich. Operation Barbarossa had not fulfilled the objective of finishing off the Soviet Union by the end of 1941, a serious failure since *Blitzkrieg* depended on instant victory. Thus, although Hitler's mastery over Europe seemed formidable, the tide was about to turn against Germany. From 1942 onwards Hitler's lightning wars were transformed into a more prolonged and destructive war of attrition – total war (see pp. 214–17).

Europe under Nazi rule 1939–45

After his conquests, Hitler constructed a Reich which was intended to last a thousand years. To ensure this he considered it essential to build a 'New Order' by which Germany would effectively dominate Europe. The two main elements of Hitler's scheme were, according to N. Rich,[95] the purification of the Germanic race and the extension of Germany's frontiers in search of *Lebensraum* in the east. Taken together, these brought about the greatest upheaval in Europe since the collapse of the Roman Empire.

Map 4 shows the extent of Hitler's domination of Europe by 1942. Most of the events leading up to this have been dealt with elsewhere, but it would be useful to draw the various threads together. The first area to be incorporated was Austria, by the *Anschluss* of 1938 (see pp. 258–9). This was followed by the dismantling of Czechoslovakia, with the absorption of the Sudetenland in 1938 and Bohemia in 1939, the latter as a German protectorate under Heydrich. Slovakia was allowed to become a puppet state under the leadership of Tiso (see pp. 293–4) until direct military occupation by the Germans after the 1944 rebellion.

The situation in south-eastern Europe was highly complex, involving a combination of Italian rule, German 'rescue missions', puppet regimes and outright conquest. On the whole, Hitler was content initially to allow Italian domination of the Balkans and the eastern Mediterranean. Albania, for example, came under Mussolini's rule in 1939. His attempt to subdue Greece, however, failed and in 1941 the Germans had to take over and partition the country. Yugoslavia was also crushed and divided, the southern part being allocated to Italy, Serbia coming under German military occupation, and Croatia establishing another puppet government, this time under Pavelich (see pp. 283–4). The other states of the area were more careful – or fortunate. Hungary allied herself to Germany until 1944, when Horthy was replaced by Szálasi's pro-Nazi Arrow Cross regime (see p. 264). Bulgaria's alliance with Germany was transformed into almost total Nazi control over Prince Cyril in 1943 (see pp. 278–9). Rumania's connection with the Reich was similarly strengthened by Antonescu (see pp. 286–7). The greatest single problem for Hitler in southern Europe was the collapse of Italy in 1943 (see pp. 126–32) and the need to pour German troops into the north to prop up Mussolini's new Salo Republic. Between

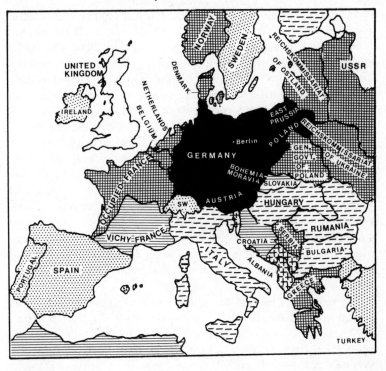

Extent of the Third Reich

States under German occupation or administration

Puppet regimes under German influence

Germany's allies, including Italy

Italian acquisitions

Neutral states

States at war with Germany and her allies

Map 4 Europe under Nazi influence by 1942

1943 and 1945 Axis co-operation and alliances throughout the region were therefore replaced by total German domination.

Western Europe came under Nazi rule in 1940. Denmark experienced least upheaval; she retained her parliamentary monarchy until 1943, although under German 'protection'. Norway was jointly administered by a German commissioner, Terboven, and a Norwegian collaborator, Quisling (see pp.295–6). The Netherlands were ruled by Reichs Commissioner Seyss-Inquart, who had previously been governor of Austria, and Belgium by General von Falkenhausen. Luxembourg was, by 1942, incorporated directly into the Reich, along with the Belgian districts of Eupen and Malmédy and the French provinces of Alsace and Lorraine. Finally, France herself was divided after being conquered in 1940. Two-thirds, including Paris and the Atlantic coast, were placed under General von Stülpnagel. The rest was allowed to establish a puppet state under Pétain and Laval, based on Vichy (see pp.297–8).

The greatest changes came in eastern Europe. Poland was conquered, plundered and destroyed in 1939 (see pp.268–9). This was followed by an attack on the Baltic States (see pp.271–2) and on Russia (see pp.68–70). Part of Poland – West Prussia, southern Silesia and Posen – was incorporated directly into the Reich. The rest formed the General Government of Occupied Polish Territories under the brutal administration of Hans Frank (see pp.268–9). The second wave of German conquests (1941–2) brought further reorganization, this time in Russia. Two vast new territories were set up, under Rosenberg. The first was Ostland, comprising the Baltic States and White Russia, the second the Ukraine. There were plans for two more, Muscovy and the Caucasus, which would have accounted for Russia up to the Urals. The whole of eastern Europe, therefore, was set aside for future German expansion in accordance with Hitler's designs in *Mein Kampf* and *Zweites Buch*.

All areas under Nazi rule were intended for maximum exploitation by the Third Reich. The basic justification for *Lebensraum* in eastern Europe was that the low productivity and cultural achievements of the 'inferior races' deprived them of a right to separate statehood and territory. The Slavs possessed far more land than their history warranted; Frank observed that the Poles 'have no historical mission whatever in this part of the world'.[96] Russia was to be set aside for the resettlement of up to 100 million Germans once the rapid population increase, projected by Hitler, had begun. Meanwhile, the peoples of the occupied countries of both eastern and western Europe would be used to enhance Germany's war effort. A severe shortage of labour had by 1942 become apparent within the Reich. Albert Speer, Minister for Armaments and War Production from 1942, managed to increase economic growth and the production of war material by deliberately promoting foreign labour – both voluntary and forced. By 1944 there were at least 7.5 million foreign civilians working in Germany.[97] A constant supply of labour was ensured by mass deportations. In some cases slave workers were provided by the Plenipotentiary for Labour, Sauckel, for use by the Reich's industrial and armaments firms. According to evidence produced at the Nuremberg Trial in 1945, eastern workers like the Tartars and Kirghiz 'collapsed like flies from bad housing, the poor quality and insufficient quantity of food, overwork and insufficient rest'.[98] Western workers were also badly treated. Krupp of Essen kept its French workers 'in dog kennels, urinals and in old baking houses. The dog kennels were three feet high, nine feet long, six feet wide. Five men slept in each of them.'[98] While people were exploited, the national wealth of the occupied states was systematically plundered. Gold and foreign holdings were removed from all the banks, and industrial produce was requisitioned on a massive scale. It has been estimated that France provided Germany with 60 billion marks and 74 per cent of her steel, while Belgium and the Netherlands lost two-thirds of their national incomes.[97]

The Nazi occupation of Europe was carried out with an unprecedented contempt for the subject peoples. This was due primarily to the racial emphasis of Hitler's rule. There were two distinct aspects here. One was a search for racial purity for the German people. This was entrusted to the SS; Himmler was made head of the RKFDV (the Reich Commissariat for the Strengthening of German Nationhood). One of the results was the large-scale kidnapping of foreign children who fitted the Aryan stereotype. At the other end of the scale were Europe's 'lower orders', including Poles and Russians, considered to be fit only for forced labour. According to Bormann, in 1942: 'The Slavs are to work for us. In so far as we don't need them, they may die. Therefore compulsory vaccination and German health services are superfluous.'[97] At the bottom of Hitler's descending racial scheme came the Jews, whose situation is dealt with on pp.172–5.

Contempt for the subject peoples bred an unimaginable brutality, evidence of which came to light in 1945 and 1946. Terror was made systematic through the extension of the SS and the SD and through basic legislation. Two examples of the latter, both in 1941, were the 'Commissar and Jurisdiction Decrees' for Russia, and the 'Night and Fog Decree' for the west. The authorities were provided with unlimited powers to uphold security, including the use of torture, arbitrary arrest and summary execution. Large-scale atrocities against the subject peoples were all too common. Three examples will suffice. In 1941, 100,000 civilians in Kharkov were forced to work all day digging a huge pit and were then machine-gunned into it.[99] The reason was that the German authorities felt that they were a threat to the levels of available foodstocks. In 1942 all the men of the town of Lidice, in Bohemia, were executed and the children and women sent to concentration camps. This was in retaliation for the assassination of Heydrich, the governor of Bohemia. A similar event occurred in 1944 when the inhabitants of Oradour-sur-Glâne, in southern France, were herded into the local church and barns and burned alive as a punishment for resistance activity. It was later discovered to be the wrong village. Vast numbers of people died in various camps, including over 4 million Soviet prisoners-of-war. Many camps, especially in Poland, became extermination factories as part of Hitler's scheme for altering the racial composition of Europe. Auschwitz, for example, killed over 1 million Jews, Treblinka 700,000, Belzec 600,000, Sobibor 250,000, Maidenek 200,000 and Kulmhof 152,000. Among the most horrific of all the Nazi activities were the appalling medical experiments carried out without anaesthetic by the likes of Josef Mengele at Auschwitz. As M.R.D. Foot writes, these 'did not advance human knowledge in any useful way whatever; unless it is useful to know how nasty man can be to man'.[99]

The very awfulness of Nazi occupation implies a high degree of efficiency. In one respect this is true; the regime took human extermination to unprecedented levels. There were, however, severe administrative problems which prevented Hitler from coming even close to establishing uniform control over Europe. There was no overall plan, merely a series of local and *ad hoc* expedients, usually lacking any central co-ordination or control. The basic problem was Hitler's own withdrawal from active administration to involve himself in the conduct of the war from the remoteness of Wolfsschanze in East Prussia. As in Germany itself (see pp.164–7) numerous administrative conflicts developed from the chaos of the conquered areas. Four examples can be cited. The first was France where there was an increasingly complex overlap of authority. The second was Norway, which saw a major conflict between Terboven and Quisling (see pp.295–6). Thirdly, Poland was the scene of a bitter clash between the new governor, Hans Frank, and Reich officials like Goering and Himmler, both of whom tried to interfere with policy decisions and administrative detail. Finally, Rosenberg had much the same problem in his attempt to run the Ukraine.[100] As he did with all political disputes, Hitler tended to ignore complaints and allow his subordinates to settle things among themselves. Overall, Hitler's policy towards the east was applied haphazardly and with an almost total lack of underlying discipline. At a conference held in July 1941, Hitler argued for initial caution and for concealing the true intention of Nazism in Russia for as long as possible in order to ease and hasten the conquest: 'we do not want to make any people into enemies prematurely and unnecessarily'. Germany's conduct towards the conquered area, he continued, should be 'first to dominate it, second to administer it, and third, to exploit it'. As events turned out in Russia and elsewhere in Europe, the ruthlessness of the occupying forces frequently lacked discipline and purpose, therefore going directly against Hitler's own instructions. The result was administrative confusion and the alienation of huge sections of the population. In Russia the Great Patriotic

War was in part provoked by unnecessary German excesses (see p.171) while in other countries the occupying authorities had to deal with an ever increasing problem of resistance movements.

Total war and the contraction of the Third Reich 1942–5

From the beginning of 1942 there were indications that the character of Hitler's war was changing. In declaring war on the United States he involved Germany against the world's greatest industrial power, while military reverses in Russia and North Africa severely tested the German economy for the first time.

The initiative for involving Germany in a conflict against the United States came from Berlin, the reverse of Washington's decision to enter the First World War. This is generally seen as one of the most irrational of Hitler's acts, and was taken without consultation with his military staff. Hitler displayed total ignorance of the United States, believing the whole nation to be deeply corrupted by its ethnic mixture and 'permanently on the brink of revolution'. But why provoke a new conflict? Why not dispose of Britain and Russia first? There is a case for saying that Hitler extended the war in order to redress the failure of the previous stage, just as the attack on Russia had been supposed to hasten the end of Britain's involvement. It is possible that Hitler's reasoning was as follows. The United States could be expected to enter the struggle eventually – clearly this would be another major problem for Germany. On the other hand, this would also upgrade the alliance between Germany and Japan since the latter would attack British and American interests in the Far East and the Pacific. This would be of vital importance, for it would divert US attention from Europe for long enough to enable Hitler to complete the destruction of Russia and to force a settlement on Britain. There would therefore be no repetition of 1918, when US troops had broken the deadlock on the western front and tipped the balance in favour of the Allies. The important thing was to ensure that Japan did not withdraw from the war prematurely. Hence, according to Jäckel, 'Japan had to do more than enter the war. It had to be kept from pulling out before victory had been won in

Europe.'[76] In fact, this was a serious miscalculation by Hitler. President Roosevelt made the decision to concentrate as much on the war in Europe as on Japan, for fear that Russia and Britain might be defeated, leaving the USA to face Germany alone. All Hitler had succeeded in doing, therefore, was to strengthen the war effort against him on the periphery – at sea and in North Africa – at the same time as his life and death struggle in Russia.

During the course of 1942 and 1943 the *Wehrmacht* suffered a series of reverses which turned the tide of the Second World War. The worst disasters occurred in Russia, with the surrender of Paulus at Stalingrad in one of the most crucial battles in modern history. But there were also crises in North Africa, with the defeat of Rommel at El Alamein. Indeed, the commitment in North Africa had a crucial effect on the campaign in Russia since it prevented Hitler from pouring in sufficient reinforcements to counter the Russian recovery. It also gave the western Allies a chance to attack Hitler's 'fortress of Europe' via its most vulnerable point of access. The result was to be the collapse of Mussolini's regime, the withdrawal of most of Italy from the war and the need for Hitler to deploy, in support of Mussolini's Salo Republic, divisions which were desperately needed in Russia.

Meanwhile, Germany was also failing to win control over the sea and air. At first, Hitler's emphasis was on creating a large surface fleet to contest with Britain's world naval supremacy. Eventually, however, he was converted by his naval commanders to a more specialized form of warfare based on U-boat attacks on merchant shipping in the Atlantic. But, despite heavy losses inflicted on Allied ships, Hitler had, in effect, lost the Battle for the Atlantic by late 1943. This was of vital importance since Hitler was unable to prevent a massive influx of supplies from the United States to Britain under 'lend–lease'. He also failed to disrupt the supply route via Murmansk through which the western Allies made a significant contribution to the Russian war effort.

Aerial warfare affected Germany more directly. The failure of Operation Sealion was due largely to the victory of the RAF in the Battle of Britain and to a rapid increase in British aircraft production. With the entry of the United States into the war came heavier saturated bombing of German targets. This was conducted 'round the clock', by the United States Air Force during the day and the RAF at night. A deliberate attempt was made to destroy German cities, and hence German morale, and also to knock out key industrial centres. The former included Hamburg, Cologne, Essen, Dortmund, Berlin and Dresden. The main industrial targets were ball-bearing plants, armaments factories and communications networks. Two arguments have been advanced as to whether this bombing made a significant difference to the outcome of the war. One is that the Armaments Minister, Albert Speer, pulled together the German economy in 1944 for a final effort; this counteracted the effect of Allied bombing, as German armaments production actually increased during the period of heaviest destruction. Thus criticism is often levelled against Bomber Command for, in effect, conducting a war on civilians. On the other hand, it could be argued that, although the attacks of 1944 may not have led to a dramatic *decrease* in production they did, nevertheless, prevent the sort of *increase* which might otherwise have occurred. In addition, catastrophic damage was inflicted by the Allies on Germany's transport and communications network; this was far more important than the destruction of cities in breaking the Nazi war effort.

By 1944 Hitler's 'Fortress of Europe', won by *Blitzkrieg*, was being breeched from three main directions. The first battering ram was applied by the Red Army, which conquered eastern Europe during the second half of 1944 and the early months of 1945. Meanwhile, the western Allies were hammering at Mussolini's Salo Republic and, in June 1944, opened up a third front with the invasion of France. Hitler now became increasingly irrational, living on false hopes and drawing comfort from the example of Frederick the Great, an eighteenth-century Prussian king who had held off, in the Seven Years War, a combination of Russia, Austria and France. Hitler firmly believed that sooner or later Russia and the western Allies could be induced to attack each other. 'All of the coalitions in history have disintegrated sooner or later. The only thing is to wait for the right moment'.[101] He did, in fact, manage two last-minute successes. He defeated in

September 1944 a British airborne invasion at Arnhem which attempted to capture the bridgeheads of the lower Rhine. He also came close in December 1944 to breaking through the Allied lines at the Ardennes in what is usually called the Battle of the Bulge. But these did no more than slow down the Anglo-American advance. The western Allies now conformed to Eisenhower's strategy of a slow and methodical thrust on Germany across the whole front rather than the British preference for a quick advance on Berlin. The result was that the Russians reached Berlin first. Hitler committed suicide on 30 April 1945 after entrusting the succession to Commander-in-Chief Admiral von Dönitz. On 7 May the German High Command surrendered. 'The Third Reich had outlasted its founder by just one week.'[102]

Hitler as a war leader

Hitler had once observed in *Mein Kampf* that Germany would be supreme in the world or it would be nothing. As far as he was concerned, there was never anything else but a choice between these two extremes. During the Second World War he pursued world power with the utmost fanaticism, even when it had become clear that defeat was a distinct probability. While he still believed that ultimate victory was possible, he saw the alternative of destruction as a just reward for failure. He told his confidants on 27 January 1942 during the first reverse in Russia: 'If the German people are not prepared to stand up for their own preservation, fine. Then they should perish.' This mentality was typical of his whole leadership. His decisions had been largely responsible for the success of *Blitzkrieg*, but were to be equally so for German failure in the second phase of the war. He committed a series of major blunders which indicated that he had learned nothing from his early success. Stalin, by contrast, learned everything from his initial failures.

In the first place, Hitler totally underestimated the individual and collective strength of his opposition. All three of the Allied powers were more effective than Germany in mobilizing for war. Britain managed to exploit a smaller economic base through severe rationing and high taxation, but based on the sort of consent that Hitler never dared expect from the

German population. The United States had a gigantic peace-time economy and had little difficulty switching to war production, despite Goering's assertion that 'The Americans can't build planes, only ice boxes and razor blades.' Under Roosevelt's lend–lease policy the United States became the 'arsenal of democracy', managing between 1940 and 1945 to manufacture 300,000 aircraft, 86,000 tanks and 71,000 naval ships. Finally, the Soviet Union managed to survive massive losses and destruction by the strategies explained on pp. 70–4. With these disparities it is obvious that Hitler was deluding himself in his belief that he could grind down his enemies through a war of attrition. The truth was that attrition was better suited to the more efficiently industrial-ized economies of the Allied powers.

Hitler also made major blunders in military organization and strategy. Perhaps the best evidence for this is provided by four men who served under him and were directly involved in the war effort. All were highly critical. One was Hitler's official war diarist, Percy Ernst Schramm, who subsequently published a detailed account of Hitler's personal life and military leadership, based on first-hand observation. The other three were Generals in the High Command: Manstein, Halder and Jodl. Halder, who replaced Beck as Chief of General Staff in 1938, wrote a totally condemnatory tract in 1949 entitled *Hitler as War Lord*. Jodl produced a memorandum in 1946, shortly before being executed at Nuremberg for war crimes. Even allowing for the fact that each of these men had reason to distance himself from Hitler, the combined weight of criticism is formidable.

On the question of Hitler's direction of the war, Halder observed that the Führer destroyed the High Command as the apex of military organization. 'He may have had a gift for mass political leadership. He had none for the leadership of a military staff.'[103] Indeed, his divide-and-rule policy 'de-stroyed a well organized system of military command which no true leader would ever have given up'. According to Jodl, Hitler allowed little influence and 'resented any form of counsel regarding the major decisions of the war. He did not care to hear any other points of view.' Instead, he had 'an almost mystical conviction of his own infallibility as a leader of the nation and of the war'. Schramm maintained that Hitler constantly interfered in military operations. He 'violated the tried and proven principle that subordinate commanders must be allowed a certain limited freedom because they are in a better position to evaluate the prevailing circumstances in their sector of the front and might be able, through swift action, to deal with a sudden crisis'.[104] Overall, Schramm adds, 'Hitler had already made himself dictator of state and society during peacetime. The war consolidated his dictatorship over the military.'[104]

Consequently, Hitler can be blamed personally for all the main strategic blunders. Schramm argues that Hitler's early success was based on huge risks which, even in retrospect, could be considered irresponsible. As the situation deteriorated he was incapable of taking a balanced decision and never saw the need for organized military retreat; he was 'unable to bring himself to make militarily necessary decisions such as the evacuation of untenable outposts'.[104] This can be supported by reference to a range of decisions in the latter phase of the war, from his refusal to let Paulus pull out of Stalingrad to his determination to hold all German outposts in France against enveloping Allied attacks. Hitler found the defensive role utterly distasteful. Instead of an orderly contraction of all his front lines, he adopted what Schramm calls a 'wave break doctrine', whereby positions had to be held even after the enemy had swept past and isolated them;[104] they could always be used as advance posts during the German recovery which Hitler hoped would occur as a result of his determination and will-power. Eventually he lost all sense of perspective. According to Halder, 'The delicate interplay between yielding pliancy and iron determination which is the essence of the art of generalship was impossible to this man, who could be termed the very incarnation of brute will.'[103] Almost exactly the same conclusion was arrived at by Manstein: 'Ultimately, to the concept of the art of war, he opposed that of crude force, and the full effectiveness of this force was supposed to be guaranteed by the strength of will behind it.'[105] Halder drew comparisons between Hitler and men of greater reason and more limited and practical objectives in what he regarded as the true German military tradition: he cited, especially, von Moltke and Bismarck. He concluded of Hitler, 'this demoniac man was no soldier leader in the German sense. And above all he was not a great General.'[103]

5
Dictatorship elsewhere

DICTATORSHIP IN SPAIN AND PORTUGAL

Portugal under Salazar

At the beginning of the twentieth century Portugal was ruled by an authoritarian monarchy. This was, however, over-thrown in 1910, to be replaced by a Republic which, in 1911, introduced a democratic constitution with a two-chamber Parliament, direct suffrage, and an executive with limited powers. Overall, the new regime was by far the most progressive in Portugal's history. Unfortunately, it was also inherently unstable. The sophisticated political system proved inappropriate to a society which was one of the most backward in Europe and in which 70 per cent of the people were illiterate. As in many other parts of Europe democracy foundered on political instability. During the 16 years of the Republic's existence there were nine presidents, 44 govern-ments, 25 uprisings and three temporary dictatorships.[1] This catalogue makes Portugal, in the words of S.G. Payne, 'the most politically chaotic of any single European ... state in the twentieth century'.[2] Political crisis was intensified by economic disaster caused by a series of incompetent budgets, an increase in inflation and a deterioration in Portugal's balance of payments. By the mid-1920s all the influential sectors of society – the professional middle class, the army and the Church – had come to the conclusion that the Republic would have to be replaced by a more stable regime. On 17 June 1926 it was therefore destroyed by General Gomes da Costa who installed a *Dictadura* (or dictatorship) in its place.

The new military rulers, however, proved equally unable to tackle Portugal's economic problems, as the cost of living soared to a level 30 times that of 1914. By 1928 the head of state, President Carmona, handed over complete responsibility for the Portuguese finances to a professor of economics at the University of Coimbra, Dr António de Oliveira Salazar. In 1932 Salazar became Prime Minister, a position he held until incapacitated by a stroke 36 years later in 1968. Throughout this lengthy period he remained in complete control, seeing himself as the only person who could reconcile the conflicting trends in Portuguese society or provide an alternative to Portugal's inefficient democracy. His power-base was a formidable array of groups disillusioned by the anarchy of the Republic. These included army officers who felt that the forces had been neglected, the Church who hated the Republic's anti-clerical policies, the upper bourgeoisie and banking interests who wanted economic stability, and, finally, right-wing intellectuals and monarchists. All trusted this remote academic far more than Portugal's more flashy military leaders.

So what sort of person was Salazar? N. Bruce describes him as a 'devout and Right-wing Catholic, a quiet and an austere man, dressed usually in a rather ill-fitting dark suit'.[1] He had little personal charisma and avoided any hint of a personality cult; in this respect he was the very reverse of Mussolini. He did, however, have a strong character and, as early as 1928 affirmed: 'I know quite well what I want and where I am going.... When the time comes for me to give orders I shall expect it [the country] to obey.'[3] His ideas were clearly and forcefully stated. He profoundly distrusted parliamentary democracy, for it had 'resulted in instability and disorder, or, what is worse, it has become a despotic domination of the nation by political parties'.[4] He therefore saw his role as establishing a paternalist regime, a government without parties. The individual should submit to this government without seeking to limit its powers. 'Let us place our liberty in the hands of authority; only authority knows how to administer and protect it.'[5] Salazar also sought to revive traditional virtues and loyalties and to develop a national pride based on the glorification of Portugal's history; for this reason his cult of empire assumed major importance. Overall, he tried to develop a state which, although based on tradition and in some ways an escape from the realities of the twentieth century, was nevertheless new in its organic development. Hence he called his model the *Estado Novo*, the New State.

The basis of the *Estado Novo* was the 1933 constitution which replaced the multi-party system with a 'unitary and corporative republic'.[6] The new lower house – the National Assembly – was elected on a list system through a restricted franchise. It also had few powers over the government and could not initiate financial legislation. A one-party system was confirmed, with the National Union (UN) acting as 'a pressure group intended to bind all sections of the community in a corporative movement'.[7] This 'corporative' system was the means whereby Salazar hoped to achieve harmony and discipline and to break the longstanding strife between labour and capital. It operated through the upper house of Parliament – the corporative chamber – which was selected from various sections of the community, including industry, commerce, agriculture, the army and the Church. Industrial relations were regulated by the National Labour Statute of 1933 which forbade workers' strikes and employers' lockouts. The whole point of corporativism was to present a viable alternative to the liberal idea, which Salazar distrusted, without adopting the collective principle as embodied in Communism, which he hated.

Salazar's *Estado Novo* had a mixed record in the period up to 1945. On the positive side, it undoubtedly provided greater political stability; the solid support from the wealthier sections of society brought to an end the pendulum of revolution alternating with counter-revolution. Above all, Salazar achieved a considerable amount in the financial sector. He produced a series of balanced budgets, stabilized the currency, reduced corruption and improved the process of tax collection. According to T. Gallagher, his methods 'were those of a careful accountant'.[3] On the other hand, the *Estado Novo* attempted few progressive reforms. Salazar was 'not an economic innovator' and balanced budgets became an obsession which served only to discourage foreign investment and loans. Industrial growth was minimal; the proportion of the workforce in industry increased hardly at all between 1920 and 1940. Agriculture, too, experienced neither fundamental changes in methods nor sustained efforts to improve irrigation. Above all, a real barrier to change was exerted by the social élite which upheld the regime. Social reform was held back by a rigid class system, something which concerned Salazar not at all. After all, he said quite openly in 1923: 'I consider more urgent the creation of élites than the necessity to teach people to read.'[8]

Salazar was always careful not to tie Portugal's foreign policy to a Fascist line. He avoided the temptation of an alliance with Italy and Germany, believing that 'in accordance with the true interests of the Portuguese nation its foreign policy is always to avoid, if possible, any entanglements in Europe'.[9] His main priority during the 1930s was to remove any possible threat from Portugal's more powerful neighbour, Spain. He was particularly concerned that the Republicans should not win the Civil War, for this might tempt a left-wing government to intervene against Portugal's *Estado Novo*. Hence Salazar backed the rebel forces under Franco and in 1939 cemented relations with his Nationalist regime in the Iberian Pact. The Second World War threatened to distabilize Salazar's position and he directed his diplomacy towards remaining neutral and, at the same time, restraining Franco from joining Hitler and Mussolini. Salazar succeeded in both aims and, as a result, he and Franco were the only two right-wing dictators still in power in 1945.

Salazar felt isolated and distinctly vulnerable in the immediate post-war period. His formula for survival was on the one hand to contribute as much as possible to the international scene and to make Portugal an indispensable link in western security while, on the other, insulating his internal dictatorship from western ideas and influences. The first of these aims was greatly assisted by the climate of the Cold War, in which the United States and Britain were more concerned with what they perceived as the new left-wing dictatorships in the eastern European countries than with the residual right-wing dictatorships of the Iberian Peninsula. Indeed, they could actually hold their noses and admit Portugal to the North Atlantic Treaty Organization in 1949.

Salazar's domestic policies, meanwhile, continued to be deeply conservative; T.C. Bruneau maintains that he 'intentionally isolated Portugal from the outside world'.[10] Salazar remained committed to old-fashioned budgetary financing and carefully restricted the use of foreign credit and investment which did so much to rebuild the shattered economies of the other states of western Europe. He was certain that rapid industrialization would weaken the social élites underpinning his regime and hence destroy the balance of the *Estado Novo*. He also emphasized the ever-growing danger of internal 'subversion'. The secret police (PIDE) was expanded, and detention without trial and the use of torture became routine. By the time of his death in 1968, Salazar had done very little to liberalize his authoritarian rule or to admit that there might be valid influences from other European countries.

Throughout its entire existence, the *Estado Novo* had one particular source of strength – and weakness. This was Portugal's overseas empire, which comprised: the Azores; Madeira; the African colonies of Guinea Bissau, the Cape Verde Islands, Principe, Sao Tomé, Cabinda, Angola and Mozambique; Goa, Damão and Diu in India; Macao in China; and East Timor in Indonesia (see Map 5). These possessions played a vital role for four reasons. First, they were of historic importance. According to Armindo Monteiro, Salazar's Minister of Colonies in the 1930s,

we now feel that we are so much the legitimate heirs of a great tradition that the generation of today is entitled to

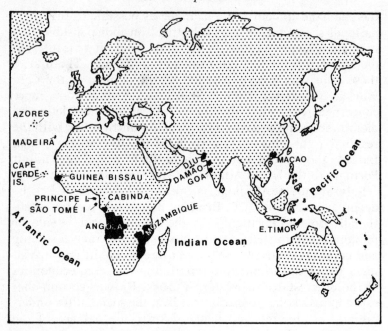

Map 5 The Portugese overseas empire in the twentieth century

invoke the past, not as a remembrance of dead things, but as a source of inspiration for the future.[11]

Secondly, it guaranteed Portugal a world role. Jorge Ameal emphasized that 'our sovereignty as a small European state spreads prodigiously over three continents and is summed up in the magnificent certainty that we are the third colonial power'.[11] Thirdly, Portugal had an historic obligation to 'civilize' and convert the peoples of Africa; 'in this heroic element is contained the most noble sentiment of our mission as a chosen people, since the task of civilizing must have, above all else, a spiritual content'.[11] Finally, the overseas empire was of economic importance, supplying Portugal with raw materials and providing markets for her finished goods.

So deep was Salazar's commitment to empire that he resisted with all his strength the trend of decolonization initiated by Britain and France in the late 1950s and early

1960s. The result was a series of colonial wars which had a profound impact on Portugal herself.

The first disaster was the Indian capture of Goa, Damão and Diu, in 1961, made possible by Britain's refusal to put pressure on a Commonwealth partner to exercise restraint. Then, from 1961, the situation also deteriorated in Portugal's African colonies. A series of guerrilla movements emerged, all committed to ejecting Portuguese rule and all receiving assistance from neighbouring Black African states or Eastern Bloc countries. Although there is some controversy as to whether the 'bush war' had been lost by 1974, the real significance lies in its impact on Portugal herself. Up to 45 per cent of the budget was allocated by Caetano (Salazar's successor from 1968) to maintaining 142,000 troops in Africa. The Portuguese army, confronted by heavy casualties in Africa and hostility from the rest of the world, suffered a decline in morale. The war also acted as a catalyst of social change in the officer corps as recruitment extended far down into the lower middle class. The new middle-ranking leadership felt less commitment to the regime and played a prominent part in the overthrow of Caetano in the coup of 25 April 1974.

The passing of the *Estado Novo* had a sense of inevitability. It had outlived its original purpose of stabilizing Portugal and was actually beginning to threaten, through diehard economic and colonial policies, whatever limited harmony had been achieved. After 1968 Salazar himself was no longer able to exert his unique blend of authority and reassurance, and his successor attracted far less support. Events in Africa convinced a large part of the population, including the army, that the time had arrived for Portugal to distance herself from her tradition and past achievements and to accept modernization. This fundamental change of attitude enabled Portugal to progress, via the coup of 1974, from dictatorship to democracy.

Spain: dictatorship to Republic 1923–30

On paper, Spain had certain assets which could well have equipped her for democracy rather than the dictatorship to which she twice succumbed between the World Wars. For example, the 1876 constitution had given her a Parliament with two chambers, one of which was elected from 1890 by universal suffrage. In practice, however, the political and social fabric faced desperate problems which eventually resulted in the collapse of the parliamentary system in 1923.

One problem was a series of external disasters. Spain became the first power to lose her imperial role, suffering in the process humiliating naval and military defeats. In 1895 Cuba rose in revolt, and Spain was defeated by the United States in the war of 1898. More serious still was a crisis in Spanish Morocco, the only significant colony left to Spain in the twentieth century. Spanish troops were pinned down by indigenous resistance movements and General Silvestre was defeated by the Riffians in 1921 at Anual, losing 12,000 of his contingent of 20,000. Military disasters were accompanied by internal instability which involved the growth of powerful opposition to central government from the left and from the regions. The former consisted of a strong trade union movement, as well as anarchist organizations influenced by the nineteenth-century philosopher, Bakunin. Left-wing radicalism frequently overlapped demands for the independence of regions like Catalonia; an example was the 1909 revolt in Barcelona in which Catalan nationalism and left-wing ideologies merged in common defiance of Madrid. Although the central government succeeded in suppressing this rebellion, it was unable to restore full confidence in its rule and resorted increasingly to graft and corruption. According to H. Thomas, 'By 1923 the Spanish parliamentary system was bruised almost to death.'[12]

The result was that the Spanish king, Alfonso XIII, acquiesced in a military coup in 1923 by Miguel Primo de Rivera. Rivera was a general who, according to Payne, was neither an intellectual nor a politician but who had become 'impatient with constitutions', preferring 'order and simplicity'.[13] He was well meaning but unsophisticated. Depending on intuition rather than reason, he convinced himself that he was most in touch with the needs and aspirations of the Spanish people. 'Your president is vigilant', he proclaimed, 'while you are asleep'. He liked to be portrayed as an Atlas who 'with his stout shoulders unshakeably avoided the collapse of the lofty roof of our beloved fatherland'.[14] He also saw himself as strengthening the Christian base of society and as a sentinel against the threat of Communism.

The best means of serving Spain, in his view, was to dispense with party politics. He was much influenced by political developments in Italy and was once introduced by Alfonso XIII on a visit abroad as 'my Mussolini'.[14] His regime was not, however, based on ideology and certainly lacked many of the features of Fascism. It was, instead, largely pragmatic. He tried at first to manage with a cabinet of military officers but came to the conclusion by 1926 that a broader based and more systematic government was necessary. He therefore introduced a 'National Assembly', a corporative chamber intended to represent different classes and interest groups. He also developed a new party, the *Unión Patriótica*, to mobilize popular support for the authoritarian system. 'This', he claimed, 'is a national movement which signifies, above all, faith in the destinies of Spain and in the grandeur and virtue of our race.'[14] As it turned out, the whole political system was too diffuse; it was neither one thing nor the other. It was not sufficiently democratic to satisfy the demands for alternative policies. Nor was it sufficiently authoritarian to stop these demands from being made.

During the six years in which he was in power, Rivera pursued bold policies, sometimes with notable success. He avoided the humiliation experienced by previous governments in dealing with Morocco and actually managed to subdue the protectorate in 1927. Internal problems were more complex. He considered Spain's most urgent need to be stability, to be achieved partly through reviving traditional virtues and partly through a process of modernization. He therefore strengthened Spain's infrastructure through the extension of public works. Unfortunately, his policies were handicapped by inadequate financing. One possible method of raising the necessary revenue was a complete overhaul of the taxation system, but this was fiercely resisted by the upper classes and the bankers. He was therefore to resort to the alternative expedient of borrowing and, in his later years, made extensive use of the 'extraordinary budget'. He aimed also at more direct government intervention in economic activity, hoping to create new industries and bring about protection through higher tariffs. There were, in fact, signs of economic improvement during the 1920s, particularly a steady increase in industrial production. According to R. Carr, however, 'the continued prosperity was to a large extent the result of favourable outside circumstances for which the regime could take no credit'.[15] It has also been pointed out that any economic reform was *not* accompanied by much-needed social changes; there was, for example, no improvement in the conditions of either industrial or agricultural workers. Rivera was not blind to the need for social reform but he was too heavily committed to the wealthier classes, upon whom he depended for support.

Rivera's dictatorship ended in January 1930, the result of overwhelming economic and political difficulties. Spain experienced a slump in share prices in the stockmarkets and an erosion of the currency. The whole basis of economic growth was threatened so that Rivera had to stop using the extraordinary budget and batten down the hatches. This signalled the end of prosperity, but the regime was not strong enough to withstand the backlash. Rivera had been unable to provide a permanent legitimacy for his government and he fell as a result of an attack from the left and the withdrawal of the support of the right. The offensive was launched by the Spanish republicans, the press, the universities and the socialists, while the conservatives saw nothing to gain in prolonging Rivera's regime. The upper classes, fearing the impact of economic decline, hoped that a change of government would regenerate confidence. Above all, the army was alienated by Rivera's attempts to reform the promotion system and eliminate some of the more blatant privileges. Given this overall lack of confidence the king requested and received Rivera's resignation in January 1930. The dictator was in poor health in any case and died only two months later.

It used to be thought that Rivera's rule was merely an interlude between the complex political developments before 1923 and after 1930. But more recently the tendency has been to stress his actual *influence* on later events. S. Ben-Ami, for example, sees his regime as a 'most significant turning point in modern Spanish history'.[14]

In the short term, the backlash against Rivera brought down the Spanish monarchy as well. Rivera's successor, General Berenguer, tried to introduce several reforms. But the republicans who had been so successful against Rivera in 1929 and 1930 were not likely now to be content with a few promises and compromises. Instead, they took full advantage of the restoration of Parliament and party politics and won a massive victory in the election of April 1931. This was taken as an overwhelming vote of no confidence in the monarchy. Fearing revolution if he tried to keep himself in power, Alfonso XIII voluntarily abdicated, expecting, no doubt, to be recalled when the political scene had quietened down. He was replaced immediately by the 'Second Spanish Republic'.

The Rivera regime not only pulled the monarchy down with its own demise; in the longer term it also helped prepare the way for a more radical right-wing dictatorship. When the Second Republic, in turn, faced crisis and collapse, it was to be replaced not, as Alfonso had hoped, by a restored monarchy, but by a more ruthless and radical right-wing dictatorship under Francisco Franco. To this development we now turn.

Spain: Republic to dictatorship 1930–9

The Second Republic lasted eight years: from 1931 to 1939. From 1936 onwards it was confronted by an all-out assault from General Franco, who eventually installed himself as *Caudillo* or dictator.

The opening years of the Republic (1931–3) were dominated by the left, first under Zamora and then Azaña. The early governments introduced a series of major reforms, intending to alter the political and social structure of Spain. Early measures included the introduction of an eight-hour working day, together with benefits and paid holidays. These were followed by attempts to reduce the top-heavy officer corps in the army through early retirement.[16] The momentum increased as the 1931 constitution introduced universal suffrage at the age of 23, abolished the nobility and, in Article 26, took extensive measures against the Church. The Republicans regarded the Church as a reactionary force which had become resistant to any progressive ideas and which therefore needed drastic change. The main measures introduced by Article 26 were the right of the state to dissolve religious orders (which now had to register officially), an end to religious education, and the forcible introduction of the type of social reform, like divorce, which had been resisted by the Church. Azaña brushed off all criticism with the words 'Do not tell me that this is contrary to freedom. It is a matter of public health.' The next reform was the 1932 statute which granted a degree of autonomy to Catalonia in such functions as education, taxation and the police. Finally, the Law of Agrarian Reform (1932) tried to narrow the gap between the landless peasantry and the enormously wealthy landlords, allowing the state to purchase in certain parts of Castile unworked lands of over 56 acres. Overall this was the most extensive package of reforms Spain had ever experienced.

Unfortunately, everything went wrong; nearly all the changes aroused bitter opposition from Spain's various vested interests. The army resented the pruning of its ranks. The Church went on to the defensive, finding a champion in Gill Robles, who set up a confederation of Catholic parties (CEDA). The landlords did everything in their power to resist the legislation on land, which was never applied effectively anyway. Azaña therefore failed to benefit Spain's lower orders and succeeded only in terrifying the privileged. In 1933 Azaña's government fell after being defeated in a general election. There then followed a swing to the centre-right, with a series of coalition governments. These proceeded to dismantle the previous reforms, or at least did everything possible to render them unworkable. This policy, in turn, provoked action by the left in industrial areas – like the Asturias Revolt of 1934, which was bloodily suppressed. The government also removed from circulation many left-wing leaders, whether or not they had been responsible for the violence. Even so, chronic instability characterized the whole period. By the time that the Assembly was dissolved in January 1936 the Republic had experienced 26 governmental crises and 72 ministers had served during a period of four-and-a-half years.[17]

There followed one of the most famous elections in modern history as much of Spain polarized into two political camps – known as 'fronts'. The left-wing parties (Communists, Socialists, Liberals, Republicans and Anarchists) combined to form the Popular Front, or Republicans. This was countered on the right by the National Front, or Nationalists, which consisted of monarchists (especially the Carlists of Navarre), conservatives, and the CEDA. Excluded from these blocs were the centre, the Basques and a new far-right-wing organization, known as the Falange, under Jose Antonio Primo de Rivera. The result of the election was a close victory for the Popular Front with 4.2 million votes to the National Front's 3.8 million.

As Azaña formed a new government, the Nationalists looked on sullenly and awaited an opportunity to seize power. Azaña proceeded to reintroduce all his earlier reforms. He exiled Franco, whom he regarded as the major threat in the army, to the Canaries. Unfortunately, the second Azaña administration did nothing to allay the fears of the right that he was drifting further to Communism. Indeed, all his policies seemed openly provocative. The right therefore opted for action and the army hatched a plot to overthrow the Republic. The *casus belli* was the murder by the state police of Sotelo, a leader of the Falange and of CEDA. General Franco, who had returned from the Canaries, led seasoned Spanish contingents from Morocco into the south, while Mola advanced from the north with support from Navarre. The Republic was to be snuffed out by the two converging forces.

At first the Nationalist offensive moved slowly. Mola gradually established a grip on northern Spain, except the Basque lands, and made Burgos the capital of the new Nationalist government, in direct defiance of Republican Madrid (see Map 6). Meanwhile, Franco invaded from Morocco, using the invaluable airlift facilities provided by the Italians and Germans. In August 1936 the two Nationalist zones linked up along the Portuguese frontier with the capture of Badajoz. The Republicans, however, still controlled the far north, part of the south, almost all the east and, of course, Madrid. Franco made an unsuccessful attempt to grab Madrid and then laid siege to the city from November 1936;

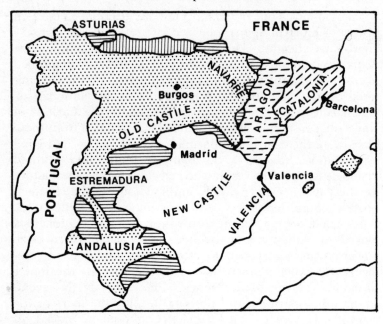

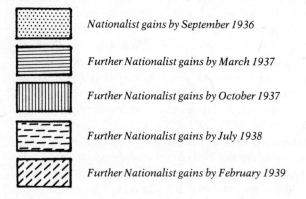

Nationalist gains by September 1936

Further Nationalist gains by March 1937

Further Nationalist gains by October 1937

Further Nationalist gains by July 1938

Further Nationalist gains by February 1939

Map 6 The Spanish Civil War 1936–9

the Republicans held out but transferred their capital to
Valencia on the east coast.

Meanwhile, foreign interest in the war was growing
rapidly. Germany and Italy stepped up their supplies to

Franco (Italy's motives are explained on pages 121–2). France was, at first, openly sympathetic to the Republicans but was manoeuvred by Britain into a more neutral stance. In 1936 the British government promoted the establishment of the Non-Intervention Committee to try to bring the war to an end by denying arms to both sides. All the major powers initially paid lip-service to the principle of the Committee, but Germany and Italy eventually defied its provisions by openly increasing the flow of war material to the Nationalists. Although the Soviet Union provided some assistance to the Republicans, the disparity between the two sides was considerable. This showed in 1937 when Franco was able to mop up Republican territory in the south, including Malaga. In the far north, meanwhile, occurred an event which provoked an international outcry – the German bombing of the Basque town of Guernica. By October 1937 the Nationalist domination of northern Spain was completed by the conquest of the Asturias.

The Republicans were not, however, finished; they had major, if temporary, successes at Guadalajara (March 1937) and Teruel (December 1937). But Franco doggedly persevered, greatly assisted by further Italian and German reinforcements. By 1938 the Nationalists had split the Republic into two, isolating Catalonia in the north-east from what was left of Republican Castile. It was now only a matter of time before the Republic was completely destroyed, especially since the international situation had become even more unfavourable to it. Britain and France, prepared to appease Hitler over Czechoslovakia, were clearly in no mood to confront him over his assistance to Franco. Russia, meanwhile, ended her commitment to the Republic which was therefore deprived of all foreign help. The Nationalists were therefore free to bomb and starve into submission the three key Republican cities – Madrid, Barcelona and Valencia. By 1 April 1939 Franco's government had been recognized by much of Europe, by democracies as well as dictatorships.

Civil war is particularly horrible and destructive. The Spanish conflict was no exception. The usual estimate of the total loss is about one million dead, although Thomas places the figure at 400,000 casualties and over 100,000 through 'malnutrition, starvation, or disease directly attributable to the war'.[18] There was certainly no shortage of information or publicity. A large number of war correspondents described or photographed battles and massacres, and writers like Hemingway and Orwell provided vivid images, as did artists like Picasso and Dali. Both the Nationalists and Republicans were responsible for atrocities and terror. The earliest examples were mainly against the Church in the Republican zone; 80 per cent of the clergy were killed in the Barbastro region. On the whole, however, terror was not normally the Republic's policy and formed no systematic part of the ideology on the left. It was the Nationalists who made terror the norm. They inflicted barbaric punishments on the areas they occupied, conducting, for example, a massacre in the bullring at Badajoz. After the end of the Civil War they probably carried out over 250,000 executions. There is therefore no doubt that the 'White Terror' was more total than any 'Red Terror'. It also spelt the end of democracy and submerged Spain into a new and ruthless dictatorship.

The sides in the Spanish Civil War

The Spanish Civil War is often seen as a fundamental divide between right and left – the first major struggle between Fascism and Communism. This view is now generally seen as an oversimplification and the result of the propaganda labels used by each side of the other. The recent tendency is to examine all the complex issues behind the confrontation. Hence, according to P. Preston, 'the Spanish Civil War was not one but many wars'.[19] The basic argument of this section is that, on the one hand, there *were* fundamental differences between the two sides, often expressed in powerful ideological terms. On the other hand, there were also many crosscurrents in Spain which tended to complicate the main issues.

As we have seen, the Civil War was fought between broad coalitions of the right (Nationalists) and left (Republicans). The Nationalist aims were the more coherent, largely because of the overwhelming influence of Franco. He projected the whole war as a crusade against the Godless left which he felt was trying to subvert the whole of Spanish society; in this respect, Franco emphasized the *defensive* nature of the uprising. He also caught the imagination of the Church by his talk of crusades, and was careful to associate his army closely with the Catholic religion, even to the extent of making the receiving of communion compulsory among his troops. In place of the corrupt 'Communist Republic', with its malfunctioning Parliament and bickering parties, its declining moral standards and growing secularization, Franco promised to revive Spain's glorious traditions. These included military power, firm personal leadership and overriding religious zeal.

The factions of the right all shared Franco's repugnance of the far left but they disagreed on long term objectives. The Carlists, for example, hoped that Franco's appeal to tradition would include the eventual restoration of the monarchy. The more moderate right wished to retain at least part of the constitutional structure, while the more radical right, the Falange, aimed to create a classless and corporatist system influenced by the Italian model. Franco steered carefully between these various positions and was able to represent them all.

The left, meanwhile, regarded its enemy with equal abhorrence: as a Fascist regime which would impose terror by means of a permanent military junta. The result would be the total exploitation of labour in the interest of the capitalist classes. The immediate task, therefore, was to defend the Republic and what it had so far achieved. The Republicans were, however, at a major disadvantage: they were by no means agreed about what was worth preserving. The moderate Republicans hoped to keep the existing institutions and to move closer towards the western democratic system once Franco's military threat had been removed. The radical left, however, wanted more fundamental changes, including the establishment of a workers' state. At this point there was a serious division within the Republican camp, as the radical left were unable to agree on a strategy for further change. One section, comprising the CNT (anarcho-syndicalists), left-wing socialists and Trotskyist Communists, all felt that the real effort should go into extending the scope of the revolution through rapid collectivization and the creation of workers' militias. This would strengthen the Republic to defeat the right. Hence, according to the anarchist Berneri, 'we shall not win the war by confining the problem to the strictly military conditions of victory but by associating these with its political and social conditions'.[20] Against this was the view of the Spanish Communist Party, on orders from Moscow, that absolute priority must be given to the defeat of Franco. According to the Party Secretary, 'We cannot achieve the revolution unless we win the war; the first thing is to win the war.'[20] To give priority to revolution would only alienate the rest of the left and risk destroying the Popular Front altogether.

To summarize, the Nationalists were fighting to destroy the Republic and impose a system which would be authoritarian, Christian and traditionalist with (via the Falange) elements of Fascism. The Republicans were obviously fighting to save the Republic but were divided on whether to keep it in its existing form or to revolutionize it. Those who advocated revolution disagreed over strategy: should priority be given to the revolution in order to win the war, or to the war in order to prepare the revolution? Given these divisions it is hardly surprising that the Republicans were unable to summon up the sort of crusading zeal experienced by Franco's Nationalists.

How did the various groups within Spain respond to the two sides? Examples particularly worth examining are the Church, the army and the regions.

The Catholic Church was torn. Many of the lower clergy supported the Republicans, partly to preserve democracy and partly for social reasons. Some of the more liberal Church leaders also preferred the left to the right – for example the Bishop of Vitoria and the Cardinal of Tarragona. But the majority of the Church establishment threw in its lot with the Nationalists. There were two main reasons for this. One was the appeal of Franco's religious crusade which, it was hoped, would arrest the secularization of what had once been Europe's most Catholic country. During the 1930s, for example, over two-thirds of the population never attended church and in some areas the proportion was as high as 99 per cent. Secondly, Franco seemed to offer the best protection against what was seen as the atheistic left. According to Pope Pius XI, it was the left, not the far right, which posed the main threat to religion in Europe. 'The first, the greatest and now the general peril, is certainly Communism in all its forms and degrees.' Spain he considered to be especially at risk. 'Satanic preparation has relighted...in neighbouring Spain that hatred and savage persecution.' Hence 'our benediction, above any political and mundane consideration, goes in a special manner to all those who assume the difficult and dangerous task of defending and restoring the rights to honour God and religion'. As for Franco himself, 'We send from our hearts the apostolic blessing, propitiator of divine favours.'[21] The Spanish bishops, meanwhile, fully justified Franco's rebellion on the grounds that it was justifiable in the defence of Christianity. They even quoted the Catholic Church's leading medieval theologian, St Thomas Aquinas. This powerful ideological undertone would seem to justify the view of M. Gallo that this was 'the last of the European religious wars.'

It is sometimes supposed that the Spanish army rose to a man against the Republic. If this had been so, the Republic would have collapsed within weeks. The reality was more complex, as the army contained a mixture of liberal and reactionary influences. Most of the senior officers remained loyal to the Republic, as they had been appointed in the first place because of their political support for the regime. The vast majority of the middle-ranking officers, by contrast, took part in the 1936 uprising. They opposed the reforms of Azaña, especially the effort to reduce the size of the officer corps through early retirement. They also came to believe that Azaña was a 'pervert who nourished hatred for the virile virtues of the army, which he intended to destroy, leaving Spain helpless and prey to freemasonry and Marxism'.[22] The role of the army was therefore to save the state, whose government, according to General Kindelán was 'in the gutter', and act as 'the guardian of the values and historical constants of the nation'.[23] The army also intended to prevent decentralization and the growth of regionalism, for this would lead eventually to the disintegration of Spain as a military power.

This brings us to the two areas which did aspire to independence from Madrid – Catalonia and the Basque country. Both declared for the Republic against the Nationalists, but for pragmatic rather than ideological reasons. Catalonia's commitment was not to the Republic as such. Rather, it saw the Republic as the only means of preserving the autonomy granted in the 1932 Catalan statute. Franco, it was well known, intended to reimpose a unitary state. During the course of the Civil War Catalonia resisted bravely and Barcelona was heavily bombed by the Nationalists in 1938 and 1939. The Basques also felt that the Republic would be more likely to uphold the autonomy which had been granted by the statute of October 1933. They, too, suffered at the hands of Franco: the bombing of Guernica became a great symbol of Fascist brutality against the Basque people and, indeed, the people of Republican Spain.

To what extent did the sides in the Civil War reflect class divisions? The general trend is obvious. According to Carr, 'Where they were free to choose, the working classes chose the Republic and the upper classes were, with few exceptions, fanatic Nationalists.'[24] The middle classes are more difficult to assess, but it seems that the young intellectuals and members of the professions were inclined to the Republic, their elder peers to Franco. Preston argues that the greatest divide was in the rural areas between the landlords and exploited peasants; this applied especially in Andalusia in the north and Extremadura in the south. The wealthy landlords did whatever possible to destroy the reforming legislation of 1931 and showed a callous indifference to the plight of the poorest peasantry. It is hardly surprising, therefore, that the peasantry and estate owners aligned themselves respectively with the Republicans and Nationalists.

Despite the self-evident political allegiance on the basis of class differences, there were some less predictable crosscurrents. One was the generational divide, which affected many families in a tragic way; younger members were more likely to commit themselves to the Republic, the elder members to Franco. Another cross-current was loyalty to regional patriotism or to the Catholic Church, both of which might displace the priority of class loyalty. Finally, the accident of where they lived decided for many people which side they supported. As in any civil war, it was taken for granted that the population of the occupied zones would act as cannon fodder for the victors.

Why did Franco win the Spanish Civil War?

A combination of factors can be used to explain the success of Franco and the Nationalists in overcoming the Second Republic and installing a permanent dictatorship in 1939.

The first of these was the contrast between the disunity of the Republicans and the cohesion of the Nationalists. The Second Republic suffered from serious divisions which undermined its war effort and military capacity; it has been argued that it experienced a 'civil war within the civil war'. There was, for example, a three-sided conflict between liberal constitutionalists, authoritarian socialists or Communists, and far-left anarchists. The ideological range was consider- able, the two extremes being western democratic theories on the one hand and the revolutionary left on the other. The latter, in turn, was divided over the primary objective of the war. One strategy was to maintain the Popular Front and to put all the effort into the defeat of Franco; this was backed by most socialists, Marxists and pro-Stalin Communists. The alternative emphasis was that of the CNT, a trade union of anarcho-syndicalists, and the POUM, a union of ultra-left Communists and Trotskyists. They wanted to progress with the 'revolution' in the belief that compromising on this would weaken the war effort. Hence, in their irreconcilable ideo- logical conflict, the groups found themselves 'polarized between war and revolution, revolution and war'. The disagreements were sometimes violently expressed; fighting, for example, broke out in Barcelona in 1937 between anarchists, socialists and Communists.

All this contrasted with the unity in the Nationalist ranks. This was due largely to the leadership of Franco. G. Jackson describes Franco as 'an authoritarian leader of immense personal prestige and a skilful politician who harnessed the contradictory forces within his camp and made good use of the diplomatic and administrative talent at his disposal'.[25] Gallo sees him as 'competent and determined'.[26] Franco certainly had shortcomings. According to D.A. Puzzo, 'His head was a cemetery of dead ideas.'[27] Nevertheless, he showed remarkable determination and commitment to his principles; these, accord..ng to B. Crozier, were 'Duty, Discipline and Order'.[28] His basic programme was single-minded and simplistic. It assumed the nature of a crusade which was fired by bigoted passion.

One of Franco's main tasks was to create unity among his supporters. As Gallo maintains, 'Like the parties of the Popular Front, the Nationalists were originally a collection of heterogeneous clans, their political diversity reflected in a variety of uniforms.'[26] Franco managed to overcome internal disputes and to balance the different Nationalist groups. He satisfied the Carlists by leaving open the question of the monarchy and in catering for their demand for legislation which favoured the Catholic Church. These moves, admittedly, were not to the liking of the more radical Falangists, but they were pacified by being allowed to direct propaganda and to influence those characteristics of a mass movement which Franco was prepared to allow; they were also pleased with his close relations with Italy and Germany. The army, bereft of any real ideas of its own, depended completely on Franco to maintain its position and influence. Franco skilfully ensured an adequate representation between the various Nationalist interests. His first National Council of October 1937 combined 20 Falangists, 8 Carlists, 5 generals and 17 others.[29] He was able to bind them together while, at the same time, preventing any of them from becoming too dominant and introducing embarrassingly radical policies. He therefore managed to avoid the sort of problems confronting Republican leaders.

Another significant reason for the victory of the Nationalists was their superior military structure and organization. The Republicans had a fair share of loyal generals but a severe shortage of middle-ranking officers, which meant that it was necessary to promote numerous inexperienced NCOs to this vitally important level. The Nationalists had a more systematic method, their 28 military academies turning out a total of 30,000 trained officers.[22] The Republican army also suffered from being less cohesive, largely because it depended on militias and elected officers. A serious disadvantage of this system was that all strategy was discussed at length, which reduced speed and efficiency and encouraged insubordination. The Nationalists had no such problems, as Franco brought all the militias under centralized control in December 1936 and imposed rigorous military discipline on all his forces. He also developed a far more efficient military administration. Carr maintains that 'Its notable achievements notwithstanding, the Popular Army, as a military machine that could be deployed by a unified command, was inferior to the Nationalist Army.'[30] As for battle strategy, Franco's was unimaginative but solid. The Republican commanders often had more dash and launched several brilliant attacks which initially succeeded. But Franco's great strength was his cautious and thorough preparation. He would never start an offensive unless he was certain that he could see it through to the end. He was often criticized by his allies abroad for his slowness but, in the end, he got results.

There is a consensus among historians that the Nationalists probably would have been unable to win the war without assistance from outside, especially from Italy and Germany. There is, therefore, agreement with Hitler's belief that 'without the help of both countries there would be today no Franco'.[31] Italy's contributions were considerable. They included over 50,000 ground troops, 950 tanks, 763 aircraft and 91 warships. Germany provided 16,000 military advisers, the latest aircraft and the services of the Condor Legion. This support proved of vital importance on three occasions. The first was the transporting of Franco's troops from Morocco into southern Spain in German and Italian aircraft, enabling Franco to conquer Andalusia in 1936. The second was the boost given to Nationalist morale, after a series of Republican victories in 1937, by a sudden increase in Italian equipment. The third was another massive flow of armaments in 1939 which made it possible for Franco to crush Catalonia.

How was all this aid paid for? At first the Nationalists faced a massive problem, for all of Spain's gold reserves were in Republican hands. But Italy and Germany soon offset this in a series of financial agreements; these, according to A. Viñas, were 'the principal way in which the Burgos [Nationalist] government could manage to make the international payments necessary to strengthen the war sector of its economy'.[32] Italy provided aid worth a total of $263 million, while Germany contributed arms worth $215 million.[33] Altogether, Franco may well have received as much as $570 million from abroad. A significant amount of business was also done with multinational companies in the western democracies; R. Whealey cites as examples the Texas Oil Company, Texaco, Shell, Standard of New Jersey, and the Atlantic Refining Company. Their role was vital; according to Whealey, 'without oil, the Generalissimo's war machines would have ground to a halt'. They also deprived the Republic of its last chance of survival. 'Multinational corporations in the sterling dollar countries...helped to crush the Spanish Republicans' hopes.'[33]

The Republic suffered more from the obstructive policies of the other powers than Franco, who could rely on more consistent support. Its most consistent ally was Stalin though even he proved eventually to be unreliable. Stalin was always unwilling to commit Russia too fully in case he should leave her vulnerable to invasion by Germany. In any case, his involvement in Spain was partly intended to stiffen the west against Fascism but, once it became clear that appeasement was the order of the day, he lost interest. Munich finally convinced Stalin that he should withdraw. Meanwhile, France was reluctant to become involved in assisting a fellow Republic. A series of governments, headed by Blum and Daladier, kept out of the conflict for fear of alienating important groups, like the Catholics, in France. The United States also kept its distance, largely to avoid complicating relations with right-wing, and pro-Franco, regimes in Latin America.

But by far the greatest obstacle to the Republic's war effort was Britain. The Governments of Baldwin and Chamberlain still hoped to come to terms with Germany and also to revive Anglo-Italian friendship. Besides, in ideological terms the real enemy was considered to be Communism, not Fascism, and therefore Stalin, not Franco. There was no question of support for the Nationalists, many of whose policies were considered repugnant. Equally, however, there appeared to be a strong case against risking a general European war for the sake of bolstering up a Republic which was inclining more and more to the left. Hence Britain put heavy pressure on France to ban all arms sales to the Republic and was also the main influence behind the formation of the Non-Intervention Committee in 1936, the purpose of which was to prevent support being given by any country to either side in the conflict. Unfortunately, while the rules of the Non-Intervention Committee were observed by the democracies, they were openly flouted by the dictatorships, who gave Franco what he wanted. Britain's role was therefore vital. According to Puzzo: 'The conclusion is inescapable that the defeat and destruction of the Spanish Republic must be attributed as much to British diplomacy in the years 1936 to 1939 as to German aircraft and Italian infantry.'[34]

The Republicans, it is true, had certain benefits; but these gradually dwindled as those of the Nationalists grew. The greatest initial advantage of the Republic was that it owned the world's fourth largest gold reserve – sufficient, it might be thought, to finance military operations against Franco. Added to this was government control over the main cities and industrial areas. The Republic, however, soon met serious difficulties in paying through normal international banking channels for arms shipments. The main reason for this was the reluctance of bankers to defy government orders on neutrality. Eventually, the Soviet Union agreed to make necessary provision. The price, however, was the transfer of Spain's gold reserves to Moscow; Stalin refused point-blank to provide the Republic with the credit being made available to Franco by Hitler and Mussolini. The Republic bought from Stalin 1000 aircraft and 200 tanks, together with the services of between 500 and 5000 advisers (who, however, arrived with Stalin's instructions to 'keep out of artillery range'). In addition, Comintern organized the International Brigades which provided a total of 40,000 volunteers from France, Britain, Canada, Yugoslavia, Hungary, Czechoslovakia, Sweden, Switzerland, Germany, Austria, Italy and 53 other countries.[35] These fought bravely but suffered heavy casualties. They were finally disbanded in 1938 as Franco made a final and successful thrust against Catalonia and Madrid.

Franco owed an enormous debt to the Fascist states who put him in power. It might therefore be thought that his future should inevitably have been linked to theirs and that their fate would be his. And yet, by 1945 both Nazi Germany and Fascist Italy lay in ruins, with their leaders dead. Franco, by contrast, was still firmly in control and managed to impose his will until his death 30 years later.

The basic reason for this was that Spain never became totally involved in the Second World War, therefore avoiding catastrophic military defeat. There was never any doubt about his sympathies for the Axis cause. General Aranda said on 5 June 1939: 'Franco is deeply and firmly convinced that his path lies by the side of Italy and Germany. He openly detests the French and does not love the British.'[36] In August 1940 Franco assured Mussolini of his intention 'to hasten our preparations with a view to entering the war at a propitious moment'.[36] But when in 1940 Hitler met Franco at Hendaye in the Pyrenees he found the *Caudillo* evasive and determined to avoid any specific military commitments. Indeed, Hitler seems to have had a bad time and later observed that he would 'rather have four teeth pulled out' than have to deal with Franco again. Franco was motivated less by caution than necessity; basically, he had no option but to remain neutral. The Spanish economy had been ruined by the Civil War and the disruption of international commerce caused by the Second World War was enough to make recovery impossible. The army was run-down and war-weary and there was a major possibility that Britain and the United States would seize Spain's Atlantic islands the moment Franco made an alliance with either Germany or Italy. He was, therefore, grateful when his neighbour and fellow-dictator, Salazar, suggested an Iberian neutrality pact.

Franco did, however, make one notable exception to his policy of non-belligerency. In fact, he referred to the existence of *two* wars. The one in the west was clearly beyond Spain's resources. But the war in the east involved a powerful ideological principle. Franco's foreign minister, Suñer, maintained that 'Russia is to blame for our civil war' and that 'the extermination of Russia is a demand of history'.[37] Hence Franco sent 18, 000 volunteers in the 'Blue Division' to assist the German invasion of Russia. By 1943, however, it had become evident that Hitler was bogged down at Stalingrad; Franco cut his losses and withdrew his remaining troops from the Russian front. He was therefore the one European dictator who managed to pull out of the Russian flame without burning his fingers. In fact, he was able to extricate himself from all hostilities so that the western Allies, much as they disliked Franco's regime, had no reason to overthrow it in their onslaught on the Axis powers.

All the same, Spain was seriously isolated in the 1940s, which meant that Franco's foreign policy was based on the search for diplomatic recognition. At first this was provided only by Salazar's Portugal and Peron's Argentina, the latter agreeing to provide grain and meat on special terms. The rest of the world was hostile. The 'Big Three' at Potsdam opposed any possible bid by Franco to join the United Nations since Franco's government did not 'in view of its origins, its nature, its record and its close association with the aggressor states, possess the qualifications necessary to justify such membership'.[38] A United Nations communiqué endorsed this view in December 1946, referring to 'a Fascist regime patterned on, and established largely as a result of aid from Hitler's Nazi Germany and Mussolini's Fascist Italy'.[39] Nor were individual European countries likely to be receptive, most of them having recently elected left-wing governments. For a while Franco shrugged off this ostracism as a deliberate conspiracy, revealing just how necessary his authoritarian regime was. 'Spaniards know what they can expect from abroad, and as history teaches them, ill-will against Spain is not something which began today or yesterday.'[40]

Gradually the situation began to improve as Spain became less obnoxious in the eyes of the western states. The basic reason was the spread of the Cold War with the perceived threat of world Communism sponsored by the Soviet Union and China. The Berlin Crisis (1947–8) and the Korean War (1950–3) both gave Franco his opportunity to end Spain's isolation and he played his diplomatic role with some skill. The result was the 1953 Madrid Pact between Spain and the

United States. This provided Spain with $226 million of aid and military equipment, in return for the use of three air bases and naval facilities. According to Gallo, this agreement was a 'triumph for the regime'. It was renewed in 1963, when it stated that any threat to Spain would be 'a common concern' to the United States. Relations also improved with West Germany and the new Fifth French Republic. Even so, Spain was still not regarded as a desirable partner in various international organizations; she was not admitted to NATO or the EEC until, in the decade after Franco's death, she had proved herself capable of sustaining basic democracy.

While he ruled Spain Franco's power was virtually absolute. He dispensed with any formal constitution, maintained complete control over the administration, dominated the courts and crippled the Parliament. His authority was strongly personalized. 'I am', he once said, 'the sentinel who is never relieved'.[41] The inscription on Spain's coinage read '*Caudillo* of Spain by the Grace of God'. Clearly he saw himself in historic succession to the great Spanish monarchs of the past, especially Philip II, with whom he often identified. For this reason he sought to revive the glories of Imperial Spain and, in the words of Gallo, 'appropriated Spanish history'. This powerful pull of tradition is an argument against applying too loosely the term 'Fascist' to Franco. Orwell, with characteristic insight, observed as early as 1937 that Franco's mutiny 'was an attempt not so much to impose fascism as to restore feudalism'.[42] Franco lacked commitment to any radical ideology and certainly did not have a mass party base. In fact, he maintained his position by balancing against each other the main groups supporting the regime. These were the army, the Church, monarchists, industrialists, financiers and – the nearest Spain came to a Fascist movement – the Falange. Hence, according to D. Gilmour, Spain was governed by 'a limited pluralism', 'not by a single party but by a reluctant coalition of diverse groups'.[43]

It would be a mistake to assume that no political changes occurred during the long period between Franco's victory and death; the regime did eventually dispense with some of its earlier horrors. Immediately after the Civil War Franco introduced the most appalling repression, with mass executions, three-minute trials, concentration camps and confessions under torture. According to Carr, 'the firing squad and prison replaced the dungeons and fires of the Inquisition'.[37] By the 1960s, however, there was evidence of some relaxation. Although Franco's personal power remained intact, much of the old bureaucratic repression was dismantled. His basic aim was no longer to terrorize the population but, rather, to neutralize and depoliticize it, encouraging it to make the most of the economic boom which Spain was experiencing during the 1960s.

This boom took some time to materialize, and only after a false start. The initial problem confronting the regime was reconstruction after the Civil War. The method chosen was autarky, or self-sufficiency, involving heavy government intervention in wage levels, import quotas and the regulation of industry.[44] The emphasis was on industrialization. The result was predictable hardship, which included widespread poverty, threatened starvation and the spread of accompanying diseases like tuberculosis. Franco used characteristically tough words to justify his policy: 'We do not want an easy, comfortable life...we want a hard life, the difficult life of a virile people.'[44] Arguably, industry benefited. By 1950 it had regained its level of pre-war production, and between 1950 and 1957 doubled its output.

This growth was, however, beset with serious problems which revealed the utter inadequacy of autarky. According to Carr, 'Autarky had ceased to be a stimulus; it had become a straitjacket'.[44] Industrial growth, for example, led to an increased demand for imports which, in turn, put a strain on the balance of trade. The government therefore recognized the necessity of creating a more balanced economy by reducing controls and depending more openly on market forces. In 1959 it introduced a Stabilization Plan to bring the economy into line with others in the west. The measures included deflation, control of the money supply, reductions of public expenditure, wage controls, the promotion of foreign investment and the reduction of trade restrictions.[44] Initial hardship was followed between 1961 and 1966 by a so-called economic miracle. The government ascribed the new-found prosperity to the Stabilization Plan and its successors, the Development Plans from 1964. It is, however, equally likely that the major cause of this recovery was *indirect*. Abandoning autarky promoted two vitally important foreign exchange earners which helped stimulate growth. One of these was tourism; the total number of foreign visitors to Spain increased from 6 million in 1959 to 21 million in 1969 and 34 million in 1972. The other boost was the large Spanish workforce abroad which sent its earnings back to the mother country. The existence of such a large Spanish workforce abroad, however, was also an indication of one of the main shortcomings of the economy, the lack of full employment. Other persistent problems were the depressed condition of agriculture and the iniquitous system of taxation which prevented the state from extracting sufficient revenue from the sectors of society who most benefited from the boom. The result was that the gap between rich and poor increased as the new-found wealth was inadequately redistributed.

What condition was the regime in by 1975? Carr refers to the 'Agony of Francoism 1969–75', an apt description of the era of growing dissent, economic strain and doubts about the future. Although opposition was still illegal, it welled up through the system in the form of working-class activism and student unrest. A more violent form was Basque separatism, the violent tactics of the organization known as ETA provoking the government into issuing the 1975 anti-terrorist law. Even the Church, once a loyal ally, now distanced itself from the regime. Its change of attitude went back to the Second Vatican Council (1962–5) when Pope John XXIII made a stand on the protection of human rights. By the 1970s the upper clergy finally withdrew their support from Franco, leaving his regime bereft of the religious sanction it had once been able to take for granted. To make matters worse, Spain was experiencing the economic problems common to other parts of Europe in the wake of the 1973 oil crisis; this threatened to cut away one of Franco's main boasts – that he had presided over unprecedented economic growth. Now the question in everyone's mind was: what type of regime would succeed the ageing and ailing dictator?

Franco's own intention was to ease the way for the return of the monarchy by grooming Prince Juan Carlos for future authority. He did not, however, have the chance to complete this to his own satisfaction. On 17 October 1975, Franco collapsed in a cabinet meeting. Doctors were summoned to the Palace and performed a tracheotomy to enable him to breathe. Rumours circulated that Franco was dying, but these were officially denied. Indeed, the surgeons made every effort to prolong Franco's life. They succeeded until 20 November, by which time he was permanently on a respirator and a kidney machine and his stomach had been removed. It was almost as if Spain dared not let him die for fear of the subsequent uncertainty.

A character as diverse and complex as Franco has inevitably been the subject of historical controversy. Two very different viewpoints can be cited. On the one hand, Franco has his defenders. One of these, Crozier, maintains that Francoist Spain was not a totalitarian state and was therefore much freer than the Soviet Union or eastern Europe. Franco's achievements were substantial, including economic well-being and all the preconditions necessary for future stability and growth. He should, therefore, be judged by the standards of Spanish history and not those of more developed countries.[45] At the other end of the spectrum, Preston denounces any attempt to defend Franco. He argues that it is a basic misconception that Franco provided social peace, for this ignores his labour camps and executions, signs of his 'brutal efficiency'. In this respect, Preston insists, 'Franco stands comparison with the cruellest dictators of the century'.[46]

DICTATORSHIP IN CENTRAL AND EASTERN EUROPE

Introduction

At the beginning of the twentieth century over three-quarters of the total area of Europe was ruled by three empires – Turkey, Austria-Hungary and Russia. By 1914 the Balkan provinces of Turkey had splintered into six independent states; their treatment after the First World War and subsequent problems are dealt with on pp. 272–92. Central and eastern Europe underwent a similar transformation in 1918 as a result of the defeat of Tsarist Russia and the disintegration of Austria-Hungary. From the territory of these two empires no fewer than eight 'successor states' were established as a result of the Treaty of Brest-Litovsk and the Paris settlement. The former (dealt with in Chapter 2) destroyed Russian sovereignty over Finland, Poland and the three Baltic states of Estonia, Latvia and Lithuania. The Paris settlement, comprising the Treaties of St Germain (1919) and Trianon (1920) acknowledged the collapse of the Habsburg monarchy and the establishment of Austria, Hungary and Czechoslovakia.

The Paris settlement ensured that Austria and Hungary were now merely the German and Magyar rumps of the old empire. The provinces of Bohemia, Moravia and Slovakia were converted into the state of Czechoslovakia. Galicia was ceded to Poland, Transylvania to Rumania, Croatia and Bosnia-Herzegovina to Serbia and South Tyrol, and Trentino to Italy. These provisions have been the subject of vigorous debate ever since and three arguments seem to represent the full range of opinion. At one extreme, the new Czech leader, Masaryk, welcomed the changes which had 'shorn national-ism of its negative character by setting oppressed peoples on their feet'. At the other extreme, some observers looked nostalgically back to the days of the multinational empire of the Habsburgs. One of these was E. Eyck, the German historian, who saw the 'dismemberment of the Austro-Hungarian state' as 'a basic error'.[47] More recently, A.J.P. Taylor has pointed to the transitory nature of the empire, but also to the difficulty of managing without it. 'The dynastic Empire sustained central Europe, as a plaster cast sustains a broken limb; though it had to be destroyed before movement was possible, its removal did not make movement successful or even easy.'[48]

An analysis of the problems confronting the 'successor states' should enable the reader to weigh the relative merits of these views. It should also explain why this part of Europe should have become the scene of a series of domestic crises, which promoted dictatorship, and of international confronta-tions, which precipitated general war.

The first of these problems was the ethnic composition of the 'successor states'. In theory, the Paris settlement was eminently reasonable; President Wilson's principle of 'national self-determination' ensured that the Slav peoples all received their own homelands, whether in Czechoslovakia, Poland or Yugoslavia. In practice, however, the settlement discriminated against both Austria and Hungary by so drawing the new boundaries that large minorities of Germans and Magyars were separated from their respective homelands. Hence 3.1 million Sudeten Germans came under Czech rule, as did the Hungarian population of Slovakia. The justification was that the Sudetenland was an industrial area which was indispensable to the economic viability of Czechoslovakia. In any case, to have left the province with Austria would have created a geographic impossibility and the Allies could hardly transfer it to Germany. There was therefore a tendency among the peace-makers to shrug off such anomalies; King Albert of the Belgians asked: 'What would you have? They did what they could.'[49] Unfortunately, the policy of favouring the Slavs at the expense of non-Slavs did not always work, for there was serious friction between the various subgroups who were brought together as co-nationals. Slovaks, for example, accused Czechs of monopolizing power, and some historians consider that the nationalist tensions which existed in the Danube area were worse after the dissolution of the empire than they had ever been before.

Ethnic conflicts were compounded by economic difficulties resulting initially from the manner in which the resources of the empire were carved up. The 'successor states' received disproportionate shares of the industries and agricultural land of Austria-Hungary. Czechoslovakia, for example, inherited only 27 per cent of the Empire's population but nearly 80 per cent of its heavy industry, sufficient to enable her to compete successfully with many western industrial states. Hungary was less fortunate. Although she received between 80 and 90 per cent of the specialized engineering and wood-processing plants, these had access to 89 per cent less iron ore and 85 per cent less timber. There was also a serious disruption in what had been a free trade area of some 55 million inhabitants in which certain areas had specialized. In the textile industry, for example, most of the spinning was concentrated in Austria and the weaving in Bohemia. From

1919, however, each of the newly independent states was forced to build up those areas of its economy which had previously been undeveloped, the purpose being to create a more balanced agricultural and industrial base. Therefore Austria had to build up her weaving and Bohemia her spinning. This, in turn, precipitated a round of tariff increases in order to protect infant industries from competition from neighbours; in their struggle for survival, many of the 'successor states' had to accept the principle of self-sufficiency even if it meant tariff wars and reduced exports. For a short period, in the second half of the 1920s, most governments managed a respectable rate of economic growth. This, however, was reversed, from 1929 onwards, by the onset of the Great Depression.

Political instability was due, in part, to economic crisis, in part to institutional defects. A great deal of thought had gone into the preparation of the constitutions of the 'successor states' in 1918 and 1919 and all the most advanced features of western democratic thought had been enshrined in the new regimes, including universal suffrage, proportional representation and strict legislative control over the presidency. One of the great disappointments of the inter-war period was that these constitutions failed to work properly in any country in central and eastern Europe, with the single exception of Czechoslovakia. In most cases there was a steady slide towards authoritarian regimes. In 1926 Pilsudski installed himself as Polish leader after a military coup, as did Smetona in Lithuania in the same year. By 1934 Austria had moved to the right under Dollfuss, while Estonia had succumbed to Päts and Latvia to Ulmanis. Hungary experienced more drastic changes which resembled violent swings of the pendulum; within the space of 26 years she was ruled by a radical left-wing 'dictatorship of the proletariat' under Béla Kun, a conservative-authoritarian regime under Horthy, and a far-right, pro-Nazi dictatorship under Szálasi. None of these states had experience of the subtleties of a constitutional democracy, since they had previously experienced only the autocracy of Tsarist Russia or the milder but authoritarian monarchy of the Habsburgs. It was, therefore, unduly optimistic to expect a country like Poland or Austria to operate the type of constitution which baffled even the experienced politicians of the Third French Republic.

The fourth problem was even more serious than the ethnic conflicts, economic difficulties and institutional defects. Feuds developed between the 'successor states' which soon interacted with the rivalries between the major powers in the area. The motives varied. Hungary followed a revisionist course, spurred on by an irredentist policy which aimed to reclaim her lost Magyar territories from Slav neighbours. Austria, deprived of her role as a major power, sought an *Anschluss*, or union with Germany, Poland aimed to expand her frontiers to those of 1772, at the expense of the Soviet Union and Lithuania. The Baltic states had to focus their attention on basic survival. After 1920 these policies resulted in the emergence of two blocs. One, which consisted of Austria and Hungary, sought to revise the Paris settlement, and gravitated rapidly towards Italy and Germany. This trend was completed by the *Anschluss* and Hungary's membership of Hitler's Anti-Comintern Pact. The second bloc comprised Poland, Czechoslovakia, Yugoslavia and Rumania. These states formed close diplomatic links with each other and, during the 1920s, could depend on French guarantees against the aggression of other powers. During the 1930s, however, French influence collapsed in central and eastern Europe. As a result, this 'Little Entente' was undermined as various states hastened to make their own additional arrangements with Germany. Czechoslovakia tried to hold out against German influence, but she was set upon in 1938 by Germany, Hungary and Poland, all intent on claiming their fellow-nationals in the Sudetenland and Southern Slovakia. The failure of the west to support Czechoslovakia was a catalyst for Soviet aggression. In August 1939 Stalin sought to wipe out the memory of Brest-Litovsk by agreeing with Hitler the partition of Poland and the division of eastern Europe into German and Soviet spheres of influence. This pact enabled Hitler to launch his *Blitzkrieg* on Poland and, in so doing, to complete the destruction of the Paris settlement.

Austria

Austria was, in 1919, the German remnant of the Austro-Hungarian monarchy. It contained a population of a mere 8 million people, of whom over one-third lived in Vienna. This transition from a major power to a state not much larger than Switzerland was so sudden that it caused 'a terrifying array of problems',[50] both internal and external. By 1933 the search for solutions in a democratic context had clearly failed and Austria drifted into a period of authoritarian government under Dollfuss (1932–4) and Schuschnigg (1934–8), which was ended by the absorption of Austria into Germany and the imposition of the Nazi dictatorship.

Austria's political problems were intensified by a loss of identity; Austrians had never wanted to be a separate entity, preferring instead *Anschluss*, or union with Germany. According to Bauer, one of the leaders of the Austrian Social Democrats, 'If we stay independent, then...we shall live the life of a dwarf state.'[51] In the event, Austrians had no choice, for *Anschluss* was explicitly forbidden by the Treaties of Versailles and St Germain. But they developed no real commitment to the separate identity thus forced upon them. The 1920s saw the steady decline of democracy; although the 1920 constitution provided for a federal republic and a strong legislature, it was rendered unworkable by the constant rivalry between the left-wing Social Democrats, under Bauer and Renner, and the conservative Christian Socialists under Bishop Seipel. Initially in coalition until 1922, the two had drifted apart and the Christian Socialists dominated most of the governments of the 1920s and 1930s. Unable to achieve a majority in Parliament, the Christian Socialists were constantly looking over their shoulder at the Social Democrats, whom they accused of trying to introduce a programme of 'Austro-Marxism'. Indeed, fear of the socialist left eventually induced the Christian Socialists to rely on a para-military force called the *Heimwehr*, the activities of which became increasingly sinister.

The main catalyst for the change from democracy to dictatorship was economic crisis which, according to K.R. Stadler, prevented 'a reasonably intelligent, civilized and industrious nation from settling down and making a success of their new state'.[51] Much of the blame has been placed on the terms of the 1919 Treaty of St Germain; according to the Austrian delegation, 'what remains of Austria could not live'.[51] Austria was now able to produce only one quarter of her food and was obliged to import most of her coal and raw materials. By 1922 the situation had deteriorated badly, with rampant inflation and hunger riots. Chancellor Seipel offered a series of solutions in the form of international loans and careful budgetary controls and, for a while, Austria experienced a small boom. This did not, however, reverse the permanent trade deficit and was, in any case, wiped out by the Great Depression. In 1931 the entire Austrian banking system, Credit Anstalt, collapsed under the strain which, in turn, resulted in the withdrawal of all foreign investment. Industrial production declined in 1932 to 61 per cent of its 1929 level, while the unemployment rate rose, in the same period, from 9.9 per cent to 21.4 per cent.[52]

Austria now entered an authoritarian phase as her leaders, unable to do much about the financial and economic crisis, sought to minimize the symptoms of political instability. The Christian Socialist leader, Dollfuss, became Minister of Agriculture in 1931 and Chancellor in 1932. This 'physically tiny and excessively vain man'[51] was a devout Catholic and implacable opponent of the left, determined to rid the country of 'godless Marxism'. Highly critical of 'so-called democracy', he aimed to establish a 'Social Christian German state of Austria, on a corporative basis, under strong authoritarian leadership'.[52] His subsequent measures certainly showed the seriousness of his intentions. In 1933 he severely weakened the Austrian Parliament and made it possible to rule by executive decree. He then turned on the parties and movements, apart from the Christian Socialists. His measures against the Social Democrats (to 'remove the rubbish accumulated under the Republic')[53] precipitated the 1934 civil war, from which Dollfuss emerged victorious. Meanwhile, under the influence of Mussolini, he had set up a mass party, the Fatherland Front, and went on in 1934 to introduce a corporative system similar to that in Italy. His own power increased dramatically as, in imitation of Mussolini, he accumulated for himself no fewer than five cabinet posts. His personal rule was abruptly terminated by his assassination in 1934 but the system was maintained in its essentials by his successor, Schuschnigg.

Throughout the period Austria experienced a complex

pattern of right-wing influences which calls for some explanation. The first major movement was the *Heimwehr*, a semi-
Fascist mass movement which was, however, increasingly
used by the conservative right, or Christian Socialists. As the
regime became, under Dollfuss, more rigidly authoritarian,
it developed, in the Fatherland Front, its own mass base,
which overlapped many of the activities of the *Heimwehr*. It
was, however, unable to control another movement of the
right – the Austrian Nazis. Openly committed to Hitler's
ideology, they regarded Dollfuss as an old-fashioned reactionary, and it was they who murdered him in 1934. Although the
Nazis did not achieve their objective of immediate union with
the Third Reich, they did play an important role in the events
leading to the downfall of Schuschnigg in 1938. It is ironical
that the *Anschluss* which Austria had always wanted could be
brought about only by internal subversion and external force
in the form of a German invasion. Why was this?

To some extent, the obstacle to voluntary *Anschluss* was the
Austrian leadership itself. Both Dollfuss and Schuschnigg
were fully in favour of union with Germany, but within the
traditional model of Austro-German dualism rather than
under the more recent Prussian domination. Schuschnigg,
especially, distrusted German militarism, the influence of
Hitler and, of course, the intentions of the Austrian Nazis
whom he saw as an enemy in the midst. He therefore pursued
a policy of maintaining Austrian independence for the
moment by manoeuvring diplomatically between Hitler and
Mussolini and avoiding direct dependence on either Italy or
Germany. Italy, however, soon lost the will to counter
German influence in Austria as her own attention was
diverted to the campaign in Ethiopia and the war in Spain.
There was little, therefore, to prevent German ascendancy in
Austria. The 1936 Austro-German Treaty tightened the link
and, in 1938, Hitler summoned Schuschnigg to Germany,
charging him with having broken this pact. Convinced that
Hitler was trying to find an excuse to take over Austria,
Schuschnigg announced a national plebiscite for a 'free',
independent and united Austria. Hitler, however, moved too
quickly for Schuschnigg. The Austrian Nazis caused so much
internal unrest that Schuschnigg was forced to resign before

the plebiscite could be held. He was succeeded as Chancellor by the Nazi leader, Seyss-Inquart, who promptly requested German intervention. There was no resistance to the German invasion and Hitler was given a rousing welcome in Vienna. The plebiscite held on 10 April 1938 returned a vote of 99.75 per cent in favour of the *Anschluss* as carried out by Seyss-Inquart and the German government.

The next seven years were probably the worst in Austria's entire history. Her very name was expunged and she was subordinated totally to the interests of the Third Reich. The administration was Nazified, the opposition was purged by the Gestapo and SS, and special courts were set up to deal with political cases. The entire economy was plundered for the German war effort, including Austria's gold reserves. Indeed, Austria suffered more severely as a result of Hitler's military ventures than did most other parts of the Reich. It is generally agreed that this experience cured forever Austria's desire to be united with Germany. In the words of the Social Democrat, Renner: 'In just three months Austria was liquidated as a state and a nation, but therewith the people's sympathies for the German Reich were also extinguished.' By 1943, E. Barker maintains, the vast majority of the population desired total independence. Resistance was attempted by a variety of groups, including Communists, Socialists, Catholics, factory workers and intellectuals; three movements of particular importance were the Austrian Freedom Movement, the Austrian Freedom Front, and the Anti-Fascist Freedom Movement for Austria. There was therefore little regret when the Allies ended the *Anschluss* in 1945. Austria recognized that her future lay in accepting that she was a small non-aligned state and not part of a massive German monolith.

Hungary

Hungary experienced between the wars a more complete range of regimes than any of the other 'successor states'. The collapse of the Habsburg monarchy in 1918 was followed by the establishment of a democratic republic under Károlyi. This, in turn, was replaced in 1919 by the Soviet Republic of Béla Kun, which soon succumbed to a counter-revolution.

Between 1920 and 1944 Hungary was ruled by a right-wing regime under Admiral Horthy, although there was some alternation between moderate and radical governments. In 1944 Horthy was overthrown by the Germans and a Nazi-style dictatorship under Szálasi was installed. With the defeat of Germany the wheel turned full circle as Hungary came under a second and, this time, permanent Communist administration.

Hungary seceded from the Austro-Hungarian Empire once it had become clear that the defeat of the Central powers was inevitable. In October 1918, a new Hungarian National Council was set up under Károlyi, which was intended as a progressive and democratic parliamentary system based on universal suffrage, secret ballot, freedom of the press and land reform. This experiment was never given a chance to work. Hungary was invaded by Czech and Rumanian detach-ments seeking to extend the boundaries of *their* states, and the western Allies denounced Károlyi for his refusal to allow his territory to be used as a base for operations against Soviet Russia. Károlyi was even denounced as a Bolshevik; this was a major blunder which served only to bring about the very Communist regime which the Allies had hoped to avoid.

For Károlyi, under severe external pressure, now felt impelled to bring the Communists into collaboration with his own Social Democrats and even thought in terms of seeking assistance from Russia to support the new regime against its numerous enemies. In March 1919 he resigned in desperation and a new, far-left coalition was set up, dominated by Béla Kun. A new Revolutionary Governing Council heralded the formation of a Soviet Republic and introduced a string of new institutions and policies, including a 'Red Army', revolution-ary tribunals, a network of councils, and extensive national-ization. Béla Kun made no secret of the narrow base of his power. He had, he said, set up 'a dictatorship of an active minority on behalf of the by and large passive proletariat'. He also considered it necessary to 'act in a strong and merciless fashion...at least until such time that the revolution spreads to the [other] European countries'.[54]

The Kun regime was not without its achievements; it introduced an eight-hour working day, increased pay and guaranteed rights for ethnic minorities in Hungary. But it collapsed, after only 133 days, for a combination of external and internal reasons. By July 1919, the invading Rumanians had broken through the Hungarian lines and were advancing on Budapest. At this time of crisis the government lacked extensive popular support, largely because of mistakes in its strategy; it had been too doctrinaire and had neglected to exploit national sentiment, it had failed to win over the peasantry by refusing to redistribute, to their private owner-ship, the land confiscated from the nobility, and it had ignored the need to maintain the support of the non-Com-munist left. Kun was therefore forced to flee Budapest and go into exile. He was eventually shot, ironically, in the Soviet Union during Stalin's purges.

The swing to the left was now followed by a lurch to the right. The 'Red Terror' was replaced by an infinitely more savage 'White Terror' as 'officers' detachments' prowled those parts of the country not occupied by the Rumanians, slaughtering workers and Jews and torturing to death any suspected members of the Béla Kun regime. This appalling phase of Hungarian history was ended in 1920 with the emergence of Admiral Horthy as the head of state, or Regent. A convinced anti-Communist, Horthy constructed an authori-tarian system which rested on the traditional power bases – the landed gentry, the industrial capitalists and the govern-ment bureaucrats. It was not, however, totalitarian; he retained the Hungarian constitution and allowed most of the parties to function, although with carefully restricted powers. Of all the 'dictatorships' covered in this book, the Horthy regime was probably the most borderline; indeed, it might be possible, for the 1920s, to dispense with the term altogether.

The lengthy period of Horthy's rule is usually divided into two distinct phases: the moderate conservatism of the 1920s and the more complex zig-zags between caution and radical-ism which characterized the 1930s.

After the bloodbath of the 'White Terror', Horthy con-centrated on providing the new regime with an aura of legitimacy. He chose as his Prime Minister Count Bethlen, a leading aristocrat who had the confidence of the capitalists and landowners. Bethlen was suspicious of democracy as applied in those countries which had not, as yet, acquired political maturity and sophistication, and hoped to reach a position halfway between 'unbridled freedom and un-restrained dictatorship'.[55] He considered it safest to return to the limited democracy of pre-war Hungary and was willing to allow many components of a constitutional system. But his concessions were cosmetic rather than functional; his franchise, for example, drastically reduced the size of the electorate. He should, nevertheless, receive some credit for a period of relative political stability and economic progress. By 1929 industry had recovered from its dreadful performance of the early 1920s and had exceeded the production figures of 1913.

The Bethlen era was ended by the Great Depression which hit Hungary as seriously as any country in Europe. The industrial growth of the late 1920s had depended heavily on foreign capital investment which was withdrawn following the collapse of the banking system in central Europe. To make matters worse, Hungary's agriculture suffered disastrously under the strain of low prices and foreign tariffs against food exports. The overall result was large-scale poverty and, in some areas, people actually starved to death. Bethlen, unable to cope with the inevitable outbursts of discontent, resigned in 1930. Horthy was now faced with a dilemma about the style of rule which he should adopt. He opted for an increased personal role and therefore extended his powers by the Regency Act of 1937. But he experienced difficulties with his choice of Prime Ministers. Basically, there were two types of premier: those who were in the conservative tradition of Bethlen, and those who had radical, even Fascist, leanings. Horthy manoeuvred uncertainly between the two styles. Between 1932 and 1936 Hungary was governed by Gömbös, a radical and, according to Pamlényi, 'an uncompromising advocate of arbitrary, totalitarian forms of government'. His real aim was the 'realization of a less concealed, total form of fascist rule free of parliamentary trappings'.[56] His death in 1936 was followed by a zig-zag sequence of conservatives like Darányi (1936–8) and Teleki (1939–41) and radicals such as Imrédy. It seemed that Horthy was unable to decide which style of right-wing rule was more appropriate to Hungary's needs.

Much the same could be said of his foreign policy. The basic influence behind Hungarian diplomacy was a powerful revisionist urge resulting from the Treaty of Trianon (1920). This had deprived Hungary of two-thirds of her territory and consigned 3.3 million Hungarians to Yugoslavia, Rumania and Czechoslovakia. According to D. Sinor, Hungary was a 'mutilated, dismembered, disarmed country, surrounded by strong and hostile neighbours'.[57] The immediate priority was to emerge from isolation. The first major development was the 1927 Treaty of Friendship with Italy and it seemed that Mussolini was the obvious ally for the future. Then, after 1933, Hitler emerged as a real alternative. The Horthy regime oscillated between distancing itself from Germany (because of its fear of German expansionism) and collaborating with Hitler in the hope of smashing the Trianon settlement. After much dithering, Prime Minister Imrédy settled for the latter course and, by the First Vienna Award (1938) Hungary benefited territorially from Hitler's destruction of Czechoslovakia.

At the same time, a succession of premiers thought that they could prevent Hungary from being sucked into Germany's European war. Teleki went so far as to refuse to allow German troops access via Hungary to Poland's southern frontier, and he even provided asylum for Polish refugees from Hitler's *Blitzkrieg*. But again irredentism – or perhaps territorial greed – prevailed. With German support, Hungary acquired, in the Second Vienna Award, some 17,000 square miles of Rumania, together with 2.5 million people.[56] Inevitably, Hitler expected in return a commitment from Hungary and this was fulfilled when, in 1941, Premier Bárdossy provided Hungarian troops for the invasion of Yugoslavia and the Soviet Union. At first it seemed that Hungary would have no cause to regret her deeper involvement, for the Axis powers appeared invincible in 1941. By 1943, however, all illusions had been destroyed in the shattering defeat inflicted on the Hungarians by the Soviet army at Voronezh, to the north of Stalingrad. Horthy tried to extricate Hungary from the war by opening negotiations with the Allies. Hitler's response, in March 1944, was the occupation of Hungary and the enforcement of the full rigours of Nazi policies, including the deportation of Hungarian Jews to the extermination camps in Poland. Horthy, in desperation, signed an armistice with the Soviet Union in October 1944. He was immediately arrested by the Germans and confined to Dachau and Buchenwald. After the end of the war he found refuge in Portugal where he lived for the rest of his life. He escaped extradition and trial for 'war crimes' largely through Stalin's intervention: 'Leave him alone, after all he did ask for an armistice.'[58]

Horthy was succeeded by one of the most fanatical regimes of the whole period – the Fascist dictatorship of Szálasi. Founder of a blatantly Nazi-style movement called the Arrow Cross, Szálasi formulated a programme of 'Hungarism' or the construction of a Greater Hungary which would cover the whole of the Danube basin.[59] He was also committed to introducing a corporate state and to nationalizing industry and mechanizing agriculture. In fact, he achieved nothing. He lost control over his movement which plundered, pillaged, tortured, and murdered over 10,000 people in the Budapest area alone until the arrival of the Russians put paid to their activities. Szálasi eventually met the fate which Horthy escaped. He was put on trial in Hungary in 1946, condemned to death and executed.

By 1945 Hungary had established, as in 1919, a coalition government dominated by the Communists. This time, however, the regime did not collapse, as it had behind it the full support of Soviet military power. The Communists had also learned, from the failure of Béla Kun's 'dictatorship of the proletariat', the importance of patriotism and efficient organization as well as ideology. The other parties were steadily undermined and eliminated so that, by 1948, the Communist Party ruled alone. This remained the case until liberalization occurred in 1989.

Poland

The First World War proved to be the turning-point in modern Polish history. It smashed the three empires which held it captive (Russia, Germany and Austria-Hungary), and created a power vacuum which a new state in eastern Europe could fill. The core of independent Poland was the former province removed from Russia by the Treaty of Brest-Litovsk (1918). To this was added territory from Germany by the

Treaty of Versailles (1919) and from Austria and Hungary by the Treaties of St Germain and Trianon (1919 and 1920). The Polish government, however, considered the eastern frontier to be too restrictive; hence, in 1919, Poland launched an attack on the Soviet Union and captured much of the Ukraine, including Kiev. The Soviet army soon recovered and drove the invaders back to Warsaw, which was subsequently besieged. Poland now appeared to be in dire peril but, with French assistance, managed to rout the Russians and re-occupy the western Ukraine, possession of which was confirmed by the Treaty of Riga (1921). To this substantial slice of territory was added Vilno, seized from Lithuania, and parts of Upper Silesia. Overall, Poland, with an area of 150,000 square miles and a population of 27 million, was one of Europe's more important states.

Unfortunately, she was confronted by a series of desperate problems. The first was the mixed composition of her population. Poles comprised only two-thirds of the total; the rest included four million Ukrainians, three million Jews, one million Germans, one million Belorussians, and smaller numbers of Russians, Lithuanians and Tartars.[60] The second problem was political instability. The constitution proved inappropriate to the ethnic structure since it provided for a centralized rather than a federal state. In theory, Poland was an advanced democracy, with guarantees of individual freedoms. Unfortunately, proportional representation encouraged the growth of small parties and prevented the formation of stable governments; altogether, there were 15 cabinets between November 1918 and May 1926, an average lifespan of only five months. The whole situation was aggravated by a major economic crisis in which inflation saw the Polish mark sink to a level of 15 million to the dollar. This inevitably hindered the task of reconstruction, promoting shortages and unemployment.

This unstable period came to a dramatic end when, in May 1926, General Pilsudski led several regiments of the Polish army into Warsaw. He replaced the democratic government with an authoritarian regime which lasted, beyond his own death in 1935, until the eventual liquidation of Poland in 1939.

Pilsudski was already something of a national hero. He had organized the Polish legions which had fought for the country's independence in the First World War. He had then become head of state between 1919 and 1922, leading the Polish offensive against Russia and organizing the defence of Warsaw in 1920. He had voluntarily stepped aside in 1922 into semi-retirement. Between 1922 and 1926, however, he watched with disgust the deteriorating political scene. At first he was not disposed to take drastic action because 'If I were to break the law I would be opening the door to all sorts of adventurers to make coups and putsches.'[61] Eventually however, he became convinced that direct action was unavoidable. His solution was a call for national unity and a common moral sense, to be promoted by a grouping called 'Sanacja'. According to J. Rothschild, his intention was to form a 'non-political phalanx of all classes and parties supposedly prepared to elevate general state interests above particular partisan and social ones'.[61] This new order would be kept together by Pilsudski himself. Ironically, he did not resume the presidency in 1926, serving, instead, in the humbler capacity of Foreign Minister with two brief spells as premier. Yet no one doubted that ultimate power lay in his hands: 'I am a strong man and I like to decide all matters by myself'.[62] To emphasize this point, he reduced the power of the legislature, arguing that 'The chicanes of Parliament retard indispensable solutions.' He saw western-style party political manoeuvres as highly destructive in Poland, since they had produced a Parliament which was in reality a 'House of Prostitutes'. He therefore broke the back of the party system and surrounded himself with loyal followers. Yet his dictatorship was never complete; his aim was not to set up a totalitarian state and a new political consciousness, but rather to depoliticize Poland and to create unity through heightened moral awareness.

What were Pilsudski's achievements? They related mainly to the restoration of the Polish state after a century and a half of foreign rule. He strengthened the executive through his changes of 1926 and the constitution of 1935 (which he did not live to see), and made the administration more professional and efficient. He revived the morale of the army and, through a skilful foreign policy, strengthened Poland's standing in Europe. On the other hand, his regime witnessed serious financial and economic problems. The Great Depression had a particularly devastating effect on Polish agriculture and, as elsewhere, caused a sudden spurt in industrial unemployment. Pilsudski resorted to an unimaginative policy of financial constraints and drastic deflation. But this only aggravated the problem, and even by 1939 Poland's per capita output was 15 per cent below that of 1913. 'Thus', observes Aldcroft, 'Poland had little to show economically for 20 years of independent statehood.'[63]

Pilsudski also showed serious flaws in his character. His rule became increasingly irksome as he himself became more and more petty. Rothschild argues that Pilsudski's best years were behind him and that he had become 'prematurely cantankerous, embittered and rigid'.[61] Overall, it could be said, he completely lost the will to temper discipline and constraint with progressive reform; his emphasis on continuity therefore precluded any possibility of meaningful change.

Pilsudski was one of the few dictators to die before the general upheaval of 1939–40. The authoritarian regime which he had established continued for the next four years but it became less personal and more ideological. The reason for this was that, cantankerous though he had been, Pilsudski proved irreplaceable; the likes of Slawek, Rydz-Smigly and Beck lacked his popularity and charisma. Faced with evergrowing pressure from the right, the *Sanacja* after Pilsudski was forced to collaborate with Poland's semi-Fascist movements,[64] since it lacked Pilsudski's confidence to defy them. Whether Poland would eventually have become a Fascist state is open to speculation, but it is interesting to note that her movement in that direction was due to the lack of leadership rather than to any personality cult. Polish 'Fascism' therefore served to conceal mediocrity rather than to project personal power.

Pilsudski and his successors were faced with the problem of upholding the security of the new Polish state. This was given some urgency by the resentment of all her neighbours against Poland's territorial gains. At first Pilsudski sought safety in an alliance with France and Rumania in 1921. Gradually, however, the will of France to assist Poland grew weaker. In 1925 France signed the Locarno Pact which, alongside Britain, Italy, Belgium and Germany, guaranteed the 1919 frontiers in western Europe but not in the east. By the early 1930s Pilsudski felt that he could no longer depend upon France and therefore sought accommodation with the powers which threatened Poland; he formed non-aggression pacts with Russia in 1932 and Germany in 1934. After Pilsudski's death, however, Poland slid towards destruction. There was a dreadful inevitability about the whole process: given Hitler's policy of *Lebensraum* and Stalin's determination to wipe out the memory of Brest-Litovsk, Poland did not stand a chance. According to K. Syrop, 'It is clear now that once Hitler and Stalin had jointly decided to wipe Poland off the map, no Polish policy and no power on earth could avert disaster.'[65]

Foreign Minister Beck showed courage in defying Hitler's demands for a Polish corridor and was bolstered by the Anglo-French guarantee of March 1939. He clearly felt that Poland stood a chance of holding off Germany, as Pilsudski had fended off Russia in 1920. This time, however, Poland was crushed by Hitler's *Blitzkrieg*. The Polish cavalry, which had triumphed over Soviet infantry were now shot to pieces by German tanks and aircraft. By mid-September the western half of Poland had been conquered by the Nazi war machine. The Polish government transferred to the east, only to be trapped by Soviet troops who were moving into position to take up the territory agreed in the Nazi–Soviet non-Aggression Pact.

Poland was therefore at the mercy of her two historic enemies. Stalin proceeded to impose Communist institutions in the east, while the German zone was divided in two. The north-west and Silesia were absorbed directly into the Third Reich and were immediately Germanized; Gauleiter Forster said that his intention was 'to remove every manifestation of Polonism within the next few years'.[66] The rest was placed under Governor-General Hans Frank, who stated that no Polish state would ever be revived. The German occupation of Poland was to prove more horrifying and destructive than in any other conquered territory. Six million people died, out of a total population of 35 million; many of these were Jews who perished in extermination camps set up at Auschwitz-Birkenau, Maidenek, Sobibor, Belzec and Treblinka. The Polish capital, Warsaw, was the only occupied city to be pulled apart, systematically, by ground demolition squads.

Yet the devastation did not destroy the Polish national spirit and three resistance organizations had come into existence by mid-1941. The first was a government in exile under Sikorski which established an army abroad and integrated Polish servicemen into the American and British forces. The second was the underground Home Army (AK), the third the Polish Workers Movement (PPR), a Communist organization led by Gomulka. At first there was co-operation between Sikorski and the Soviet Union but, as the Soviet victory over Germany became more and more likely, Stalin did everything possible to weaken Sikorski and the AK. His task was made easier by the Yalta and Potsdam Conferences of 1945. The western Allies were, of course, unhappy about Poland falling under Soviet influence but were unable to prevent it. Hence, when recreated, Poland eventually became one of Stalin's satellite states, with a regime which was far more systematically pervasive than Pilsudski's had ever been. It was not until 1989 that the monopoly of the Communist Party was broken.

Estonia, Latvia and Lithuania

The Baltic enclaves Estonia, Latvia and Lithuania, originally provinces of Tsarist Russia, had been occupied by Germany in the First World War. Like Poland, they filled the power vacuum left by the defeat of both Germany and Russia. By 1920, the last foreign troops had been withdrawn and the newly independent republics could concentrate on internal consolidation.

In this they appeared to be assisted by liberal constitutions guaranteeing individual freedoms, rights for ethnic minorities, proportional representation and powerful Parliaments. Unfortunately, in the Baltic republics, as elsewhere, these principles proved extremely difficult to operate. One of the main problems was the proliferation of parties competing for power; in 1925, for example, the Latvian Parliament (*Saeima*) contained no fewer than 26 parties. The result was political instability, as Estonia saw 17 governments in 14 years, Latvia

16 in the same period and Lithuania 11 in seven years.[67] All this occurred at a time when political continuity was particularly important to tackle a wide range of economic and social problems, especially land reform and industrialization.

The first move to the right occurred in Lithuania in 1926. After a prolonged economic depression many prominent Lithuanians questioned the relevance of democratic institutions. The most important of these was Smetona, who seized power with the help of the military and established an authoritarian regime not unlike that of Pilsudski in Poland. Democracy lasted somewhat longer in the other two states but was wrecked eventually by the Great Depression which caused a decline in exports, an increase in unemployment, and misery in the rural areas. In 1934, therefore, they followed Lithuania's example. Dictatorships were set up by Päts in Estonia and Ulmanis in Latvia.

The three regimes had much in common. All imposed the usual measures associated with dictatorship, including restrictions on political parties, the strengthening of presidential powers and dependence on the army. Smetona went further than either of his contemporaries, transforming Lithuania into a one-party state and developing the aura of a personality cult – he was known as Leader of the People (*Tautos Vadas*). But none of the regimes had an ideological base. Indeed, all were as suspicious of the extreme right as they were of the radical left. The Fascist movements which developed in the Baltic states (the Thunder Cross of Latvia, the Estonian Freedom Fighters and the Lithuanian Iron Wolf) were regarded as a major danger, to be disciplined or even banned.

The three Baltic dictators have attracted far less condemnation than the others. V.S. Vardis, for example, argues that 'As dictatorships go...their rule was the mildest in Europe.'[67] The repressive measures were by no means complete and left considerable room for manoeuvre. The press, for example, was less constrained than elsewhere and was still able to convey left-wing views. There was no attempt to introduce a complete corporate system and private enterprise continued to flourish. The Baltic peoples recovered reasonably well from the worst impact of the Depression and certainly enjoyed a higher standard of living than their contemporaries in the Soviet Union. By the late 1930s two of the three, Estonia and Latvia, showed signs of returning to a more obvious democratic base.

Yet, in 1939, the independence of all three Baltic republics was snuffed out, never to be rekindled. Two contrasting explanations have been provided for this.

One is that the three states were, like Poland, condemned by their geo-political position in Europe, strategically placed as they were between Germany and the Soviet Union. A. Dallin argues that their demise was as near as possible inevitable and that 'whatever these countries did or failed to do was ultimately immaterial'.[68] It could certainly be argued that the situation which brought the states into existence at the end of the First World War was unique and never to be repeated – the almost simultaneous collapse of *both* major powers in the region. But it was hardly to be expected that this power vacuum would remain or that Russia would countenance the permanent loss of her Baltic territories. Hence the fate of the republics was decided when the Nazi–Soviet Non-Aggression Pact of August 1939 allocated Estonia and Latvia to Stalin, and Lithuania to Hitler.

An alternative view is that the Baltic states did too little to help themselves. They failed to set up an effective security system or to co-operate sufficiently to mobilize the 500,000 men available. Any attempts which were made at alliance were unsatisfactory. A pact was drawn up in 1921 but Latvia and Estonia refused to admit Lithuania because they were afraid of being drawn into a border conflict between Lithuania and Poland. The 1934 Treaty of Friendship and Co-operation did include Lithuania but provided only for consultation on foreign policy and not on military planning. By 1939 there were, in fact, three divergent approaches; Latvia wanted to remain strictly neutral, Estonia was primarily anti-Russian and Lithuania anti-German.[69] E. Anderson has argued:

It would be idle to pretend that the Baltic states were a factor of first importance in European affairs; nevertheless, placed as they were between Russia, Poland and Germany, if united, they could have played a respectable role in north-eastern Europe. Their fate during the months that followed, then, would probably have been somewhat different.[69]

Late in 1939 Estonia, Latvia and Lithuania had to sign pacts with the USSR allowing the Red Army to be stationed on their territory. Stalin systematically tightened his grip, assisted by Hitler's transfer of Lithuania to the Soviet sphere in exchange for an additional slice of Poland. In 1940 the area was brought under direct Soviet rule but proved extremely difficult to govern. Revolts occurred in all three states and the Baltic peoples had high hopes of independence when, in 1941, Germany attacked the Soviet Union. But Hitler's plans were even more unpleasant than Stalin's. All three states came under Rosenberg's Ministry for the Occupied Eastern Territories and experienced systematic terror and exterminations. The Nazi dictatorship ended in 1944 with the fall of Tallinn and Riga to the Red Army but the price was the reimposition of Stalinism and their transformation into Soviet Socialist Republics. The Baltic republics were, therefore, the only creations of the Brest-Litovsk and Paris settlements not to be revived at the end of the Second World War.

DICTATORSHIP IN THE BALKANS

Introduction

The one common link between all the Balkan peoples was their historic subjugation to the Turks; all of the states of south-eastern Europe were originally part of the Ottoman Empire. Greece became independent in 1830, followed by Serbia and Rumania after the Crimean War, Bulgaria in 1878 and Albania in 1912. The First World War saw a division of loyalties. Bulgaria allied herself to Germany, Austria-Hungary and Turkey (known collectively as the Central powers). Serbia and Albania were invaded and occupied by the Central powers, while Rumania and Greece opted to join the Allies. All but Bulgaria emerged from the peace settlement either intact or enlarged. It seemed that their futures were guaranteed and that they would benefit from liberal and progressive rule.

Appearances were, however, deceptive and this initial optimism was not fulfilled. The Balkan states faced massive economic, social and political problems which led inexorably to dictatorship.

The first failures occurred in the agricultural policies of the various governments. The immediate post-war priority was to redistribute land to the peasantry but, in every case, the reform programme was either incomplete or did not affect a high enough proportion of the population. There remained a large and discontented rural proletariat which placed intolerable pressure on the land and aggravated the problem of low productivity. The other half of the economy, industry, also experienced difficulties. The most serious was inadequate domestic sources of investment, which made most of the Balkan states a prey to external influence; Albania, for example, came to depend too heavily on Italy, while Rumania and Bulgaria found themselves ensnared by Germany.

Although it is hazardous to generalize about an area as complex as the Balkans, there does seem to have been an identifiable political trend. At first the Balkan states operated as democracies, with radical governments (like that of Stambuliski in Bulgaria) attempting radical reforms. There followed a drift to the right as the parliamentary system was undermined by bickering parties and a rapid sequence of weak governments. The eventual outcome was a series of authoritarian regimes. Albania was the first to succumb as Ahmed Zogu proclaimed himself president in 1924 and King Zog in 1928. Yugoslavia, too, came under a royal dictatorship, in the form of Alexander I, from 1929. Rumania's equivalent was King Carol (1903–40) and Bulgaria was ruled with an iron hand by King Boris from 1935. Greece experienced a more ideologically based dictatorship under General Metaxas (1936–41).

All of these regimes found themselves caught up in hectic diplomacy and bitter rivalry. Before the First World War the Balkans had been the 'powder keg' of Europe, always threatening to transform a local crisis into a general conflagration between the major powers. After 1918 the area of greatest potential danger shifted to central Europe but the south-east remained unstable and volatile as some of the defeated states sought to reconstitute their former power.

Bulgaria and Hungary, in particular, advanced revisionist claims against their neighbours. The latter, fully conscious of the resentment of Bulgaria and Hungary, sought security in two major multilateral agreements. The first was the Little Entente (1920–1) in which Rumania, Yugoslavia and Czechoslovakia sought to isolate Hungary and to prevent the possibility of a Habsburg restoration. The second was the Balkan Pact of 1934, comprising Rumania, Yugoslavia, Turkey and Greece and directed, among other objectives, towards the containment of Bulgaria. There was also a considerable amount of bilateral diplomacy between individual Balkan states. The overall result was that, by 1939, a precarious balance of power had been achieved in which uneasy détente had come to replace active confrontation. What happened was that this balance was destroyed by the involvement of the great powers, and the Balkan states were sucked one by one into the Second World War.

Albania

The main developments in Albania between the wars were the internal dominance of Ahmed Zogu, later proclaimed King Zog, and the ever-growing influence of Fascist Italy, resulting in 1939 in direct rule.

Albania established itself as an independent state in 1912, after the First Balkan War. Almost immediately it encountered external threats to its very existence. During the First World War, for example, it was occupied by no fewer than seven armies,[70] while both Greece and Italy had expectations of Albanian territory as a reward for having joined the Allies. Their claims to Albanian territory so delayed international consideration of the future of this tiny state that the Albanians impatiently took matters into their own hands. Setting up a Regency Council and a Committee of National Defence, they managed to evict an Italian occupation force of 20,000 men. By 1920 Albania was a fully independent state and a member of the League of Nations. Indeed, a report commissioned by the League was full of optimism about Albania's future: 'It seems clear that the essential elements of a prosperous Albania exist' and that 'it possesses all the condition necessary for the formation of a politically and economically independent state.[70]

Unfortunately Albania was to suffer from serious instability which led to political chaos and dictatorship. The problem was partly economic and social: inadequate development and the long-standing conflict in the south between the Muslim landowning aristocracy and the Christian agricultural workers. It was also political. Albania was torn by the rivalry between Bishop Noli and Ahmed Zogu, the former much influenced by western ideas, the latter entirely indigenous. At first they served in the same government but, in 1922, Noli withdrew to form an opposition. In 1924 Zogu did badly in an election and considered his position so perilous that he fled to neighbouring Yugoslavia. Noli, who now replaced him, attempted to introduce a series of reforms but his government lacked internal unity and effective leadership. In 1924, therefore, Zogu was able to make a sudden comeback. Invading Albania with his own followers, a thousand Yugoslav volunteers and 40 officers of the White Russian army, he overthrew Noli and had himself proclaimed president. He took immediate action to consolidate his power and, in 1928, elevated his title to 'Zog I, King of the Albanians'. He was backed by a new constitution which remained in existence until 1939.

There is little disagreement about the nature of Zog's rule. S. Pollo and A. Puto argue that 'Zogu's return meant the establishment of a totally reactionary dictatorship in Albania.' It is true that order was restored, but 'it was the worst possible kind of stability'.[71] A. Logoreci maintains that the monarchy was 'a pitiful incongruity' which made Albania 'the laughing stock of Europe'.[72] L.S. Stavrianos, too, believes that any reforms attempted were only 'skin deep'.[70] Zog did make a superficial effort to retain the parliamentary system but, at the same time, rigged elections, eliminated opponents and even hired assassins to deal with prominent Albanians in exile. He was determined, in his own words, to 'establish exemplary order and discipline throughout the country'.[71]

Much, of course, would depend on economic stability. This, in turn, provided a link between domestic and foreign policy. Zog identified Albania's main need as foreign aid, and Italy as the most likely source. He therefore signed a series of agreements with Mussolini. The first, in 1925, allowed the Italians to finance a new National Bank and a Company for the Economic Development of Albania. In return, Mussolini expected to be given increased control over Albania's military security and foreign affairs. Zog went further down this perilous road in the 1926 Treaty of 'friendship and security' and the 1927 defensive military alliance. By 1933 he was uncomfortably aware of Albania's dependence on Italy. He therefore openly defied the Italian dictator and refused his demands for a customs union. Mussolini, however, won his point because, by 1935, Albania was in urgent need of further Italian loans to wipe out the large budgetary deficit which had accumulated during this brief period of conflict.

The process of Italian colonization was well advanced by 1939. It remained only to transform this into direct political control. Feeling the need to keep up with the hectic pace of Hitler's foreign adventures, Mussolini invaded Albania on 7 April 1939 and overthrew the Zog regime. Albania came under the direct rule of Victor Emanuel III, and the diplomatic corps and army were united with those of Italy. This arrangement continued until the surrender of Italy in September 1943. From this date Germany was the occupying power, a transition which marked an increase in the number of savage atrocities.

The Albanians are, historically, the most fiercely independent of the Balkan peoples. A powerful resistance movement developed in 1941, with the assistance of Yugoslavia, and based on Hoxha's Albanian Communist Party. The military arm was the National Liberation Front (NLC) which co-ordinated a series of successful guerrilla attacks against German units and increased its own numbers by the end of 1944 to about 70,000.[73] Hoxha aimed for a social revolution to be accomplished alongside the eviction of the Germans and his new government was dominated from the start by the Communists. He remained in firm control until his death in 1984, establishing in the process the sort of personality cult which had completely eluded Zog.

Bulgaria

Bulgaria was the only Balkan state to have allied itself during the First World War to the Central powers. As one of the defeated combatants, Bulgaria was treated severely by the

Allies, losing Western Thrace to Greece, the Dobruja to Romania and several key frontier areas to Yugoslavia. The Treaty of Neuilly (1919) also ended military conscription, reduced Bulgaria's army to 33,000 and imposed an indemnity of 450 million dollars, payable over 38 years. Bulgaria's leaders, therefore, faced considerable problems in adjusting to the country's loss of territory, prestige and status; this was reflected in the wide variety of regimes experienced between the wars. Bulgaria's first government, under Stambuliski, was radical and reformist. After this had been overthrown in 1923, Bulgaria reverted to a more traditional style of politics. This, however, proved so chaotic that another coup, this time in 1934, set up a right-wing regime which was gradually converted by King Boris into a royal dictatorship. After a period of German influence, Bulgaria emerged from the Second World War with all the components of a pro-Moscow Communist system.

Between 1919 and 1923 Bulgaria was led by Stambuliski, son of a peasant and a former school teacher. He intended to transform Bulgaria into 'a model agricultural state'[74] by means of a programme which redistributed land to benefit the poorer peasantry; by 1926 about 80 per cent of the rural masses owned plots. Stambuliski's popularity was apparent in the 1923 elections, in which his Agrarian Party won 212 of the 245 seats in the legislature. But this could not guarantee the survival of his government. He was confronted by numerous enemies which included liberals, the army (which was concerned about his leftist leanings) and a terrorist group called the Internal Macedonian Revolutionary Organization (IMRO).[75] In June 1923 Stambuliski was ousted by a military coup. He was handed over to the IMRO, at whose hands he met a horrifying end; he was tortured, mutilated, and finally shot.

He was succeeded by a series of short-lived coalitions led by nonentities. Between 1923 and 1934 the incidence of violence rapidly increased as the IMRO intensified their activities. Relations with neighbouring states also caused concern; in October 1925, for example, the Greeks invaded Bulgaria to settle a frontier dispute and left only when confronted by a rare show of collective unity in the League of Nations. In 1934

Bulgaria's vulnerability increased as a result of the formation, among her neighbours,[75] of the Balkan Entente. Meanwhile, of course, the economy had been shattered by the impact of the Great Depression. The whole unstable edifice was eventually brought down in 19 May 1934 by a coup conducted by Colonel Velchev.

At first the new regime was faceless; Stavrianos has called it 'dictatorial but not fascist'.[75] It did not have the ideological base of Fascism, and premier Georgiev had little upon which to construct a personality cult. Waiting in the wings, however, was a ruthless, dynamic and elegant figure. King Boris intended to take control of the new regime when the opportunity presented itself. According to R. Ristelhueber, he showed 'a combination of flexibility and subtlety'.[76] In 1935 he issued a manifesto which announced major changes. There would, he insisted, be 'no going back'[75] to the unstable era of party politics; hence all political parties were banned. In 1937 he drew up a new constitution which guaranteed the place of a legislature in the Bulgarian system but placed tight conditions on the purpose and conduct of elections. It was possible, for example, to elect only candidates who had no party attachment and voting was made into something of an ordeal as a result of heavy police surveillance. In defence of Boris, it has been argued that he did much to reduce the level of political extremism and terrorist violence and that he tried to stabilize the economy. On the other hand, Bulgaria became, in effect, a police state in which terror now came from above. As for his attempt to pull Bulgaria out of the grips of the Depression, the cost was almost total dependence on Nazi Germany which was by 1939 taking 68 per cent of all Bulgaria's exports and providing 66 per cent of her imports.[75] This, in turn, pulled Bulgaria directly into the Axis political and diplomatic orbit.

Like most other states in eastern Europe and the Balkans, Bulgaria sought at first not to become involved in Hitler's war. Then, in 1941, Boris allowed the Germans to use his country as a base for operations against Greece and Yugoslavia, in return for territory to be extracted from these two victims. By 1943, however, Boris's commitment to the Axis cause was being questioned and he died in suspicious circumstances in August 1943 after an interview with Hitler. His place was taken by Prince Cyril who acted as regent for the six-year-old king, Simeon. Cyril strengthened the links with Germany, effectively transforming Bulgaria from an autonomous dictatorship into a puppet regime under full Nazi control. This was eventually disposed of in 1944 as a result partly of internal resistance from the Fatherland Front under the leadership of Dimitrov and partly of the Russian invasion. By 1946 it had become clear that Bulgaria would be a Communist state with close links with the Soviet Union. It was not until 1989 that this was liberalized sufficiently to allow for opposition groups.

Yugoslavia

Yugoslavia was one of the most diverse and heterogeneous of the smaller states of Europe. Its original core was the pre-war kingdom of Serbia, to which was added a significant number of territories in 1918. These included provinces of the former Austro-Hungarian monarchy, like Croatia, Slavonia, Dalmatia, Carniola, Styria, Carinthia, Istria, Baranja, Backa, the Banat, Prekomurje, Medjumurje, and Bosnia-Herzegovina. Small but important frontier areas were received by the Treaty of Neuilly, from Bulgaria and, finally, the previously independent state of Montenegro was added in the south. The result of these gains was a considerable ethnic mix. The new nation had a total of 12 linguistic groups, of which three were predominant. These were the Serbs, Croats and Slovenes which, between them, accounted for ten million out of the total population of 12 million.[77] The generous boundary changes meant that there were also significant numbers of Germans, Magyars, Albanians and Turks.

This conglomerate was at first called the 'Kingdom of the Serbs, Croats and Slovenes'. It adopted a new constitution in 1921 which provided for a parliamentary monarchy under King Alexander, recognized the existence of political parties and based the electoral system on proportional representation. This constitution could not, however, provide a guarantee of permanent stability. The country faced two sets of serious problems, economic and political. Serbia had been devastated during the First World War and had experienced, proportionately, among the heaviest population loss in

Europe. Post-war recovery was made extremely difficult by the impoverishment of the peasantry, and the persistent threat of economic instability served only to destabilize the political scene. This, in any case, was threatening enough. The main problem was the mutual distrust, often hatred, between the Serbs and Croats. The former were Orthodox in religion and socially conservative; the latter tended to be Catholic and more open to progressive western influences. The main area of conflict between them was the type of regime to be established. The Serbs wanted a centralized state (in effect a Greater Serbia) which they won in the 1921 constitution. The Croats, by contrast, aimed at a decentralized federation and did everything possible to undermine the predominantly Serb governments of the 1920s. A major crisis occurred in 1928 when the Croatian leader, Radich, was assassinated in the Parliament, or *Skupshtina*.[78] In the riots that followed there were open demands for an end to the power of Serbia and for the creation of a 'free Croatia'.

At this point King Alexander seized the initiative and imposed the sort of royal dictatorship which was to set the pattern for other Balkan states. He moved rapidly to close the Parliament and abolish the 1921 constitution. He was motivated by an impatience with party bickering, which he found repugnant; he had, in any case, developed a profound suspicion of western democratic systems from his earlier contacts with the court of Imperial Russia. According to V. Dedijer, he was 'autocratic by temperament'[79] and unable to share power: he frequently screamed at his ministers. He saw himself as the saviour of his state, which he decided to rename Yugoslavia. In his proclamation of 6 January 1929 he observed:

> I am sure that all, Serbs, Croats and Slovenes will loyally support my efforts, whose sole aim will be to establish as rapidly as possible such administration and organization of the state as will best conform with the general needs of the people and the interests of the state.[80]

To accomplish this he scrapped the old local government boundaries and set up nine new units, or *banovine*, which were superimposed across the old ethnic areas. He failed, however, to draw the sting of the problem. In 1931 the numerous Croatian exiles appealed to the League of Nations, making allegations that Alexander had imposed a reign of terror in Croatia and was making systematic use of brutality and torture.

In fact, Alexander tried to modify his rule by granting in 1931 a new constitution which officially ended the period of dictatorship. Two views have been put forward to explain his action. One is that this was a phased return to normality after a period of tough discipline. An alternative view is that the new concessions were 'merely a fig leaf for the royal dictatorship, which continued as before.'[78] Several points seem to support the second argument. The 1931 constitution greatly reduced the power of the Parliament, maintained the structure of the police state, introduced an Italian-style electoral sytem, and abolished the secret ballot. Far from leading Yugoslavia back to democracy, Alexander only narrowed the base of his regime. In the process, he alienated not only the Croats but also a large number of the more progressive Serbs. At the same time, he faced a growing economic crisis which included a trade deficit, a collapse of agricultural prices and the end of foreign investments and credits. The picture looked bleak indeed when, in October 1934, Alexander was assassinated, while on a visit to Marseilles, by a Macedonian terrorist.

He was succeeded by his son Peter, who, at eleven, was too young to rule. The regent, therefore, was Prince Paul who, according to Stavrianos, was 'ill suited for his task, being a dilettante and more interested in his art collection'.[78] Paul delegated most of his powers to his Prime Minister, Milan Stoyadinovich, who inclined towards Fascism and built up a mass movement of green-shirted youths. Stoyadinovich also projected himself as the '*Vojda*' or leader, but failed the ultimate test of maintaining law and order. The threat from Croatia grew more and more serious until, in 1939, Stoyadinovich was replaced by Tsvetkovich, who had a more moderate and less repressive answer to Croatian separatism. On 26 August 1939, Croatia was given full autonomy and her own assembly, within, of course, a Yugoslav federation.

One of the reasons for this concession was developments

elsewhere in Europe. Hitler, for example, had shown the utmost ruthlessness in Czechoslovakia, turning the Slovaks against the Czechs and promoting internal dissolution to make possible external invasion and German occupation. The Yugoslav government wanted to avoid the same thing happening between Croatia and Serbia. The solution seemed to be to remove the sort of irritants which had encouraged the Slovaks to connive at the destruction of their partnership with the Czechs.

To make doubly sure that the Czech experience would not be repeated, Yugoslavia maintained and intensified her already close relations with the Axis powers. This process had been under way since the early 1930s and had involved a shift of original policy. During the 1920s Yugoslavia had depended on French support to offset the threat of Italy over the Fiume issue. Then, during the last year of his life, King Alexander had taken the initiative of moving closer to Germany. During the regency of Paul, Yugoslavia became more and more dependent on German economic acid, as was shown by the trade agreements of 1934 and 1936. By 1939 Yugoslavia seemed a willing enough client state to Germany, although extremely wary of Hitler's habit of exploiting the resentment of ethnic minorities. It seemed, therefore, that the safest course of action was to keep close links with Germany, somehow satisfy the Croats, and sit tight.

By 1941 Paul had become sufficiently confident to follow a more active policy. He was now convinced that the Axis powers would win the war and that the best guarantee of Yugoslavia's external security would be to join the Tripartite Pact between Germany, Italy and Japan. This, however, had drastic consequences. Paul's regime was overthrown in a wave of anti-Axis feeling, intensified by fears that Yugoslavia was about to be forced into war on the orders of Hitler. In fact, the immediate threat now came from Italy. Mussolini used the internal chaos in Yugoslavia as an opportunity to launch an invasion from Albania, which Italy had already occupied in 1939. Mussolini had always expressed the most profound contempt for Yugoslavia, regarding this new country as an 'artificial contrivance of Versailles'.[81] The Italian offensive was not, however, entirely successful, and

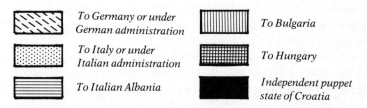

To Germany or under German administration	To Bulgaria
To Italy or under Italian administration	To Hungary
To Italian Albania	Independent puppet state of Croatia

Map 7 The dismemberment of Yugoslavia 1941

needed German assistance. Eventually the Yugoslav state was dismembered (see Map 7). Slovenia in the north was partitioned between Germany and Italy, the southern provinces were added to Bulgaria and Italian Albania, Serbia passed under German administration, and Croatia became a pro-Nazi puppet regime under its own *Poglavnik* (*Führer*), by the name of Pavelich. The collapse of Yugoslavia was accompanied by serious disorder and appalling massacres as old ethnic scores were settled. No other state in the whole of Europe must have appeared so unlikely ever to be resurrected in the future.

Yet Yugoslavia became the centre of the most effective partisan activity in Europe. According to Dedijer, this was the 'first massive uprising in Hitler's "Fortress of Europe" ';[81] it was, in fact, 'one of the high points in the history of struggle against tyranny'. The two main branches of resistance were the right-wing and predominantly Serbian-based Chetniks, under Mihailovich, and the Communist partisans under Josip Broz, better known as Tito – himself a Croation. Of the two resistance movements, Tito's partisans were the more successful. Tito followed a non-doctrinaire strategy and tried to attract as wide a range of support as possible. He employed highly effective hit-and-run tactics and made maximum use of Yugoslavia's mountainous terrain. He devised a political programme which was likely to appeal to all parts of Yugoslavia, with emphasis on federalism and self-determination. The partisans were, it is true, helped by Hitler's constant need to drain off German troops from Yugoslavia to fight on the Russian front; they also received direct aid from the Red Army in 1944 and 1945. But it is usually acknowledged that the prime credit for the liberation of Yugoslavia should go to the partisans. Yugoslavia was, in effect, one of the very few occupied states to free herself.

This was of enormous importance in Yugoslavia's post-war history. Tito carried out his promises, by introducing a federal structure, but also determined that Yugoslavia should never again fall under the influence of a great power. His independent line, in fact, resulted in Yugoslavia being excluded from the Soviet orbit in 1949. Yugoslavia eventually emerged as one of Europe's very few neutral states and as a key member of the world's 'non-aligned movement'.

Rumania

Rumania entered the First World War in August 1916. She was rapidly defeated by Austria-Hungary but, on the latter's collapse, ended up as one of the main beneficiaries of the peace settlement. By the Treaty of Trianon she received 31.5 per cent of the area of the former kingdom of Hungary[82] and emerged as one of the largest of the Balkan states.

The political scene, however, was to prove extremely unstable. The first stage was a coalition government between the Nationalist Party of Transylvania and the Peasant Party of Wallachia, under the leadership of Vaida. This was committed to a policy of economic and social reform. It failed, however, to gain the approval of King Ferdinand who dismissed the entire government in a royal coup in 1920, substituting a more authoritarian regime under Averescu. This in turn, was replaced in 1922 by a liberal government under Bratianu, which had some major achievements to its credit; a new constitution was drawn up in 1923, based on western democratic principles. Unfortunately, the reforming impetus broke down and, in 1928, the government was resoundingly defeated by the main opposition, the National Peasants. The new Prime Minister, Maniu, hoped to revive a policy of social and economic reform. This time, however, good intentions were destroyed by the impact of the Depression and the emergence of another royal dictator.

Ferdinand died in 1927, leaving the succession open. The main claimant was Carol who had, however, been excluded from the throne earlier because of widespread disapproval of his sexual activities. The National Peasant Government now pursued an ultimately fatal policy. Hoping to win Carol's permanent support and wanting to demonstrate that it was not morally prudish, it assisted Carol's return to Bucharest. Soon after his coronation, however, Carol dismissed Maniu and his cabinet. He was convinced that the only solution to Rumania's political and economic problems was a regime based on 'dynastic authoritarianism'.[83] He expressed strong reservations about parliamentary systems and openly admired Mussolini's regime. He therefore proceeded to install a series of puppet governments and, in 1938, abolished the 1923 constitution introducing, instead, an imitation of Mussolini's corporate state. He also replaced the traditional party structure with his own 'Front of National Rebirth'. Although some observers claim that Carol was a 'monarcho-Fascist', this term is not particularly appropriate. Carol was never inclined to any systematic ideology and remained traditional and conservative in his policies.

Besides, Rumania had developed a Fascist movement which actually *opposed* Carol; this was an alternative force on the right which was far more radical than royal dictatorship. It is possible to see Carol's measures as a defence against two evils, as he saw them. One was liberal parliamentarianism; the other was radical, even revolutionary, Fascism. The latter originated, in 1927, with the formation by Codreanu of the League of the Archangel Michael. In 1930 this developed a para-military organization known as the Iron Guard. The 'Guardists' were violently antisemitic and typically Fascist in offering a 'third way' between middle-class capitalism and Communism. Codreanu also stressed the importance of mass enthusiasm. Describing a campaign in 1930 he said: 'We looked like crusaders. And crusaders we wanted to be, knights who in the name of the cross were fighting the godless Jewish powers to liberate Rumania.'[84] At first King Carol was prepared to ally himself with the Fascist right and even to make use of its mass base. Soon, however, he found it an encumbrance and a threat to internal security. In 1938, therefore, he took the drastic step of banning the Iron Guard, along with Rumania's political parties. Codreanu was prosecuted for treason and sentenced to serve ten years in prison. There he died in suspicious circumstances, probably strangled by the prison guards. The whole episode provides an example of the bitter distrust between the reactionary right, in the form of royal absolutism, and the radical right, in the form of Fascism.

Subsequent events were even more tortuous. King Carol had to abdicate in 1940, in utter humiliation. The immediate reason was that Rumania was forced to give up territory to three aggressive neighbours: Bessarabia and Northern Bukovina to Russia, Northern Transylvania to Hungary, and Southern Dobrudja to Bulgaria.[85] Carol was succeeded by King Michael, who tried to prevent the complete disintegration of Rumania by entrusting power to a military dictatorship under General Antonescu. At first Antonescu was prepared to collaborate with the revived Iron Guard, now under Sima. Indeed, he went so far as to proclaim a National Legionary State with himself as leader, or *'Conducator'*.

Before long, however, the Iron Guard once again became troublesome, seeking total power and a more extreme regime. Antonescu therefore purged the Guard, dismissed Sima and destroyed, once and for all, the influence of home-grown Fascism in Rumania.

At the same time, Antonescu strengthened links with Germany. Rumania played a significant part in the invasion of Russia and was largely responsible for the conquest of the Crimea. Then, at Stalingrad, the Rumanian army was shattered, and with it Antonescu's reputation. By 1944 Rumania was under threat of Soviet attack. King Michael tried at the last minute to win the support of the western Allies by sacking Antonescu and installing, in turn, Generals Senatescu and Radescu. In the process, he deliberately distanced Rumania from Germany, thereby reversing Antonescu's policy.

Michael's initiative was doomed. The western Allies had already secretly consigned Rumania to the Soviet sphere of influence, in return for a Soviet guarantee of the security of Greece. Under Soviet influence a new National Democratic Front was established, coming increasingly under the control of the Communists. The previous leaders were dealt with one by one; Antonescu, for example, was tried and executed as a war criminal in 1946, and Michael was forced to abdicate in 1947. Finally, in 1948, a new constitution was drawn up, based on that of the USSR. The country remained under a neo-Stalinist regime until the overthrow of Nicolae Ceausescu in December 1989.

Greece

Greece was the oldest of the Balkan states, winning her independence from the Ottoman Empire in 1830. Her territory had been greatly extended by the Treaty of Sèvres (1920), by which she received from Turkey Eastern Thrace, many of the Aegean Islands and the administration of Smyrna. From Bulgaria she gained Western Thrace (see Map 8). Yet, despite being one of the victors in the First World War, Greece deteriorated into prolonged chaos during the 1920s and 1930s, eventually succumbing to the dictatorship of Metaxas.

Her problems were both external and internal. The

 Greece before 1918

 Ceded by Bulgaria; Greek possession confirmed by Treaty of Neuilly 1919

 Ceded by Turkey by Treaty of Sèvres 1920; restored to Turkey by Treaty of Lausanne 1923

Map 8 Greece after the First World War

external crisis was the more immediate and urgent. The Greek government found its territorial gains from Turkey difficult to digest. In 1920 the Ottoman Sultan was overthrown and a dynamic leader, Mustapha Kemal, set up a new Turkish Republic in Ankara. Kemal's main objective was to destroy the Treaty of Sèvres and, in particular, to drive the Greeks out of Turkish territory. The Greek government found itself isolated diplomatically from its former allies, and fought a disastrous war in Turkey. The Greek army was badly equipped and had severe problems of communication. By 1922 the Greeks were defeated and, by the Treaty of Lausanne (1923), were obliged to give up Eastern Thrace. The whole episode was a triumph for rejuvenated Turkish nationalism over Greek pretensions to imperialism.

Foreign problems acted as a catalyst for internal political instability as Greece experienced numerous changes of regime between 1920 and 1935. At first the conflict was between a discredited monarchy and the republicans, but the abdication of King Constantine in 1922 did little to guarantee peace as his successor, George II, also had to renounce the throne. Party politics in the new republic, formed in 1924, became so chaotic and boisterous that the military decided to intervene, with General Pangalos imposing a brief dictatorship in 1926. Democracy had a second chance when Venizelos was elected to power in 1928, but the parliamentary system was destabilized by the disastrous impact of the Depression on the Greek economy, especially on shipping and tourism. Greece reverted in the early 1930s to a series of short and unstable regimes, punctuated by attempted coups and counter-coups. This sorry state of affairs continued until 1935 when General Kondyles forced the Greek Parliament to abolish the Republic. He then arranged a plebiscite which produced a suspiciously large majority in favour of the return of the monarchy – in the person of George II. The new king dispensed with the services of Kondyles but, in 1936, appointed an even more authoritarian premier in the form of General Metaxas, who dominated Greece for the next four years.

The traditional view of Metaxas is that he was typical of Balkan dictators, comparable in his conservative policies to Carol of Rumania and Alexander of Yugoslavia. But, according to J.V. Kofas, his regime was more radical than is generally realized, with a powerful 'quasi-Fascist' element.[86] Can this view be justified?

Some of the ideas of Metaxas could be seen as old-fashioned

in their anti-liberalism, especially between 1936 and 1938. He conceived a powerful dislike of parliamentary politics which, he thought, would 'throw us into the embrace of communism'.[86] He was also élitist in his support of a pyramid class structure with a nobility at the apex. But he went much further than the other Balkan leaders in the style of his leadership and the totality of his vision. He fostered a personality cult, proclaiming himself leader (*Archigos*), 'First Peasant' and 'First Worker'. He aimed to replace constitutional democracy with an entirely new system, the keynote of which would be the suppression of individualism to the interests of the state; his programme would therefore be radical rather than conservative. The spirit behind his changes would be historic and racial: he aimed to revive the glories of the Greek past. He spoke of the three phases of Greek civilization. The first was the Golden Age of Pericles in the fifth century BC, the second was Medieval Byzantium. The third would be the emergence of a racially pure Hellenic order under Metaxas himself.

Metaxas began his dictatorship with a proclamation of martial law and a ban on normal political activity: 'There are no more parties in Greece. . . . The old parliamentary system has vanished forever.'[87] He also imposed a censorship which was so severe that it applied even to blank spaces in newspapers. Gradually he constructed a network of terror and indoctrination on a scale not seen elsewhere in the Balkans. Indeed, he was clearly influenced by the Third Reich; the Athens police headquarters displayed pictures of Hitler and Goebbels, and Greek security was based heavily on the SS and Gestapo. *Mein Kampf* was widely read and became a major influence behind the National Organization of Youth (EDN) which, according to Kofas, provided the regime with a 'fascist base'. Overall, Metaxas made Greece the most thoroughly Germanized state in south-eastern Europe.

At the same time, he did try to maintain an independent foreign policy and to avoid becoming a mere puppet of the Axis powers. He was initially more suspicious of Italy than of Germany, largely because of Mussolini's aggressive designs on Corfu (see Chapter 3). Then, in 1939, he came to the conclusion that Germany, too, needed watching: Hitler's designs on Czech and Polish territory caused a wave of apprehension even in states which sympathized ideologically with Nazism. Hence, shortly after the Italian invasion of Albania, the Greek government, along with Rumania, accepted an Anglo-French guarantee of security of the kind which had already been extended to Poland. The hollowness of this promise was, however, demonstrated in September 1939, when nothing could be done to prevent the German invasion of Poland. Metaxas decided that his only course of action was to keep Greece neutral no matter what happened elsewhere in Europe.

But this was to prove impossible. In October 1940 Mussolini issued an ultimatum to Metaxas demanding Italian military bases on Greek territory. When Metaxas refused, Mussolini launched a full-scale invasion. At first, Metaxas showed effective leadership and organized a successful military counter-offensive. He emphasized that Greece 'has a debt to herself to remain worthy of her history'.[88] The Italians encountered a series of defeats, the worst at Metsovo. By the end of 1940 Greece had succeeded in liberating herself. The worst, however, was yet to come, although Metaxas did not live to see it. In spring 1941, Hitler launched a German onslaught to rescue Mussolini from total humiliation. Despite help from British troops, the Greek mainland and islands were rapidly conquered. The country was partitioned between Germany, Italy, Albania and Bulgaria, and ruled by puppet regimes led by Tsolakoglou, Logothetopoulos and Rhalles. Like Metaxas, these men were ideologically sympathetic to Nazism. Unlike Metaxas, however, they lacked the Hellenic drive which placed Greek nationalism above all other considerations.

They also failed to gain from the Greek people the sort of collaboration received from the puppet regimes of Hungary, Croatia, Rumania and Bulgaria. Part of the reason was that the Greek population suffered more severely than almost any other: 7 per cent of all Greeks died under German occupation and 30 per cent of the national wealth was removed. Greeks, it has been argued, were actually *driven* to resistance.[89] Certainly there was massive support for the National

Liberation Front (EAM) and its National Popular Liberation Army (ELAS). These organizations scored a number of notable successes against the occupying forces and, by 1944, were setting up administrations in newly liberated areas. The Greek effort was assisted not by the Russians, as elsewhere in the Balkans, but by the British, who made a series of landings from 1943 onwards.

The anti-German Greek government in exile returned to Athens in October 1944. But the eviction of the Nazis did not mean the end of Greece's internal problems. Between 1946 and 1949 the country lapsed into civil war as the various ex-resistance groups competed for power. The main threat was from the Greek Communists, supported by Greece's neighbours and the Soviet Union. Eventually the Communist insurgency was overcome by a pro-western government, largely with American political and economic support under the label of the Truman Doctrine. Between 1950 and 1967 Greece followed a democratic course but fell to a vicious military junta which is sometimes compared with the earlier dictatorship of Metaxas. This nightmare lasted until 1974, when defeat in the Cyprus war discredited the colonels' regime and made possible the restoration of a parliamentary system.

PUPPET DICTATORSHIPS FROM DEMOCRACIES

Introduction

All the states dealt with so far in this chapter developed their own dictatorships before the Second World War. Some, like Rumania, Hungary and Bulgaria, became German satellites and allies. Others, like Poland, Albania, Greece, Yugoslavia and the Baltic states, were conquered and partitioned. Two – Spain and Portugal – managed to remain neutral.

The experience of the democracies also varied. A few, like Britain, Ireland, Sweden, Switzerland and Finland, remained intact. The others were conquered and came under foreign military occupation for the duration of the war; they are dealt with on pp. 207–14. Three of these, however, form a special category. Slovakia, Norway and Vichy France all became collaborationist regimes with home-produced dictators who, having failed to achieve power democratically, owed their sudden change of fortunes to German victory. Two of these leaders – Quisling and Laval – were among the most detested of the entire period.

Slovakia

Czechoslovakia was the only state in central and eastern Europe, apart from Finland, to hold on to a genuine parliamentary government during the 1920s and 1930s. Under her two presidents, Masaryk and Beneš, she rose above serious internal difficulties and survived the Depression and regional separation. What she could not do was resist the intolerable pressure applied from outside by Hitler, who was clearly determined to destroy the Czechoslovak nation. His initial strategy was to use the German minority in the Sudetenland to make massive demands on the Czech government. At the same time, he used the threat of war to deter Britain and France from supporting Beneš. The result was three visits to Germany by the British Prime Minister, Chamberlain, which culminated in the Munich settlement. This meant the cession to Germany of 10,000 square miles of territory and 3½ million peoples. By the same agreement Poland received Teschen, and Hungary southern Slovakia. The Munich settlement was clearly a major step towards the disintegration of Czechoslovakia. In March 1939, Hitler despatched German troops to occupy Prague and bring the whole of Bohemia into the Third Reich. At the same time he backed the claim of the province of Slovakia to autonomy and established a German protectorate under the presidency of Monsignor Jozef Tiso, a cardinal in the Catholic Church.

The new republic did possess certain advantages. It had a fairly widespread support, particularly from the Church, and gained a positive response to the new constitution of July 1939. Tiso hoped to maintain a considerable degree of independence from Germany and to promote conservative Christian values like those of Dollfuss and Schuschnigg in Austria or Salazar in Portugal. Increasingly, however, Tiso was pressurized by the radicals in his Slovak People's Party. His Prime Minister, Tuka, and other leading politicians, like Mach and Durcansky, were openly pro-Nazi. Despite Tiso's efforts, Slovakia came more and more under Germany's influence. The armaments industry was subordinated to the Nazi war effort and Slovakia contributed over 50,000 men to the invasion of Russia in 1941. Above all, the Nazis had a major say in the treatment of Slovakia's Jews. At first Tiso and the pro-Nazi radicals in his government constructed a package of limited antisemitic policies like the exclusion of Jews from business and the professions. Then Tuka and Mach seized the initative, pursuing a Nazi scheme for the resettlement of Slovak Jews in Poland. Although Tiso went along with this, he called a halt on the orders of the Pope and for two years resisted a resumption of the deportations.[90] The fate of the Jews, however, was sealed when Slovakia was brought under direct German military administration in September 1944.

Whatever Tiso's claims to the contrary, the Slovak Republic was closely tied to the fortunes of Germany. From 1943 onwards this made for extreme vulnerability. As the German military machine was breaking down in Russia, domestic resistance grew against Slovakia's involvement in this futile war. The banned parties collaborated, in exile, to form a Slovak national council which was committed to ending the link with Germany and to reinstating Czechoslovakia, this time as a federation. In 1944 several army officers hoped, with popular support, to overthrow the pro-Nazi government. By October, however, the Germans had succeeded in crushing the rebellion. They had also installed, under Stefan Tiso (a relative of the previous president) a more subservient regime. This was described by J.K. Hoensch as 'a mere puppet of, and executioner for, the German occupation force'.[90] German occupation was ended by the arrival of Soviet troops in April 1945. The Slovak Republic was instantly liquidated and the former state of Czechoslovakia revived, with Beneš installed as the first post-war president. Under Soviet influence, the early broad-based and multi-party governments gave way between 1948 and 1949 to an exclusively Communist regime which remained until brought down by popular movements in 1989.

Norway

Norway had been a typical example of Scandinavian political stability. She had survived the Great Depression, through consensus rather than confrontational politics, a model of the effective operation of proportional representation. She had also been strongly committed to peace and neutrality. In 1938, Norway had signed with Denmark, Sweden, Finland and Iceland a neutrality pact. Unfortunately, this was not based on strength; Norway's defences had deteriorated badly during the 1920s and 1930s.[91] The Norwegian government tried to keep out of the Second World War but the Germans launched a surprise attack in April 1940, drawn by Norway's mineral resources and strategic position in the North Atlantic. The Norwegian armed forces resisted for as long as possible but were eventually forced to surrender in June. King Haakon withdrew in temporary exile to London and the whole country fell to German control.

This was exercised by two dictators. One was Josef Terboven, previously *Gauleiter* of Cologne, now appointed Reich's Commissar for Norway. The other was Vidkun Quisling. He had set up a Norwegian Nazi party in the 1930s but this had never been popular with the electorate: it seemed, therefore, that he had no chance of attaining power by his own merits. He made secret contacts with Germany in the period 1939–40 and was suitably rewarded after the German conquest in 1940. He acquired more and more responsibility until, in February 1942, he became Minister President of Norway, in the process competing directly with his official superior, Terboven. According to K.F. Larsen, 'Quisling was allowed to do as he pleased in most internal affairs, and became more and more brutal and tyrannical.'[91]

Quisling's ideas were strongly influenced by Nazism, and in particular by Alfred Rosenburg. He had a vision of the regeneration of Norway under his own leadership as '*Forer*'; he developed a private army which was similar to the SA and SS; and he totally condemned parliamentary politics, probably as a result of his own disastrous showing in the 1936 elections. He also projected extreme views on race. He was strongly antisemitic and believed in the utmost importance of Nordic racial purity and supremacy. His initial hope was that Norway could work to promote peace and co-operation between Britain and Germany to form a great Nordic peace union. By 1940, however, he had become convinced that Britain had succumbed to Jewish influence and was therefore no longer worthy of such a destiny. He therefore decided to throw in Norway's lot entirely with Germany: 'in the Greater German community we shall have a leading position in the working of the New Order'.[92]

Under Quisling and Terboven, Norway was heavily exploited to meet the needs of Hitler's war effort in Europe. The Germans appropriated the funds of the Norwegian national bank, depleted the industrial stock and increased the national debt ninefold.[91] Most of the population remained quiet, if sullen and resentful, but a variety of resistance activities developed. Non-violent forms included Church manifestos, protesting against the occupation and style of leadership, and a massive increase in the number of illegal publications. Military resistance, meanwhile, was co-ordinated in London, and conducted on behalf of the government in exile. Commando groups, for example, carried out daring raids on German positions. The Norwegian merchant navy also played an important role in the war against Germany. Those ships which had escaped German hands carried vital supplies across the Atlantic, assisted at the evacuation of Dunkirk in 1940, and convoyed troops for the Normandy landings in 1944.[91] Even so, Norway did not have the strength to liberate herself and the main impetus of the attacks of the western Allies was in the Mediterranean and France, not Scandinavia. Norway therefore had to wait until the final surrender of the German armed forces in May 1945.

As soon as this happened, King Haakon returned Norway to her customary democratic government. The general election of October 1945 produced a coalition government which gave priority to reconstruction. It also dealt with the collaborators. Terboven had already committed suicide but Quisling was captured. He was put on trial and eventually executed for treason. It has been pointed out that Quisling's role was no worse than that of the other collaborators elsewhere in Europe. Still, it is he rather than they 'who is remembered above all as the archetypal traitor'.[92]

France

Like Norway, France became a dictatorship as a direct result of military defeat by Germany in 1940. It is difficult to see how Fascism could have come to power in any other way. France had managed to sustain democracy throughout the inter-war period, usually through broad-based governments either of the right or of the left; these included the *Bloc National* under Clemenceau (1919), the *Cartel des Gauches* under Herriot (1924), Poincaré's National Union (1926) and Blum's Popular Front (1936). These had compensated for the Third Republic's tendency towards political instability. What destroyed this Republic was the most catastrophic military reverse in the whole of France's history. This resulted from the triumph of the German *Blitzkrieg* strategy over the French defensive system based on the Maginot Line.

France's humiliation was followed by an armistice with the Germans. A new government under Marshal Pétain, the hero of the first World War, secured partial independence for Vichy France, the rest of the country coming under direct German administration. The Vichy Government also contained French Fascists like Pierre Laval and Raphaël Alibert, who sympathized openly with Nazi ideas. Pétain and Laval introduced a 'National Revolution', the tone of which was unmistakeably authoritarian with the emphasis on 'Work, Family, Country' rather than 'Liberty, Equality, Fraternity'.[93] The democratic past was denounced, especially the Third Republic which had brought France to defeat and ruin.

There is some evidence to show that Pétain was reasonably popular in 1940, offering as he appeared to do a way out of total defeat and disaster. But gradually the Vichy regime lost all credibility. The Germans imposed more and more demands on the French economy and looked to Laval to maintain the closest possible co-operation between Vichy and Berlin. Pétain tried to retain at least some autonomy by dismissing Laval in December 1940 but was forced by strong German pressure to reinstate him in April 1942. From this time onwards Laval was the real dictator, a Nazi puppet in every sense of the word. He thought in terms of a German-dominated Europe, with France playing an important peripheral supporting role. He also hoped for a negotiated peace with the United States which would enable Germany to finish off Russia and, perhaps, reduce its heavy demands on France. His dreams dissipated when, later in 1942, the

Germans occupied Vichy and reduced the once autonomous area to the level of the rest of France.

The reason for this was the growing resistance to the regime, and the threat from outside. Up to 1942 Vichy had kept up at least the pretence of independence and had even possessed colonies in North Africa. These, however, were conquered by British and American troops and the Vichy government was deprived of any significant role. Many Frenchmen therefore switched their support to resistance movements like General de Gaulle's Free French. The real impetus came with the invasion of France by the western Allies during the course in 1944, the north falling in June, the south in August. De Gaulle was allowed by the British and Americans to liberate Paris. He subsequently introduced a programme for national recovery which included the construction of the Fourth Republic and the involvement of France in key diplomacy on the future of Germany. One of the Allied leaders, President Roosevelt, considered de Gaulle a possible danger. He pointed to certain authoritarian tendencies and warned that de Gaulle might establish another dictatorship. Time was to show that de Gaulle avoided this trap, settling instead for a leadership which was paternalist but firmly rooted in democracy.

6
Dictatorships compared

TOTALITARIAN AND AUTHORITARIAN DICTATORSHIPS

Throughout this book references have been made to the terms
'totalitarian' and 'authoritarian' dictatorships. The purpose
of this chapter is to draw together these references and to
attempt an overall distinction between the two types of
regime.

Although both dispensed with the normal process of
parliamentary government and were critical of democracy,
their basic intentions differed. Authoritarian regimes used
dictatorship in a conservative way: the aim was to preserve
traditional values and often the traditional social structure.
This was to be accomplished neither by revolution nor by
rousing the masses. Quite the contrary. As K.D. Bracher
argues, authoritarian regimes arrived at the neutralization or
'immobilization of all other forces in the state'.[1] Totalitarian
regimes, by contrast, had a more radical programme of
change, and deliberately mobilized the masses to serve a
'revolutionary monopolist movement'. They were also

permeated by an ideology or 'a quasi-religious philosophy with a claim to exclusivity'.

The term 'totalitarian' was, according to W. Laqueur, 'coined to cover common features of communist and fascist states'. Certainly this is the approach used by recent experts like H. Arendt, R. Macridis, or C. Friedrich and Z. Brzezinski. Using a synthesis of their, and other, views, it is possible to construct a definition of totalitarianism, as follows.

First, all totalitarian regimes possessed a distinctive ideology which formed a 'body of doctrine covering all vital parts of man's existence'.[2] Everything was subordinated to it and society was restructured according to its goals.[3]

Second, the political system was under the control of a single party, presided over by a leader who was invested with the cult of personality. This party aimed at mobilized mass support, particularly among the youth, and generated para-military activity. Party politics were ended and the legis-lature brought under the control of the executive.

Third, the individual was completely subordinated to the dictates of the state through a process of coercion and indoctrination. The former could involve 'a system of terror, whether physical or psychic, effected through party and secret police control'.[2] Indoctrination sought the destruction of cultural pluralism and the shaping of education, literature, art and music to the objectives of political ideology.[3]

Fourth, the totalitarian state sought to impose complete control over the economy by establishing the basic objectives and providing 'bureaucratic co-ordination of formerly independent corporate entities'.[2]

Using these criteria, it should be possible to establish which of the dictatorships can be described as 'totalitarian' and to which the term 'authoritarian' would be more appropriate.

In many respects the most effective of all the 'totalitarian' systems was Stalin's Russia, since it fulfilled all the cate-gories mentioned. Marxism–Leninism was an all-embracing ideology which was used extensively as a social engineering force. The political structure was dominated by the CPSU, in turn subordinated to a leader who took the personality cult to an unprecedented extreme. Stalinist purges accounted for the elimination of millions, while indoctrination was accomplished through the medium of Socialist Realism. The economy, of course, was strictly regulated by a series of five year plans. Yet while there seems little doubt about the totalitarian nature of Stalin's regime, there has been some reservation as to whether the same label can be applied to Lenin's. Arendt, for example, did not consider Lenin's Russia as genuinely totalitarian, but rather as a 'revolutionary dictatorship'; she concludes that 1929 was the 'first year of clear-cut totalitarian dictatorship in Russia'.[4] In support of this view it could certainly be argued that Lenin considered many of his more coercive measures as temporary, even reversing policies like War Communism and relaxing the use of terror by dissolving the Cheka. On the other hand, those historians, like G. Leggett, who emphasize the continuity between Lenin and Stalin claim that the difference between the two regimes was one of degree rather than principle. By this approach it would seem that Lenin's Russia was less totalitarian than Stalin's, but totalitarian nevertheless.

The situation in Germany is also complex. On the one hand there is plenty of evidence that the Nazi regime was totalitarian. It was based on an ideology which was more frightful than any yet devised and which was imposed upon the population by extensive coercion and indoctrination. The masses were radicalized and mobilized in support of a single party under the personal authority of an irreplaceable Führer. And yet, it has been argued, Germany was an 'imperfect totalitarianism'.[5] It is certainly true that the Nazi Revolution swept away far fewer of the institutions of the previous regime than did the Bolshevik Revolution and Hitler was satisfied with a less rigidly centralized and planned economy. In Italy, Mussolini's objectives were undoubtedly totalitarian but their actual enforcement was patchy and inconsistent, as is shown in Chapter 3. There was, it is true, a more systematic economic theory than in Germany, but even the so-called corporate state was incomplete. In virtually every sector – political, social and economic – radical theory was undermined by a remarkably persistent status quo.

Of the lesser states, two might be described as totalitarian for the brief period they were ruled by Fascist regimes under the protection of Nazi Germany. These were Croatia under the Ustashi regime and Szálasi's Hungary. All the others are more aptly termed 'authoritarian'. It is true that some had common features with the totalitarian states. Greece, for example, openly imitated the Nazi security system and Metaxas was undoubtedly influenced by Hitler's ideology. Hungary under Gömbös and Poland after Pilsudski flirted with milder forms of Fascism, while Austria under Dollfuss and Salazar's Portugal tried out local variants of corporativism. Several factors, however, prevent these and the other regimes from being regarded with Italy as even partly totalitarian. With the possible exception of Greece they lacked any consistent attempt to mobilize the masses behind the regime. In fact, quite the reverse: they aimed to neutralize and depoliticize. This was partly because leaders like Salazar and Franco relied upon traditional ideas, although in a regenerated form, and distrusted anything which was remotely radical or revolutionary. Finally, authoritarian leaders were content to let the individual remain within his traditional social context and there was rarely any attempt at mass indoctrination.

The rest of this chapter will develop these points and draw general comparisons, under four main headings, between the various regimes covered by this book.

THE IDEOLOGICAL BASIS OF DICTATORSHIP

The term ideology is normally understood to mean an organized set of ideas and ideals intended to deal with problems and, perhaps, to institute sweeping change. The totalitarian ideologies had in common a desire to destroy the existing system and to recreate according to an ideal form – often called a utopia. In fact, Friedrich and Brzezinski believe that 'totalitarian ideologies are typically utopian in nature'.[6] Authoritarian regimes, by contrast, were usually unable to produce a distinctive ideology. Although they often aimed to change the existing political system, they were much more prepared to adapt to more traditional influences and ideas. Hence they tended to be backward looking, even reactionary, in contrast to the revolutionary nature of totalitarian ideologies.

It is usual to categorize three inter-war ideologies as totalitarian: Marxism–Leninism, Nazism and Fascism. Of these, Marxism–Leninism was by far the most coherent, based on a systematic doctrine derived from the ideas of Hegel, Marx and Engels, as redefined by Lenin and Stalin. It incorporated an economic theory (economic determinism), a series of historical laws (dialectical materialism) and a belief in eventual progress towards a higher form of human organization called the 'classless society' (see Chapter 1). Fascism and Nazism owed to nineteenth-century writers like Nietzsche, Gobineau and H.S. Chamberlain such concepts as racial inequality and the inevitability of struggle. But neither possessed the disciplined structure of Marxism–Leninism, partly because, in the words of Bracher, neither had 'the kind of classic bible that Marxism possessed'.[7] Hitler's ideas, for example, were expounded very loosely in *Mein Kampf*, which was little more than an autobiography, while Mussolini's most explicit doctrinal statement was confined to a short article in *Encyclopedia Italiana*. Neither of these sources had the coherence and weight of Marx's *Das Kapital* or Lenin's *The State and Revolution*. Bracher goes so far as to call Nazism 'an eclectic "ragbag" ideology, drawn from a multitude of sources'.[7] As for the lesser dictators, few even attempted a systematic statement of beliefs beyond a simple reformulation of traditional ideas. This applied to all authoritarian leaders, whether military men like Franco and Pilsudski or academics like Salazar. Some of the more radical, potentially totalitarian dictators, who came to power as Nazi puppets during the Second World War, did have a go at organizing their thoughts. A typical example was Szálasi of Hungary; but, as E. Weber points out, Szálasi's writing is unsystematic and 'steadfastly ignores grammar, style and sense'.[8]

Marxism–Leninism, Nazism and Fascism had in common the desire to transform the previous system through revolution. All three involved the manipulation of history and the movement towards an ideal. There were, however, major differences in the nature of that ideal. The Marxist utopia involved two distinctive phases (see Chapter 1). The first was the 'dictatorship of the proletariat' which was intended to eliminate all obstacles to achieving the second, and very different phase, the 'classless society'. Force and struggle

were therefore a means to an end. This end was fundamentally different in that it would see the decline of organized
coercion and the conclusion of the 'prehistoric phase' of
man's existence. According to Engels there would be 'a leap
from slavery into freedom; from darkness into light'.[9] In
complete contrast, Nazi and Fascist utopias envisaged one
stage only – uninterrupted and unending movement towards
total domination and power. Fascism has been described as a
'national-imperial mission ideology' which made a 'powerful
state the highest value';[10] this process, the opposite to the
'classless society', is sometimes called 'étatisme'. It also
involved the perpetual glorification of war and struggle for, in
Mussolini's words, 'war is to the man what maternity is to the
woman'.[11] Nazism also focused on struggle, although the
vehicle was race rather than the state, Aryanism rather than
étatisme. According to Hitler, 'All of nature is one great
struggle between strength and weakness, an eternal victory of
the strong over the weak.'[12] The victims were to be the race
enemies, for 'All eugenic progress can begin only by eliminating the inferior.' These ideas were to be sublimated in the
most horrifying way in the gas chambers of Auschwitz-
Birkenau.

Elsewhere the purpose of ideology was less to transform
than to revive. It was therefore less forward-looking and more
traditional, even nostalgic. History was regarded less as a
transition to a higher phase, more as providing *past* examples
for imitation. The clearest example of this was Salazar's
stress on '*Deus, Pátria, Família*' (God, country, family) and on
the historic role of Portuguese imperialism 'to defend western
and Christian civilisation'.[13] Franco, in turn, aimed quite
consciously at reviving the virtues of the historic Spain
destroyed, he considered, by the Second Republic; he regarded himself therefore as the political reincarnation of
Philip II. Even the more radical 'Hungarism' of Szálasi and
the 'Hellenism' of Metaxas were essentially a glorification of a
national past. In more other states presidential or royal
absolutism lacked any systematic ideas and based itself on
pragmatic commonsense and an appeal to patriotism.

Which of the main ideologies proved to be of the most
practical use? Marxism–Leninism certainly appears the most

elusive in its ultimate aim: the 'classless society' and the 'withering away' of the state could occur only after a profound change in human nature. Nazism and Fascism, by contrast, intended to exploit and accentuate the most basic human instincts – the struggles for survival and domination. And yet events proved Marxism–Leninism a more efficient tool than either Fascism or Nazism for transforming society, the economy and political institutions. The reason was that the practical application of Marxism–Leninism by Stalin stopped well short of the ultimate ideal of the 'classless society' and concentrated on the organization and coercion necessary for the phase of the 'dictatorship of the proletariat'. Fascism and Nazism lacked the capacity for complete institutional reorganization and for the mobilization of the economy for total war, even though the latter featured so strongly in their scheme. On balance, therefore, Stalin had at his disposal a far more powerful ideological weapon than had either Hitler or Mussolini.

THE POLITICAL STRUCTURE OF DICTATORSHIP

Totalitarian regimes aimed to transform the political establishment. The three states normally seen as totalitarian went about this in very different ways.

The Russian leadership introduced by far the most extensive changes, aiming to eradicate all previous institutions. The three constitutions of the period provided for a system of soviets, dominated at all stages by the Party. The Party was able to exercise total control through its Central Committee which, in turn, was subdivided into the Orgburo, Politburo and Control Commission. The Nazi leadership also sought political change, although in practice it stopped far short of the sort of transformation seen in the Soviet Union. Instead of sweeping away the old system altogether, Hitler carried out some drastic surgery on it; for example, he perpetuated the emergency powers of the executive by means of the Enabling Act and, by merging the Presidency and Chancellorship, destroyed the checks and balances within the constitution. Mussolini's Italy followed the German rather than the Soviet pattern. The effect, however, was still less complete; the superstructure of the monarchy remained intact and was eventually to become the focal point of opposition to the *Duce*. Elsewhere the dictators were far less ambitious. One of the characteristics of authoritarian regimes was to stabilize and restore rather than to transform, even though constitutional amendments were often involved. Examples of attempts to emphasize tradition and order can be seen in Salazar's *Estado Novo* (1935) and the constitutions in the various Balkan states which granted increased powers to their respective monarchs.

What importance did the dictators attach to a party base and to radicalizing the masses? Again, the approach in the totalitarian states varied. Russia used the 'vanguard' method, by which the Party dominated the entire system. Rather than attempting to generate mass involvement it operated through the principle of 'democratic centralism', whereby a small élite acted on behalf of the entire population. Membership of the Party was strictly limited and, during the 1930s, Stalin was able, through his purges, to reduce even this. The Nazi and Fascist Parties possessed more genuine mass bases, which did much to radicalize politics and promote right-wing revolutionary fervour. But penetration by the Parties of state institutions was far less complete than in Russia. (This theme is examined at length in Chapters 3 and 4.) Elsewhere the development of a one-party system was intended to neutralize, defuse and depoliticize rather than to create a resurgent mass. This, for example, was the motive behind Salazar's National Union (UN), Rivera's *Unión Patriotica* (UP), the Fatherland Front of Dollfuss and Pilsudski's *Sanacja*.

All the dictatorships covered by this book depended upon the leadership of a single commanding figure. The most extreme cases of this were Russia, Germany and Italy. In theory, Stalin was subject to collective leadership and the ideology of Communism was supposed to prevent any excessive accumulation of personal power. In practice, Stalin elevated his authority to heights which were unprecedented even in a country with an almost uninterrupted history of autocracy. The situation in Germany was perhaps the reverse of this. In theory, Hitler was in total command, with no conceivable constraints. According to Broszat,

Hitler's power as Führer exceeded that of any monarch. The notion of "divine right" was replaced by the claim that the Führer was the saviour appointed by Providence and at the same time the embodiment and medium of the unarticulated will of the people.[14]

In practice, however, Hitler was frequently isolated at the pinnacle of the Party and state apparatus; Chapter 4 deals with the effect of this on the actual exercise of his authority. Mussolini's power was never as strong as Hitler's, even in theory. He remained, officially, the appointee of Victor Emanuel and it was to the king, not to the *Duce*, that the army and state officials owed their ultimate allegiance. The 'authoritarian' states also depended on the strong-man image. Both Rivera and Franco used the imagery of the 'sentinel', while a range of titles sprang up, all loosely translatable as 'leader'. Franco was known as *Caudillo*, Smetona as *Tautos Vadas*, Antonescu as *Conducator* and Metaxas as *Archigos*. None of these 'leaders', however, found it necessary to adopt the cult of personality which played so important a part in the totalitarian states. This was because they aimed to quieten the population, not to rouse it; this could be more successfully accomplished by a more remote type of authority.

No dictatorship could have survived without the support of the army. There was, however, a contrast between those regimes which tried to *absorb* the military and those which allowed the army to remain as an independent and privileged institution. Once again, the most complete transformation was achieved in Russia. The Bolshevik regime built an entirely new army and subordinated it to the Party by means of commissars; under Stalin these were known as *Zampolits* (Deputy Commanders for Political Affairs). At the head of the whole system was the GPUVS or the Main Political Administration of the Soviet Armed Forces.[15] In Germany control over the army was accomplished more gradually. Hitler had to earn its support in 1934 in the Night of the Long Knives but, by 1938, felt sufficiently confident to reorganize the high command. He subsequently used the *Waffen SS* to politicize the army and infuse it with Nazi ideology. Italy, never a good example of a totalitarian state, did not experience a comparable process. Mussolini, in fact, claimed that he did 'not intend to use the army as a political arm'.[15] He also failed to produce an equivalent to the *Waffen SS*, which meant that there was nothing to prevent the officers from taking part in a plot to depose him in 1943.

Elsewhere the army achieved or retained a high status. In Portugal it had a special relationship with Salazar, until, that is, it was destabilized by the experience of the African wars. In Spain it was directly elevated and protected by Franco who was, of course, the Commander-in-Chief. The same applied in Poland, although Pilsudski was less able than Franco to adjust to a civilian role. These and other leaders did whatever was necessary to prevent the penetration of the armed forces by radical right-wing groups, realizing that a disaffected officer corps could engineer a military coup.

THE STATE, SOCIETY AND INDIVIDUAL

The individual exists within a society; the society is contained within a state. An important characteristic of a totalitarian state is that it aims to subordinate both the individual and society. According to Buchheim, 'Totalitarian rule attempts to encompass the whole person, the substance and spontaneity of his existence, including his conscience.'[16] This trend was most marked in Russia. Lenin intended to create a 'new type of man', the purpose of society being to impart to him the new political values and culture as directed by the state. There was a similar emphasis in both Germany and Italy, on a radical change of attitudes and beliefs, although in practice neither régime succeeded in subordinating society as successfully as in Stalinist Russia. In the smaller states there was no place for social transformation. The intention, instead, was to restore the traditional social balance. One example was Salazar's Portugal, of which Bruce writes: 'the state was never to swallow up the groups – hence it was never to be "totalitarian" – it was simply to act as the co-ordinating agent of these groups.'[17] Franco's regime, according to Payne, followed the 'intolerant, ultra-Catholic norms of Spanish history',[18] while the main influence on Pilsudski's *Sanacja* was Polish civic virtue, based very much on social tradition.

How completely did the totalitarian regimes reach the individual? One of the most important methods used was propaganda. According to Friedrich and Brzezinski, 'The nearly complete monopoly of mass communication is generally agreed to be one of the most striking characteristics of totalitarian dictatorship.'[19] Each state had its own means of achieving this monopoly. Within the Soviet Union state ownership prevailed, in contrast to private ownership under state licence, as sometimes existed in Italy and Germany. The Nazi and Fascist systems placed greater emphasis than the Soviet Union on the use of radio, probably because Hitler and Mussolini were more adept than Stalin at the use of the spoken word. All systems tried to manipulate culture, whether through Socialist Realism or Aryanism; as shown in Chapter 3, Italy was probably the least successful in this respect. All redesigned the structure and function of education, although in different ways. The Nazi and Fascist approach was to close minds in order to make them unreceptive to anything but carefully programmed propaganda. The result would be a simplification of the whole intellectual process. Soviet education was based, in theory, on *expanding* the intellect so that it could deal with the complexities of the dialectic and other elements of Marxist ideology. In practice, however, Soviet education under Stalin stultified the intellect by demanding the complete acceptance, as an act of faith, of the ideas passed down from the leadership. Stalinist Russia was probably best placed to carry out Buchheim's description of the end result of indoctrination: 'The successfully indoctrinated person is prepared with prefabricated answers to all questions directed at him.... He sees the world exclusively from the point of view and in the light of the ideology.'[16] He is, in fact, 'intellectually and morally synchronized with the practical course of the totalitarian exercise of power'.

Propaganda and indoctrination were invariably backed up by terror. Totalitarian states, indeed, made a permanent connection between the two processes. Authoritarian states, although never strong on indoctrination, often pursued a brutal form of repression. The purpose of terror in the totalitarian states was the identification and elimination of all enemies, whether 'racial' as in Germany or 'class' as in Russia. The methods used included some of the most notorious institutions ever devised. Russian security evolved through the *Cheka*, GPU, OGPU, NKVD, MGB, MVD and, after the death of Stalin, the KGB. German institutions comprised the SA, SS, SD and Gestapo. Of the two systems, Germany's committed the more appalling atrocities sinking, in the process, to the depths of barbarism. Stalin's, however, proved more efficient and sophisticated in its operations and in identifying and eliminating opposition. Italy's system, based on the OVRA, never achieved the same notoriety; according to Friedrich and Brzezinski, it was 'less total, less frightful, and hence less "mature" than in Germany and the Soviet Union'.[20] Elsewhere methods varied considerably. Some states had no organized terror as such: examples included Horthy's Hungary, the Baltic states, Austria under Dollfuss, and Pilsudski's Poland. Others developed a machinery for repression which was actually more efficient than Italy's. Franco executed far more people than Mussolini, Salazar introduced the notorious PIDE, while Metaxas patterned his security system directly on the Gestapo.

The main devices of terror were purges and penal camps. The use of purges was most extensive in Russia. The reason was that Stalin was the most obsessed about the security of his position: unlike Hitler and Mussolini, he had not been the original inspiration behind the new system and needed to place firmly upon himself the mantle of Lenin. He therefore resorted to the massive show trials, based upon their manufactured confessions; as M. Latey observes, 'Other revolutions have devoured their own children; it was reserved to Stalin to make them vomit in public first.'[21] In Germany purges served a more specific purpose. The Night of the Long Knives was Hitler's method of rooting out the radical wing of the Nazi movement in order to guarantee military support for the new regime. It was not, however, followed by a clean sweep through the rest of the Party leadership. One can only speculate on whether this would have happened had the Third Reich outlived Hitler. Would Goering, Himmler,

Bormann or Goebbels eventually have become a Stalin?

One of the most notorious features of the Hitler and Stalin regimes was their use of camps. More details are known about the German camps because of the publicity given to them during the Nuremberg trials. Stalin, as one of the victors, was able to conceal some of the worst defects of his own system. The overall conception of the German camps was the more horrifying because of their eventual connection with the deliberate extermination of six million people. There was no Soviet equivalent to the RHSA, to Auschwitz-Birkenau, to the gas chambers or ovens. Stalin's camps were more traditional; they were labour or concentration camps, not designed for mass killings. In terms of overall numbers, more victims were probably processed through the GULAG system than through the SS network. It could even be that more people died in captivity in Russia than in Germany. These deaths, however, were the result of neglect and overwork rather than a policy of genocide. The Stalinist system always retained a theoretical emphasis on correction and rehabilitation while the Nazi ideology demanded a policy of disposal.

THE ECONOMIES OF THE DICTATORSHIPS

Within the totalitarian states the government sought to impose overall economic control. This was most complete in the Soviet Union which, as in the political sphere, destroyed the previous system and started again from scratch. Stalin's method was the five year plan, co-ordinated by Gosplan which, by 1938, had subdivided into 54 departments. His basic intention was to impose upon all sectors of the economy the principle of collective ownership while, at the same time, preparing the Soviet Union to resist an invasion from the west. The Fascist states, by contrast, aimed to adapt rather than destroy the previous system. Germany's programme was based on *Gleichschaltung*, Italy's on the corporate state (see Chapters 3 and 4). In both cases the emphasis was on state direction but with a degree of private enterprise; the state allied with big business rather than seeking to destroy it. The ultimate objectives of both Hitler and Mussolini were autarky and the pursuit of *Lebensraum*, the assumption being that only territorial expansion would enable the German and Italian economies to reflect the industriousness of their respective peoples.

Elsewhere, the smaller states varied in their economic policies. Some, like Spain, Austria and Portugal, were clearly influenced by Mussolini's corporate state although they avoided some of its Fascist connotations. Others struggled on with open economies based on private enterprise and minimal state direction; eventually, however, the impact of the Depression forced Bulgaria, Rumania, Yugoslavia and Greece into making trade agreements with Germany. These, in turn, dragged them into the vortex of German diplomatic and political influence.

The key test of the success of the planned economies was their capacity for mobilization in war time. The Soviet system of the 1930s may have appeared appallingly wasteful, but it did make the most successful adjustment to the demands of total war. The reason was partly that the consumer had already been so heavily subordinated to the dictates of industrialization that the economic hardship of the Second World War was no worse than the stringency of the 1930s. After the initial disasters of 1941 and 1942, war brought out of the best in the Soviet economy, as productivity increased and the workforce responded effectively to the demands placed upon it. The experience of the Fascist states was very different. The Italian economy reacted badly to being stretched by conflict in the 1930s. The Ethiopian campaign and the Spanish Civil War brought it close to collapse, while the campaigns in the Balkans and North Africa finished it off. Germany was geared specifically to a war of conquest followed by the absorption of large areas to consolidate the economic base. But since Hitler never dared inflict on the German consumer the sort of demands taken for granted by Stalin in Russia, this conquest had to be rapid. As long as Germany could depend upon a successful *Blitzkrieg* the economy functioned smoothly and efficiently. Faced with the prospect of total war, however, Germany fell far behind the Soviet Union in armaments production. By the time that Speer had managed to introduce more radical measures it was already too late: Soviet troops were closing in on the Third Reich.

All of the totalitarian regimes were severely tested by the special problems posed by agriculture. Tight centralized control was particularly difficult in an economic activity which was essentially local and which required the exercise of on-the-spot initiative. It might have been possible to co-ordinate all decision-making in the industrial sector, but how could the same process take into account the diverse and unpredictable conditions faced by agriculture? The Soviet experience was catastrophic. Stalin's enforced collectivization alienated huge sections of the peasantry, and his determination to use agriculture to subsidize industrial development created an imbalance which permanently crippled the Soviet economy. Mussolini's policies were similarly disastrous for Italy. Although he avoided a social upheaval by not seeking to alter the pattern of land ownership, he did cause serious disruption to agricultural productivity. In insisting that farmers should switch to crops like wheat to enable to government to win its 'Battle for Grain', he created an imbalance which post-war Italy has struggled to resolve. Hitler managed to avoid the direct disruption inflicted by Stalin and Mussolini. It could, however, be argued that his belief in a strong peasantry underlay his policy of *Lebensraum*: he envisaged the settlement of German rural communities across the whole of eastern Europe. *Lebensraum*, in turn, conditioned Hitler's whole economic and military strategy, with all the implications examined in Chapter 4.

Some of the smaller states experienced agricultural reforms in the early 1920s; Stambuliski, for example, sought to redistribute land among the peasantry of Bulgaria in what was really the reverse of Stalin's policy. But the onset of the Depression forced the authoritarian regimes to abandon virtually all attempts to direct agriculture. The smaller dictators valued the support of the landed gentry too much to risk incurring their wrath by interfering with the status quo. In this respect, as in many others, they considered that things were best left as they were.

Conclusion: Since 1945

The period between the two World Wars experienced an unprecedented variety of regimes. These can be classified in two ways.

First, it is possible to make a three-way distinction between democracies, left-wing dictatorships (Russia) and right-wing dictatorships (Germany, Italy and many smaller states).

The alternative division is between democracy and dictatorship, the latter subdividing into totalitarian regimes (Stalinist Russia, Nazi Germany and possibly Mussolini's Italy) and authoritarian states.

This book has looked at both types of classification. The first was considered explicitly in Chapter 1, the second in Chapter 6. Both were used implicitly throughout Chapters 2 to 5.

The post-war period has seen major political changes. After 1945 the regimes of the far left were greatly strengthened while, elsewhere, parliamentary democracy was revived. The far right, by contrast, was gradually squeezed out of Europe altogether.

The collapse of the right-wing dictatorships was a direct result of military defeat in the Second World War at the hands of the western democracies and the Soviet Union. The scope and extent of this defeat utterly discredited Fascism as a doctrine or as a vehicle for political activism. It is true that the word itself survives. It is normally used to describe small parties of the far right which aspire, so far unsuccessfully, to reviving a totalitarian form of nationalism. It is also sometimes used as a term of abuse against regimes or governments more appropriately called reactionary or traditionalist. Since 1945 Europe has seen only three manifestations of the far right, all of which were authoritarian rather than Fascist. Spain and Portugal survived as dictatorships, against the general trend, because they had avoided involvement in the Second World War. Neither, however, was able to outlive its founder: Portugal moved towards democracy after the 1974 revolution, Spain more gradually under the guidance of King Juan Carlos. Greece presents a different case. Between 1967 and 1974 the colonels briefly recreated the Metaxas era, but their regime was eventually doomed by its isolation, ostracism and defeat in war. Since 1975 there has not been a single example of a rightwing dictatorship whose capital is based in Europe.

As a result of the decline of the far right, Europe polarized between parliamentary democracy and the Communist left (see Map 9). The reason was that western Europe felt vulnerable after the Second World War to the threat which it perceived from the new Soviet superpower and came to depend on a renewed connection with the United States in the form of NATO. The Soviet Union, in turn, tightened its control in eastern Europe by means of Comecon and the Warsaw Pact. The west saw itself as the 'free world' and the Soviet bloc as the main threat to this freedom.

This situation lasted well into the 1980s, when a change occurred. Imperceptible at first, this accelerated with breathtaking speed towards the end of the decade. Gorbachev dismantled much of the remaining neo-Stalinist apparatus in the Soviet Union. While 1989 saw political transformation in

 Communist states under the influence of the USSR

 Communist states eventually outside the Soviet bloc

States experiencing right-wing regimes but eventually establishing parliamentary democracies

Parliamentary democracies

Map 9 Types of regime in Europe after the Second World War
(until 1989)

Poland, Hungary, East Germany, Bulgaria, and Romania. Terms like 'dictatorship' and 'totalitarian' had become more and more difficult to apply to eastern Europe.

It could be argued that the disastrous political instability and confusion which characterized the inter-war period moved after

1945 from Europe to the Third World. The result, once again, was a long list of dictatorships — of both the far left and the far right. These, too, have been categorized; in 1982 the US administration drew a distinction between authoritarian states of the right and totalitarian states of the Communist left, adding that the former were less dangerous and aggressive than the latter. Other statesmen feel that there are 'lessons' to be learned from Europe of the 1930s which can be applied to the modern world. Inasmuch as these 'lessons' profoundly influence international relations, Europe's dictators continue to speak from beyond the grave.

Notes

A COMMENT ON THE TERM 'DICTATORSHIP'

1 H. BUCHHEIM: *Totalitarian Rule: Its Nature and Characteristics* (Middletown, Conn. 1968); Ch. 1.
2 M.R. CURTIS: Dictatorship (entry in *Encyclopedia Americana*).

1 THE SETTING FOR DICTATORSHIP

1 J.S. HUGHES: *Contemporary Europe* (Englewood Cliffs, NJ 1961); Ch. 2.
2 K.D. BRACHER: *The Age of Ideologies* (London 1984); Part II, Ch. 2.
3 J.A.S. GRENVILLE (ed.): *The Major International Treaties 1914–1973* (London 1974); Document: President Wilson's Fourteen Points, 8 January 1918.
4 A. COBBAN: *The Nation State and National Self-Determination* (London 1969); Part I, Ch. 4.
5 H. KOHN: *Political Ideologies of the Twentieth Century* (New York 1949); Ch. 13.
6 K.J. NEWMAN: *European Democracy Between the Wars* (trans. K. Morgan) (London 1970); Ch. 3.
7 H. KOHN: op. cit.; Ch. 12.
8 R.C. MACRIDIS: *Contemporary Political Ideologies* (Boston 1983); Ch. 9.
9 Quoted in D. SMITH (ed.): *Left and Right in Twentieth Century*

Europe (Harlow, Essex 1970); Ch. 1.

10 E. WEBER in W. LAQUEUR (ed.): *Fascism. A Reader's Guide* (Harmondsworth 1979).

11 P. FEARON: *The Origins and Nature of the Great Slump 1929–1932* (London 1979); Ch. 1.

2 DICTATORSHIP IN RUSSIA

1 A. ASCHER (ed.): *The Mensheviks in the Russian Revolution* (London 1976); Introduction.

2 E.H. CARR: *The Bolshevik Revolution* (London 1950); Vol. I, Ch. 4.

3 A.E. ADAMS (ed.): *The Russian Revolution and Bolshevik Victory* (Lexington, Mass. 1974); extract by M. FAINSOD.

4 See *A History of the Communist Party of the Soviet Union* (Moscow 1970).

5 S.N. SILVERMAN (ed.): *Lenin* (New York 1966); Ch. 2.

6 J.L.H. KEEP (ed.): *The Debate on Soviet Power: Minutes of the All-Russian Central Executive Committee of Soviets* (Oxford 1979); Introduction.

7 P. KENEZ: 'The ideology of the White Movement', *Soviet Studies*, xxxii, 1, Jan. 1980.

8 C. HILL: *Lenin and the Russian Revolution* (London 1947); Ch. 7.

9 S.N. SILVERMAN (ed.): op. cit.; Ch. 2.

10 R. GREGOR (ed.): *Resolutions and decisions of the Communist Party of the Soviet Union: Vol 2. The Early Soviet Period 1917–1929* (Toronto and Buffalo 1974); Document 2.9.

11 G. LEGGETT: 'Lenin, terror and the political police', in *Survey*, Autumn 1975.

12 E.H. CARR: op. cit.; Ch. 7.

13 G. LEGGETT: *The Cheka: Lenin's Political Police* (Oxford 1981); Epilogue.

14 G. LEGGETT: op. cit.; Ch. 14.

15 D. LANE: *Politics and Society in the USSR* (London 1970); Ch. 3.

16 R. MEDVEDEV: *The October Revolution* (London 1979); Part IV.

17 A. ERLICH: *The Soviet Industrialization Debate 1924–1928* (Cambridge, Mass. 1967); Ch. 1.

18 A.G. MAZOUR (ed.): *Soviet Economic Development: Operation Outstrip 1921–1965* (Princeton, NJ 1967); Ch. 2.

19 L. TROTSKY: *History of the Bolshevik Revolution*, Vol. 1.

20 A. KERENSKY: 'The policy of the Provisional Government of 1917', *The Slavonic and East European Review*, XI, 31, July 1932.

21 R. GREGOR (ed.): op. cit.; Introduction.

22 C. HILL: *Lenin and the Russian Revolution* (London 1947); Ch. 8.

23 E. MANDEL: 'Solzhenitsyn, Stalinism and the October Revolution', *New Left Review*, 86, 1974.

24 G. LEGGETT: op. cit.; Epilogue.

25 E.H. CARR: 'The Russian Revolution and the West', *New Left Review*, III, 1978.

26 L. SCHAPIRO: *1917: The Russian Revolutions and the Origins of Present Day Communism* (Hounslow 1984); Epilogue.

27 L. COLLETTI: 'The question of Stalin', *New Left Review*, 61, 1970.

28 M. MCCAULEY: *Stalin and Stalinism* (Harlow, Essex 1983); Ch. 1.

29 E.H. CARR: *Socialism in One Country 1924–1926* (London 1958); Ch. 4.

30 N. KRASSÓ: 'Trotsky's Marxism', *New Left Review*, 44, 1967.

31 R. HUTCHINGS: *Soviet Economic Development* (Oxford 1967); Ch. 6.

32 E.H. CARR: 'Revolution from above', *New Left Review*, 44, 1967.

33 L. PIETROMARCHI: *The Soviet World* (London 1965); Ch. 7.

34 D. LANE: *Politics and Society in the USSR* (London 1970); Ch. 3, Reading 6.

35 M. MCCAULEY: op. cit.; Part II.

36 R.C. TUCKER: *The Soviet Political Mind* (London 1972); Ch. 3.

37 A. ULAM: 'The price of sanity', in G.R. URBAN (ed.): *Stalinism. Its Impact on Russia and the World* (London 1982).

38 M. MCCAULEY: op. cit.; Ch. 2.

39 I. DEUTSCHER: *Stalin. A Political Biography* (London 1949); Ch. 9.

40 D. LANE: op. cit.; Document 15.

41 ibid.; Ch. 11.

42 R. HINGLEY: *Russian Writers and Soviet Society 1917–1978* (London 1979); Ch. 2.

43 ibid.; Ch. 9.

44 M. MCCAULEY: op. cit.; Part II.

45 A. FONTAINE: *History of the Cold War from the October Revolution to the Korean War, 1917–1950*, trans. D.D. Paige (London 1968); Ch. 1.

46 A.Z. RUBINSTEIN: *Soviet Foreign Policy Since World War II* (Cambridge, Mass. 1981); Ch. 1.

47 G.F. KENNAN: *Soviet Foreign Policy 1917–1941* (Princeton, NJ 1960); Document 8.

48 R.C. TUCKER: 'The emergence of Stalin's foreign policy', *Slavic Review*, xxxvi, 4, Dec. 1977.

49 W. LAQUEUR: *Russia and Germany: A Century of Conflict* (London 1965); Ch. 11.

50 J.A.S. GRENVILLE: *The Major International Treaties 1914–1973* (London 1974); pp.195–6.

51 *A Short History of the Communist Party of the Soviet Union* (Moscow 1970); p.247.

52 W. LAQUEUR: op. cit.; Ch. 12.

53 G.F. KENNAN: *Soviet Foreign Policy 1917–1941* (Princeton, NJ 1960); p.104.

54 I. GREY: *Stalin: Man of History* (London 1979); Ch. 24.

55 T.H. RIGBY (ed.): *Stalin* ('Great Lives Observed' series) Englewood Cliffs, NJ 1966); p.121.

56 I. DEUTSCHER: *Stalin: a Political Biography*; Ch. 11.

57 A. BULLOCK: *Hitler: A Study in Tyranny* (London 1952); Ch. 12.

58 See pp.53–4.
59 For further details of the war in Eastern Europe see Chapter 5.
60 M. GARDER: *A History of the Soviet Army* (London 1966); Ch. 10.
61 V.M. KULISH: 'Russia strikes back', in *Purnell's History of the 20th Century*, Vol. 5 (London 1968); p.1936.
62 I. DEUTSCHER: op. cit.; Ch. 13.
63 G.S. KRAVCHENKO: 'Stalin's war machine' in Purnell's *History of the Second World War*, Vol. 3 (London 1966).
64 A. FONTAINE: op. cit.; Ch. 8.
65 J. ELLENSTEIN: *The Stalin Phenomenon* (London 1976); Ch. 5.
66 *History of Soviet Society* (Moscow 1971); p.273.
67 R. HUTCHINGS: op. cit.; Ch. 7.
68 J. ELLENSTEIN: op. cit.; Ch. 5.
69 C. SETON WATSON: 'The Cold War–its origins', in J.L. HENDERSON, (ed.): *Since 1945: Aspects of Contemporary World History* (London 1966).
70 A.Z. RUBINSTEIN: *Soviet Foreign Policy since World War II* (Cambridge, Mass. 1981); Ch. 3.
71 R.C. TUCKER: op. cit.; Ch. 6.
72 This subject is covered thoroughly in R.C. TUCKER: 'The rise of Stalin's personality cult' in *American Historical Review*, 1979.
73 M. MCCAULEY: op. cit.; Part III.
74 I. GREY: op. cit.; extracts from Preface and Ch. 23.

3 DICTATORSHIP IN ITALY

1 A. CASSELS: *Fascist Italy* (London 1969); Ch. 4.
2 A.J.P. TAYLOR: *The Origins of the Second World War* (London 1961); Ch. 3.
3 A. DE GRAND: *Italian Fascism: Its Origins and Development* (Lincoln, Neb. 1982); Ch. 1.
4 D. MACK SMITH: *Italy: A Modern History* (Ann Arbor, Mich. 1959); Ch. 37.
5 A. DE GRAND: op. cit.; Ch. 2.
6 A.J. GREGOR: *Young Mussolini and the Intellectual Origins of Fascism* (Berkeley, London and Los Angeles 1979); Ch. 10.
7 See A. CASSELS: op. cit.; Ch. 2.
8 A. LYTTELTON: 'Italian Fascism' in W. LAQUEUR (ed.): *Fascism – A Reader's Guide* (London 1976).
9 M. GALLO: *Mussolini's Italy* (New York 1973); Ch. 5.
10 L. BARZINI: 'Benito Mussolini', *Encounter*, July 1964.
11 R. MACGREGOR-HASTIE: *The Day of the Lion* (New York 1963); p.29.
12 M. GALLO: op. cit.; Ch. 2.
13 See D. MACK SMITH: *Mussolini* (London 1981).
14 C. HIBBERT: 'Fallen idol', *Spectator*, 19 June 1964; a review of Sir I. Kirkpatrick's *Mussolini, Study of a Demagogue*.
15 Sir I. KIRKPATRICK: *Mussolini, Study of a Demagogue* (London

1964); Ch. 6.

16 MUSSOLINI: 'The political and social doctrine of Fascism', *International Conciliation*, 306, Jan. 1935.

17 A. DE GRAND: op. cit.; Ch. 10.

18 M. GALLO: op. cit.; Ch. 7.

19 R. WOLFSON: *Years of Change* (London 1978); Ch. 11.

20 See P. MELOGRANI: 'The Cult of the Duce in Mussolini's Italy' in G.L. MOSSE (ed.): *International Fascism: New Thoughts and New Approaches* (London and Beverly Hills 1979).

21 D. MACK SMITH: *Italy: A Modern History* (Ann Arbor, Mich. 1959); Ch. 49.

22 P.V. CANNISTRARO (ed.): *Historical Dictionary of Fascist Italy* (Westport, Conn. and London 1982); Manifesto of Anti-Fascist Intellectuals.

23 ibid.; Cinema.

24 M. GALLO: op. cit.; Ch. 13.

25 *Historical Dictionary of Fascist Italy*; Antisemitism.

26 M. VAN CREVELD: 'Beyond the Finzi-Contini Garden. Mussolini's "Fascist Racism"', *Encounter*, Feb. 1974.

27 MUSSOLINI: *My Autobiography* (London 1928); p.276.

28 E.R. TANNENBAUM: *Fascism in Italy* (London 1973); Ch. 7.

29 P.C. KENT: *The Pope and the Duce* (New York 1981); overall argument summarized in Preface.

30 G. JACKSON (ed.): *Problems in European Civilization: The Spanish Civil War* (Lexington, Mass. 1967); extract by F.J. TAYLOR.

31 A. CASSELS: *Fascist Italy* (London 1969); p.58.

32 A. DE GRAND: op. cit.; Ch. 8.

33 *Historical Dictionary of Fascist Italy*; Industry.

34 D. MACK SMITH: *Italy: A Modern History*; Ch. 28.

35 A.J. GREGOR: *Italian Fascism and Developmental Dictatorship* (Princeton, NJ 1979); Ch. 8.

36 See S. MARKS: 'Mussolini and Locarno: Fascist foreign policy in microcosm', *Journal of Contemporary History*, July 1979.

37 See P.G. EDWARDS: 'Britain, Mussolini and the Locarno–Geneva System', *European Studies Review*, Jan. 1980.

38 R.B. BOSWORTH: 'The British Press, the Conservatives and Mussolini 1920–34', *Journal of Contemporary History*, April 1970.

39 A. LYTTELTON: 'A demogogue and his effects', *Times Literary Supplement*, 9 April 1982.

40 H. THOMAS: *The Spanish Civil War* (London 1961); Appendix 3.

41 W. SHIRER: *The Rise and Fall of the Third Reich* (London 1960); Ch. 9.

42 CIANO: *Diary 1937–38*, trans. A. Mayor (London 1948); p.29.

43 R. DE FELICE: *Fascism: An Informal Introduction to its Theory and Practice* (New Brunswick, NJ 1976), quoted in D. SMYTH: 'Duce Diplomatico', *The Historical Journal* 21, 4 (1978).

44 G. CAROCCI: *Italian Fascism*, trans. I. Quigly (Harmondsworth 1974); Ch. 7.

45 D. MACK SMITH: *Mussolini's Roman Empire* (London 1976); Preface.
46 M. KNOX: *Mussolini Unleashed 1939–1941* (Cambridge 1982).
47 F.W.D. DEAKIN: *The Brutal Friendship* (London 1962); Ch. 1.
48 D. MACK SMITH: *Mussolini's Roman Empire*; Ch. 13.
49 ibid.; Ch. 17.
50 C. LEEDS: *Italy under Mussolini*; Ch. 5.
51 M. GALLO: op. cit.; Ch. 15.
52 *Historical Dictionary of Fascist Italy*; Italian Social Republic.
53 L. BARZINI: 'Benito Mussolini', *Encounter*, July 1964.

4 DICTATORSHIP IN GERMANY

1 L. SNYDER (ed.): *The Weimar Republic* (Princeton, NJ 1966); Reading No. 3.
2 ibid.; Reading to No. 18.
3 A. BULLOCK: *Hitler: A Study in Tyranny* (London 1952); Ch. 2.
4 J. NOAKES and G. PRIDHAM: (eds): *Documents on Nazism 1919–1945* (London 1974); Ch. 1, Document 12.
5 See A. BULLOCK: op. cit.; Ch. 2.
6 J. NOAKES and G. PRIDHAM: op. cit.; Ch. 3; Document 4.
7 E. EYCK: *A History of the Weimar Republic* (Cambridge, Mass. 1962); Vol. 1, Ch. 10.
8 H. BOLDT: 'Article 48 of the Weimar Constitution, its historical and political implications', in A. NICHOLLS (ed.): *German Democracy and the Triumph of Hitler: Essays in Recent German History* (London 1971).
9 K. SONTHEIMER: 'The Weimar Republic and the prospects of German democracy', in E.J. FEUCHTWANGER (ed.): *Upheaval and Continuity* (London 1973).
10 E. FRAENKEL: 'Historical handicaps of German parliamentarianism', in *The Road to Dictatorship 1918–1933* (London 1970).
11 L. SNYDER: op. cit.; Ch. 9.
12 S. TAYLOR: *Germany 1918–1933* (London 1983); Ch. 4.
13 HITLER: *Mein Kampf*; Vol. 2. Ch. 11.
14 ibid.; Vol. 1, Ch. 6.
15 P.D. STACHURA: 'Who were the Nazis? A socio-political analysis of the National Socialist *Machtübernahme*', *European Studies Review*, II, 1981.
16 R.F. HAMILTON: *Who Voted for Hitler?* (Princeton, NJ 1982).
17 H. TREVOR-ROPER: *The Last Days of Hitler* (London 1947); Ch. 1.
18 J. NOAKES: 'Nazi Voters', *History Today*, August 1980.
19 See D. MÜHLBERGER: 'The sociology of the NSDAP: The question of working-class membership', *Journal of Contemporary History*, 15, 1980.
20 D.G. WILLIAMSON: *The Third Reich* (Harlow, Essex 1982); Ch. 3.
21 J. NOAKES and G. PRIDHAM: op. cit.; Ch. 5, Document 7.
22 M. BROSZAT: *The Hitler State: The Foundation and Development*

of the Internal Structure of the Third Reich (London 1981); Ch. 3.

23 J. NOAKES and G. PRIDHAM: op. cit.; Ch. 7, Document 2.

24 ibid.; Ch. 8, Document 1.

25 M. BROSZAT: op. cit.; Ch. 6.

26 J. NOAKES and G. PRIDHAM: op. cit.; Ch. 8, Document 4.

27 Sir J. WHEELER-BENNETT: *The Nemesis of Power: The German Army in Politics 1918–1945* (London 1953); Part III, Ch. 2.

28 H. ROSINSKI: *The German Army* (New York 1966); Ch. 6.

29 R. GRUNBERGER: *A Social History of the Third Reich* (London 1971); Ch. 10.

30 J. NOAKES and G. PRIDHAM: op. cit.; Part III.

31 Information from M. BROSZAT: op. cit. and J. NOAKES and G. PRIDHAM: op. cit.

32 K.D. BRACHER: *The German Dictatorship* (New York 1970).

33 Extracts which follow are quoted in I. KERSHAW: *The Nazi Dictatorship: Problems and Perspectives of Interpretation* (London 1985); Ch. 4; K. HILDEBRAND: *The Third Reich* (London 1984); Part II; M. BROSZAT: op. cit.; Ch. 8.

34 D. IRVING: *Hitler's War* (New York 1977); Introduction.

35 Information from J. NOAKES and G. PRIDHAM: op. cit.; Ch. 10.

36 ibid.; Ch. 10, Document 8.

37 H. HOLBORN: *A History of Modern Germany, Vol. 3, 1840–1945* (London 1969); p.747.

38 ibid.; pp.747–8.

39 J NOAKES and G. PRIDHAM: op. cit.; Ch. 10, Document 30.

40 I. KERSHAW: op. cit.; Ch. 3.

41 D. SCHOENBAUM: *Hitler's Social Revolution* (London 1967); Ch. 7.

42 K.D. BRACHER: op. cit.; Ch. 5.

43 M.J. THORNTON: *Nazism 1918–1945* (London 1966); Ch. 7.

44 R. GRUNBERGER: op. cit.; Ch. 27.

45 J. NOAKES and G. PRIDHAM: op. cit.; Part IV.

46 R. GRUNBERGER: op. cit.; Ch. 19.

47 ibid.; Ch. 20.

48 Summary of debate and quotation in I. KERSHAW: op. cit.; Ch. 5.

49 Summary of debate and quotation in K. HILDEBRAND: op. cit.; Part II, Ch. 5.

50 K.D. BRACHER: op. cit.; Ch. 7.

51 J. NOAKES and G. PRIDHAM: op. cit.; Ch. 13.

52 D.G. WILLIAMSON: op. cit.; Ch. 7.

53 Extract in R.G.L. WAITE (ed.): *Hitler and Nazi Germany* (New York 1965).

54 R. GRUNBERGER: op. cit.; Ch. 14.

55 R. KNAUERHASE: *An Introduction to National Socialism 1920–1939* (Columbus, Ohio 1972).

56 D.G. WILLIAMSON: op. cit.; Document 7.

57 J. NOAKES and G. PRIDHAM: op. cit.; Ch. 12.

58 K.D. BRACHER: op. cit.; Ch. 7.

59 R. GRUNBERGER: op. cit.; Ch. 29.

60 I. KERSHAW: op. cit.; Ch. 7.

61 R.O. PAXTON: 'The German opposition to Hitler: a non-Germanist's view', *Central European History*, 1981.

62 J. NOAKES and G. PRIDHAM: op. cit.; Ch. 11.

63 K. HILDEBRAND: op. cit.; Ch. 2.

64 J.C.G. RÖHL: *From Bismarck to Hitler* (Harlow, Essex 1970); Ch. 5, Document 1.

65 J.W. HIDEN: *The Weimar Republic* (Harlow, Essex 1974); Ch. 4.

66 J.C.G. RÖHL: op. cit.; Ch. 5, Document 7.

67 H.W. GATZKE: *Stresemann and the Rearmament of Germany* (Baltimore 1954); Ch. 6.

68 H. HOLBORN: op. cit.; Ch. 12.

69 G.A. CRAIG: *Germany 1866–1945* (Oxford 1978); Ch. 19.

70 J. NOAKES and G. PRIDHAM: op. cit.; Ch. 18.

71 Quotations in this paragraph are from *Mein Kampf* and *Zweites Buch*. Material and quotations also from H. VON MALTITZ: *The Evolution of Hitler's Germany* (New York 1973); Ch. 3.

72 Quoted in D.G. WILLIAMSON: op. cit.; Ch. 9.

73 A. HILLGRUBER: *Germany and the Two World Wars*, trans. W.C. Kirby; Cambridge, Mass. and London 1981; Ch. 5.

74 E. JÄCKEL: *Hitler in History* (Hanover and London 1984); Ch. 2.

75 See I. KERSHAW: op. cit. for summary of debate and for quoted extracts.

76 E. JÄCKEL: op. cit.; Ch. 4.

77 A. HILLGRUBER: 'England's place in Hitler's plans for world dominion', *Journal of Contemporary History*, 9, 1974.

78 Quotations from A.J.P. TAYLOR: *The Origins of the Second World War* (London 1961); Ch. 7.

79 Quoted in K.H. JARAUSCH: 'From Second to Third Reich: the problem of continuity in German foreign policy', *Central European History*, 12, 1979.

80 A. BULLOCK: op. cit.; Ch. 8.

81 A. BULLOCK: contribution to *Hitler and the Origins of the Second World War; Proceedings of the British Academy LIII* (Oxford 1967).

82 See F. FISCHER: *Germany's Aims in the First World War* (London 1967).

83 J. NOAKES and G. PRIDHAM: op. cit.; Ch. 16.

84 J.L. SNELL (ed.): *The Outbreak of the Second World War* (Boston 1962); extract from the Nuremberg Judgement.

85 R.J. SONTAG: 'The last months of peace, 1939'; *Foreign Affairs*, XXV, 1957.

86 H. TREVOR ROPER: 'A.J.P. Taylor, Hitler and the War', *Encounter*, XVII, 1961.

87 J. FEST: *Hitler* (London 1974); Interpolation Three.

88 T.W. MASON: 'Some origins of the Second World War', *Past and Present*, 1964.

89 R. HENIG: *The Origins of the Second World War* (London 1985); Section III.

90 J. NOAKES and G. PRIDHAM: op. cit.; Ch. 19.
91 D.G. WILLIAMSON: op. cit.; Ch. 10.
92 G.A. CRAIG: op. cit.; Ch. 20.
93 W.L. SHIRER: *The Rise and Fall of the Third Reich* (London 1960); Ch. 19.
94 K. HILDEBRAND: op. cit.; Ch. C1.
95 N. RICH: *Hitler's War Aims: The Establishment of the New Order* (London 1974); Vol II.
96 K. SYROP: *Poland: Between Hammer and Anvil* (London 1968); Ch. 16.
97 M.J. THORNTON: op. cit.; Ch. 9.
98 W.L. SHIRER: op. cit.; Ch. 27.
99 M.R.D. FOOT: 'Nazi wartime atrocities', in *Purnell's History of the Twentieth Century*, Vol. 5 (London 1968).
100 See D.G. WILLIAMSON: op. cit.; Ch. 11.
101 T.L. JARMAN: *The Rise and Fall of Nazi Germany* (London 1955); Ch. 15.
102 A. BULLOCK: op. cit.; Ch. 14.
103 F. HALDER: *Hitler as War Lord*, trans. P. Findley (London 1950).
104 P.E. SCHRAMM: *Hitler: The Man and the Military Leader* (London 1972); Ch 2.
105 J.P. STERN: *Hitler: The Führer and the People* (London 1975); Ch. 22.

5 DICTATORSHIP ELSEWHERE

1 N. BRUCE: *Portugal: The Last Empire* (London 1975); Ch. 1.
2 S.G. PAYNE: 'Epilogue' in L.S. GRAHAM and H.M. MAKLER (eds): *Contemporary Portugal: The Revolution and its Antecedents* (Austin, Tex. 1979); p.345.
3 T. GALLAGHER: *Portugal: A Twentieth-Century Interpretation* (Manchester 1983); Ch. 3.
4 H. KAY: *Salazar and Modern Portugal* (London 1970); Ch. 5.
5 ibid.
6 T. GALLAGHER: op. cit.; Ch. 4.
7 H. KAY: op. cit.; Ch. 4.
8 T. GALLAGHER: op. cit.; Ch. 5.
9 R.A.H. ROBINSON: *Contemporary Portugal: A History* (London 1979); Ch. 3.
10 T.C. BRUNEAU: *Politics and Nationhood: Post-Revolutionary Portugal* (New York 1974); Ch. 1.
11 J.E. DUFFY: *Portuguese Africa* (Cambridge, Mass. 1959); Ch. 9.
12 H. THOMAS: *The Spanish Civil War* (London 1961); Ch. 2.
13 S.G. PAYNE: *Falangé: A History of Spanish Fascism* (Stanford, Cal. 1961); Ch. 1.
14 S. BEN-AMI: 'Dictatorship of Primo de Rivera: a political reassessment', *Journal of Contemporary History*, Jan. 1977, pp. 65–84.
15 R. CARR: *Modern Spain 1875–1980* (Oxford 1980); Ch. 7.

16 ibid.; Ch. 8.
17 H. THOMAS: op. cit.; Ch. 10.
18 ibid.; Appendix II.
19 P. PRESTON: 'War of words: the Spanish Civil War and the historians', in P. PRESTON (ed.): *Revolution and War in Spain 1931–1939* (London 1984).
20 R. CARR and J.P. FUSI: *Spain: Dictatorship to Democracy* (London 1979); p. 26.
21 F. JAY TAYLOR: *The United States and the Spanish Civil War* (New York 1956).
22 M. ALPERT: ' Soldiers, politics and war', in P. PRESTON: op. cit.
23 R. CARR: op. cit.; Ch. 8.
24 ibid.; Ch. 9.
25 G. JACKSON: *The Spanish Republic and the Civil War 1931–39* (Princeton, NJ 1965); Ch. 24.
26 M. GALLO: *Spain under Franco*, trans. J. Stewart (London 1973); Introduction.
27 D.A. PUZZO: *The Spanish Civil War* (New York 1969); Ch. 2.
28 B. CROZIER: *Franco: A Biographical History* (London 1967); Part IV, Ch. 6.
29 S. PAYNE: *Falangé: A History of Spanish Fascism* (Stanford, Cal. 1961).
30 R. CARR: *Modern Spain 1875–1980*; Ch. 9.
31 D. SMYTH: 'Reflex reaction: Germany and the onset of the Spanish Civil War', in P. PRESTON: op. cit.
32 A. VIÑAS: 'The financing of the Spanish Civil War', in P. PRESTON: op. cit.
33 R. WHEALEY: 'How Franco financed his war – reconsidered', *Journal of Contemporary History*, 12, 1977.
34 D.A. PUZZO: *Spain and the Great Powers 1936–1941* (New York 1962); Conclusions.
35 Information on International Brigades from H. THOMAS: op. cit.; Appendix III.
36 M. GALLO: op. cit.; Part I, Ch. 2.
37 R. CARR: *Spain 1808–1975* (Oxford 1966); Ch. 18.
38 M. GALLO: op. cit.; Part II, Ch. 2.
39 M. GALLO: op. cit.; Part II, Ch. 3.
40 J.D.W. TRYTHALL: *Franco: A Biography* (London 1970); Ch. 8.
41 ibid.; Ch. 11.
42 D. GILMOUR: *The Transformation of Spain: From Franco to the Constitutional Monarchy* (London 1985); Ch. 1.
43 ibid.; Ch. 2.
44 R. CARR: *Spain 1808–1975* (Oxford 1966); Ch. 20.
45 B. CROZIER: op. cit.; Part VII.
46 P. PRESTON: 'From rebel to Caudillo: Franco's path to power', *History Today*, Nov. 1983.
47 E. EYCH: *A History of the Weimar Republic*, Vol. I. Ch. 4.
48 A.J.P. TAYLOR: *The Habsburg Monarchy* (London 1948); Epilogue.
49 S. MARKS: *The Illusion of Peace* (London 1976); Ch. 1.

50 E. BARKER: *Austria 1918–1972* (London 1973); Part I.
51 K.R. STADLER: *Austria* (London 1971); Ch. 4.
52 E. BARKER: op. cit.; Ch. 9.
53 ibid.
54 A.C. JANOS: *The Politics of Backwardness in Hungary, 1825–1945* (Princeton, NJ 1982); Ch. 4.
55 ibid.; Ch. 5.
56 E. PAMLÉNYI (ed.): *A History of Hungary* (London 1975); Ch. 9.
57 D. SINOR: *History of Hungary* (London 1959); Ch. 32.
58 P. IGNOTUS: *Hungary* (London 1972); Ch. 9.
59 E. WEBER (ed.): *Varieties of Fascism* (New York 1964); Reading 3A: Ferencz Szálasi: The Way and the Aim.
60 K. SYROP: *Poland: Between the Hammer and the Anvil* (London 1968); Ch. 14.
61 J. ROTHSCHILD: *Pilsudski's Coup d'État* (New York and London 1966); Conclusion.
62 K. SYROP: op. cit.; Ch. 15.
63 Z. LANDAU and J. TOMASZEWSKI: *The Polish Economy in the Twentieth Century* (London 1985); Editor's Introduction by D.H. ALDCROFT.
64 See J. HOLZER: 'The political right in Poland 1918–39', *Journal of Contemporary History*, 12, 1977.
65 K. SYROP: op. cit.; Ch. 15.
66 ibid.; Ch. 16.
67 V.S. VARDIS: 'The rise of authoritarian rule in the Baltic states', in V.S. VARDIS and R.J. MISIUNAS (eds): *The Baltic States in Peace and War 1917–1945* (University Park, Penn. and London 1978).
68 B. MEISSNER: 'The Baltic Question in world politics', in VARDIS and MISIUNAS: op. cit.
Also A. DALLIN: 'The Baltic states between Nazi Germany and Soviet Russia', in VARDIS and MISIUNAS: op. cit.
69 E. ANDERSON: 'The Baltic Entente: phantom or reality' in VARDIS and MISIUNAS: op. cit.
70 L.S. STAVRIANOS: *The Balkans Since 1453* (New York 1958); Ch. 36.
71 S. POLLO and A. PUTO: *The History of Albania*, trans. C. Wiseman and G. Cole (London 1981); Ch. 9.
72 A. LOGORECI: *The Albanians* (London 1977); Ch. 3.
73 L.S. STAVRIANOS: op. cit., Ch. 38.
74 B. JELAVICH: *History of the Balkans Vol. 2: Twentieth Century* (Cambridge 1983); Ch. 5.
75 L.S. STAVRIANOS: op. cit.; Ch. 33.
76 R. RISTELHUEBER: *A History of the Balkan Peoples*, trans. S.D. Spector (New York 1971).
77 F. SINGLETON: *Twentieth-Century Yugoslavia* (London 1976); Ch. 5.
78 L.S. STAVRIANOS: op. cit.; Ch. 32.
79 V. DEDIJER: 'Yugoslavia between Centralism and Federalism', in

v. DEDIJER *et al.* (eds): *History of Yugoslavia* (New York 1974).

80 R.W. SETON WATSON and R.G.D. LAFFAN: 'Yugoslavia between the Wars', in s. CLISSOLD (ed.): *A Short History of Yugoslavia* (Cambridge 1966).

81 v. DEDIJER: 'The subjugation and dismemberment of Yugoslavia', in v. DEDIJER *et al.*: op. cit.

82 L.S. STAVRIANOS: op. cit.; Ch. 30.

83 s. FISCHER-GALAȚI: *Twentieth Century Rumania* (New York and London 1970); Ch. 3.

84 F.L. CARSTEN: *The Rise of Fascism* (London 1967); Ch. 5.

85 L.S. STAVRIANOS: op. cit.; Ch. 35.

86 J.V. KOFAS: *Authoritarianism in Greece: The Metaxas Regime* (New York 1983); Ch. 2.

87 L.S. STAVRIANOS: op. cit.; Ch. 34.

88 B. JELAVICH: op. cit.; Ch. 6.

89 L.S. STAVRIANOS: op. cit.; Ch. 38.

90 J.K. HOENSCH: 'The Slovak Republic', in v.s. MAMATEY and R. LUZA (eds): *A History of the Czechoslovak Republic 1918–1948* (Princeton, NJ 1973).

91 K.F. LARSEN: *A History of Norway* (Princeton, NJ 1948); Ch. 21.

92 P.M. HAYES: *Quisling* (London 1971); Ch. 9.

93 H. TINT: *France Since 1918* (London 1970); Ch. 7.

6 DICTATORSHIPS COMPARED

1 K.D. BRACHER: *The Age of Ideologies* (London 1984); Part II, Ch. 1.

2 C.J. FRIEDRICH and Z.K. BRZEZINSKI: *Totalitarian Dictatorship and Autocracy* (Cambridge, Mass. 1956); Ch. 2.

3 R.C. MACRIDIS: *Contemporary Political Ideologies* (Boston 1983); Part II.

4 Quoted in R.C. TUCKER: *The Soviet Political Mind* (London 1971); Ch. 2.

5 G.R. URBAN (ed.): *Stalinism: Its Impact on Russia and the World* (London 1982); extract by L. Kolakowski.

6 C.J. FRIEDRICH and Z.K. BRZEZINSKI: op. cit.; Ch. 7.

7 K.D. BRACHER: op. cit.; Part II, Ch. 4.

8 E. WEBER: *Varieties of Fascism* (New York 1964); Reading 3, Introduction.

9 R.C. MACRIDIS: op. cit.; Ch. 5.

10 K.D. BRACHER: op. cit.; Part II, Ch. 3.

11 H. KOHN: *Political Ideologies of the Twentieth Century* (New York 1966); Ch. 10.

12 J. REMAK: *The Nazi Years* (Englewood Cliffs, NJ 1969); Ch. 3.

13 T. GALLAGHER: *Portugal: A Twentieth-Century Interpretation* (Manchester 1983); Ch. 7.

14 M. BROSZAT: *The Hitler State* (London 1981): Ch. 6.

15 C.J. FRIEDRICH and Z.K. BRZEZINSKI: op. cit.; Ch. 26.

16 H. BUCHHEIM: *Totalitarian Rule: Its Nature and Characteristics*

(Middletown, Conn. 1968); Ch. 1.

17 N. BRUCE: *Portugal: The Last Empire* (London 1975); Ch. 2.

18 S.G. PAYNE: *Franco's Spain* (London 1968); Ch. 2.

19 C.J. FRIEDRICH and Z.K. BRZEZINSKI: op. cit.; Ch. 11.

20 ibid.; Ch. 14.

21 M. LATEY: *Tyranny: A Study in the Abuse of Power* (London 1969); Ch. 6.

Select bibliography

The previous section listed the works which have been used in compiling this book. This final section is intended to select from these a few titles to introduce the reader to further study.

GENERAL ISSUES (INTERNATIONAL RELATIONS, INSTITUTIONS AND IDEOLOGIES)

The various foreign policies are covered in the context of the individual states. The most accessible collection of documents on international relations covering the whole period is J.A.S. GRENVILLE (ed.): *The Major International Treaties 1914–1973* (London 1974). Now well established, but as fresh and controversial as ever is A.J.P. TAYLOR: *The Origins of the Second World War* (London 1961). Two introductions to the period can be strongly recommended: R. HENIG: *Versailles and After* (London 1984) and R. HENIG: *The Origins of the Second World War* (London 1985). A more detailed analysis is provided by S. MARKS: *The Illusion of Peace, International Relations in Europe 1918–1933* (London 1976) and a reinterpretation of the Versailles Settlement is contained in M. TRACHTENBERG: *Reparation in World Politics* (London 1980). Several titles in the series *Problems in European Civilization* (Lexington, Mass.) provide a useful survey of different viewpoints, although they do not always include some of the latest research. Examples include: I.J. LEDERER (ed.): *The Versailles Settlement*; L.F. SCHAEFFER (ed.): *The Ethiopian Crisis*; J.L. SNELL (ed.): *The Outbreak of the Second World War*.

On institutions and ideologies I found the following particularly informative and enlightening: K.J. NEWMAN: *European Democracy Between the Wars*, trans. E. Morgan (London 1970); H. BUCHHEIM: *Totalitarian Rule: Its Nature and Characteristics* (Middletown, Conn. 1968); K.D. BRACHER: *The Age of Ideologies* (London 1984); R.C. MACRIDIS: *Contemporary Political Ideologies* (Boston 1983); C.J. FRIEDRICH and Z.K. BRZEZINSKI: *Totalitarian Dictatorship and Autocracy* (Cambridge, Mass. 1956); G.L. MOSSE (ed.): *International Fascism* (London and Beverly Hills 1979); E. NOLTE: *Three Faces of Fascism* (New York 1963); M. KITCHEN: *Fascism* (London 1976); F. CARSTEN: *The Rise of Fascism* (London 1967); S.J. WOOLF (ed.): *Fascism in Europe* (London 1981); and I. DEUTSCHER: *Marxism in Outline* (London 1972).

DICTATORSHIP IN RUSSIA

Substantial general works on the Lenin era include: E.H. CARR: *The Bolshevik Revolution 1917–23* (3 vols; London 1950); E.H. CARR: *The Russian Revolution from Lenin to Stalin 1917–1929* (London 1979); C. HILL: *Lenin and the Russian Revolution* (London 1974); L. SCHAPIRO: *1917: The Russian Revolutions and the Origins of Present Day Communism* (Hounslow 1984); L. FISCHER: *The Life of Lenin* (London 1965); R. MEDVEDEV: *The October Revolution* (London 1979). Two more detailed works which can be recommended are: A. ASCHER (ed.): *The Mensheviks in the Russian Revolution* (London 1976); and G. LEGGETT: *The Cheka: Lenin's Political Police* (Oxford 1981).

The controversies relating to both Lenin and Stalin are best followed up through the notes to the relevant sections of Chapter 2. The basic works on Stalin include. I. DEUTSCHER: *Stalin: A Political Biography* (Oxford 1949); A.B. ULAM: *Stalin: The Man and his Era* (London 1973); T.H. RIGBY (ed.): *Stalin* (Englewood Cliffs, NJ 1966); I. GREY: *Stalin: Man of History* (London 1979); R. HINGLEY: *Joseph Stalin: Man and Legend* (London 1974); A. NOVE: *Stalinism and After* (London 1975); M. MCCAULEY: *Stalin and Stalinism* (London 1983). More specific material can be found in: R. CONQUEST: *The Great Terror* (London 1968); R. HUTCHINGS: *Soviet Economic Development* (Oxford 1967); D. LANE: *Politics and Society in the USSR* (London 1970); G.F. KENNAN: *Soviet Foreign Policy 1917–1941* (Princeton, NJ 1960); R. HINGLEY: *Russian Writers and Soviet Society 1917–1978* (London 1979).

Articles on a variety of topics (mentioned in the Notes) can be found in journals like *Soviet Studies, The Slavonic and East European Review, New Left Review* and *Slavic Review*.

DICTATORSHIP IN ITALY

Among the main general works on Mussolini's Italy are: A.
CASSELLS: *Fascist Italy* (London 1969); D. MACK SMITH: *Mussolini*
(London 1981); M. GALLO: *Mussolini's Italy* (New York 1973);
R. MACGREGOR-HASTIE: *The Day of the Lion (New York 1963);* Sir
I. KIRKPATRICK: *Mussolini: Study of a Demagogue* (London 1964);
C. HIBBERT: *Mussolini* (Harmondsworth 1975); and R. COLLIER:
Duce!: The Rise and Fall of Mussolini (London 1971).

On more specific issues, the following are recommended: A. DE
GRAND: *Italian Fascism: Its Origins and Development* (Lincoln,
Neb. 1982); A.J. GREGOR: *Young Mussolini and the Intellectual
Origins of Fascism* (Berkeley, London and Los Angeles 1979);
P.V. CANNISTRARO (ed.): *Historical Dictionary of Fascist Italy*
(Westport, Conn. and London 1982); P.C. KENT: *The Pope and the
Duce* (New York 1981); A.J. GREGOR: *Italian Fascism and Develop-
mental Dictatorship* (Princeton, NJ 1979); R. DE FELICE: *Fascism:
An Informal Introduction to its Theory and Practice* (New Brunswick,
NJ 1976); G. CAROCCI: *Italian Fascism* (Harmondsworth 1974);
D. MACK SMITH: *Mussolini's Roman Empire* (London 1976); and
M. KNOX: *Mussolini Unleashed* (Cambridge 1982).

Articles can be found in the following journals: *Encounter,
Spectator, Journal of Contemporary History* and *European Studies
Review*.

DICTATORSHIP IN GERMANY

By far the most useful collection of primary sources is J. NOAKES
and G. PRIDHAM (eds): *Documents on Nazism 1919–1945* (London
1974). Others include L. SNYDE: *The Weimar Republic* (Princeton, NJ
1966); J.W. HIDEN: *The Weimar Republic* (Harlow, Essex 1974); and
D.G. WILLIAMSON: *The Third Reich* (Harlow, Essex 1982).

The list of secondary sources is now too long to condense effec-
tively. Among the best known are A. BULLOCK: *Hitler: A Study in
Tyranny* (London 1952); W.L. SHIRER: *The Rise and Fall of the Third
Reich* (London 1960); J. FEST: *Hitler* (London 1974); N. STONE: *Hitler*
(London 1980); and A.J. NICHOLLS: *Weimar and the Rise of Hitler*
(London 1968).

Especially recommended are several now well-established overall
interpretations of the Nazi era; I have attempted to provide an
introduction to these in Chapter 4. These include M. BROSZAT: *The
Hitler State* (London 1981); K.D. BRACHER: *The German Dictatorship*
(New York 1980); E. JÄCKEL: *Hitler in History* (Hanover and London
1984); and A. HILLGRUBER: *Germany and the Two World Wars*
(Cambridge, Mass. and London 1981). Three recent publications
provide a valuable analysis of recent ideas and historical research.
These are K. HILDEBRAND: *The Third Reich* (London 1984); J. HIDEN
and J. FARQUHARSON: *Explaining Hitler's Germany: Historians and*

the Third Reich (London 1983); and I. KERSHAW: *The Nazi Dictatorship: Problems and Perspectives of Interpretation* (London 1985).

The Notes for Chapter 4 contain references to useful articles from *European Studies Review, History Today, Journal of Contemporary History, Central European History, Foreign Affairs* and *Past and Present.*

DICTATORSHIP ELSEWHERE

I found the most readable books on Salazar's Portugal to be T. GALLAGHER: *Portugal: A Twentieth-Century Interpretation* (Manchester 1983); and H. KAY: *Salazar and Modern Portugal* (London 1970). Among the plethora of books on Spain there are several standard works. These include H. THOMAS: *The Spanish Civil War* (London 1961); G. JACKSON: *The Spanish Republic and the Civil War 1931–39* (Princeton, NJ 1965); and S.G. PAYNE: *Franco's Spain* (London 1968). Of R. CARR's general works I found *Modern Spain 1875–1980* (Oxford 1980) the most useful. Among recent publications, a series of particularly interesting essays can be found in P. PRESTON (ed): *Revolution and War in Spain 1931–1939* (London 1984).

Central and eastern Europe are effectively covered in E. BARKER: *Austria 1918–1972* (London 1973); K.R. STADLER: *Austria* (London 1971); E. PAMLÉNYI: *A History of Hungary* (London 1975); D. SINOR: *History of Hungary* (London 1959); K. SYROP: *Poland: Between the Hammer and the Anvil* (London 1968); and V.S. VARDIS and R.J. MISIUNAS (eds.): *The Baltic States in Peace and War 1917–1945.* The Balkans and south-eastern Europe are dealt with comprehensively in L.S. STAVRIANOS: *The Balkans Since 1453* (New York 1958) and B. JELAVICH: *History of the Balkans, Vol.2: The Twentieth Century* (Cambridge 1983). Books on individual countries are mentioned in the Notes for Chapter 5.

Articles, especially on Spain, can be found in *Journal of Contemporary History* and *History today.* In locating articles on any topic within any journal, the *Humanities Review* is invaluable as a starting point.

Index